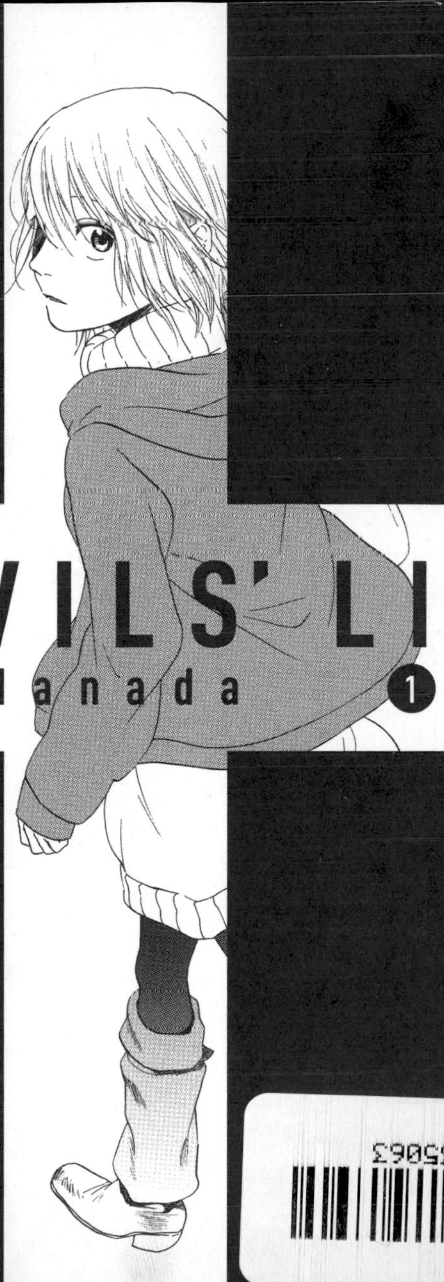

DEVILS' LINE

Ryo Hanada 1

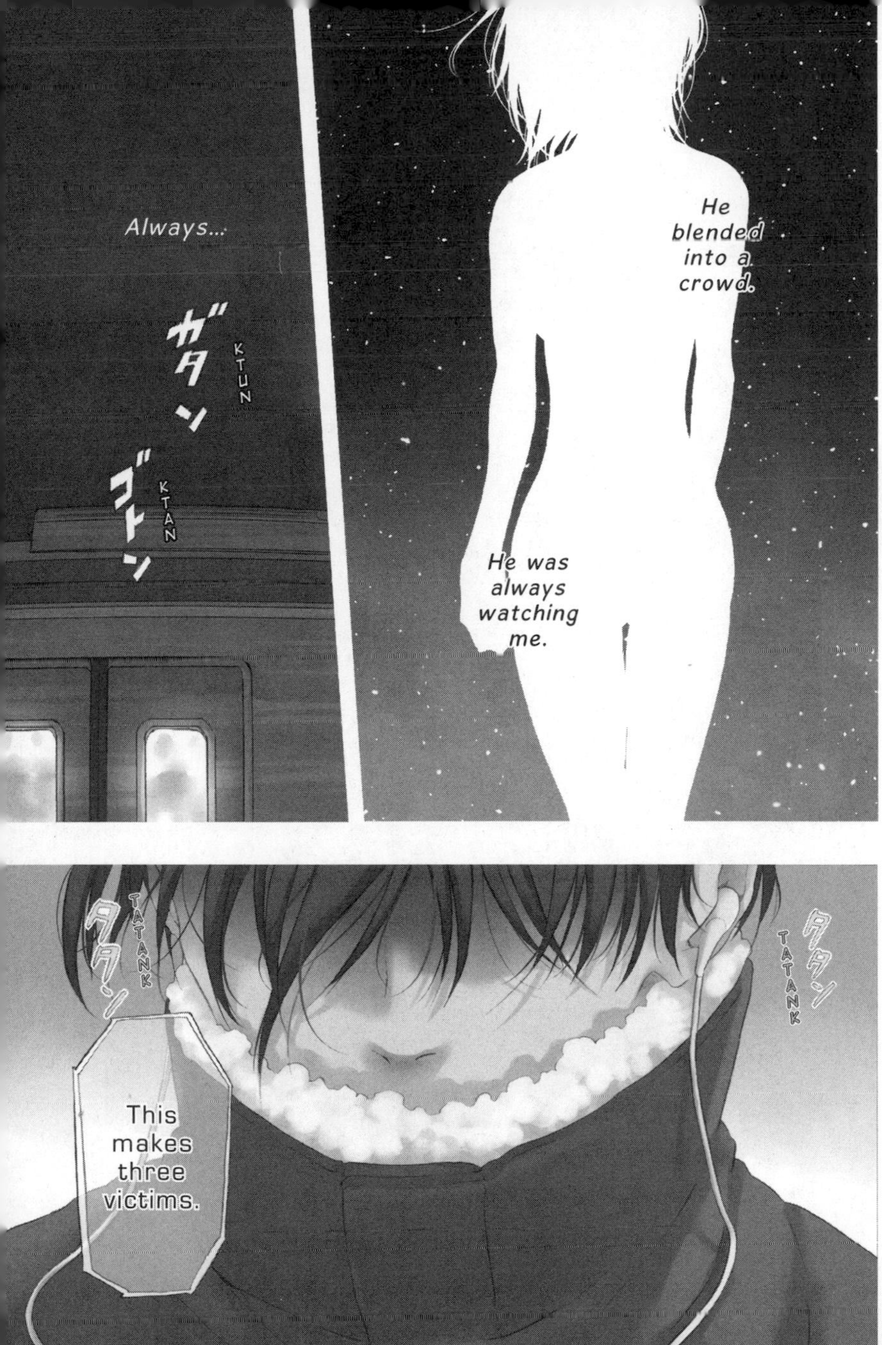
He blended into a crowd.
He was always watching me.
Always...
ガタン
KTUN
ゴトン
KTAN
タタン
TATANK
タタン
TATANK
This makes three victims.

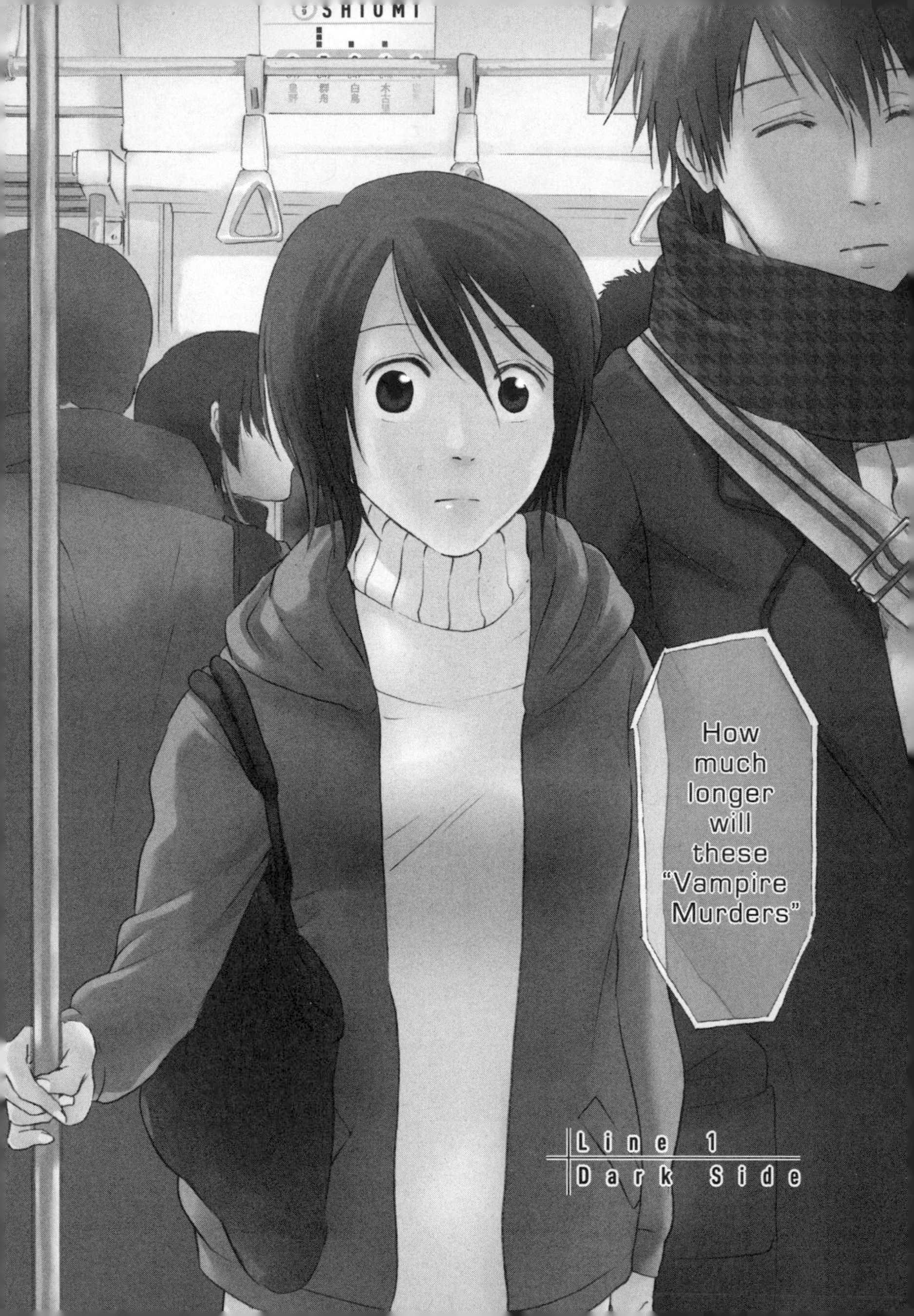
SHIOMI
How much longer will these "Vampire Murders"
Line 1
Dark Side

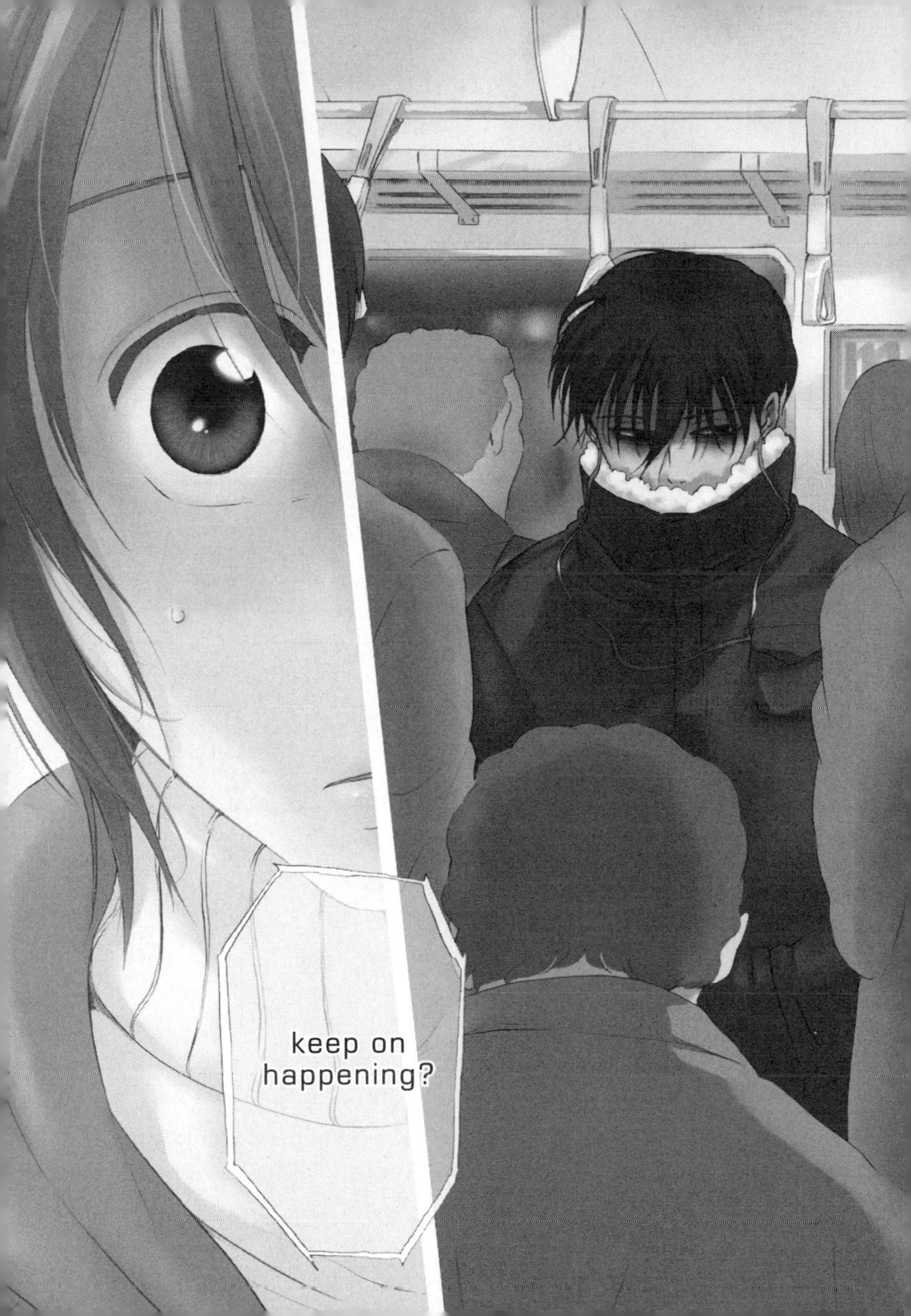
keep on
happening?

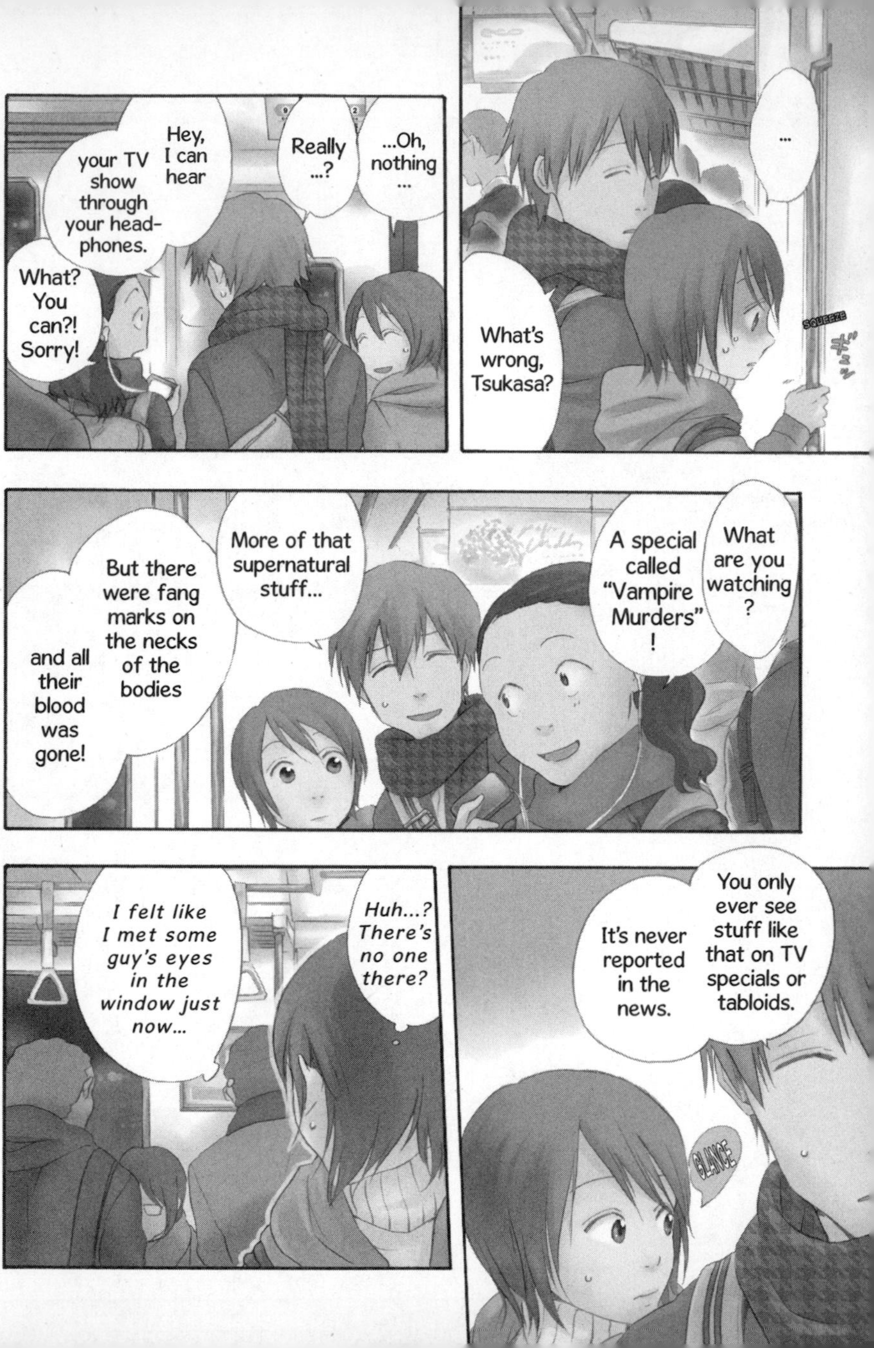
...
What's wrong, Tsukasa?
SQUEEZE
...Oh, nothing ...
Really ...?
Hey, I can hear your TV show through your head-phones.
What? You can?! Sorry!
What are you watching?
A special called "Vampire Murders"!
More of that supernatural stuff...
But there were fang marks on the necks of the bodies and all their blood was gone!
You only ever see stuff like that on TV specials or tabloids.
It's never reported in the news.
GLANCE
Huh...? There's no one there?
I felt like I met some guy's eyes in the window just now...

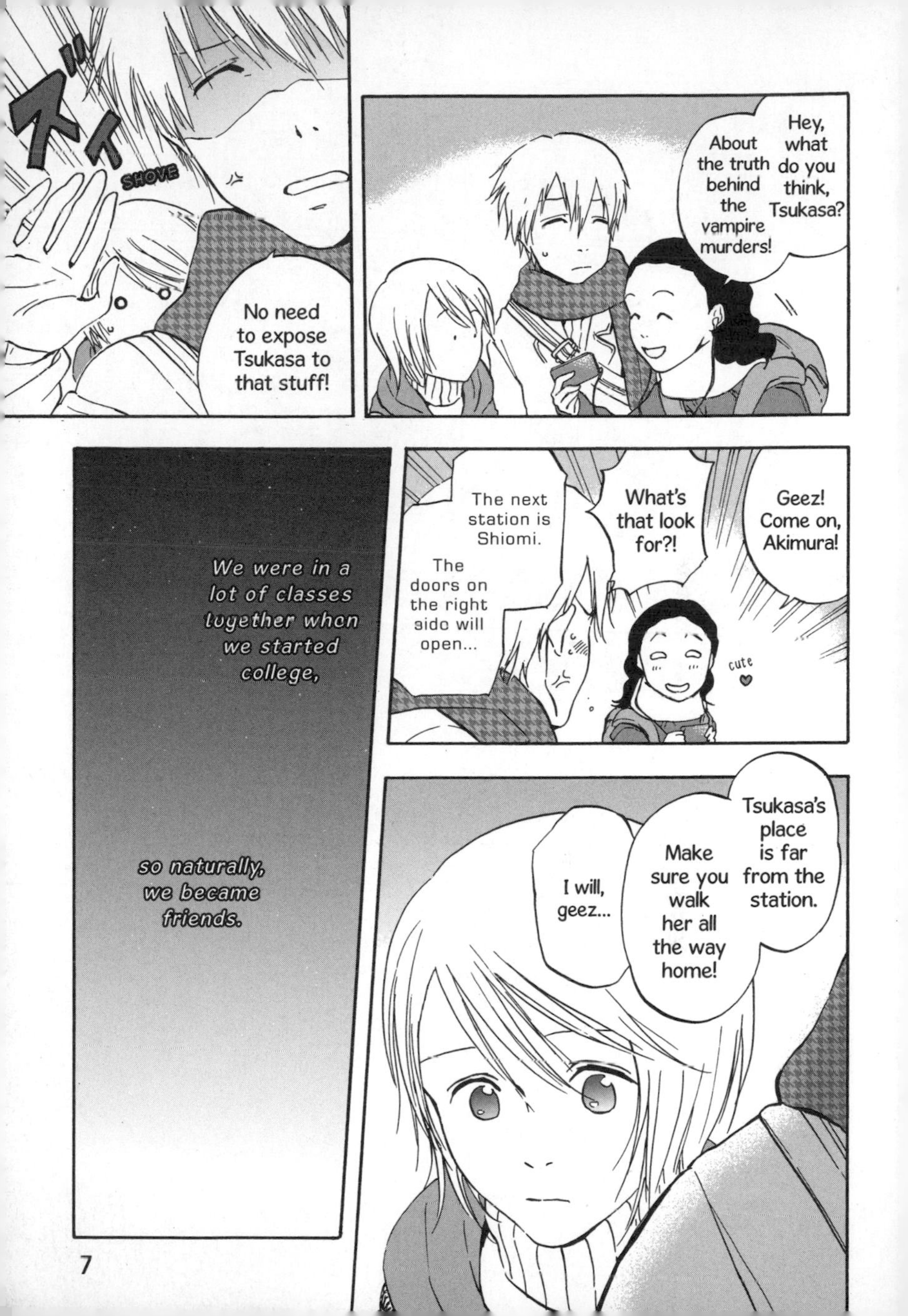

Hey, what do you think, Tsukasa?
About the truth behind the vampire murders!
ズイ
SHOVE
No need to expose Tsukasa to that stuff!
Geez! Come on, Akimura!
What's that look for?!
The next station is Shiomi.
The doors on the right side will open...
cute
Tsukasa's place is far from the station.
Make sure you walk her all the way home!
I will, geez...
We were in a lot of classes together when we started college,
so naturally, we became friends.

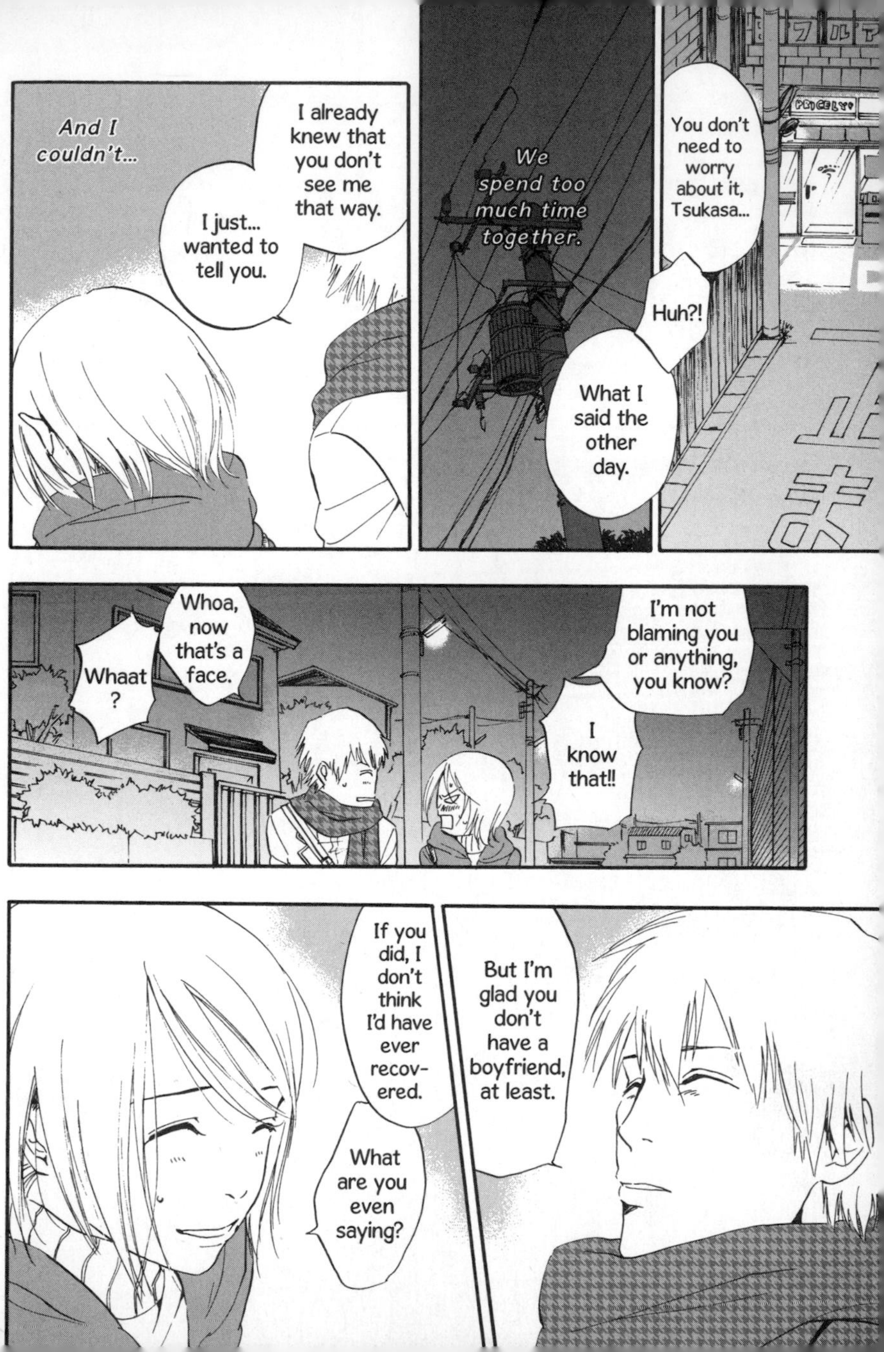
You don't need to worry about it, Tsukasa...
Huh?!
What I said the other day.
We spend too much time together.
I already knew that you don't see me that way.
I just... wanted to tell you.
And I couldn't...
I'm not blaming you or anything, you know?
I know that!!
Whoa, now that's a face.
Whaat?
But I'm glad you don't have a boyfriend, at least.
If you did, I don't think I'd have ever recovered.
What are you even saying?

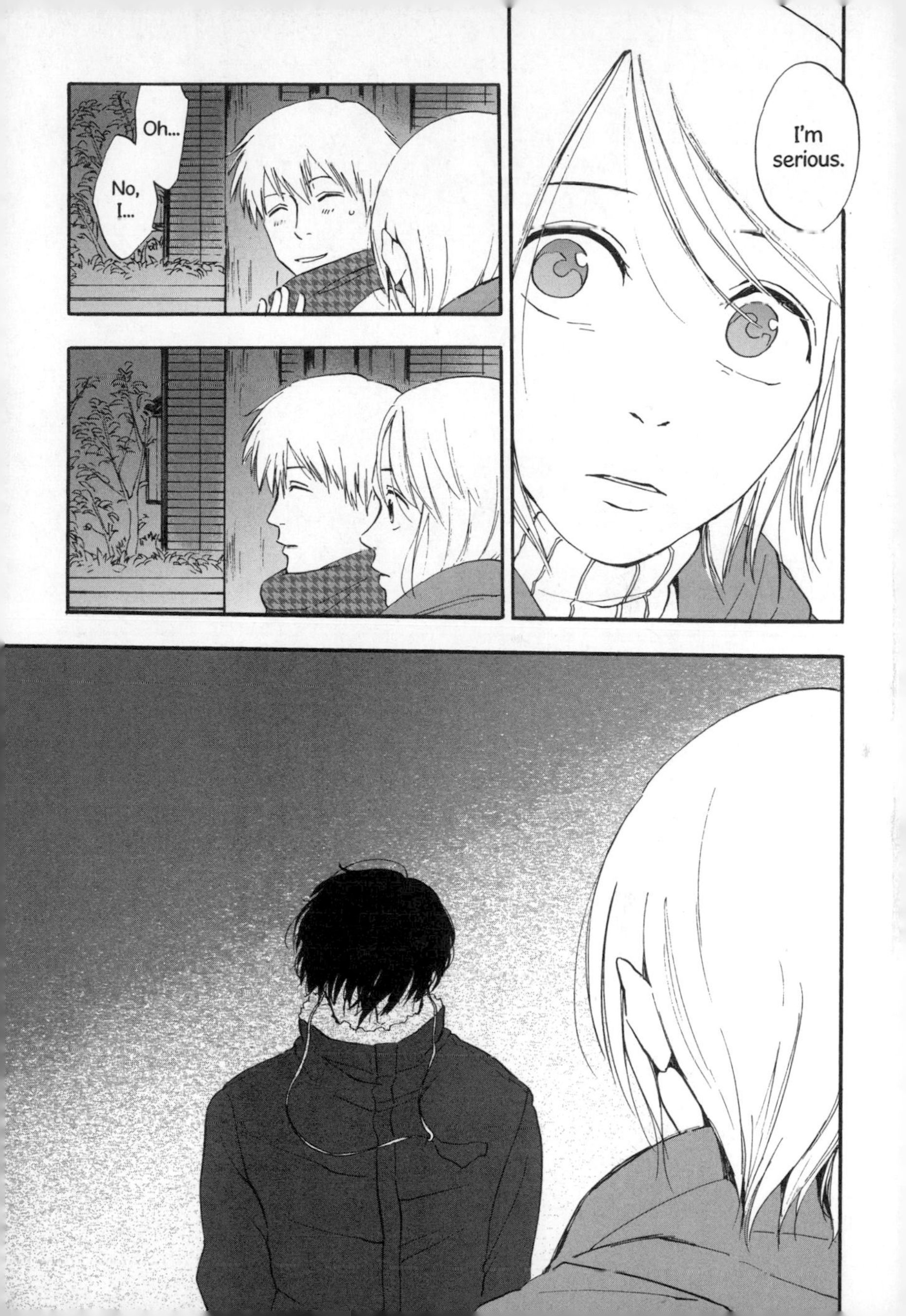
I'm serious.
Oh...
No, I...

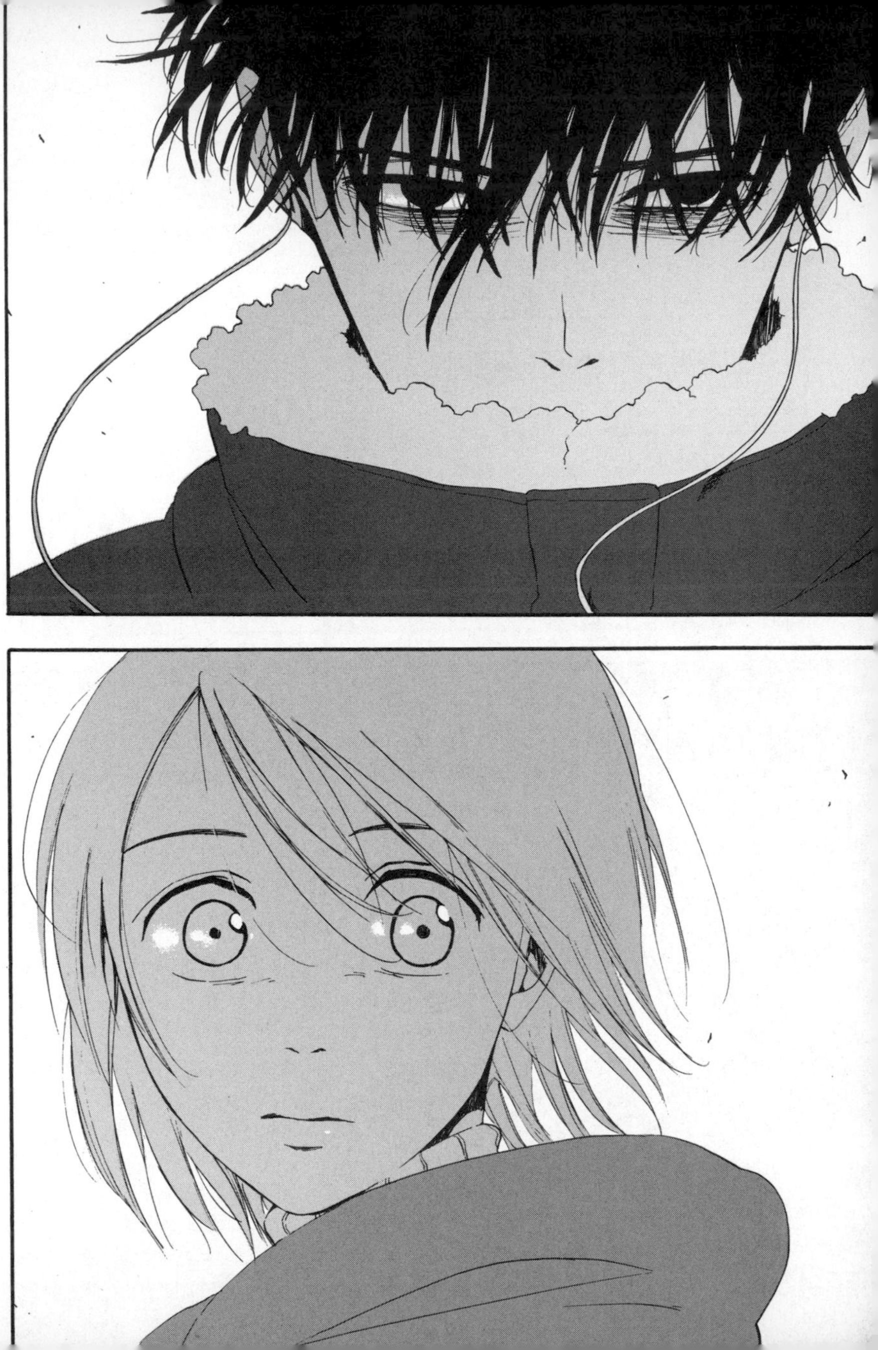

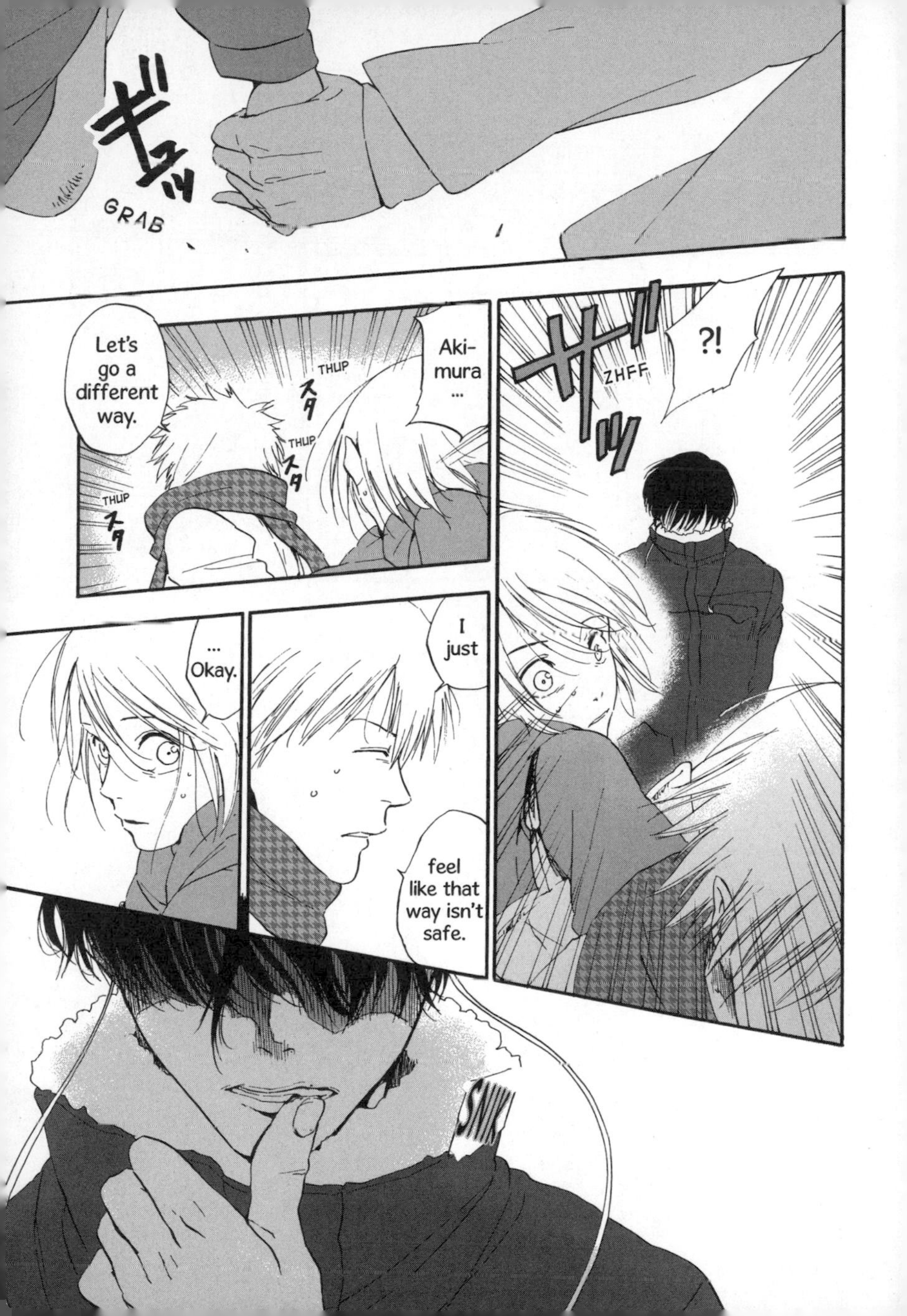
ギュッ
GRAB
ザッ
ZHFF
?!
Aki-mura ...
Let's go a different way.
スタ
THUP
スタ
THUP
スタ
THUP
I just feel like that way isn't safe.
... Okay.
SNIK

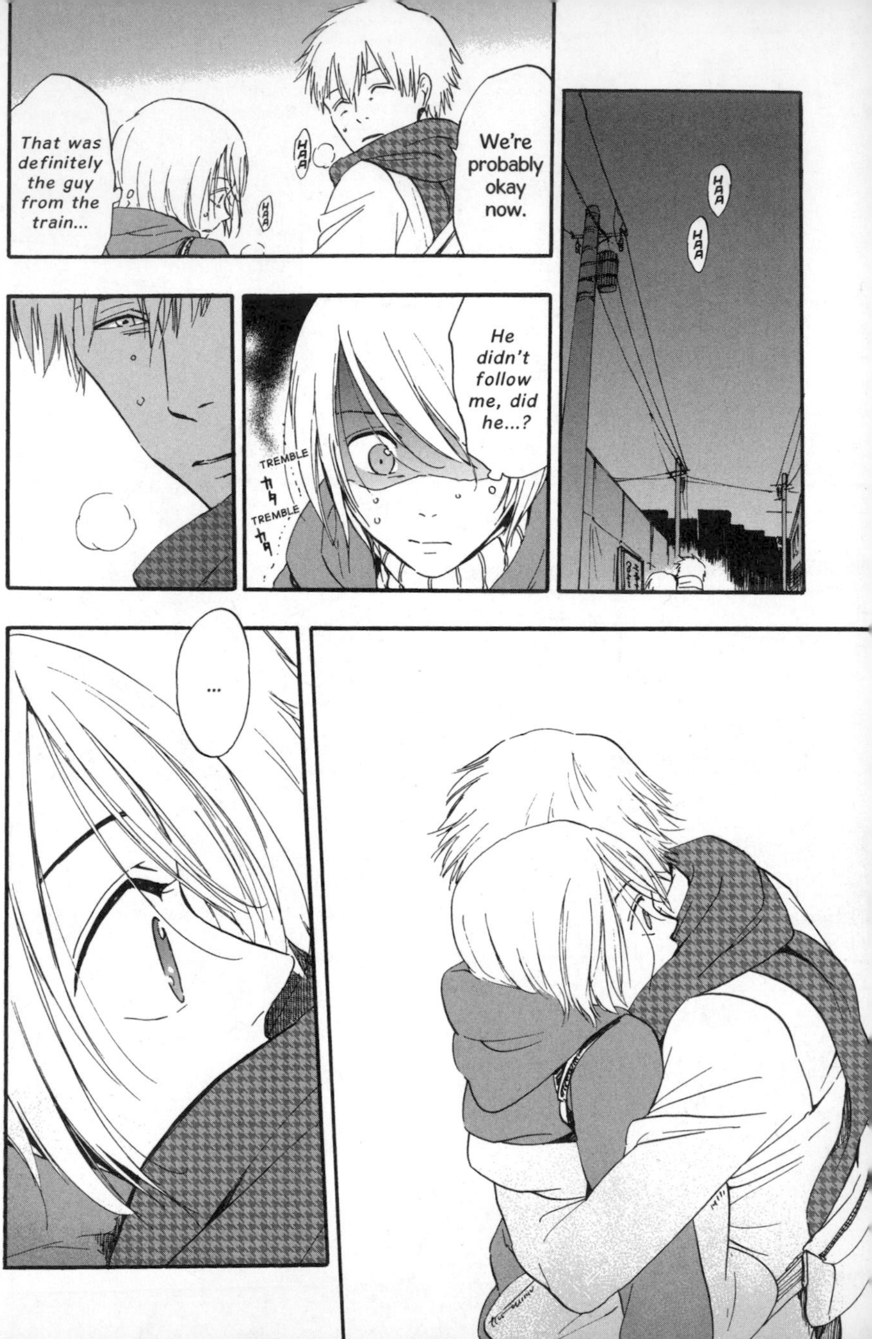
HAA
HAA
We're probably okay now.
HAA
HAA
That was definitely the guy from the train...
He didn't follow me, did he...?
TREMBLE
TREMBLE
...

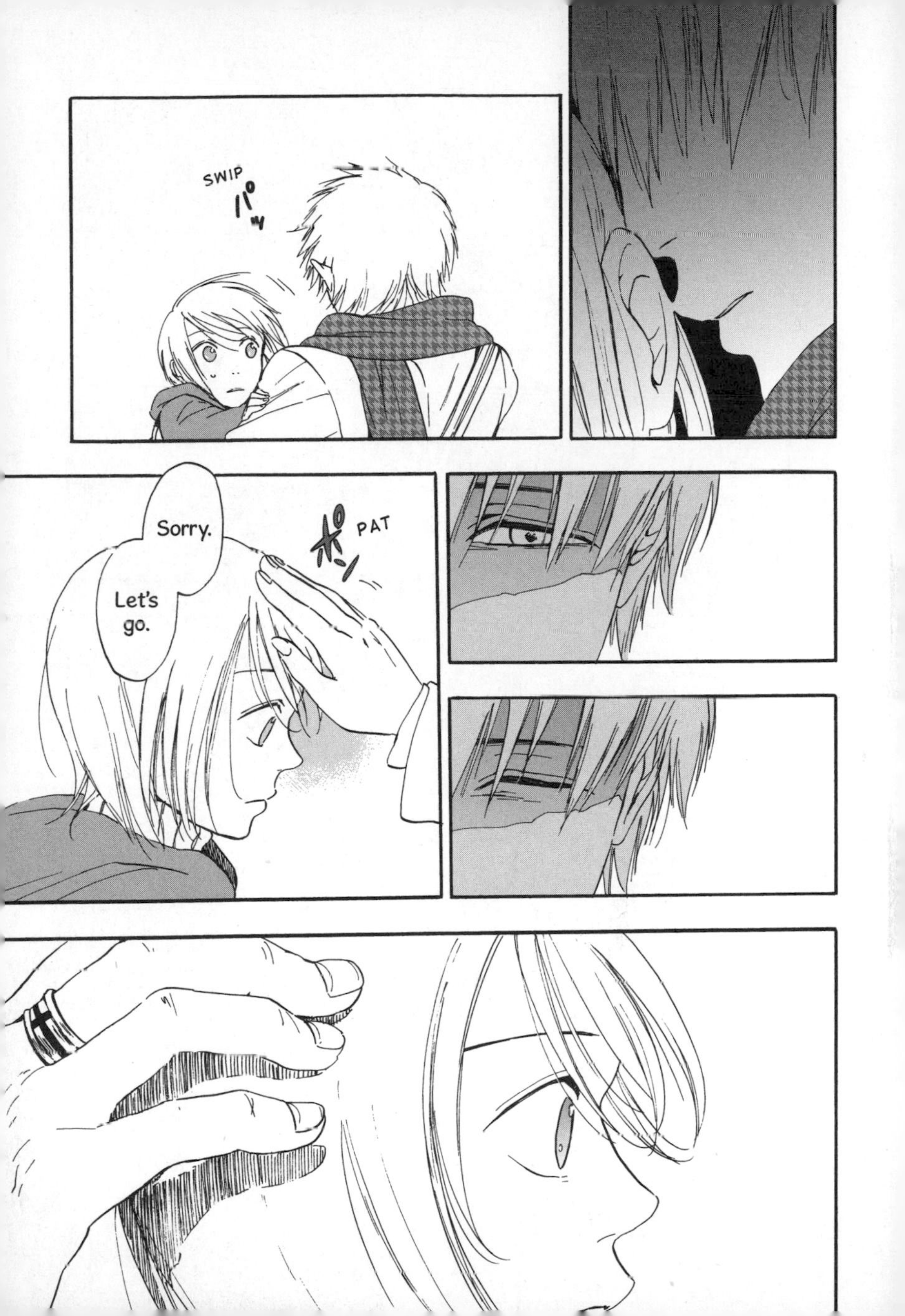
SWIP
パッ
PAT
ポン
Sorry.
Let's go.

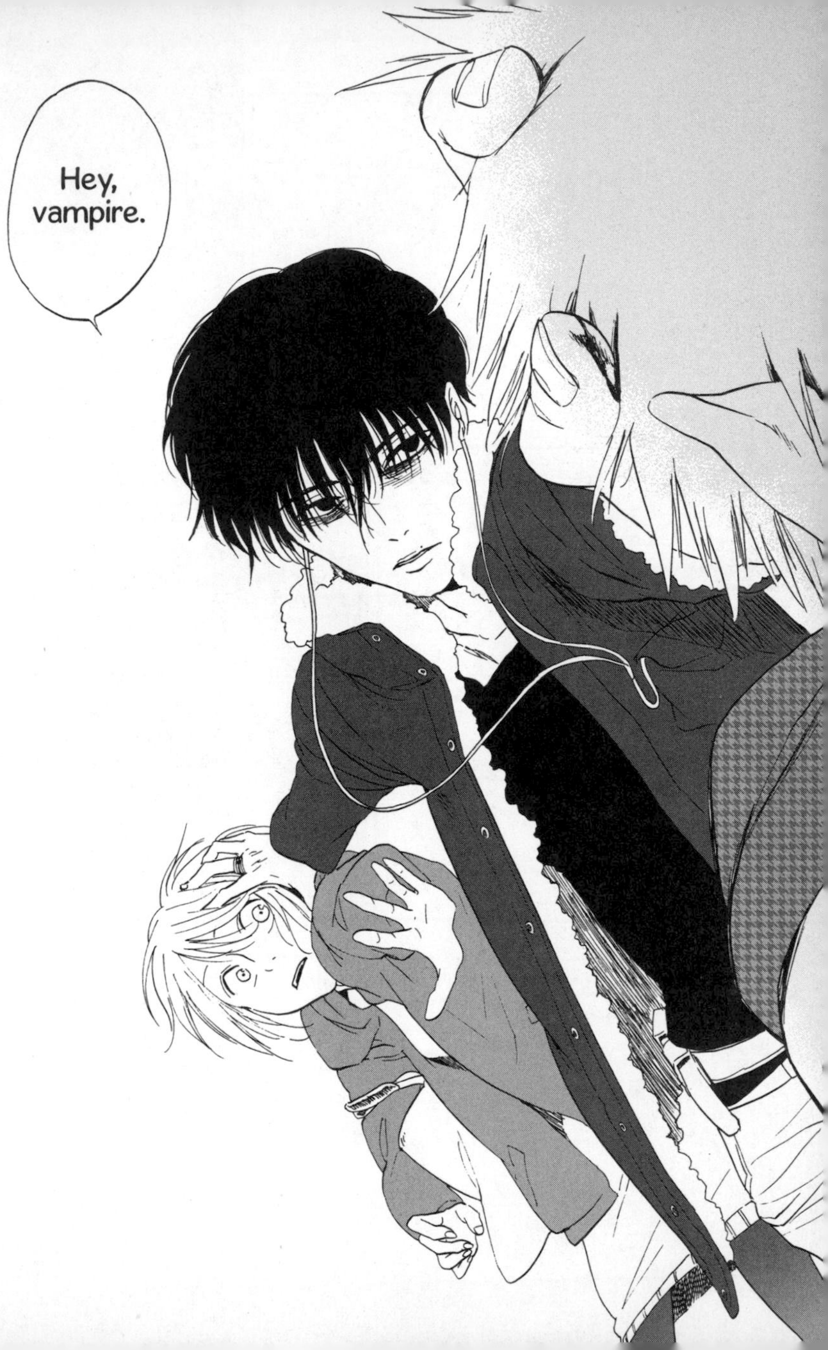
Hey, vampire.

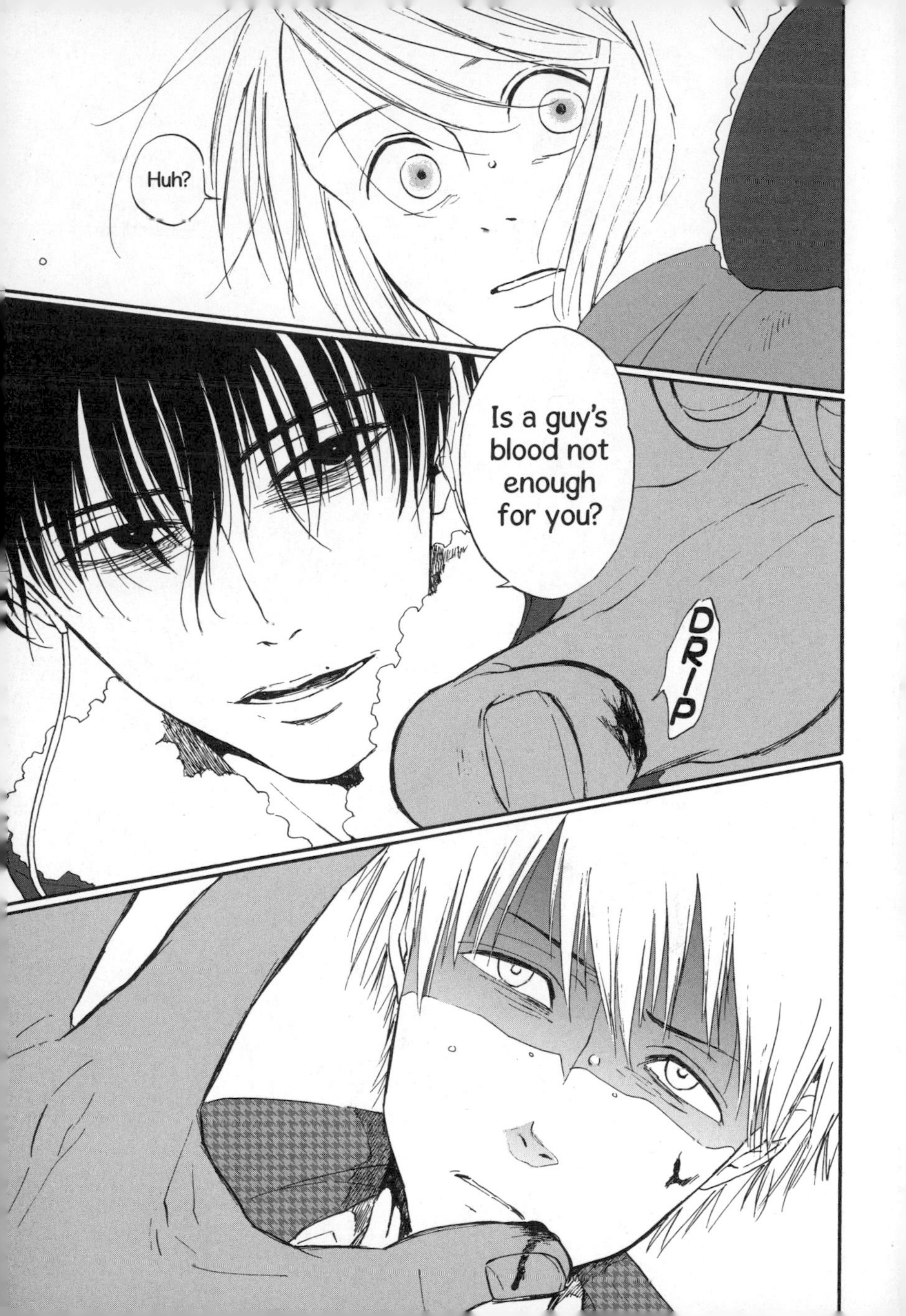
Huh?
Is a guy's blood not enough for you?
DRIP

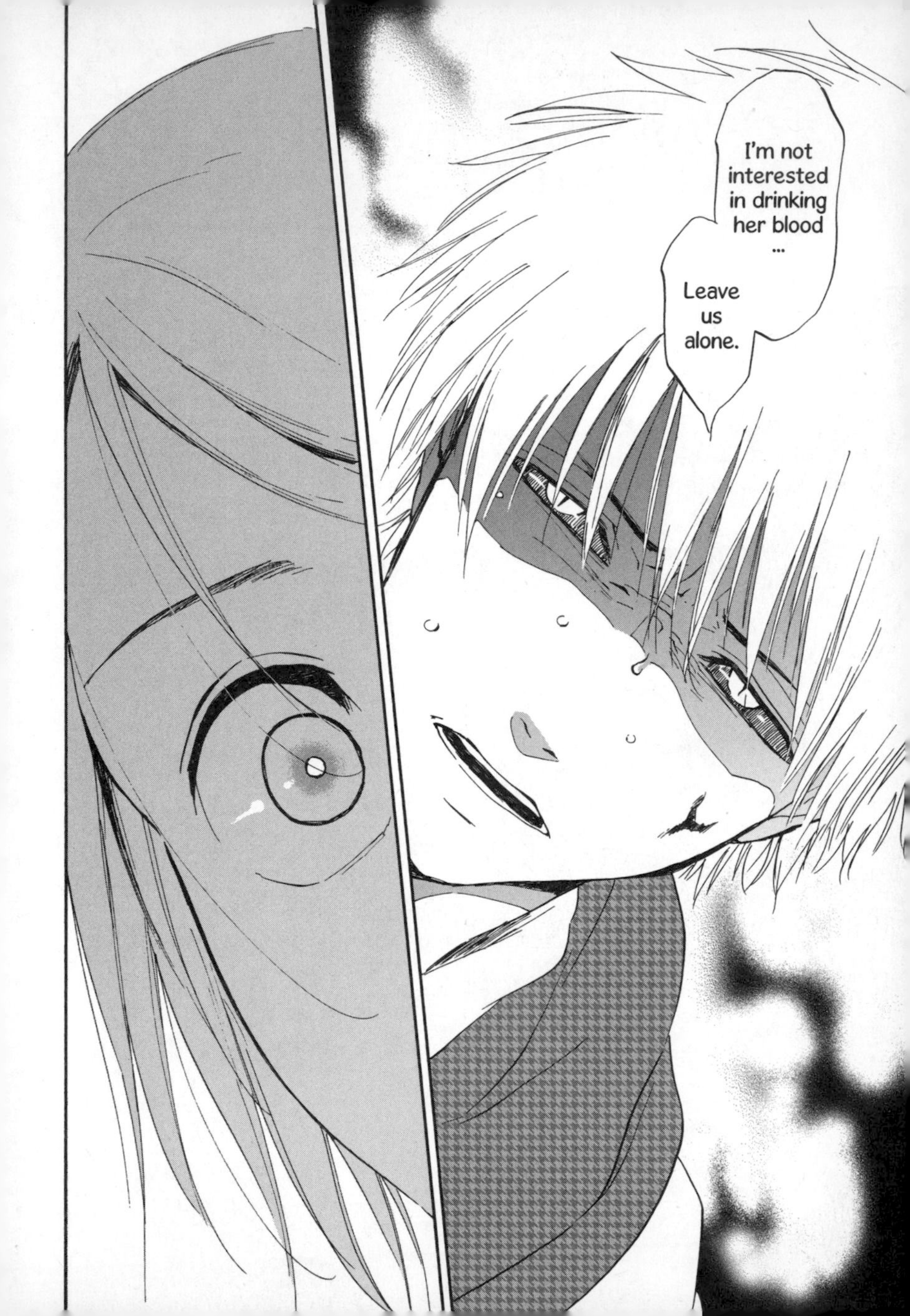
I'm not interested in drinking her blood ...
Leave us alone.

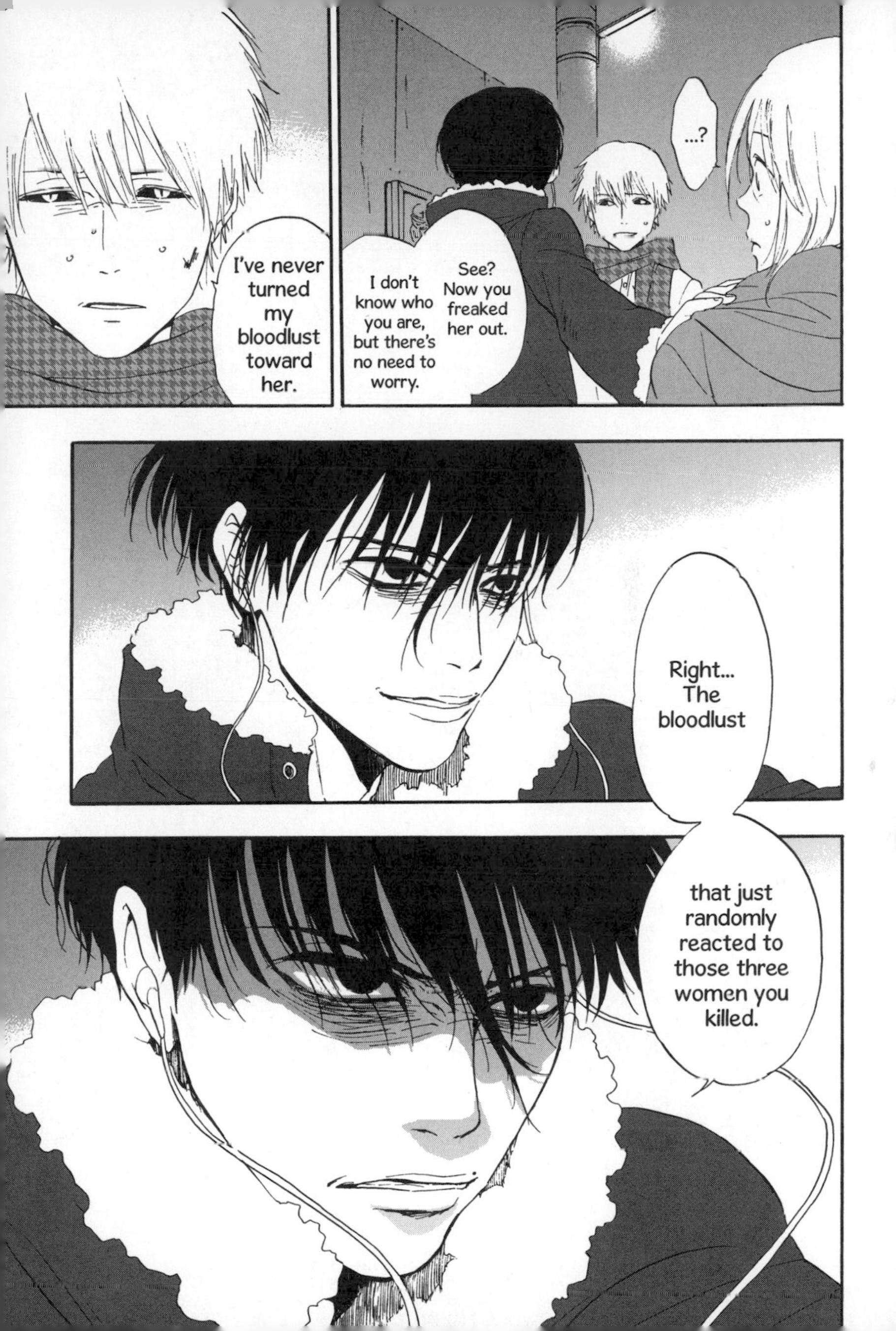
...?
See? Now you freaked her out.
I don't know who you are, but there's no need to worry.
I've never turned my bloodlust toward her.
Right... The bloodlust
that just randomly reacted to those three women you killed.

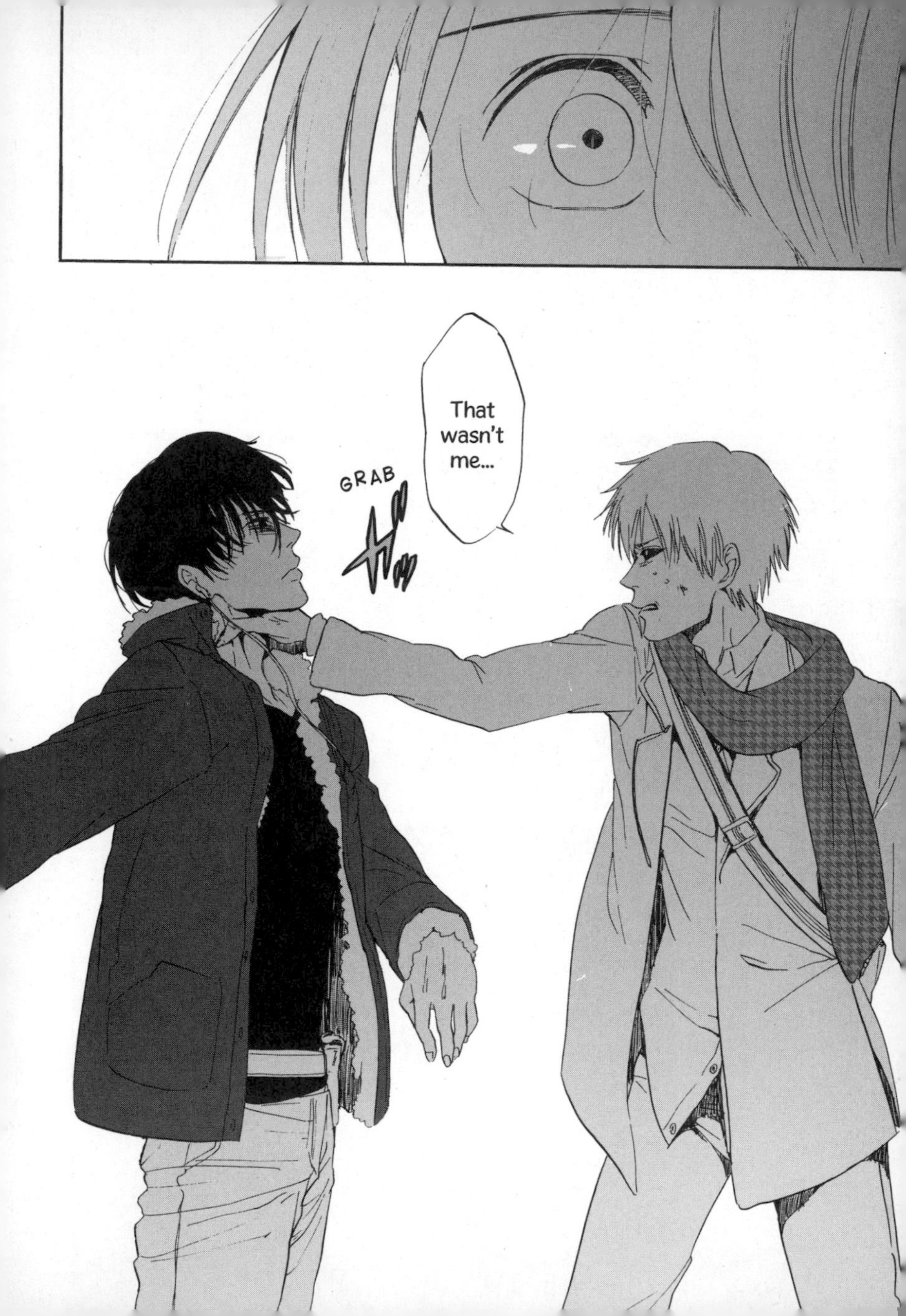
That wasn't me...
GRAB

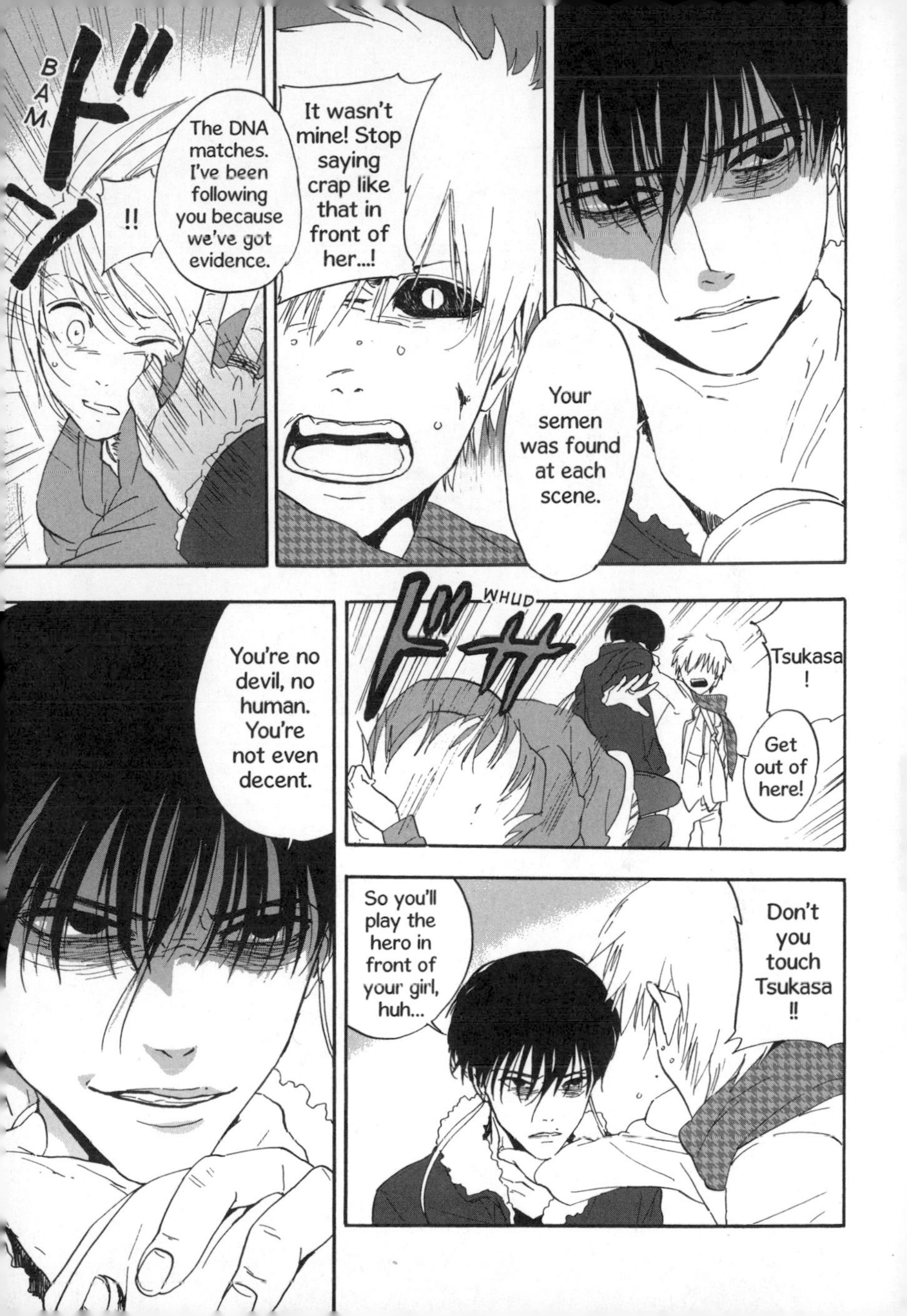
Your semen was found at each scene.
It wasn't mine! Stop saying crap like that in front of her...!
BAM
!!
The DNA matches. I've been following you because we've got evidence.
WHUD
Tsukasa!
Get out of here!
Don't you touch Tsukasa!!
So you'll play the hero in front of your girl, huh...
You're no devil, no human. You're not even decent.

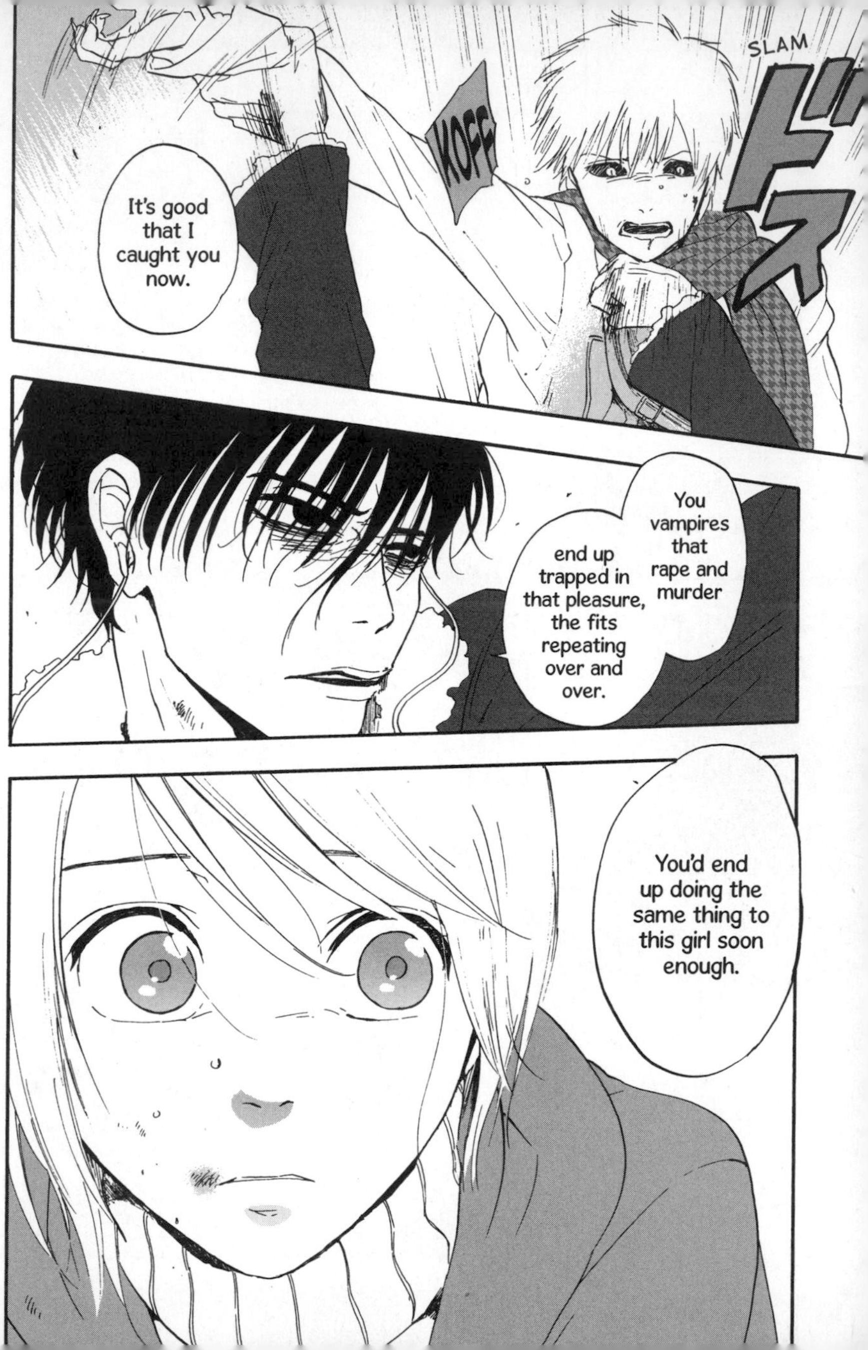
SLAM
ドス
KOFF
It's good that I caught you now.
You vampires that rape and murder
end up trapped in that pleasure, the fits repeating over and over.
You'd end up doing the same thing to this girl soon enough.

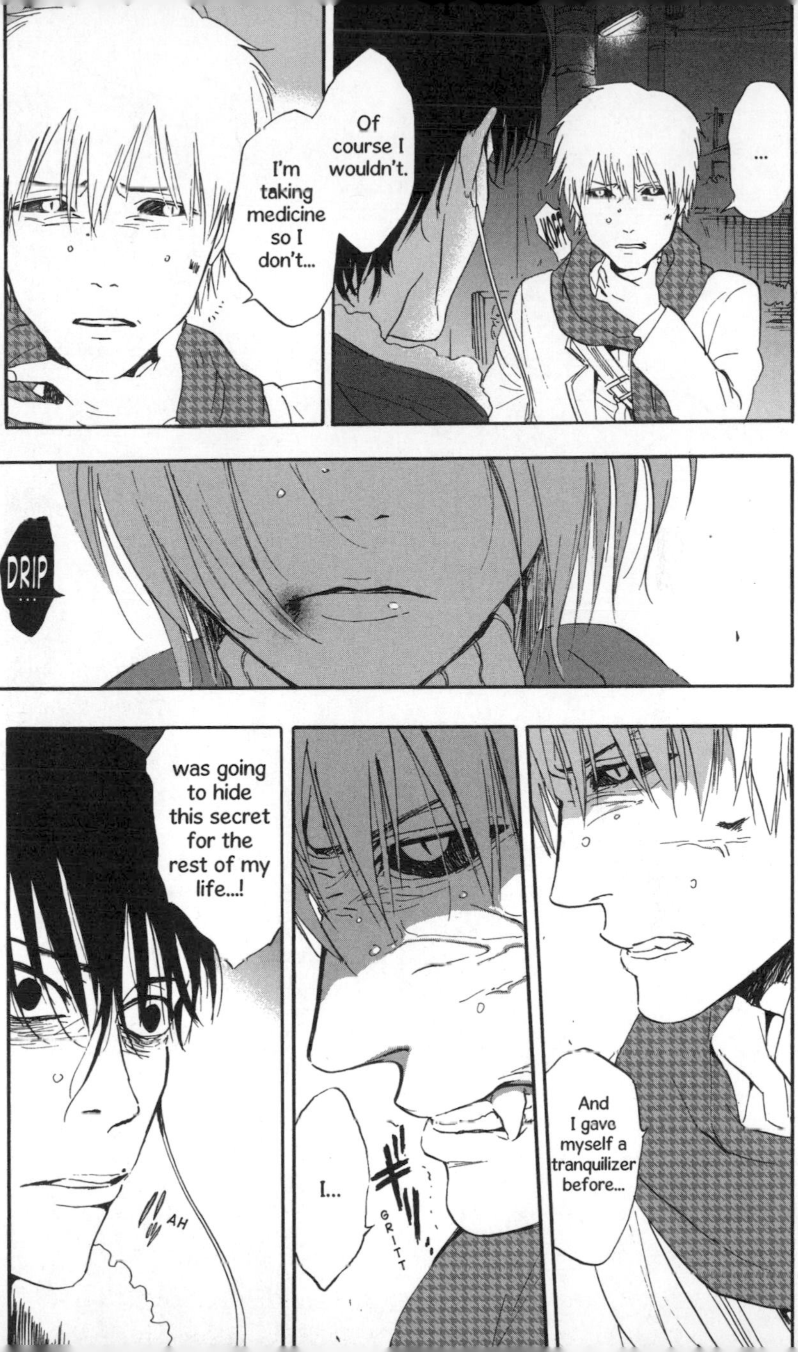
...
KOFF
Of course I wouldn't.
I'm taking medicine so I don't...
DRIP ...
And I gave myself a tranquilizer before...
I...
GRITT
was going to hide this secret for the rest of my life...!
AH

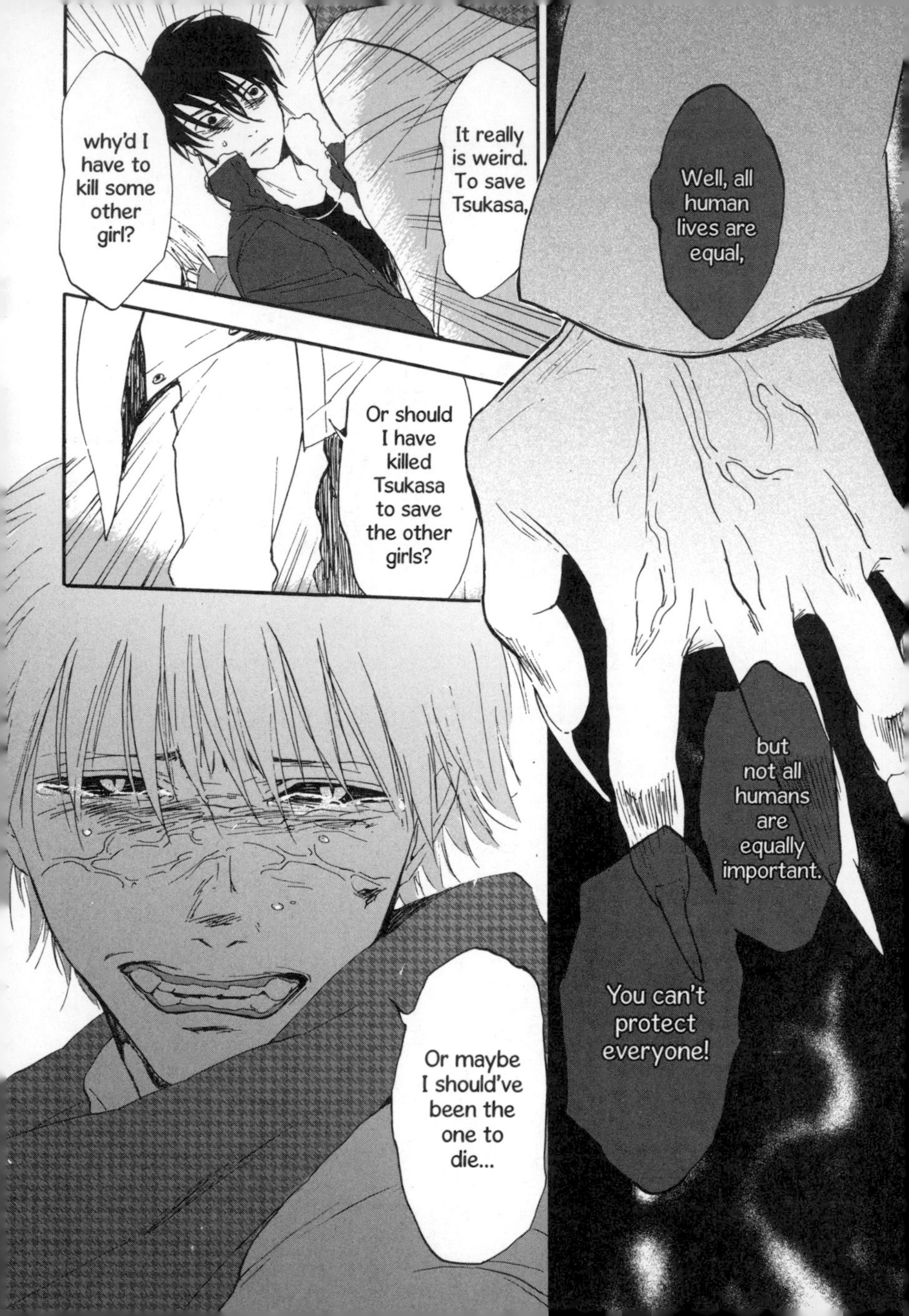
Well, all human lives are equal,
but not all humans are equally important.
You can't protect everyone!
It really is weird. To save Tsukasa,
why'd I have to kill some other girl?
Or should I have killed Tsukasa to save the other girls?
Or maybe I should've been the one to die...

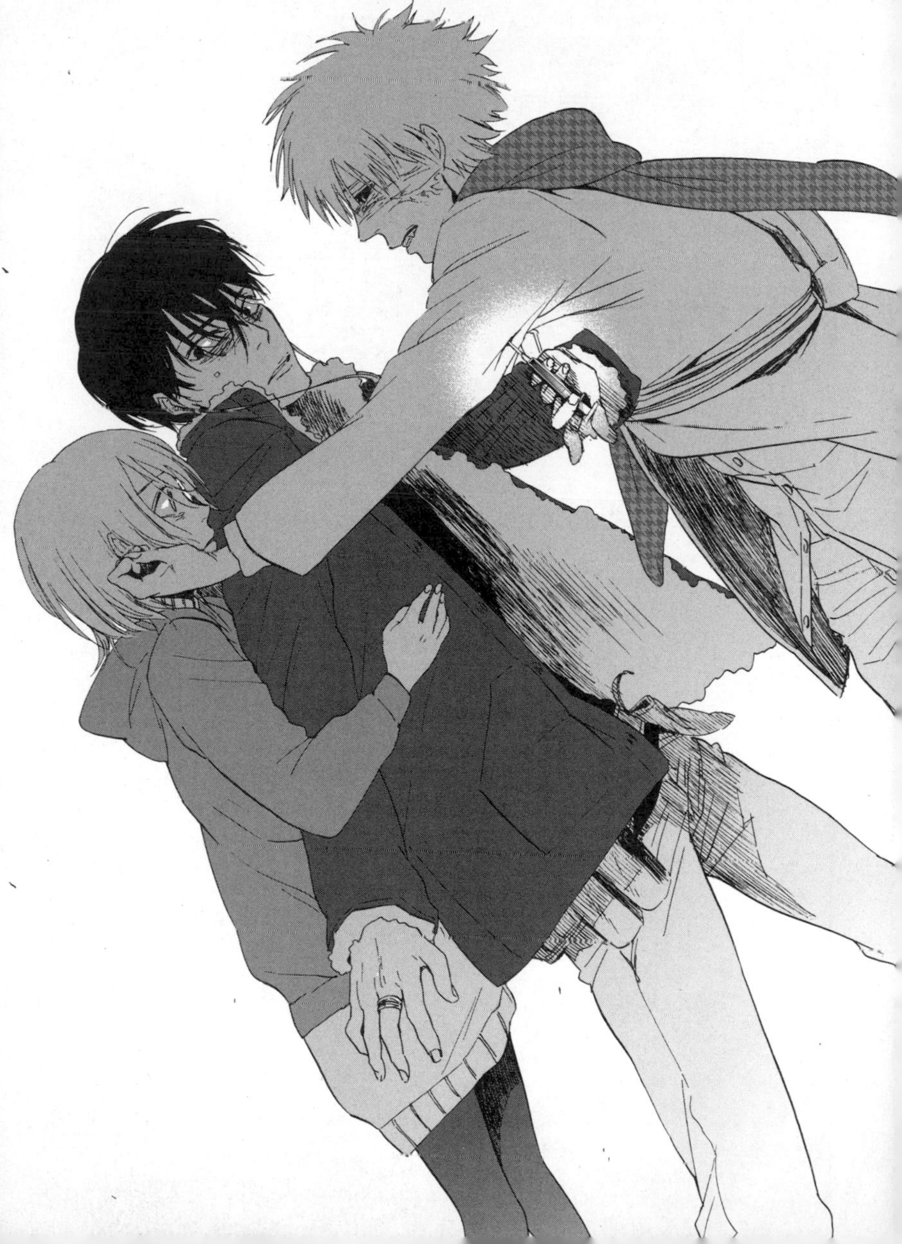

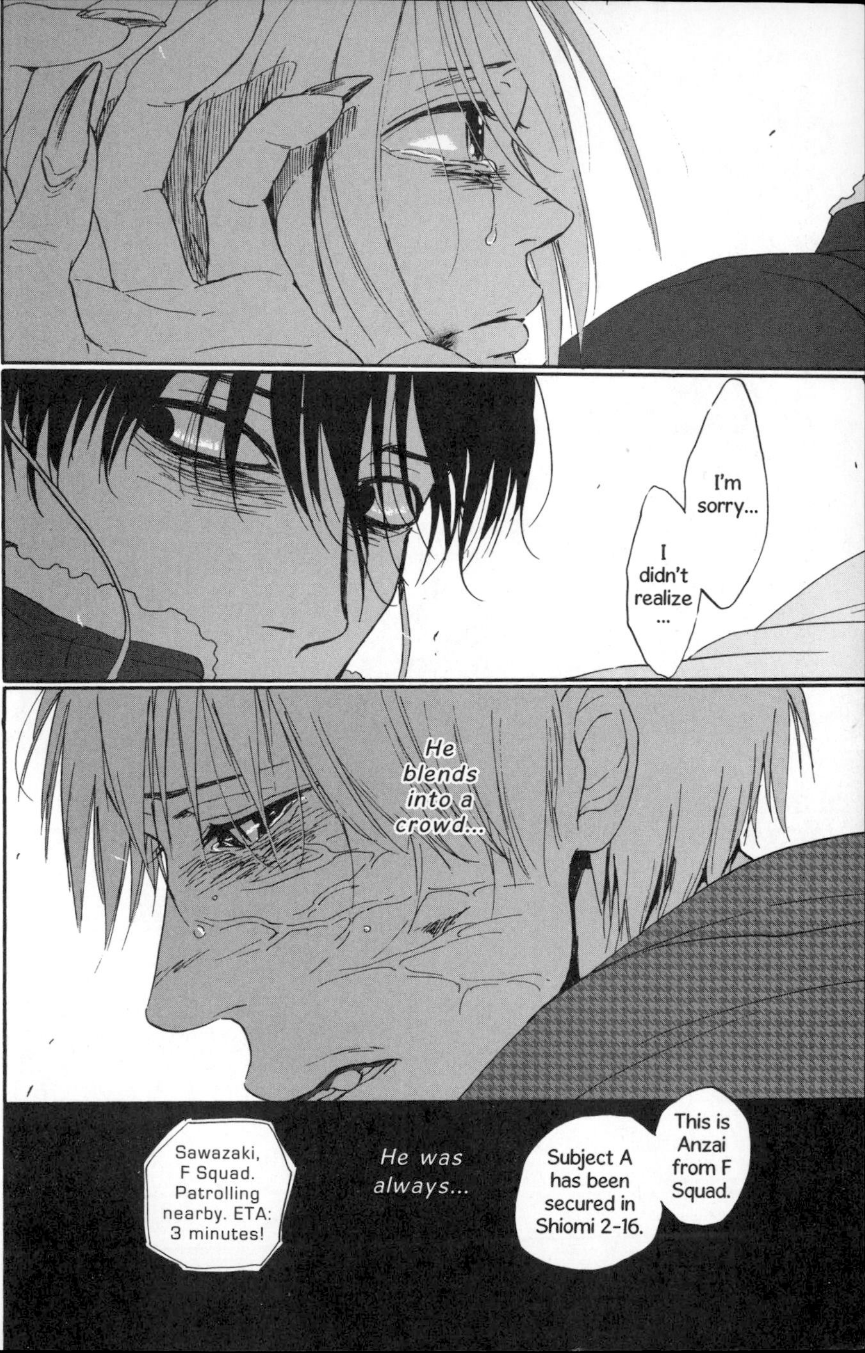
I'm sorry...
I didn't realize ...
He blends into a crowd...
This is Anzai from F Squad.
Subject A has been secured in Shiomi 2-16.
He was always...
Sawazaki, F Squad. Patrolling nearby. ETA: 3 minutes!

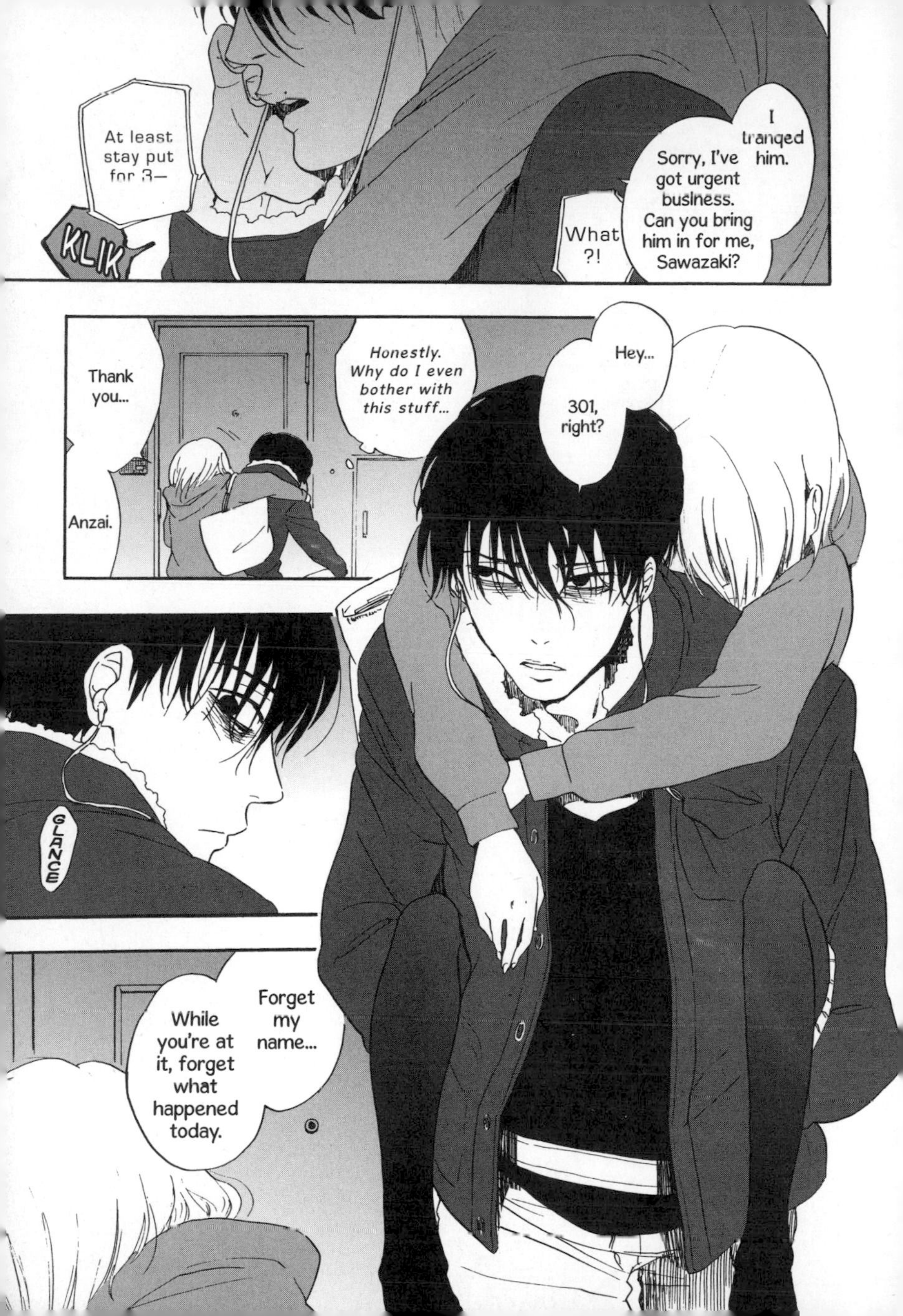
I tranqed him.
Sorry, I've got urgent business. Can you bring him in for me, Sawazaki?
What?!
At least stay put for 3—
KLIK
Hey...
301, right?
Honestly. Why do I even bother with this stuff...
Thank you...
Anzai.
GLANCE
Forget my name...
While you're at it, forget what happened today.

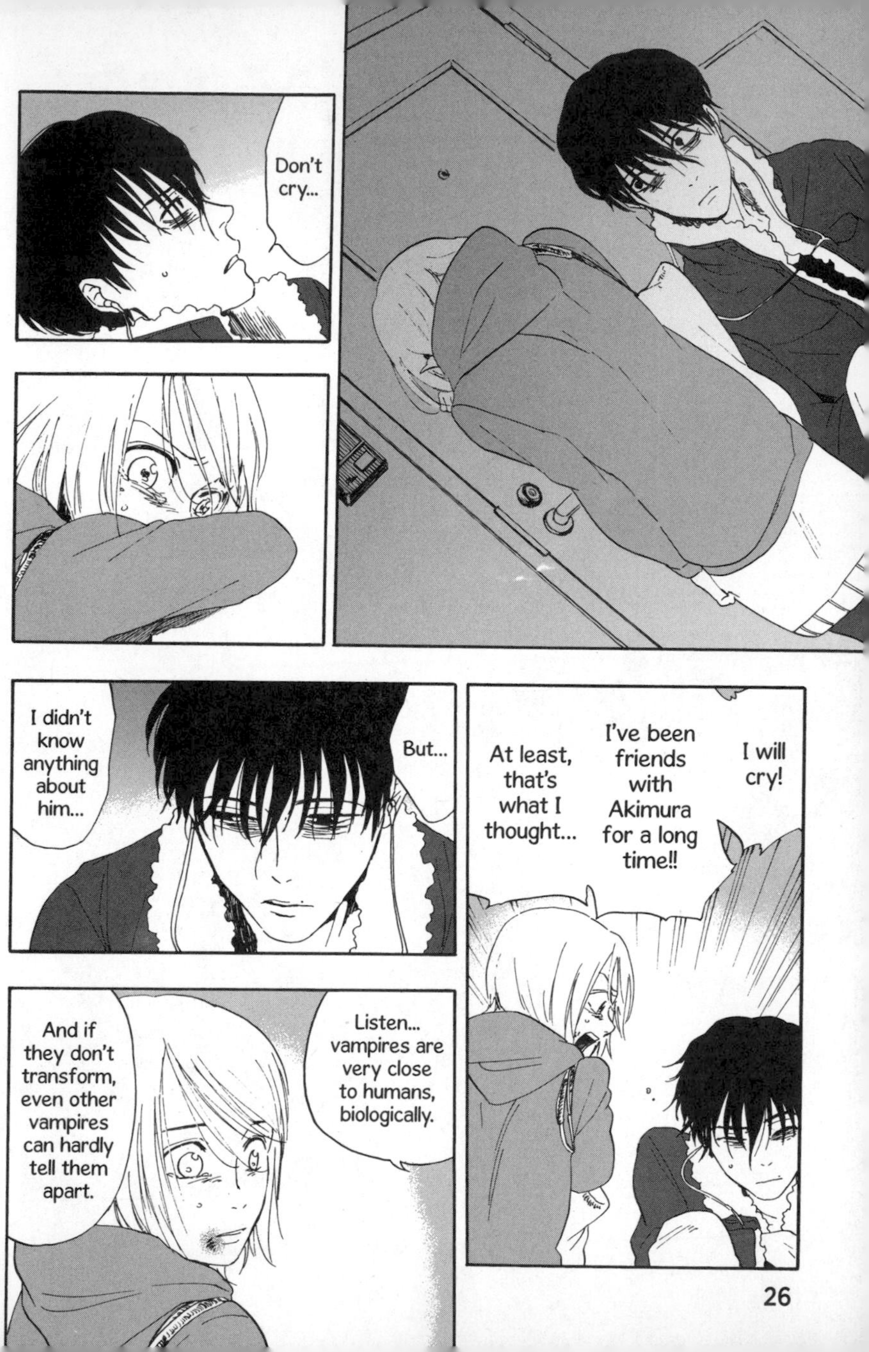

Don't cry...
I will cry!
I've been friends with Akimura for a long time!!
At least, that's what I thought...
But...
I didn't know anything about him...
Listen... vampires are very close to humans, biologically.
And if they don't transform, even other vampires can hardly tell them apart.

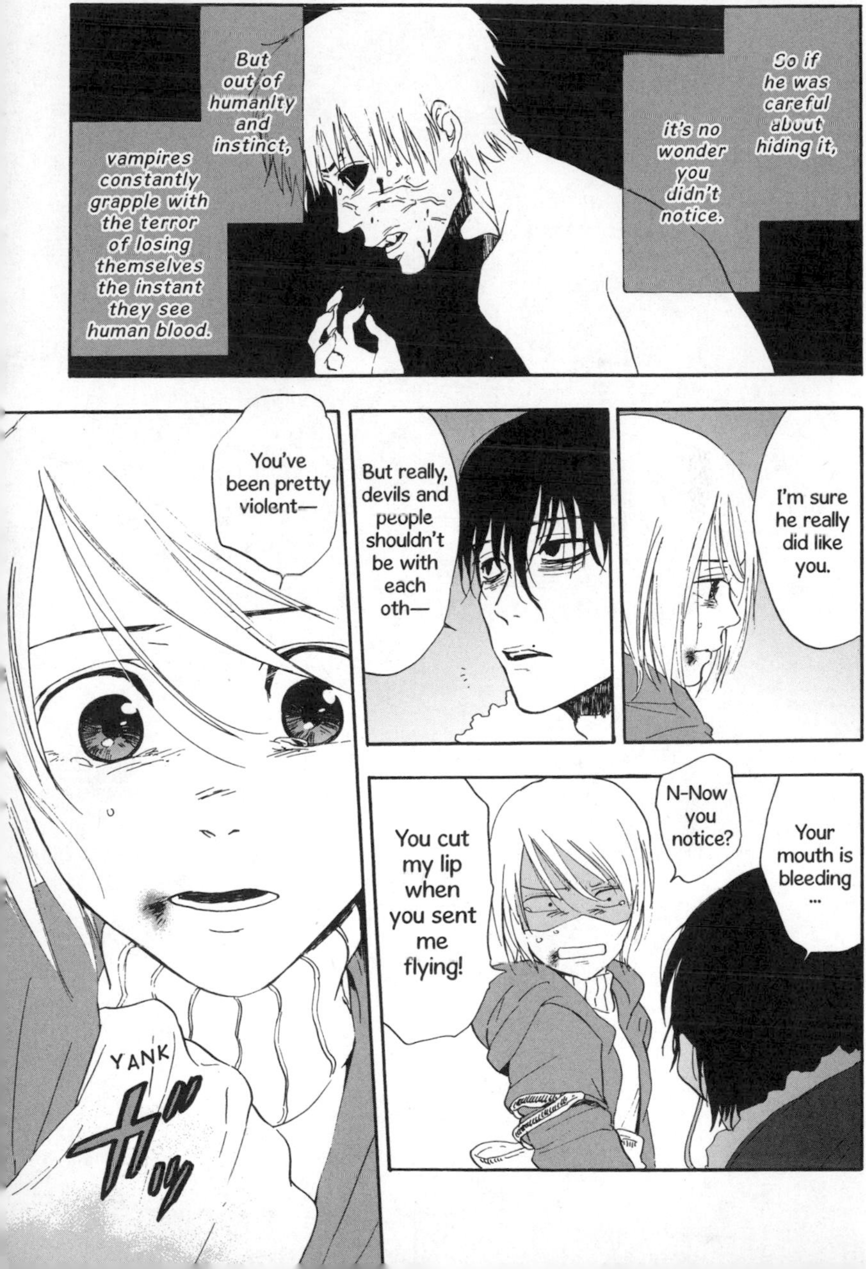
So if he was careful about hiding it,
it's no wonder you didn't notice.
But out of humanity and instinct,
vampires constantly grapple with the terror of losing themselves the instant they see human blood.
I'm sure he really did like you.
But really, devils and people shouldn't be with each oth—
Your mouth is bleeding ...
N-Now you notice?
You cut my lip when you sent me flying!
You've been pretty violent—
YANK

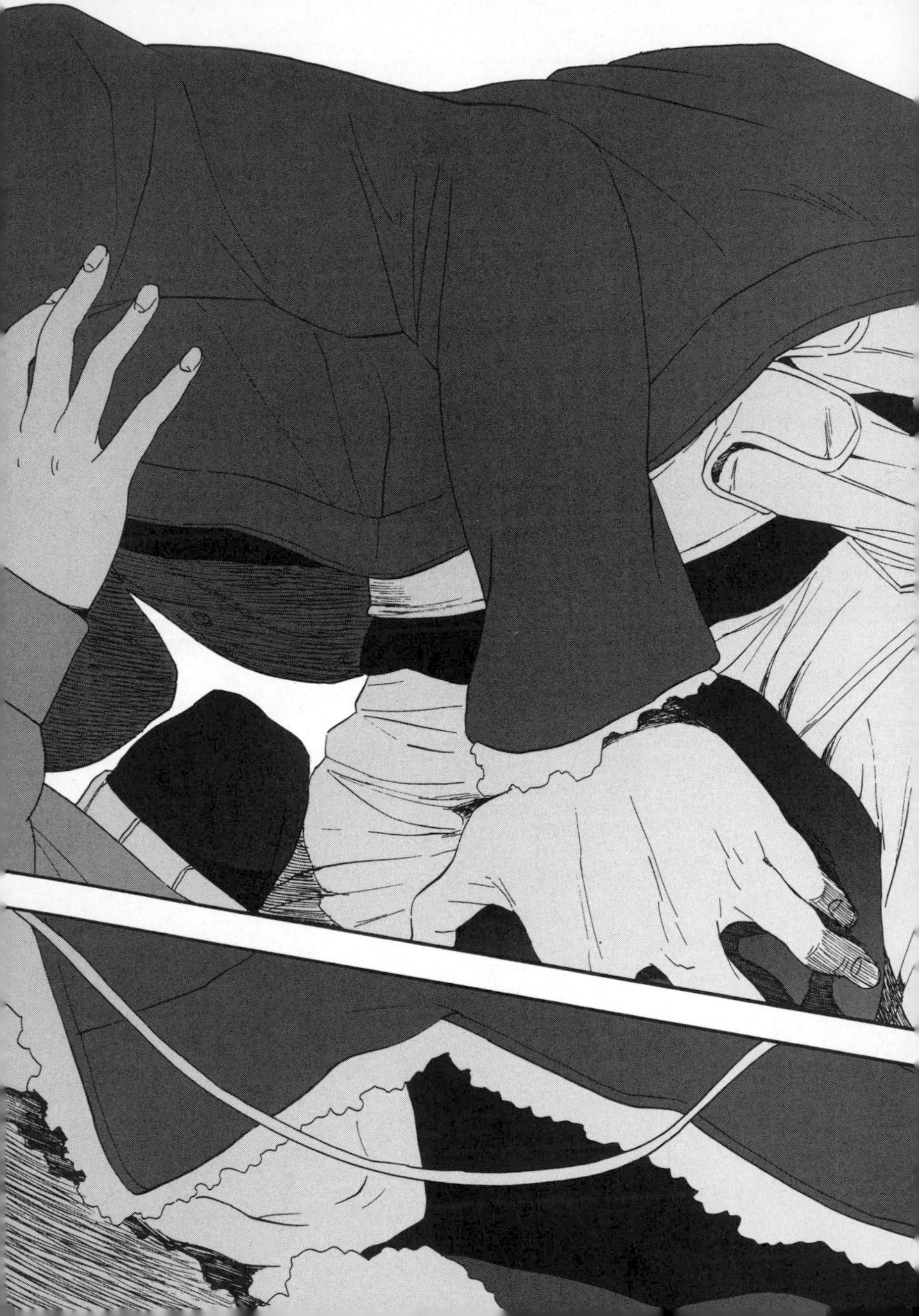

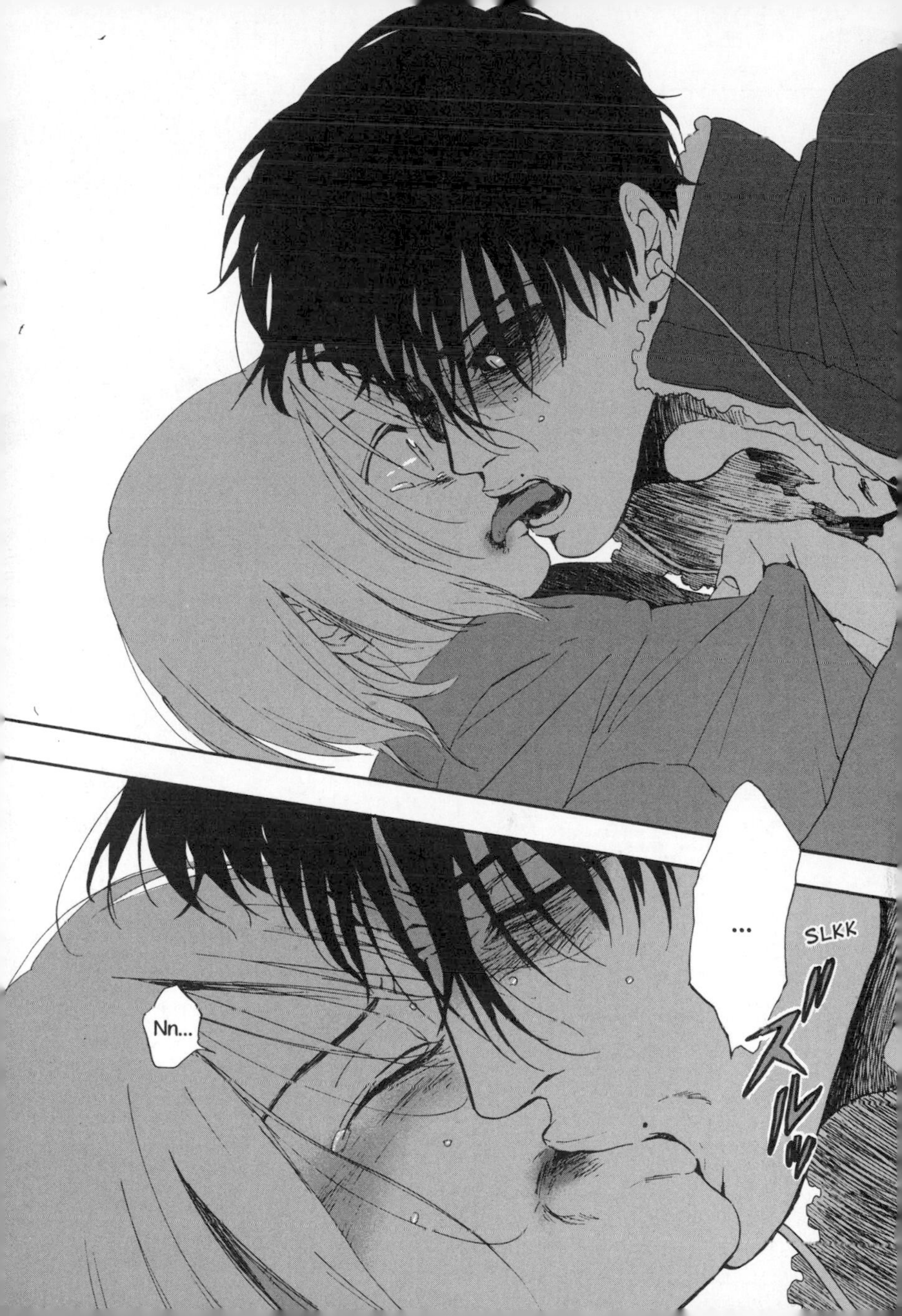
...
SLKK
ズルッ
Nn...

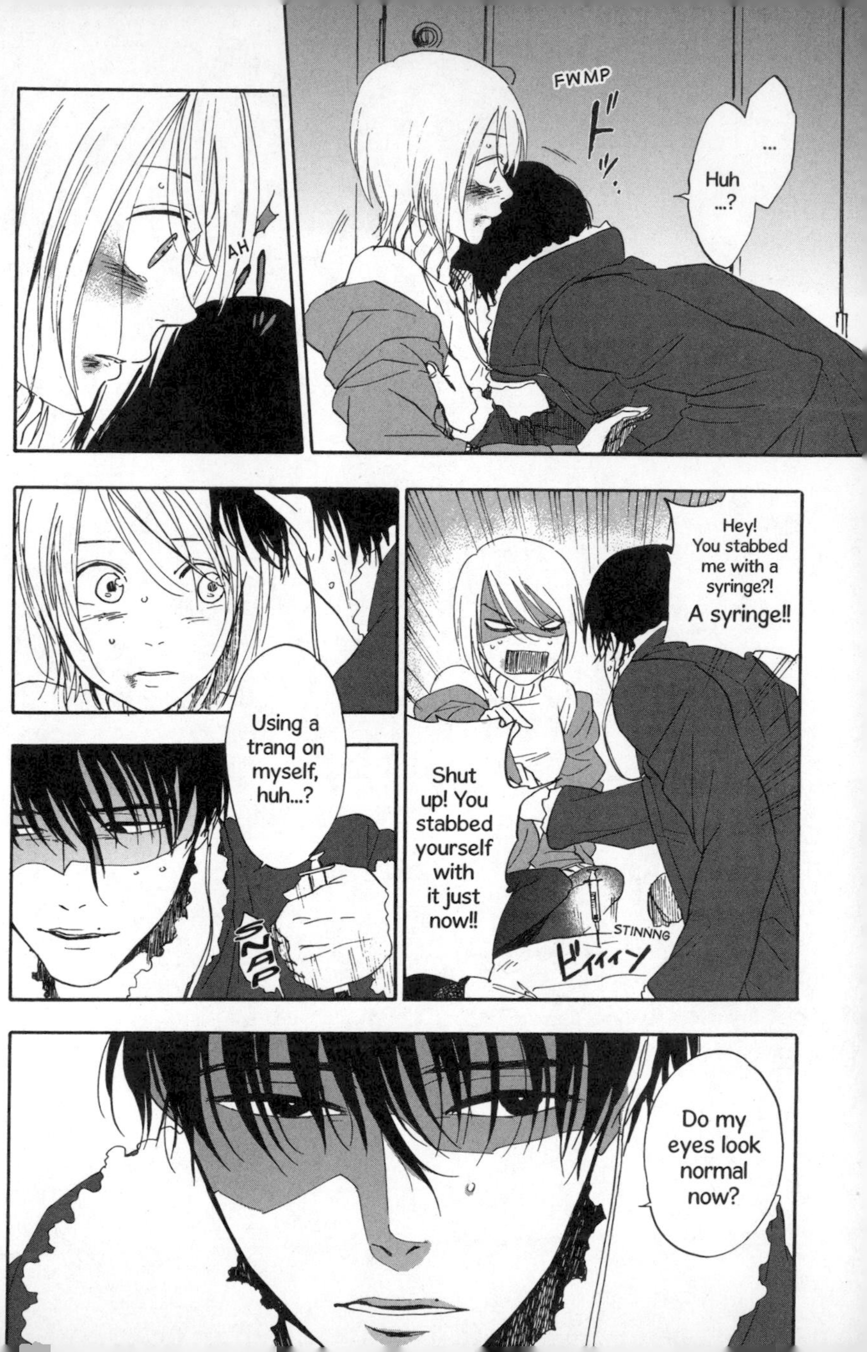
FWMP
ドッ…
...
Huh ...?
AH
Hey! You stabbed me with a syringe?!
A syringe!!
Shut up! You stabbed yourself with it just now!!
STINNNG
ビイイイン
Using a tranq on myself, huh...?
SNAP
Do my eyes look normal now?

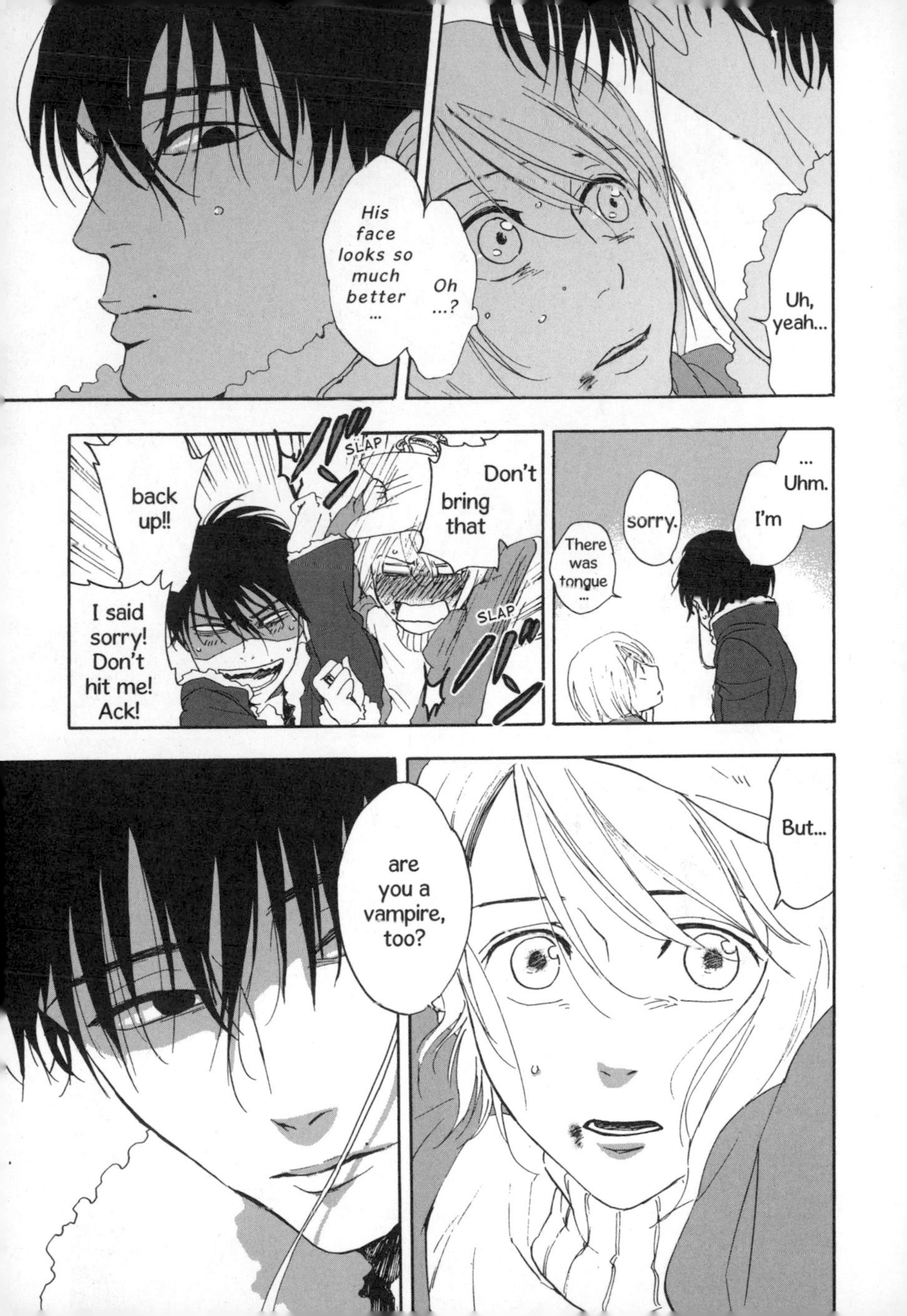
Uh, yeah...
Oh ...?
His face looks so much better ...
... Uhm.
I'm
sorry.
There was tongue ...
SLAP
Don't bring that
back up!!
SLAP
I said sorry! Don't hit me! Ack!
But...
are you a vampire, too?

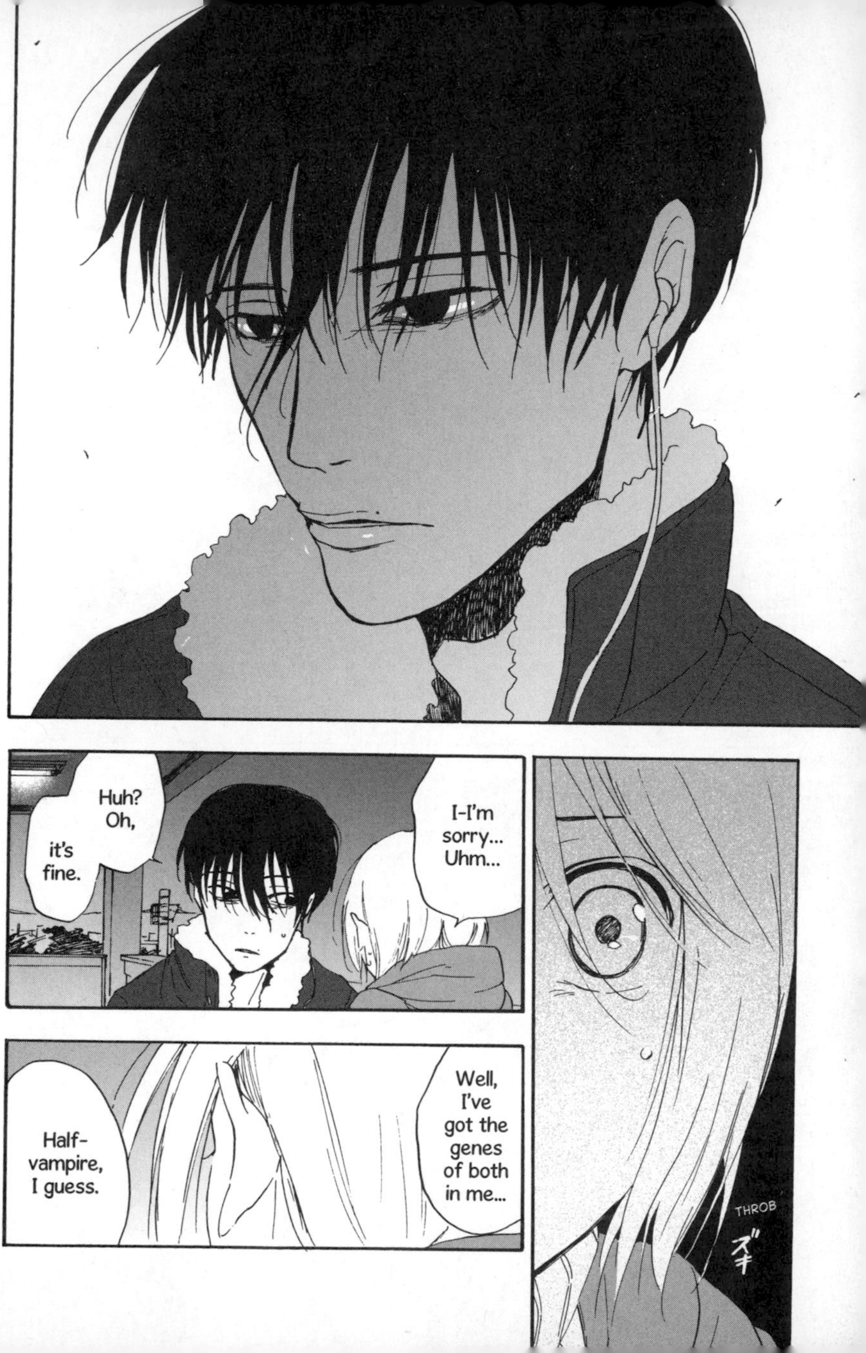
THROB
ズキ
I-I'm sorry... Uhm...
Huh? Oh,
it's fine.
Well, I've got the genes of both in me...
Half-vampire, I guess.

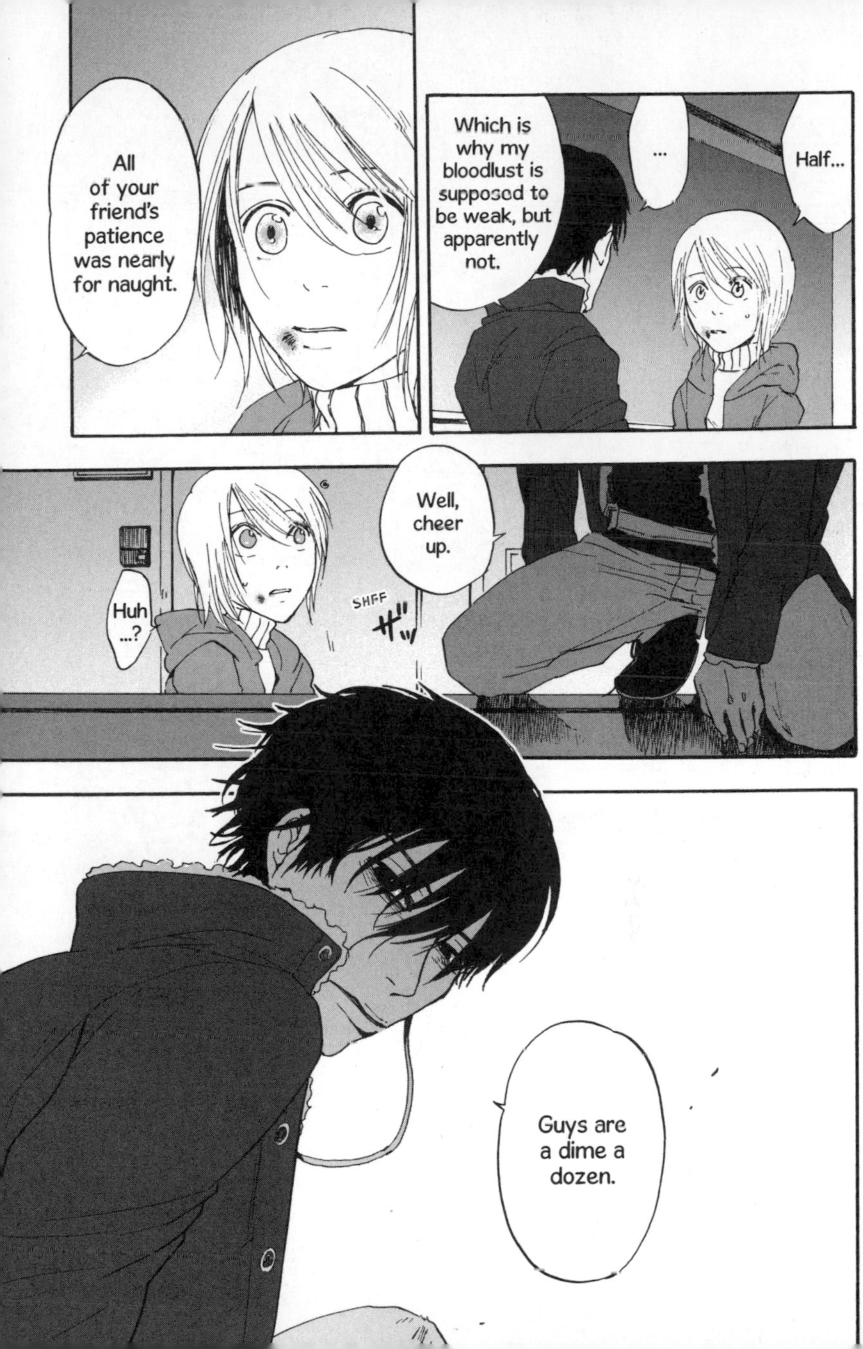
Half...
...
Which is why my bloodlust is supposed to be weak, but apparently not.
All of your friend's patience was nearly for naught.
Well, cheer up.
SHFF
Huh ...?
Guys are a dime a dozen.

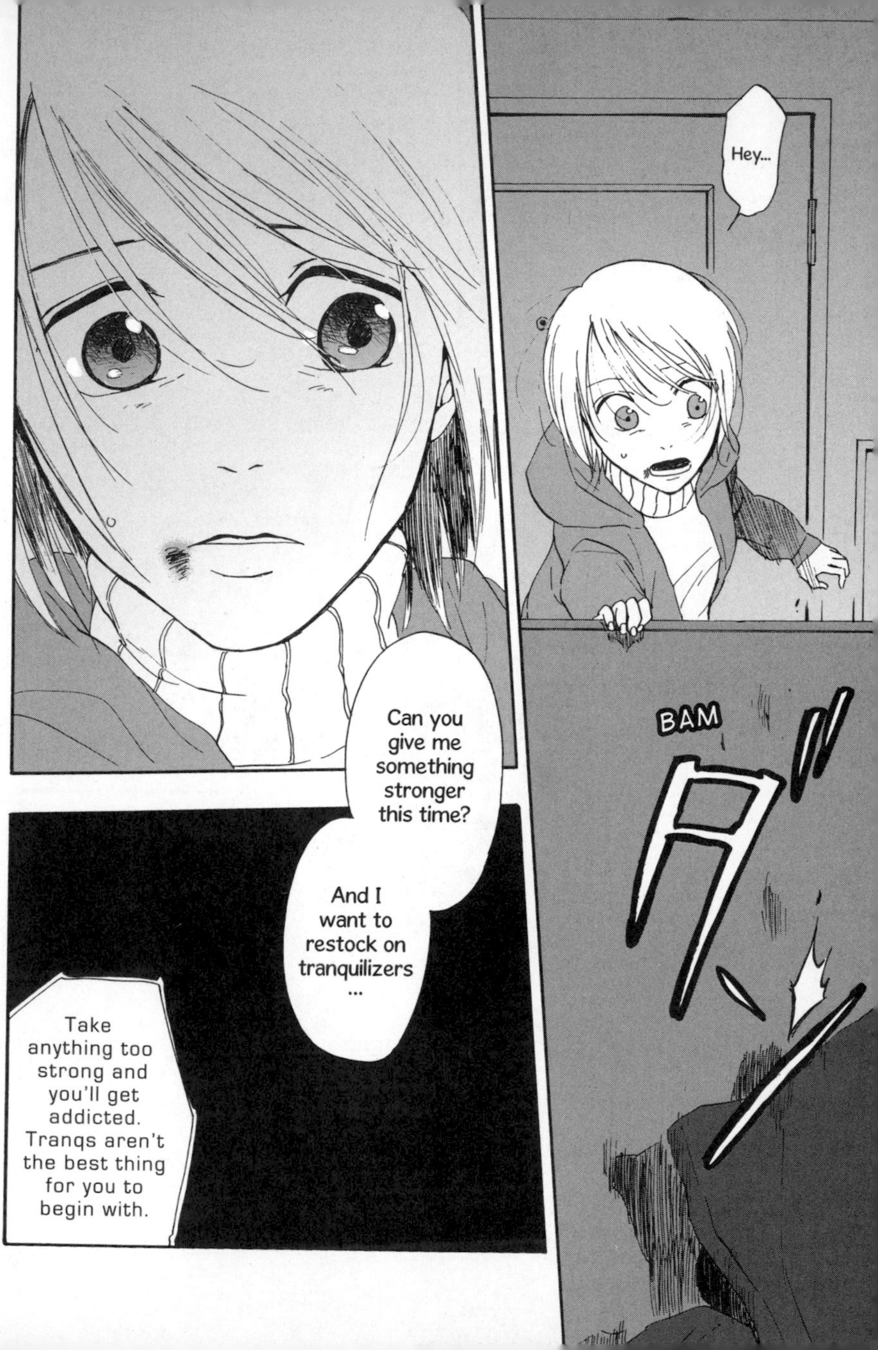
Hey...
BAM
Can you give me something stronger this time?
And I want to restock on tranquilizers ...
Take anything too strong and you'll get addicted. Tranqs aren't the best thing for you to begin with.

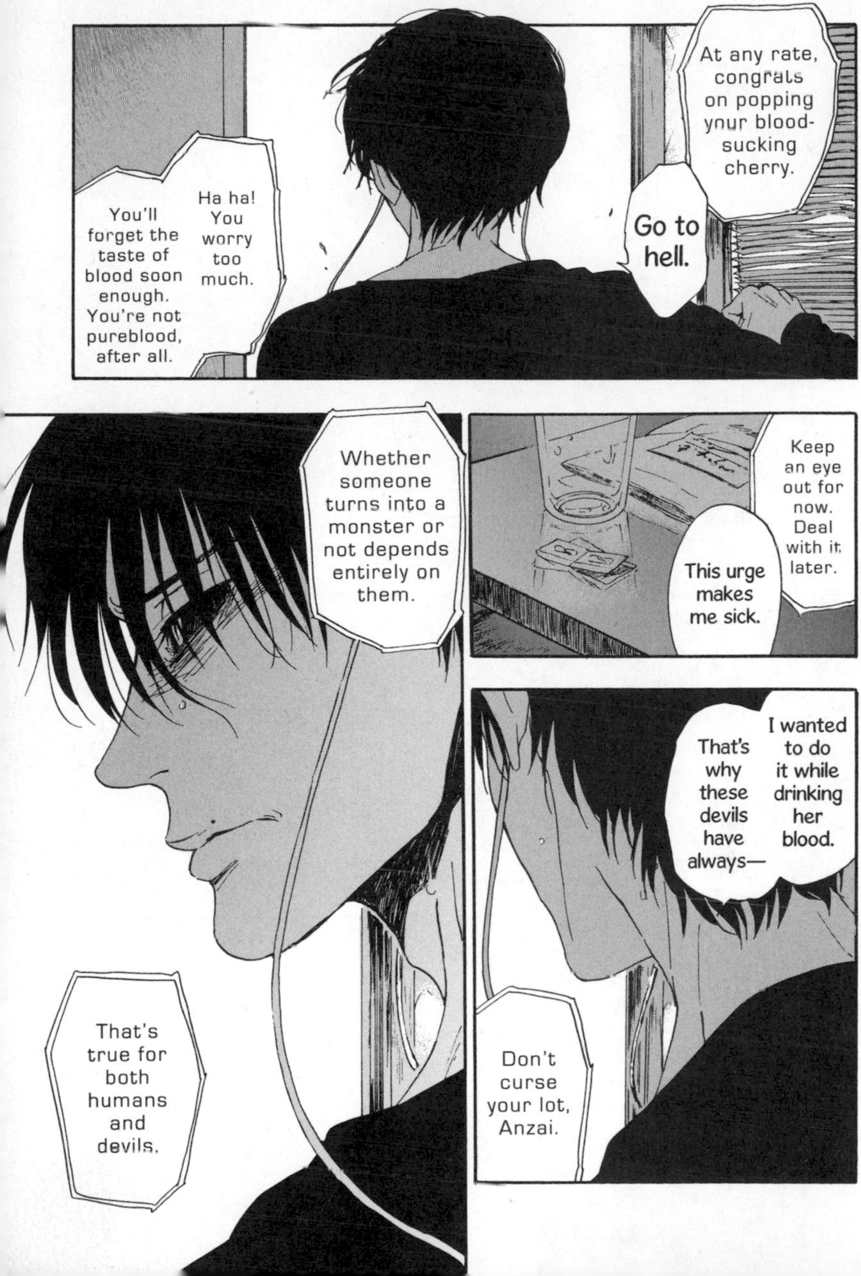
At any rate, congrats on popping your blood-sucking cherry.
Go to hell.
Ha ha! You worry too much.
You'll forget the taste of blood soon enough. You're not pureblood, after all.
Keep an eye out for now. Deal with it later.
This urge makes me sick.
I wanted to do it while drinking her blood.
That's why these devils have always—
Don't curse your lot, Anzai.
Whether someone turns into a monster or not depends entirely on them.
That's true for both humans and devils.

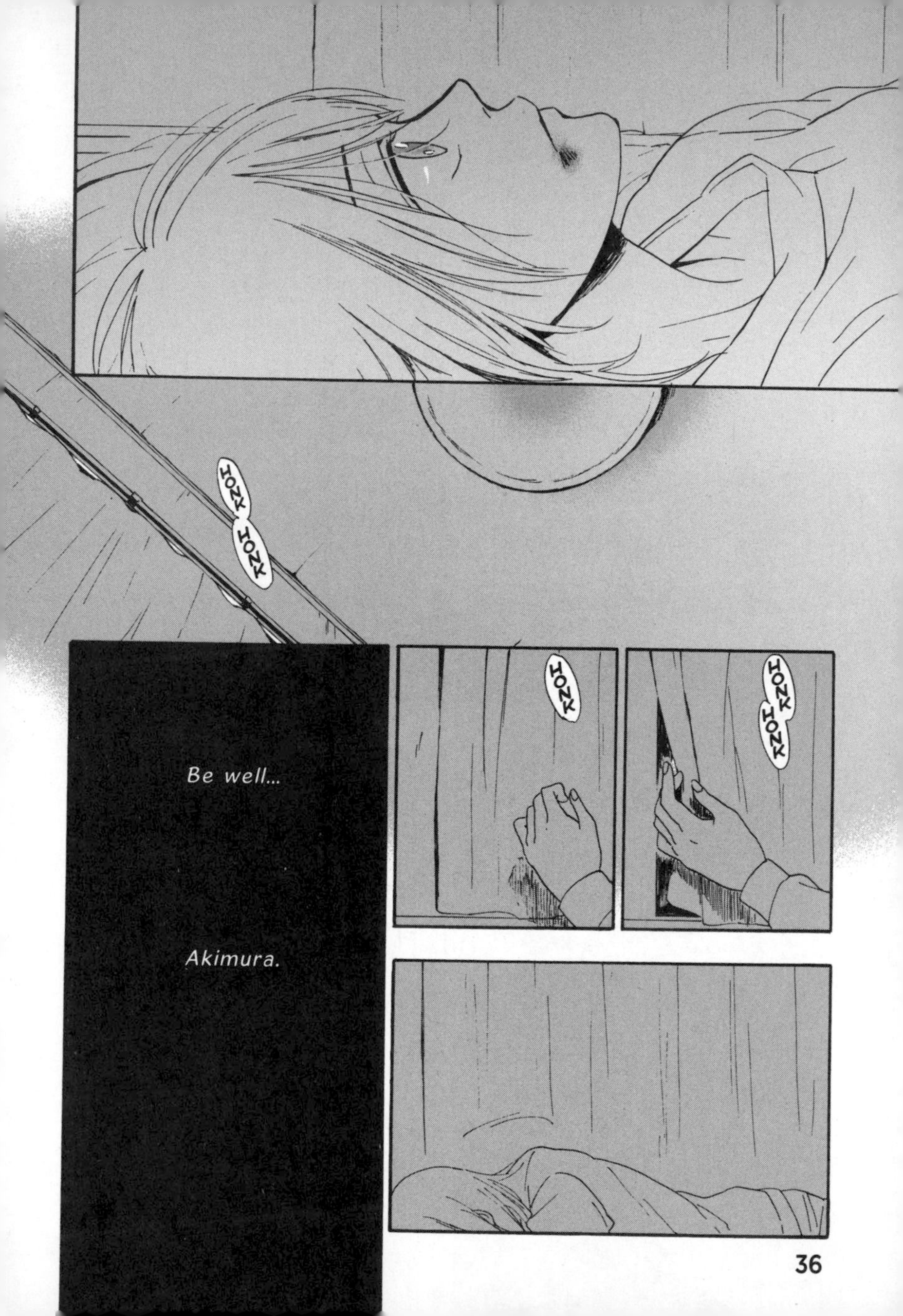
HONK HONK
HONK
HONK HONK
HONK
Be well...
Akimura.

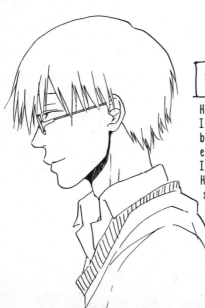

Shouta Akimura

He wore glasses when
I first thought him up,
but at some point, he
ended up losing the glasses.
I think he's nearsighted.
He's in love with Tsukasa,
so maybe he wanted to
  look more attractive and
    decided to wear contacts
    instead.

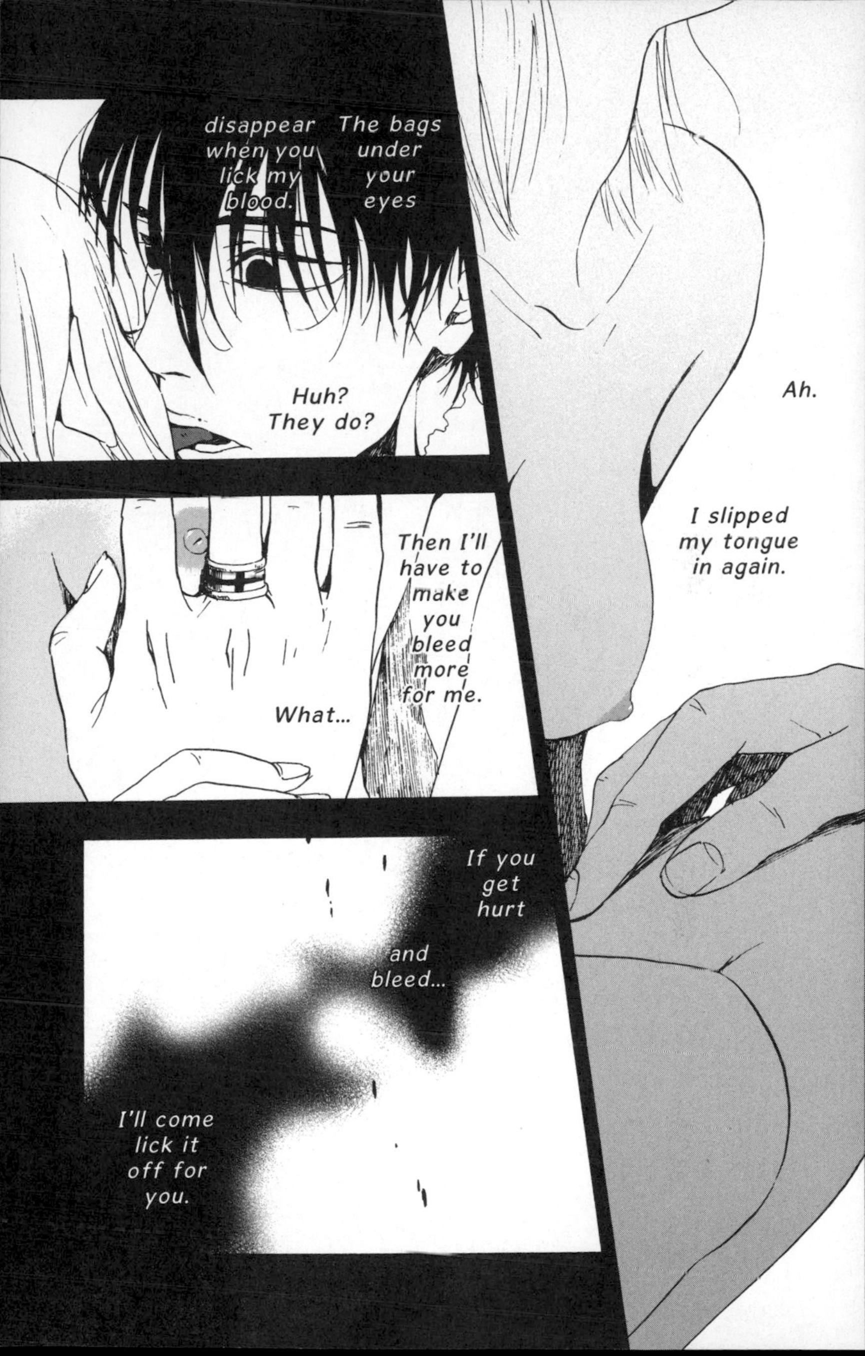
Ah.
I slipped my tongue in again.
The bags under your eyes
disappear when you lick my blood.
Huh? They do?
Then I'll have to make you bleed more for me.
What...
If you get hurt
and bleed...
I'll come lick it off for you.

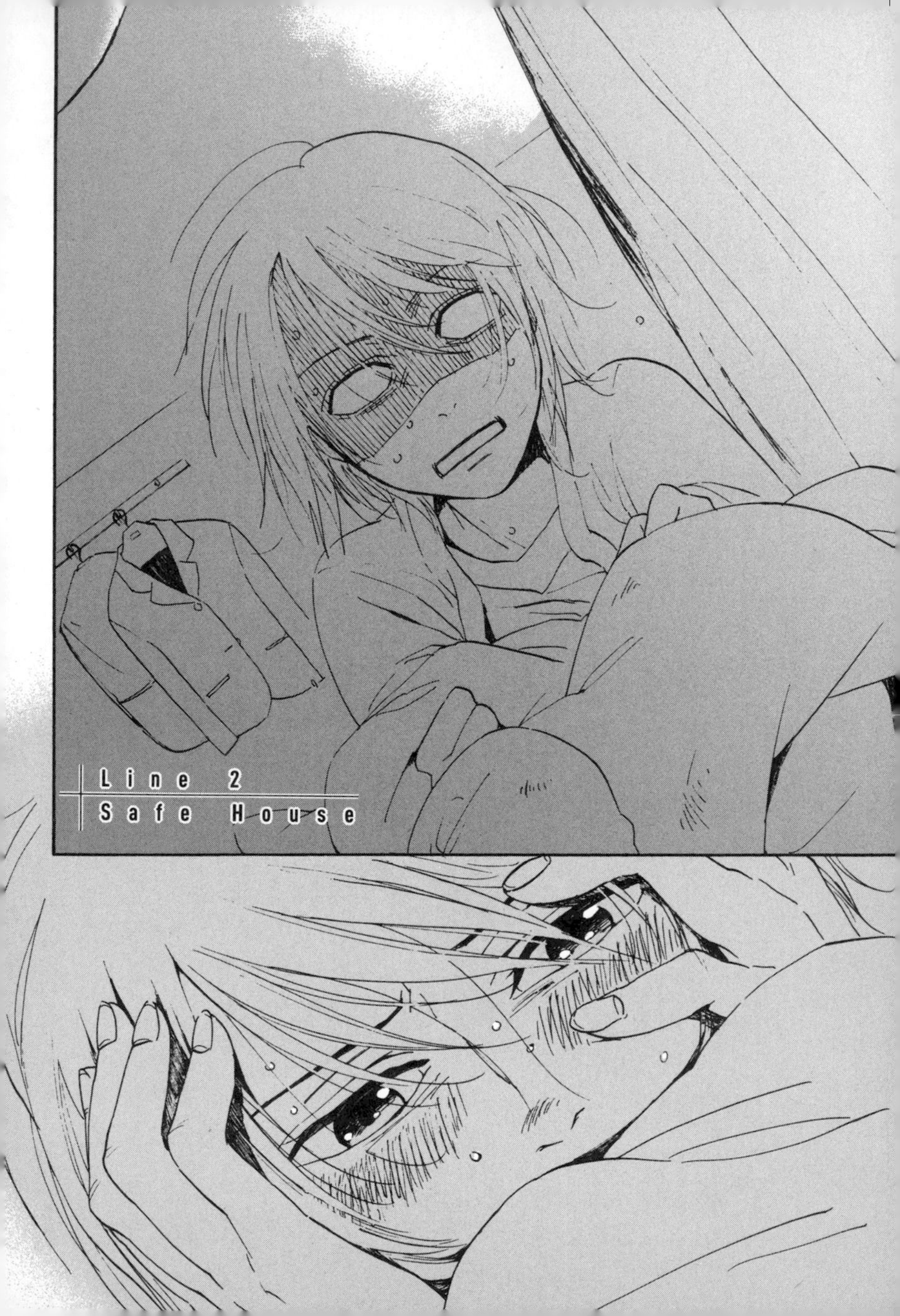
Line 2
Safe House

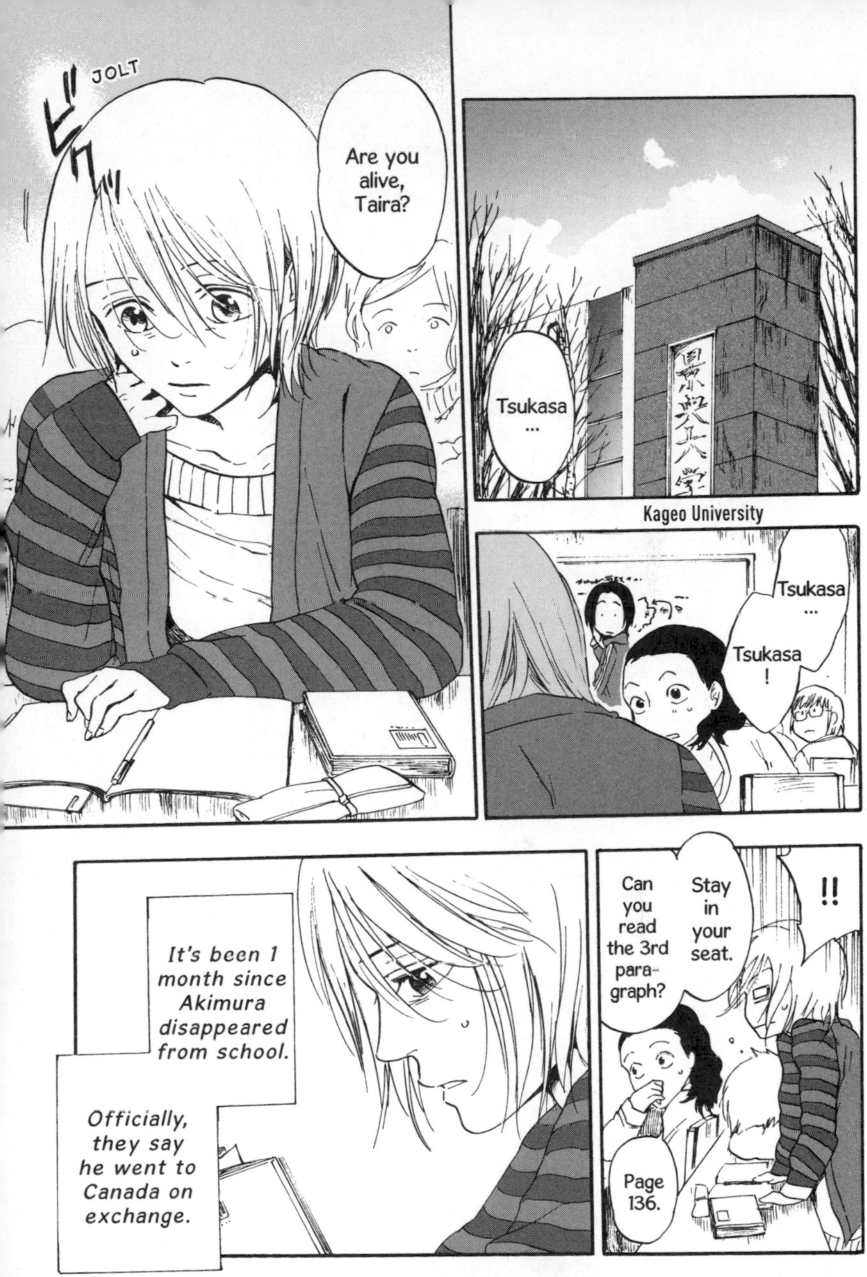
Tsukasa...
Kageo University
Tsukasa...
Tsukasa!
JOLT
Are you alive, Taira?
!!
Stay in your seat.
Can you read the 3rd para-graph?
Page 136.
It's been 1 month since Akimura disappeared from school.
Officially, they say he went to Canada on exchange.

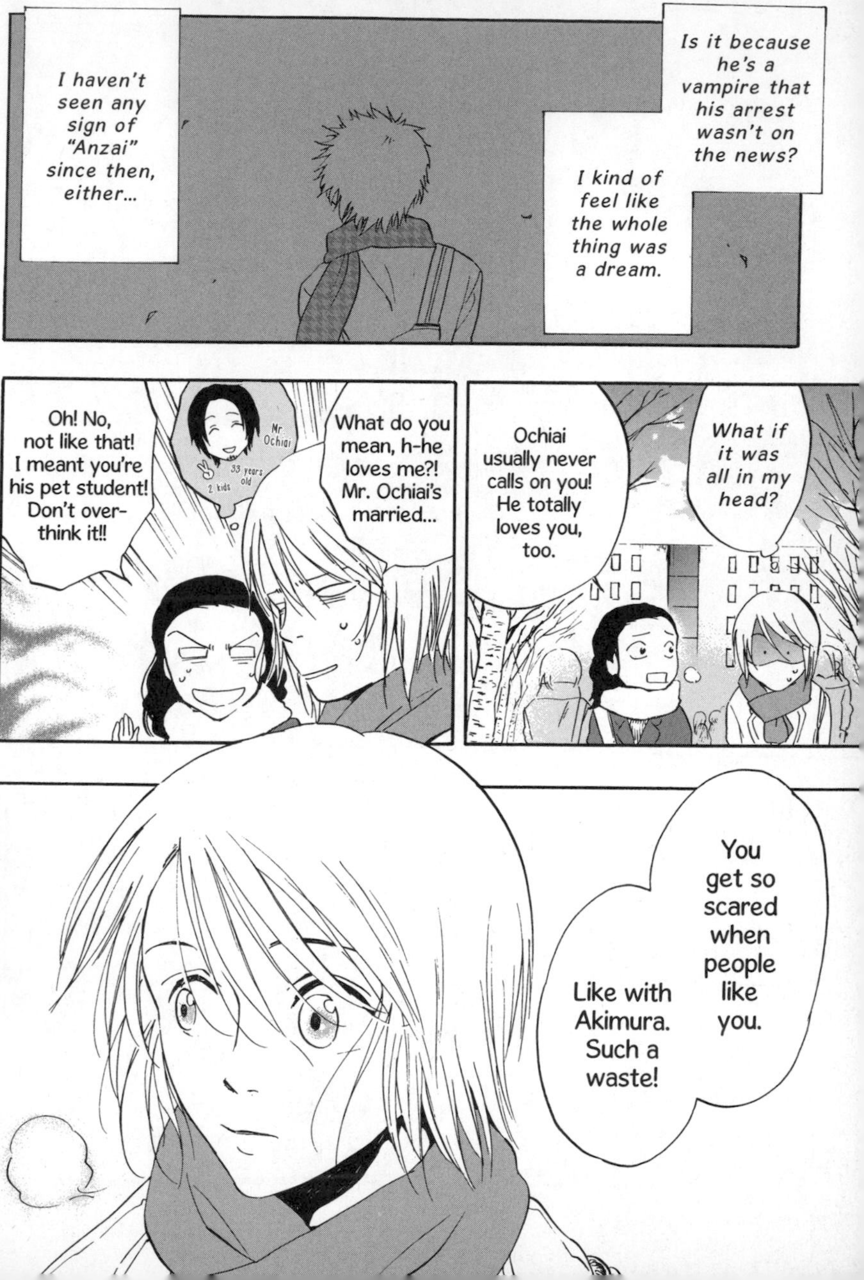
Is it because he's a vampire that his arrest wasn't on the news?
I kind of feel like the whole thing was a dream.
I haven't seen any sign of "Anzai" since then, either...
What if it was all in my head?
Ochiai usually never calls on you! He totally loves you, too.
What do you mean, h-he loves me?! Mr. Ochiai's married...
Mr. Ochiai
33 years old
2 kids
Oh! No, not like that! I meant you're his pet student! Don't over-think it!!
You get so scared when people like you.
Like with Akimura. Such a waste!

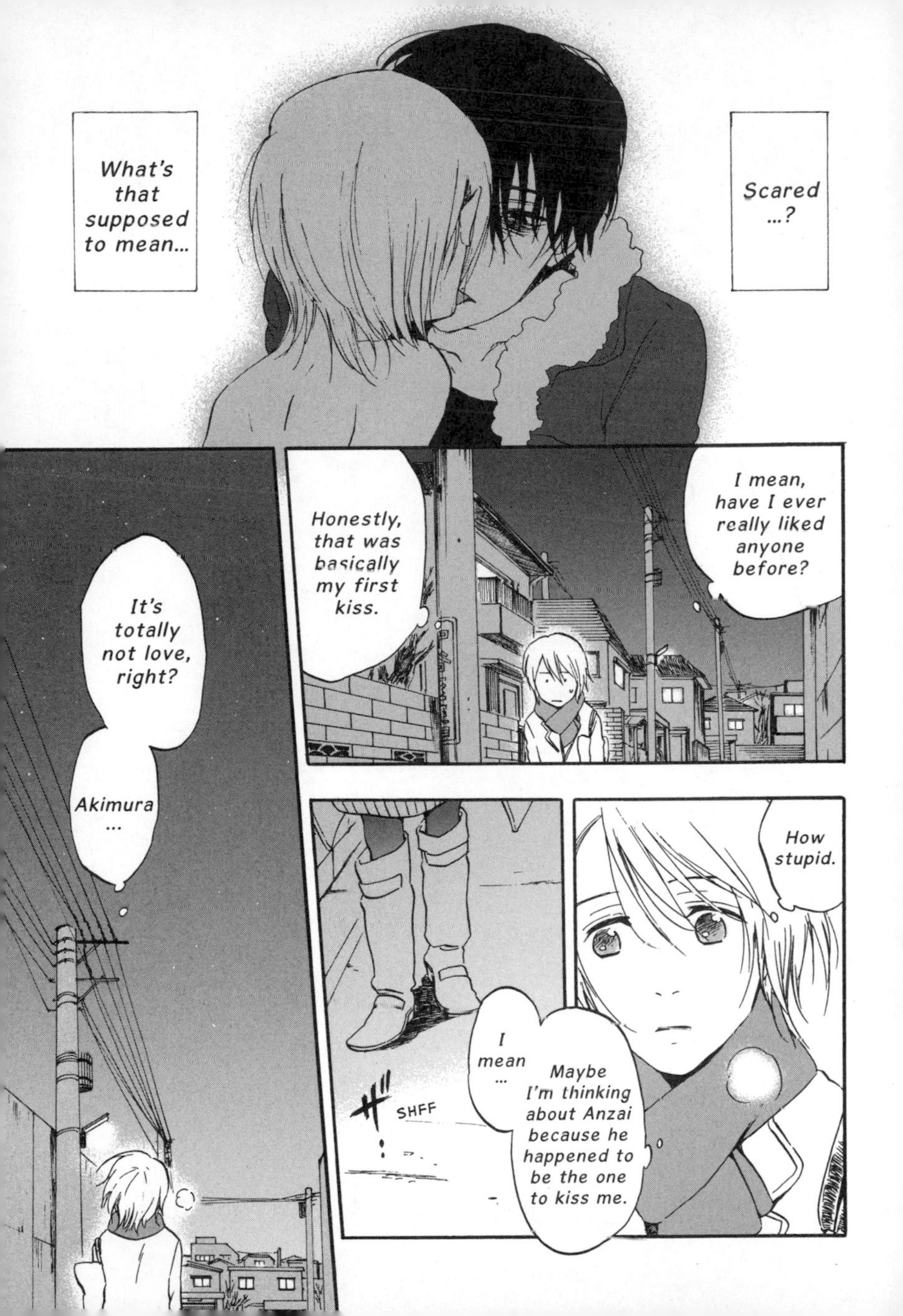
Scared ...?
What's that supposed to mean...
I mean, have I ever really liked anyone before?
Honestly, that was basically my first kiss.
How stupid.
I mean ...
Maybe I'm thinking about Anzai because he happened to be the one to kiss me.
SHFF
It's totally not love, right?
Akimura ...

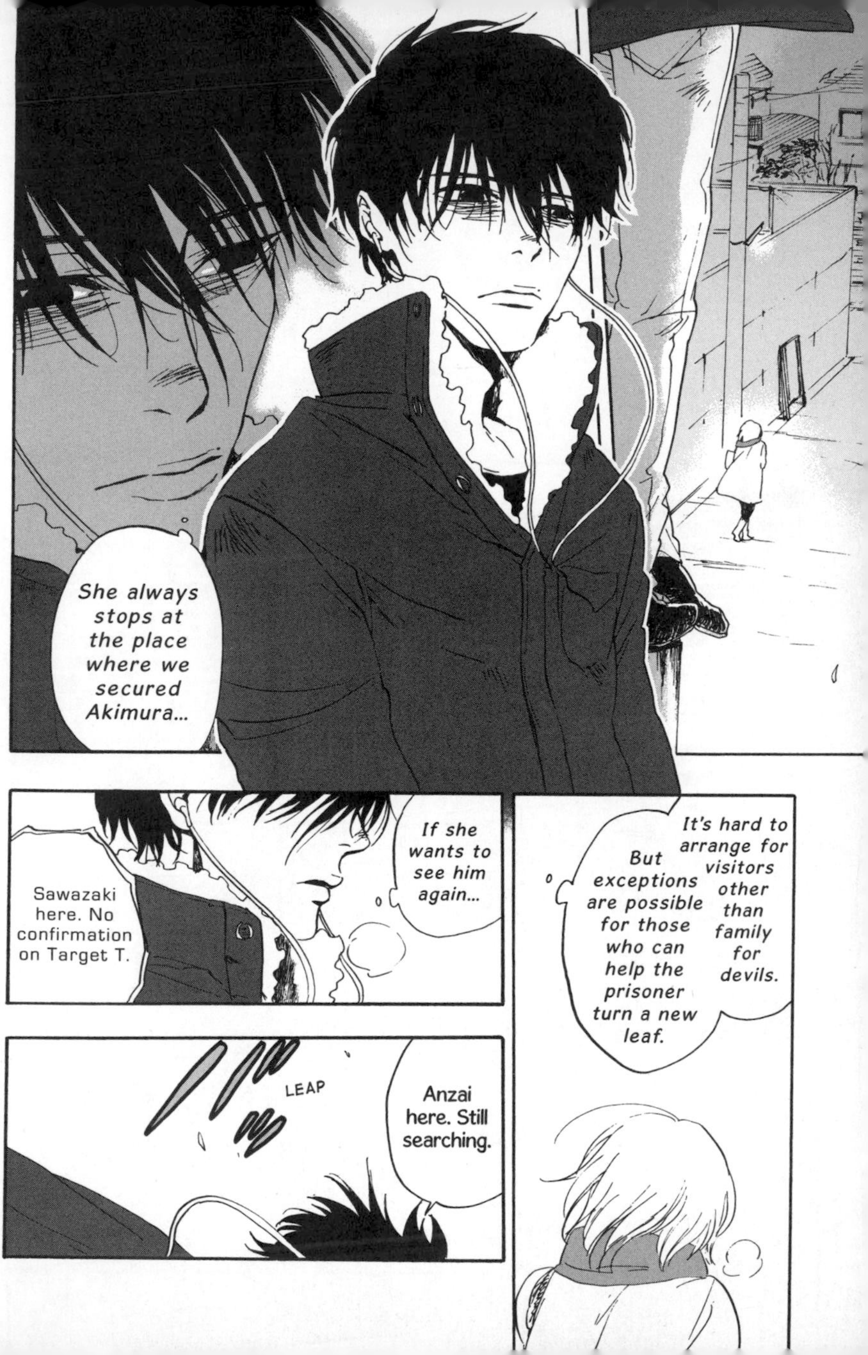
She always stops at the place where we secured Akimura...
It's hard to arrange for visitors other than family for devils.
But exceptions are possible for those who can help the prisoner turn a new leaf.
If she wants to see him again...
Sawazaki here. No confirmation on Target T.
Anzai here. Still searching.
LEAP

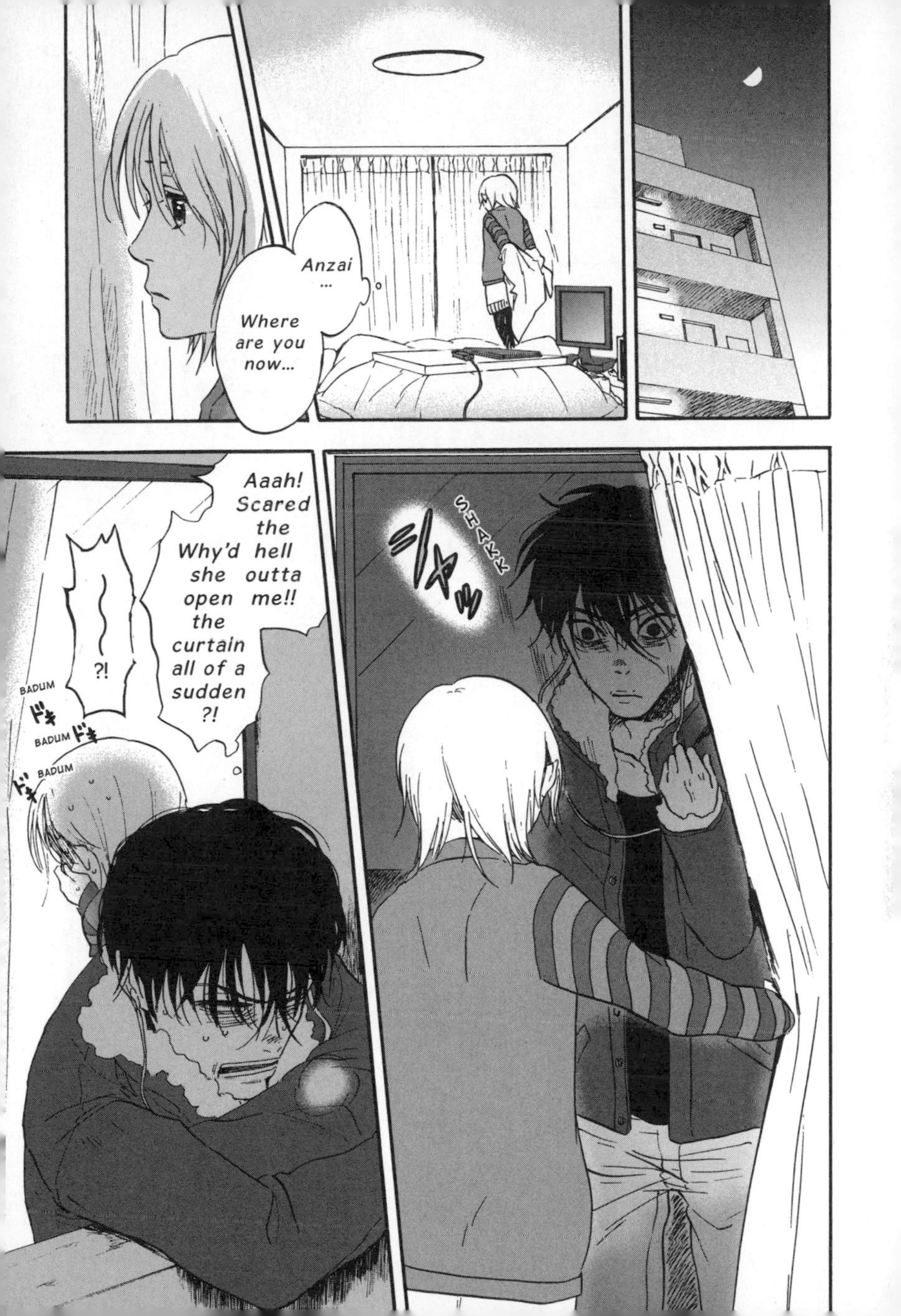

Anzai ... Where are you now...
SHAKK
Aaah! Scared the hell outta me!!
Why'd she open the curtain all of a sudden?!
?!
BADUM
BADUM
BADUM

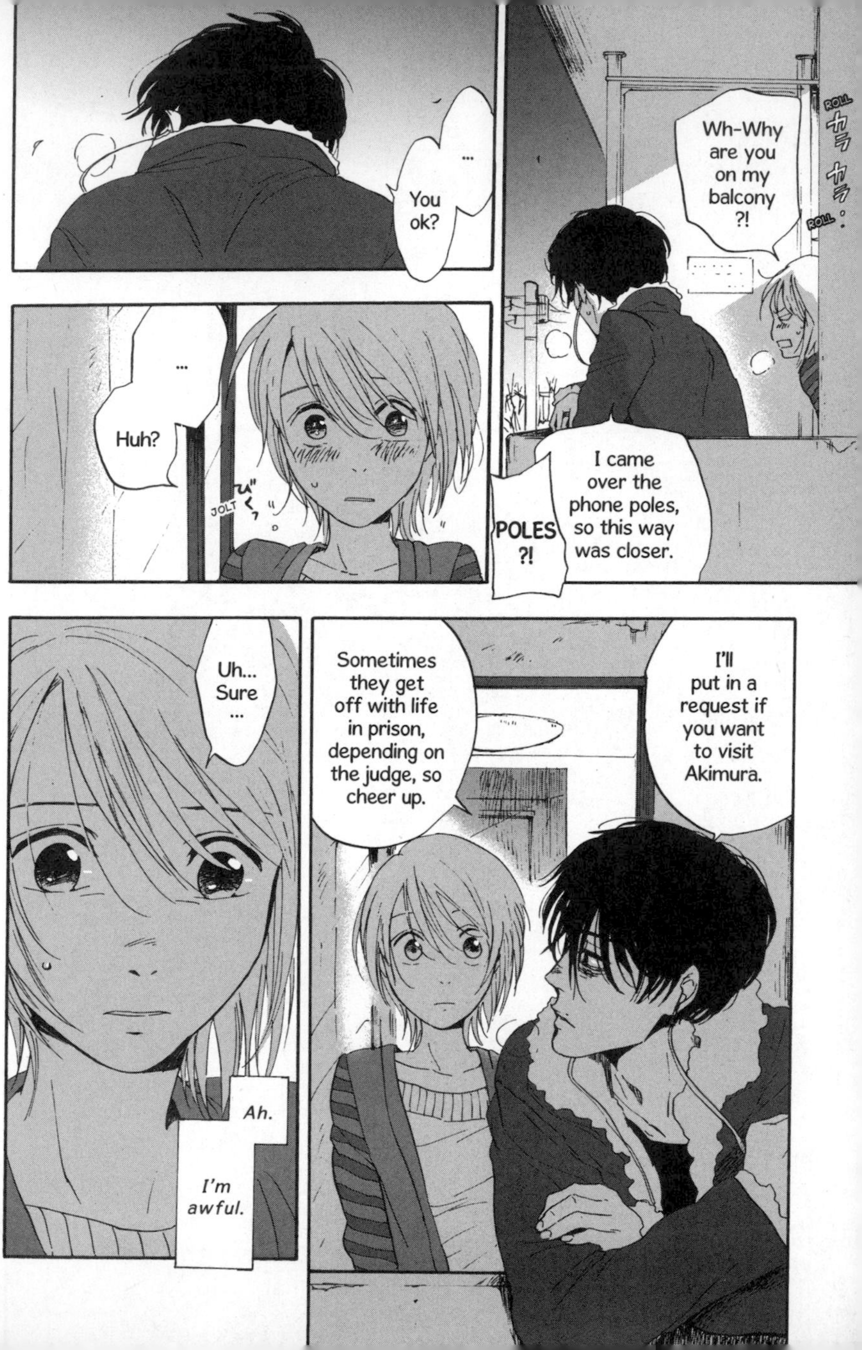
ROLL
カラ
カラ
ROLL
Wh-Why are you on my balcony ?!
I came over the phone poles, so this way was closer.
POLES ?!
... You ok?
... Huh?
びくっ
JOLT
I'll put in a request if you want to visit Akimura.
Sometimes they get off with life in prison, depending on the judge, so cheer up.
Uh... Sure ...
Ah.
I'm awful.

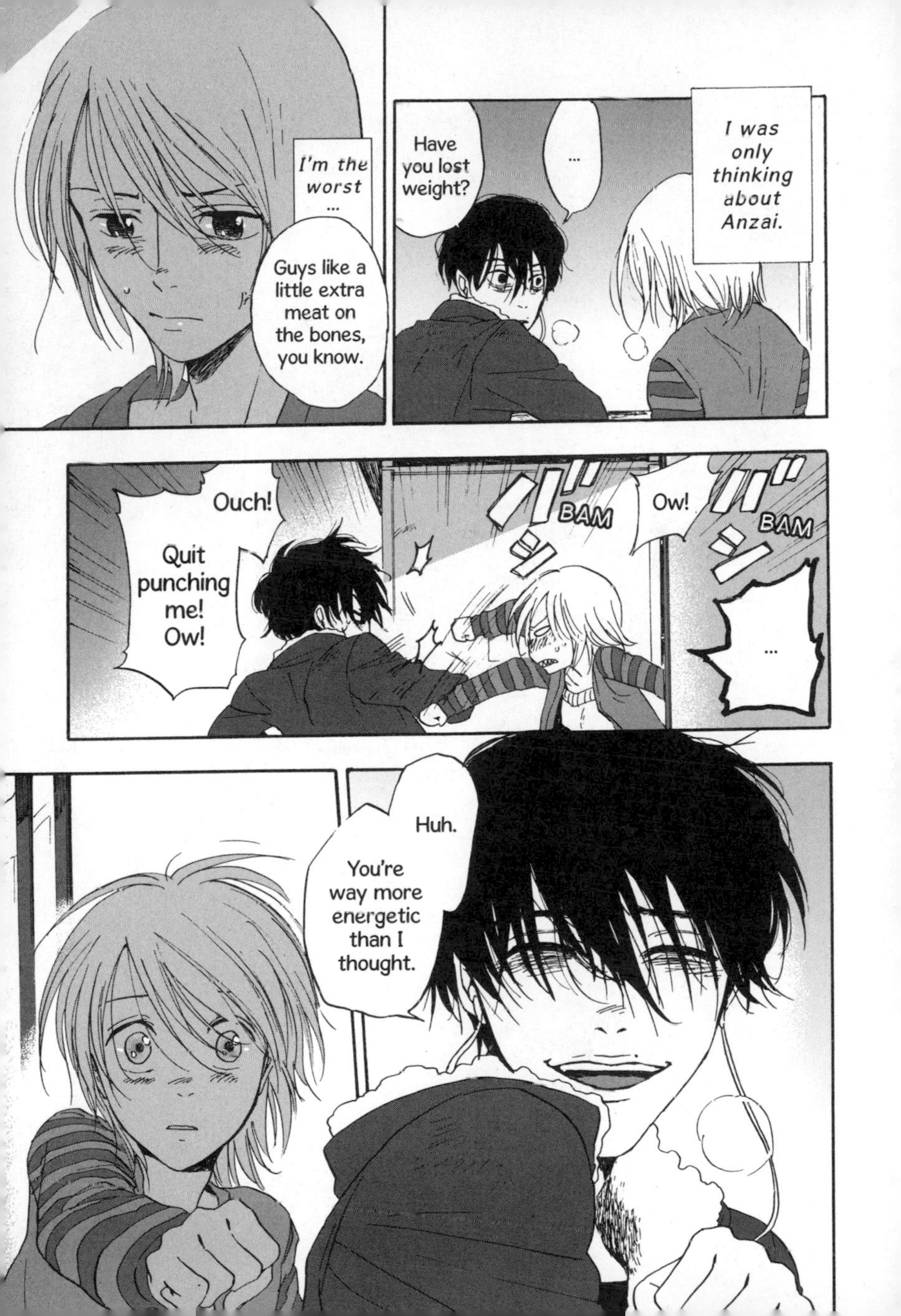
I was only thinking about Anzai.
...
Have you lost weight?
I'm the worst ...
Guys like a little extra meat on the bones, you know.
BAM
Ow!
...
BAM
Ouch!
Quit punching me! Ow!
Huh.
You're way more energetic than I thought.

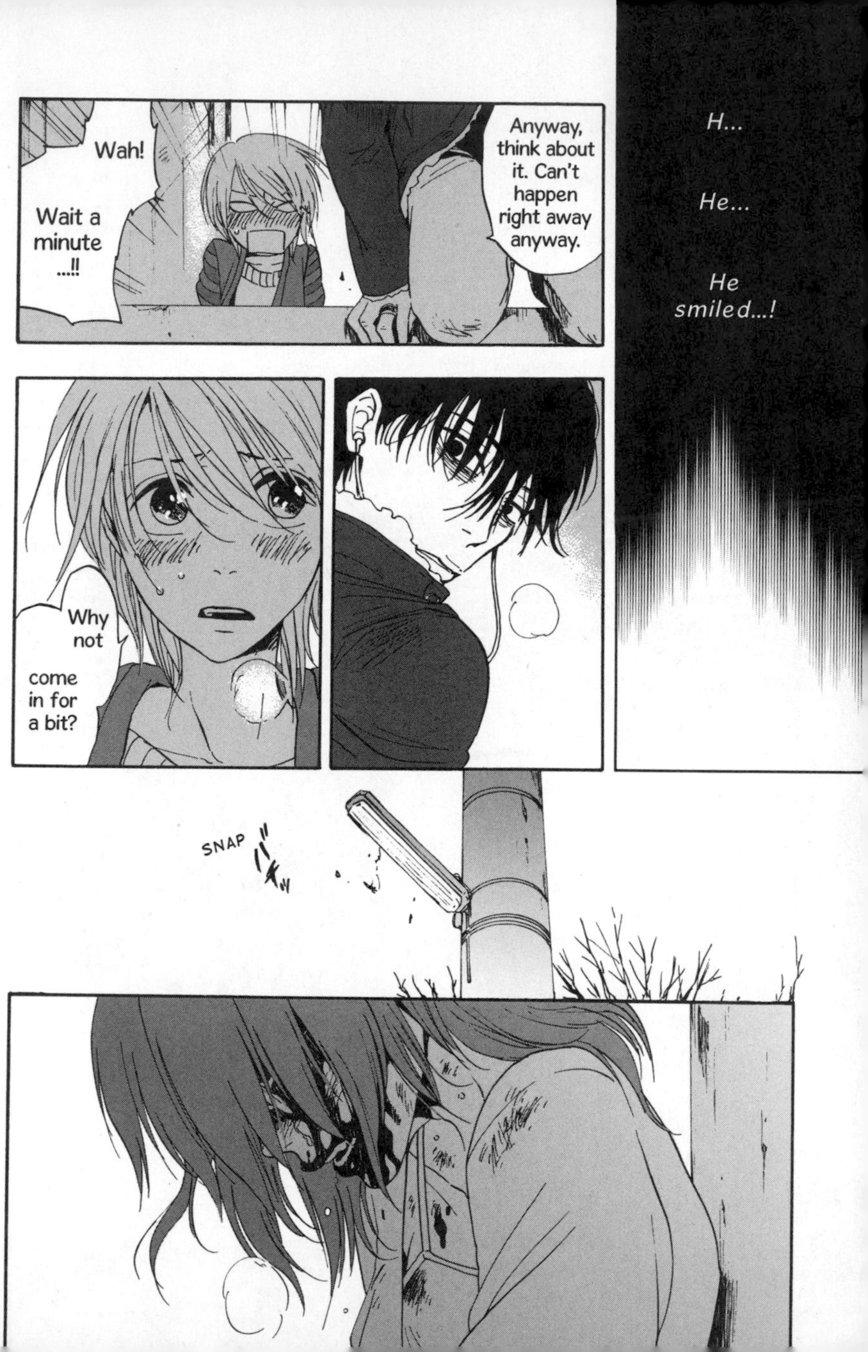
H...
He...
He smiled...!
Anyway, think about it. Can't happen right away anyway.
Wah!
Wait a minute ...!!
Why not
come in for a bit?
SNAP

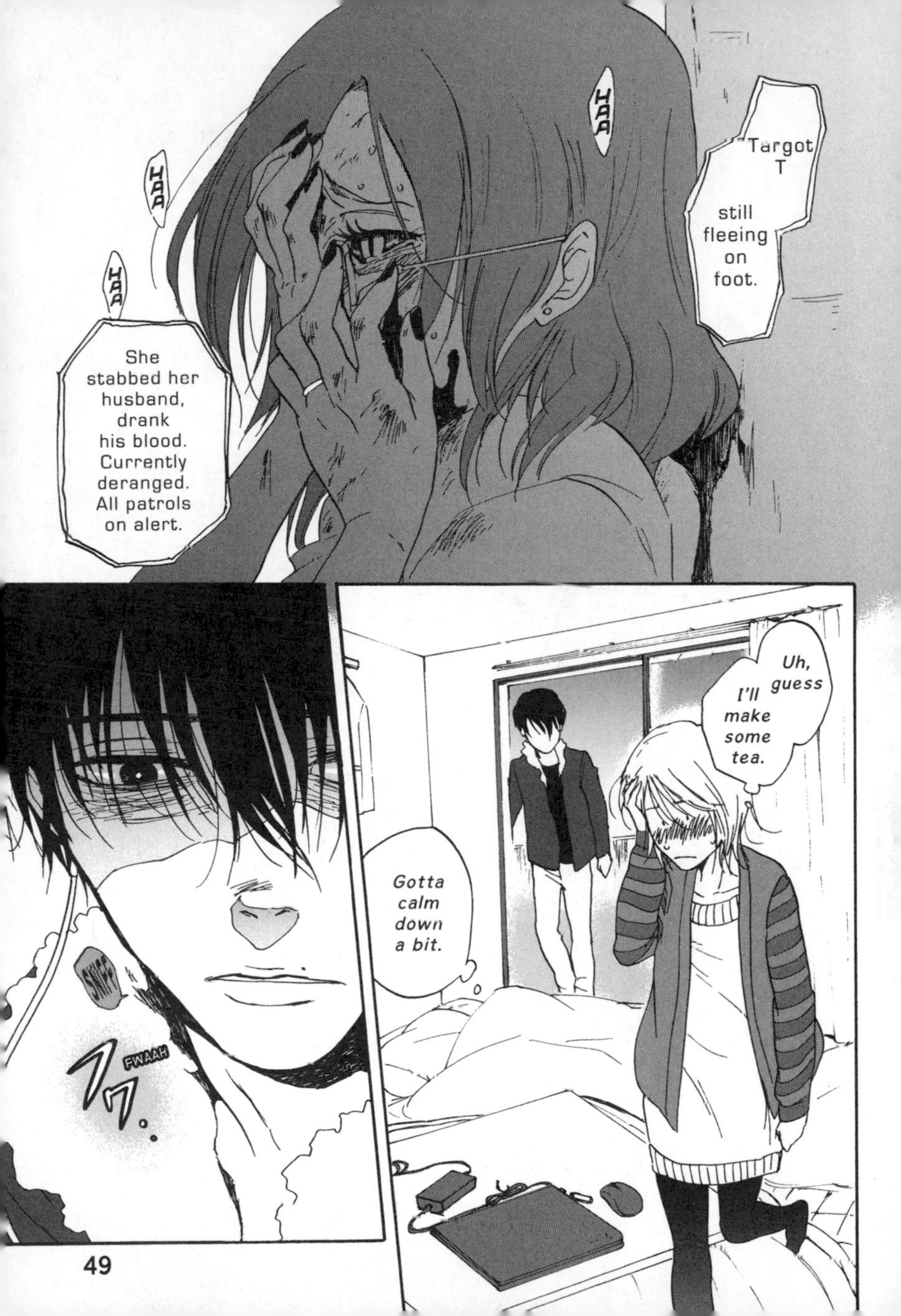
Targot T
still fleeing on foot.
HAA
HAA
HAA
She stabbed her husband, drank his blood. Currently deranged. All patrols on alert.
Uh, guess I'll make some tea.
Gotta calm down a bit.
SNIFF
FWAAH

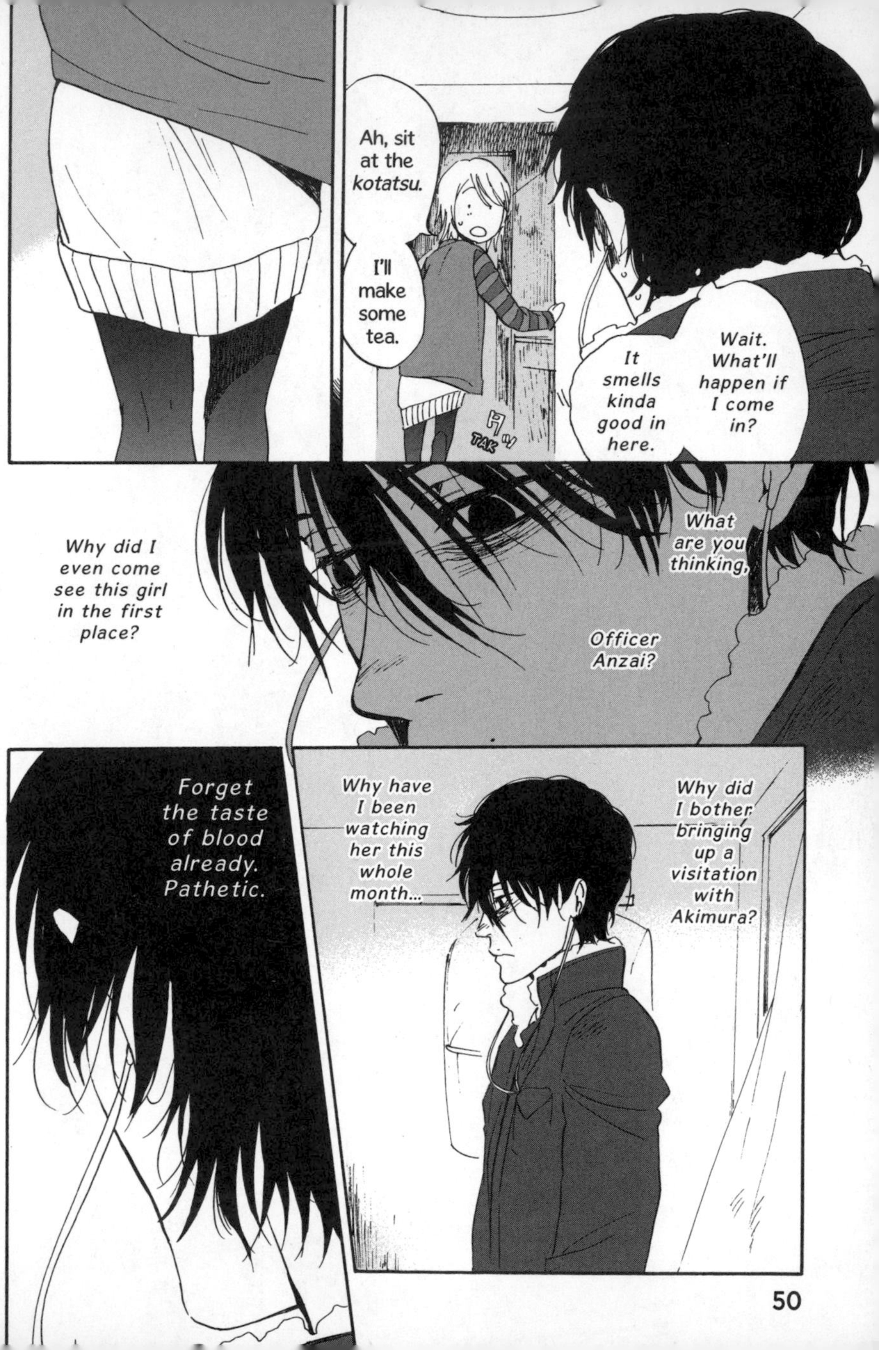
Wait. What'll happen if I come in?
It smells kinda good in here.
Ah, sit at the kotatsu.
I'll make some tea.
TAK
What are you thinking,
Officer Anzai?
Why did I even come see this girl in the first place?
Why did I bother bringing up a visitation with Akimura?
Why have I been watching her this whole month...
Forget the taste of blood already. Pathetic.

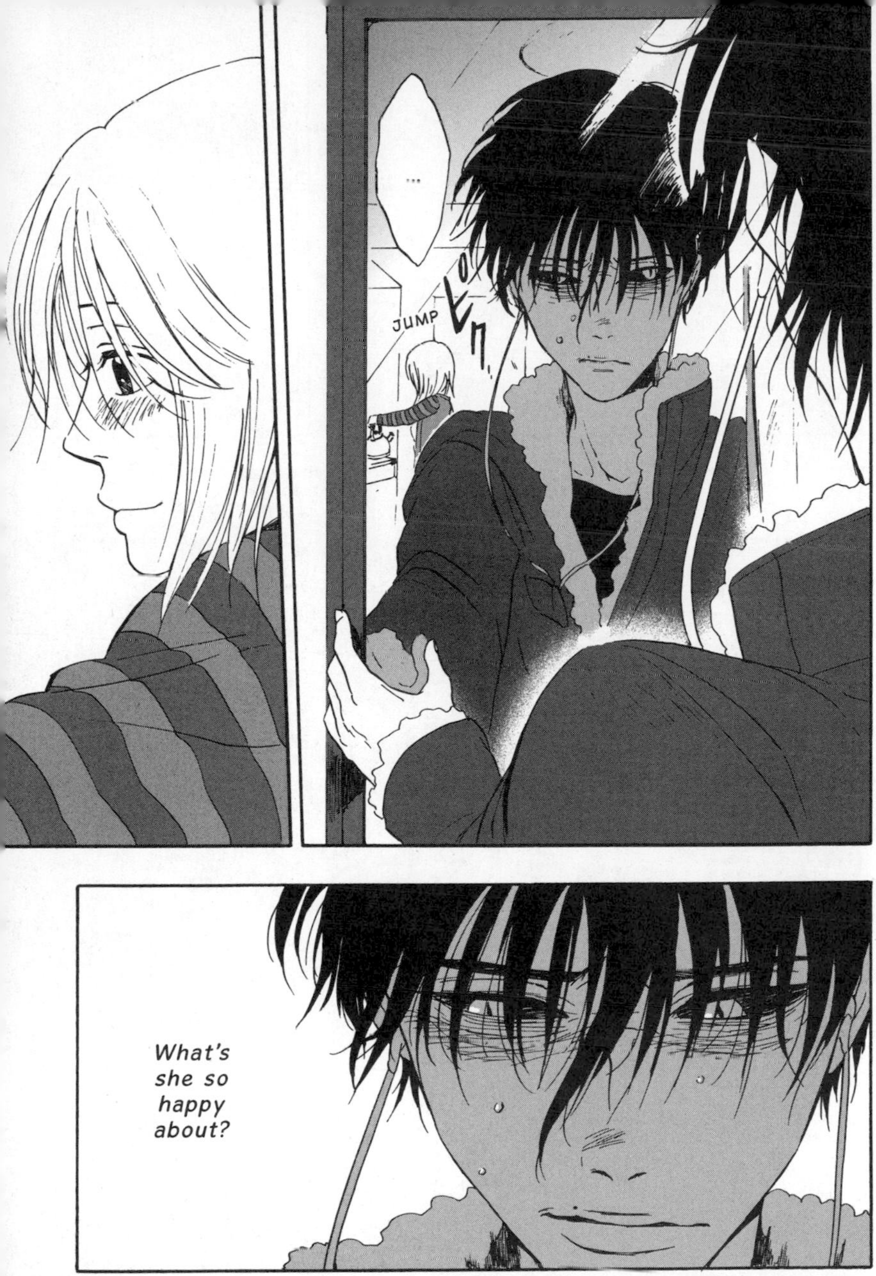
...
JUMP
What's she so happy about?

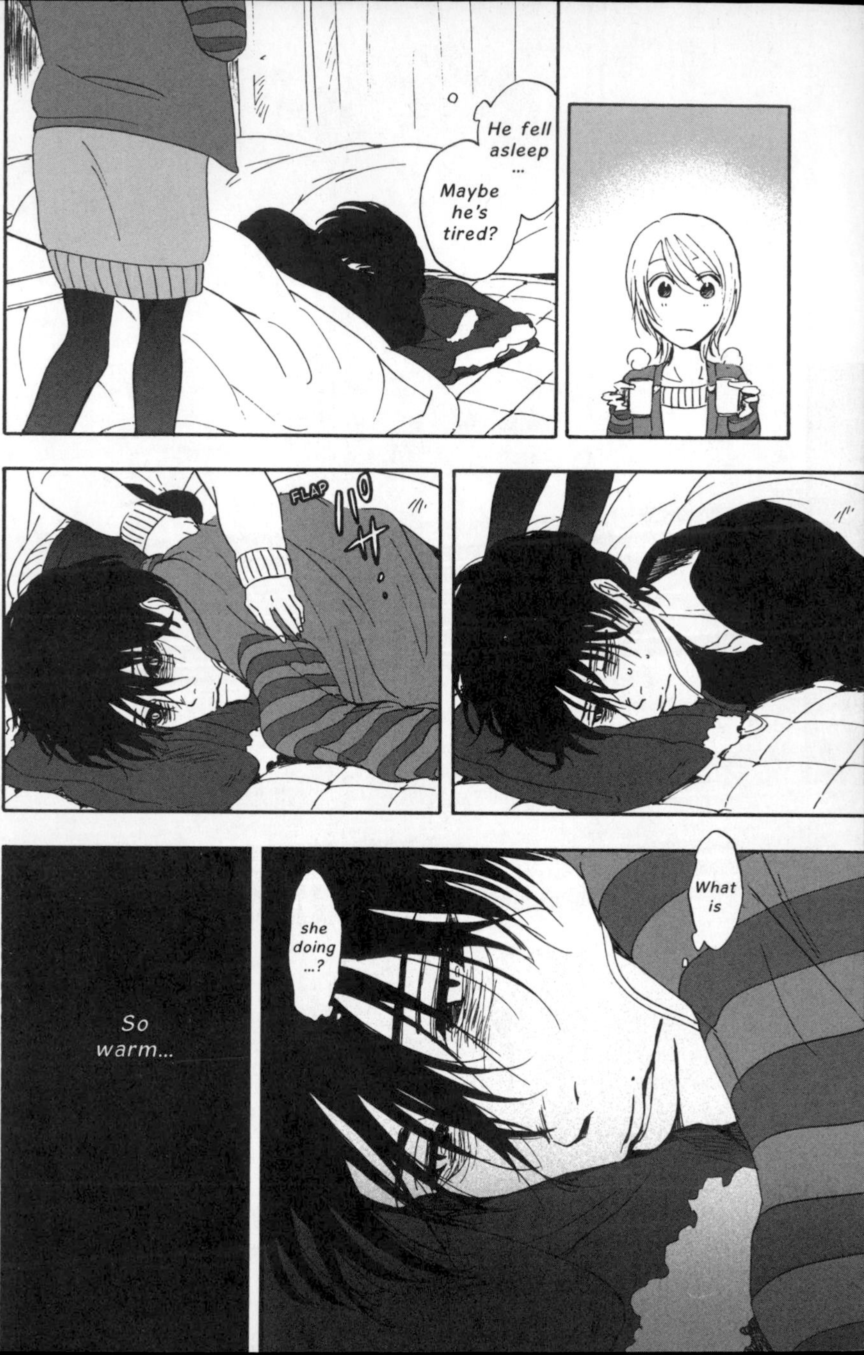
He fell asleep ... Maybe he's tired?
FLAP
What is
she doing ...?
So warm...

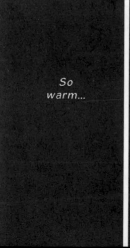

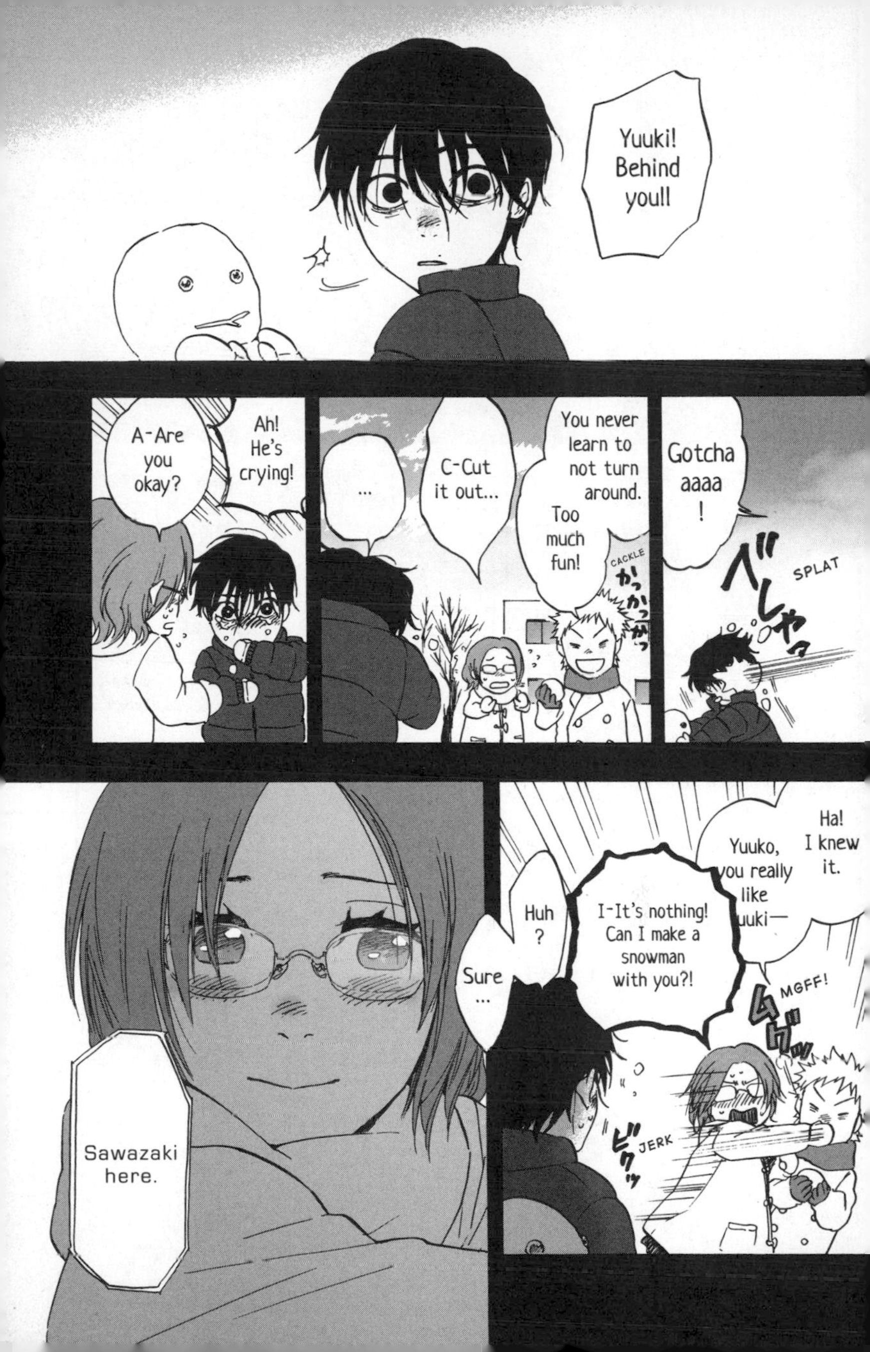
Yuuki! Behind you!!
Gotcha aaaa !
ベシャッ
SPLAT
You never learn to not turn around.
Too much fun!
CACKLE
かっかっかっ
C-Cut it out...
...
Ah! He's crying!
A-Are you okay?
Ha! I knew it.
Yuuko, you really like uuki—
I-It's nothing! Can I make a snowman with you?!
ムグッ
MGFF!
Huh ?
Sure ...
ビクッ
JERK
Sawazaki here.

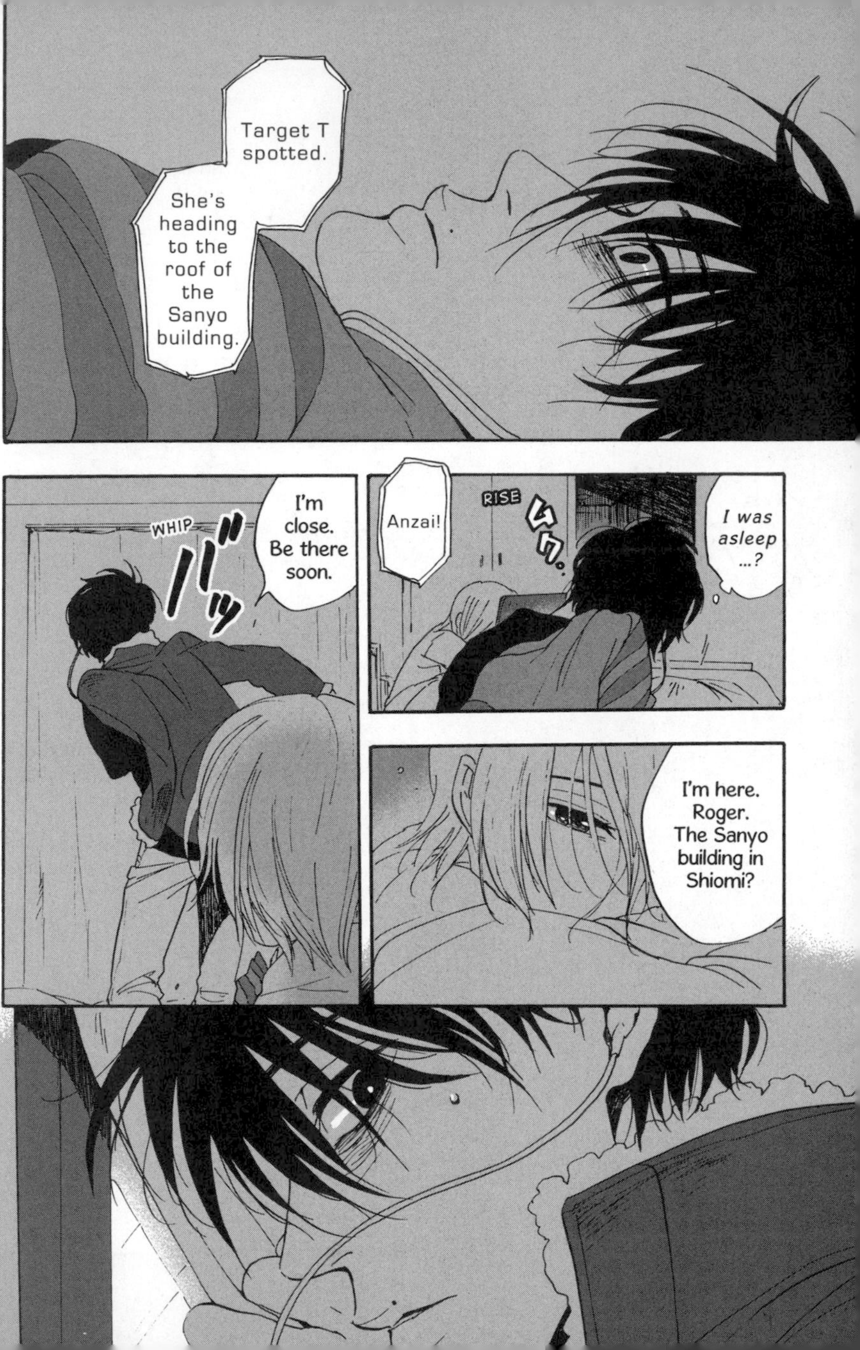
Target T spotted.
She's heading to the roof of the Sanyo building.
I was asleep ...?
RISE
Anzai!
I'm here. Roger. The Sanyo building in Shiomi?
WHIP
I'm close. Be there soon.

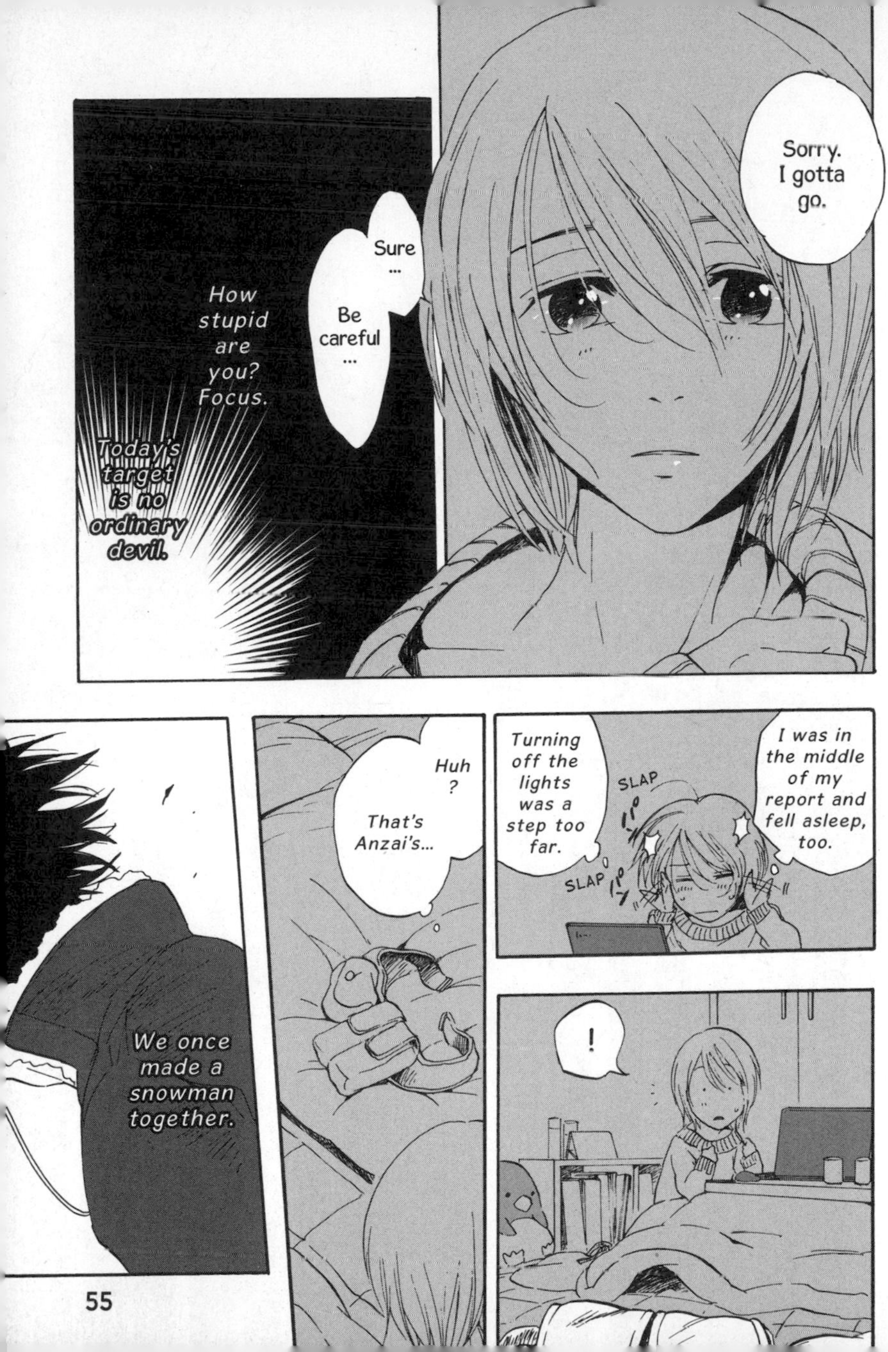
Sorry. I gotta go.
Sure...
Be careful...
How stupid are you? Focus.
Today's target is no ordinary devil.
I was in the middle of my report and fell asleep, too.
Turning off the lights was a step too far.
SLAP
SLAP
!
Huh?
That's Anzai's...
We once made a snowman together.

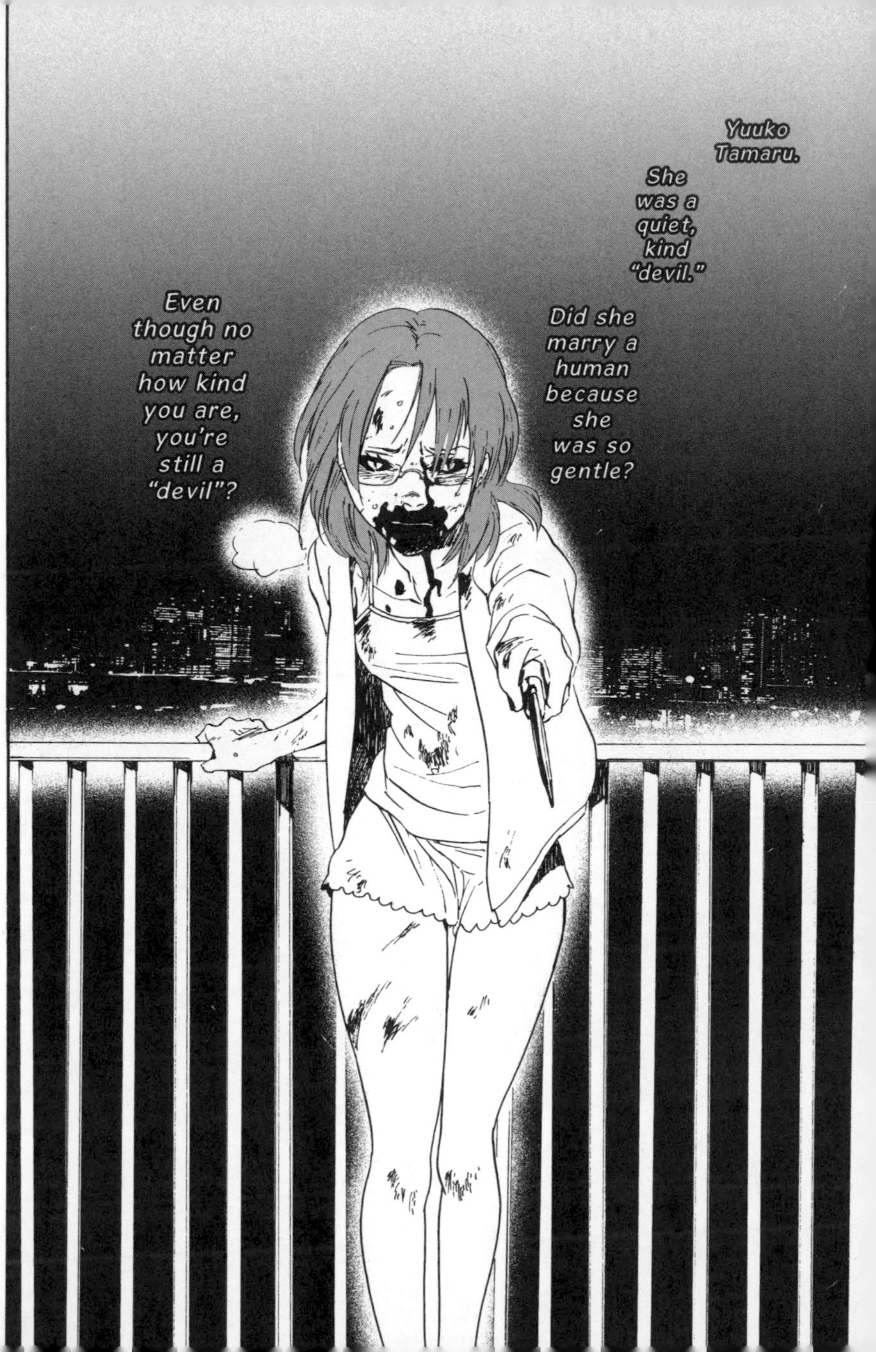
Yuuko Tamaru.
She was a quiet, kind "devil."
Did she marry a human because she was so gentle?
Even though no matter how kind you are, you're still a "devil"?

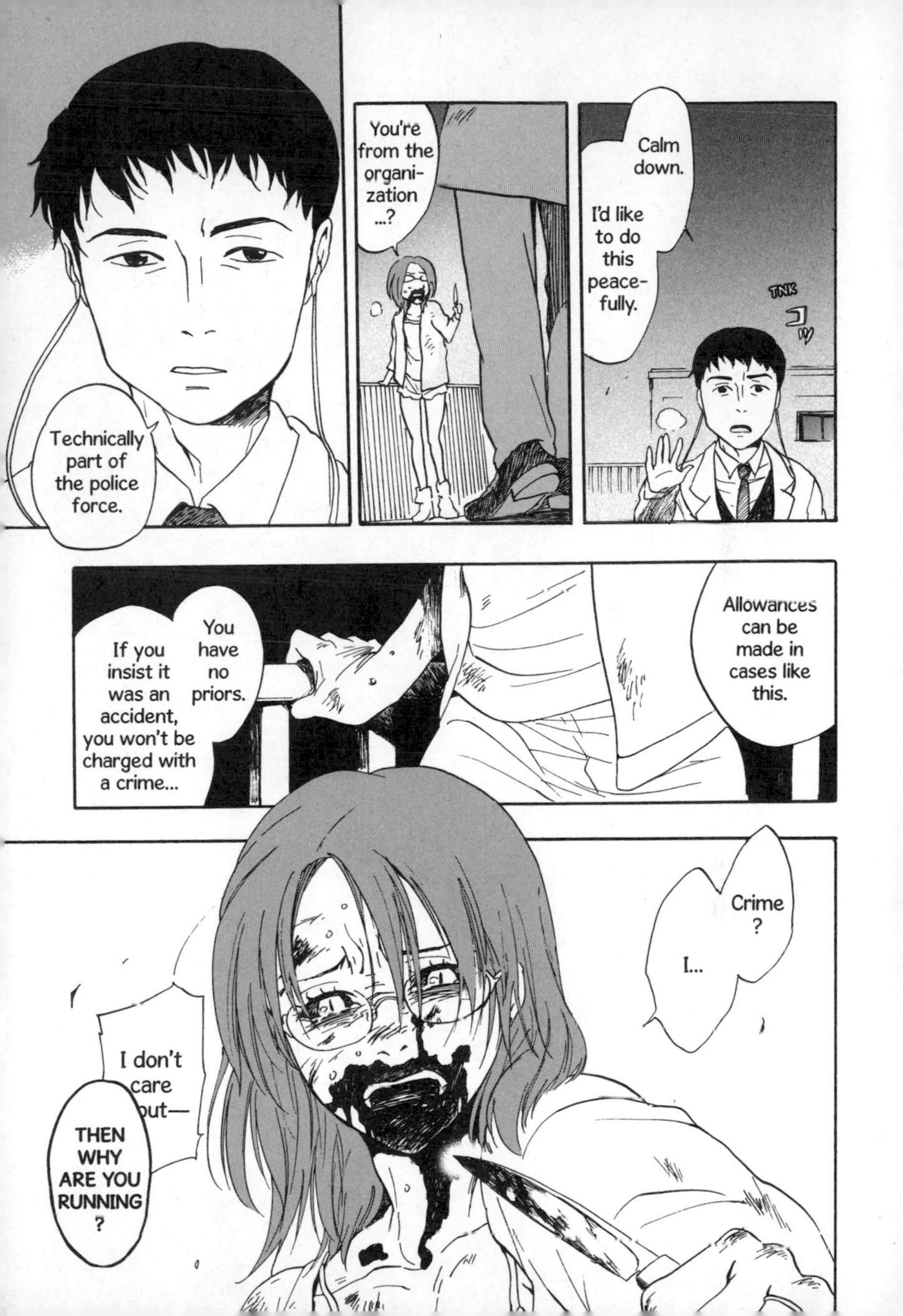

Calm down.
I'd like to do this peacefully.
TNK
You're from the organization...?
Technically part of the police force.
Allowances can be made in cases like this.
You have no priors.
If you insist it was an accident, you won't be charged with a crime...
Crime? I...
I don't care about—
THEN WHY ARE YOU RUNNING?

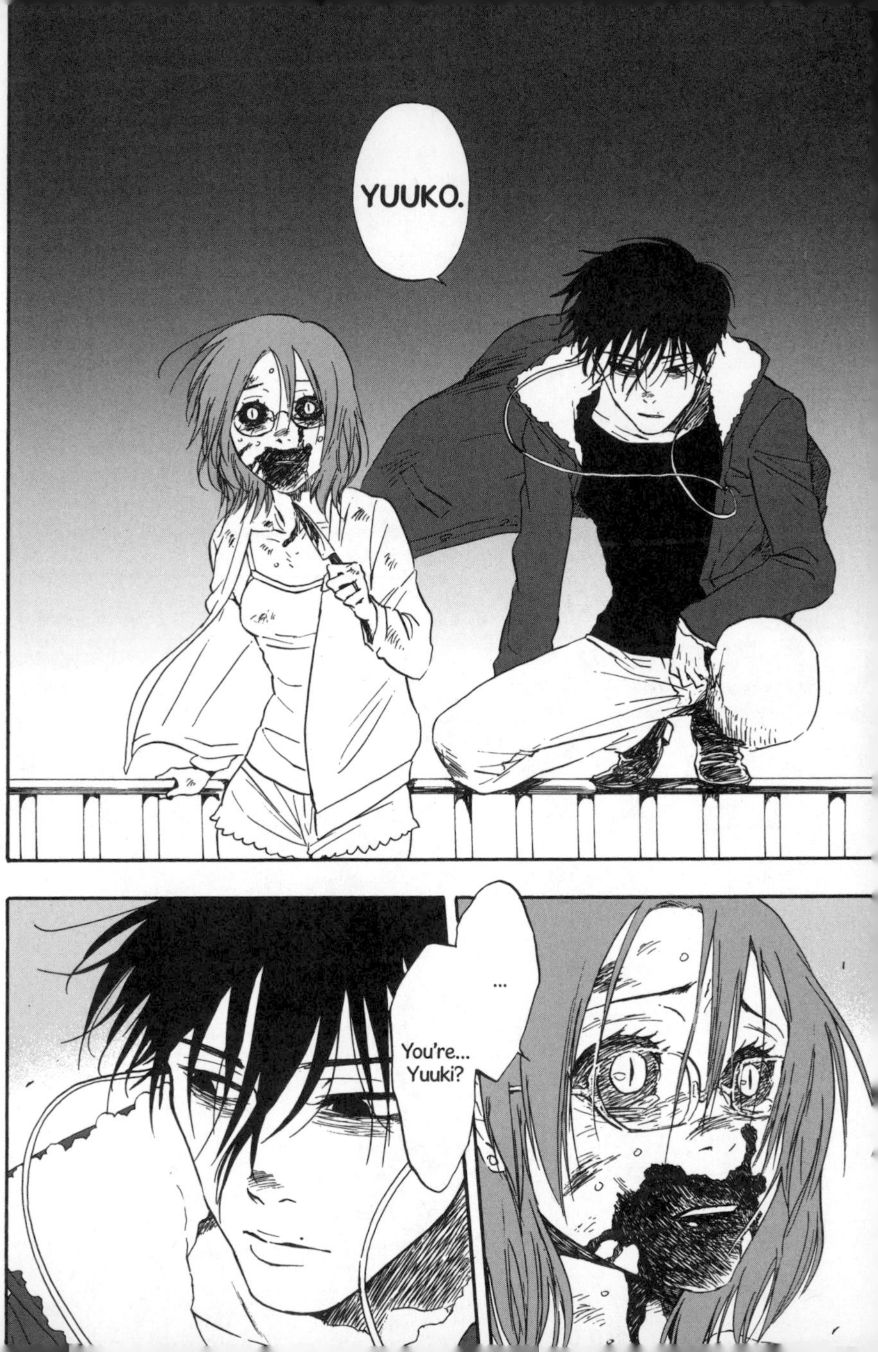
YUUKO.
...
You're...
Yuuki?

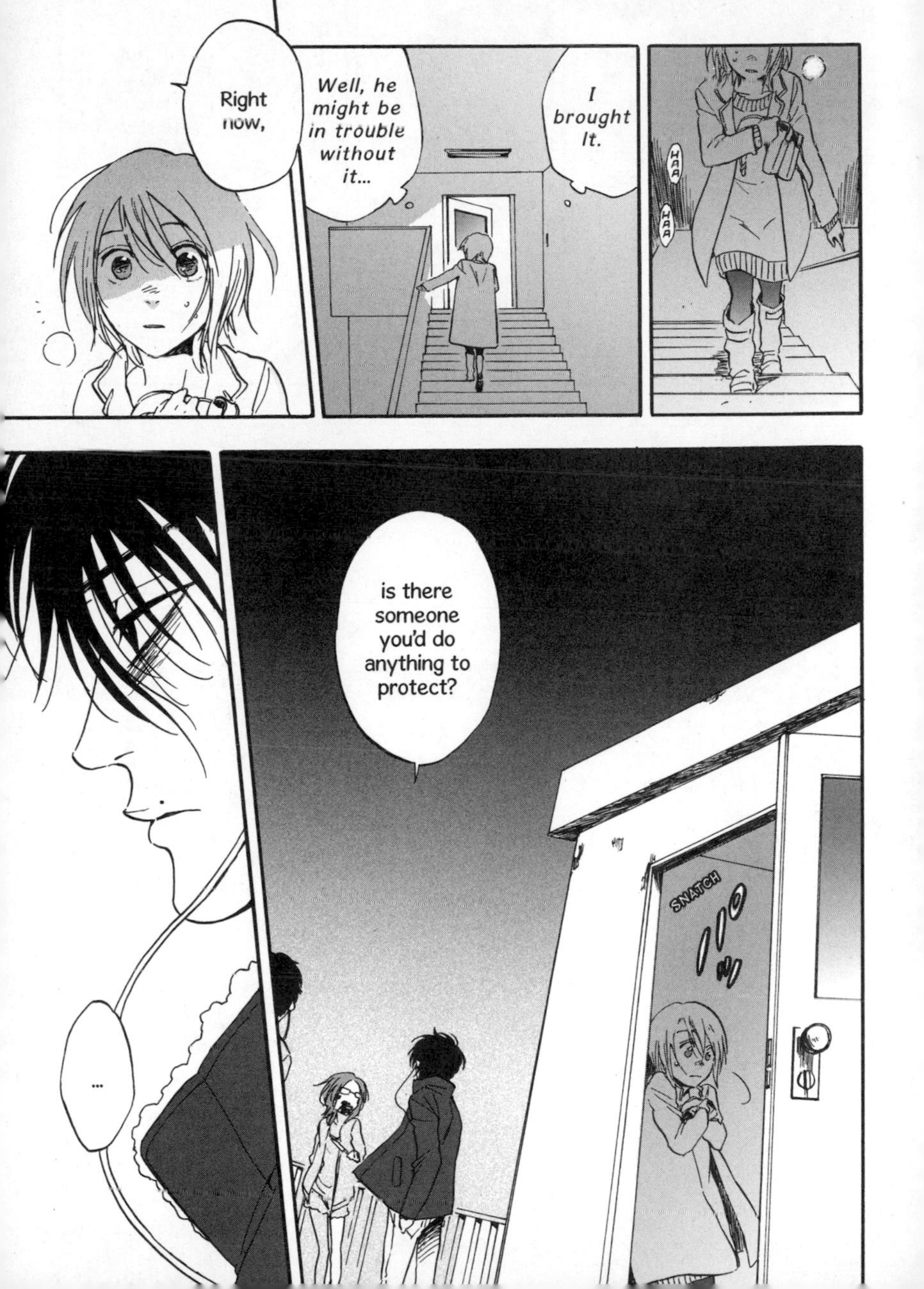
HAA
HAA
I brought It.
Well, he might be in trouble without it...
Right now,
SNATCH
is there someone you'd do anything to protect?
...

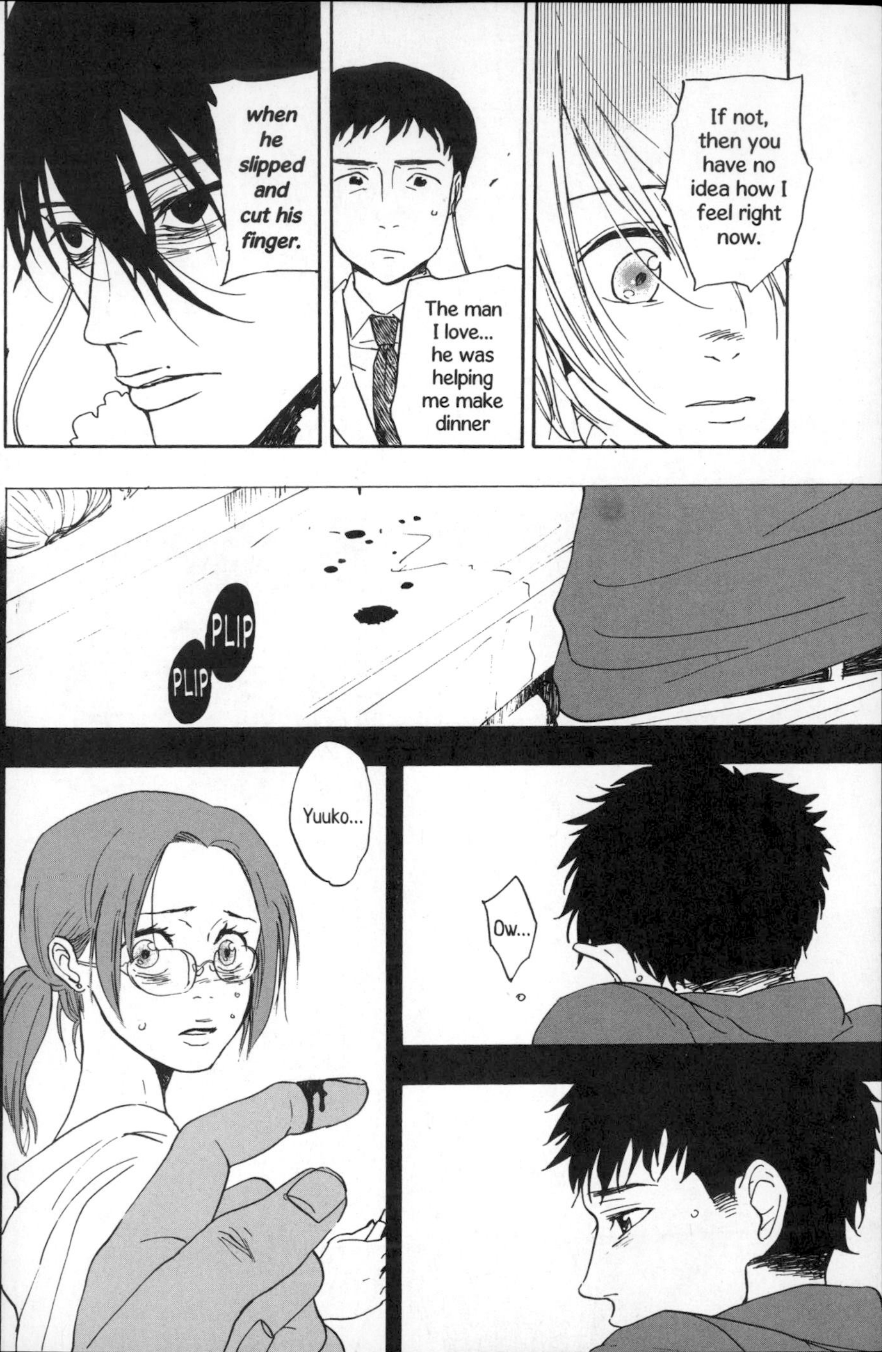
If not, then you have no idea how I feel right now.
The man I love... he was helping me make dinner
when he slipped and cut his finger.
PLIP
PLIP
Ow...
Yuuko...

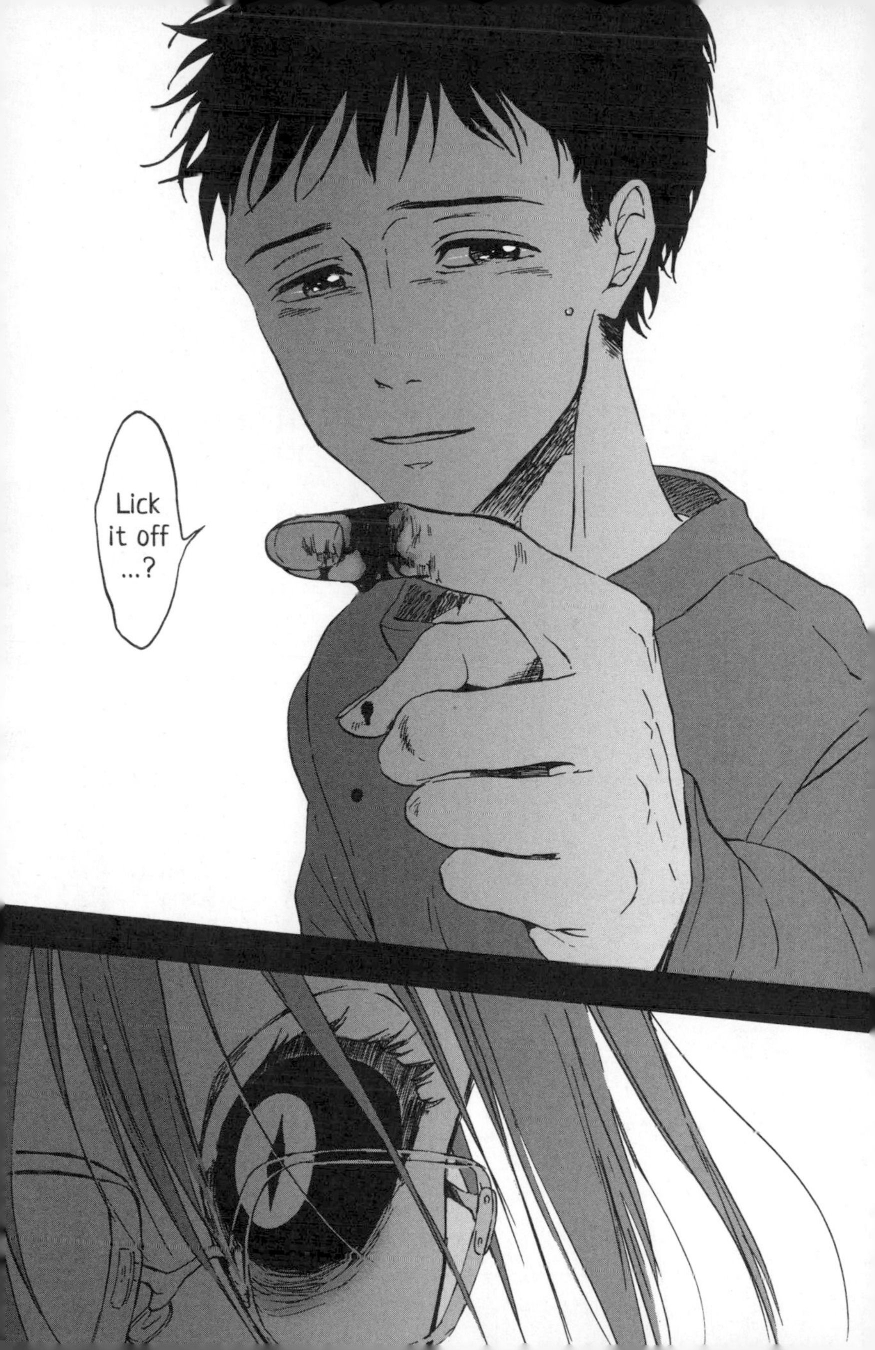
Lick it off ...?

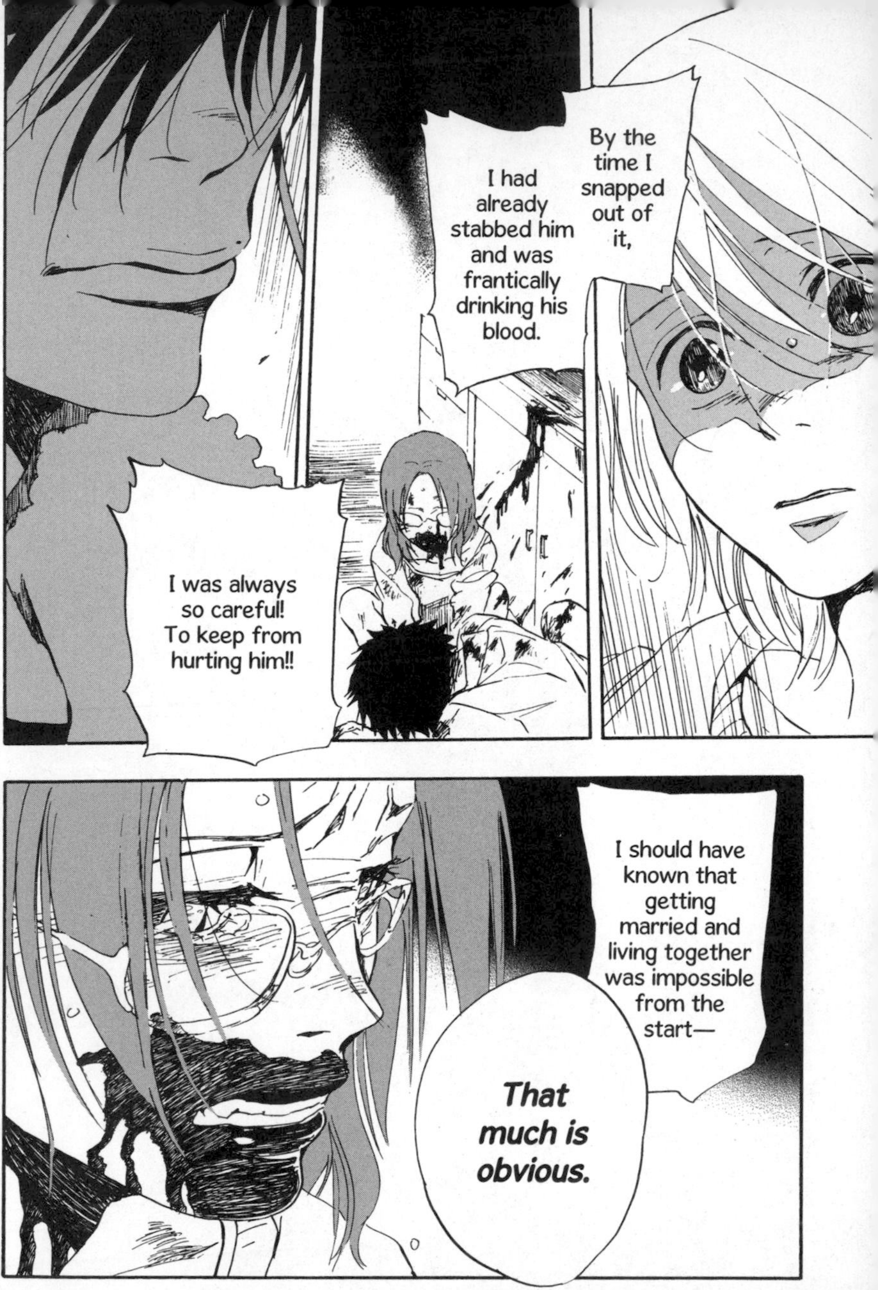
By the time I snapped out of it,
I had already stabbed him and was frantically drinking his blood.
I was always so careful! To keep from hurting him!!
I should have known that getting married and living together was impossible from the start—
That much is obvious.

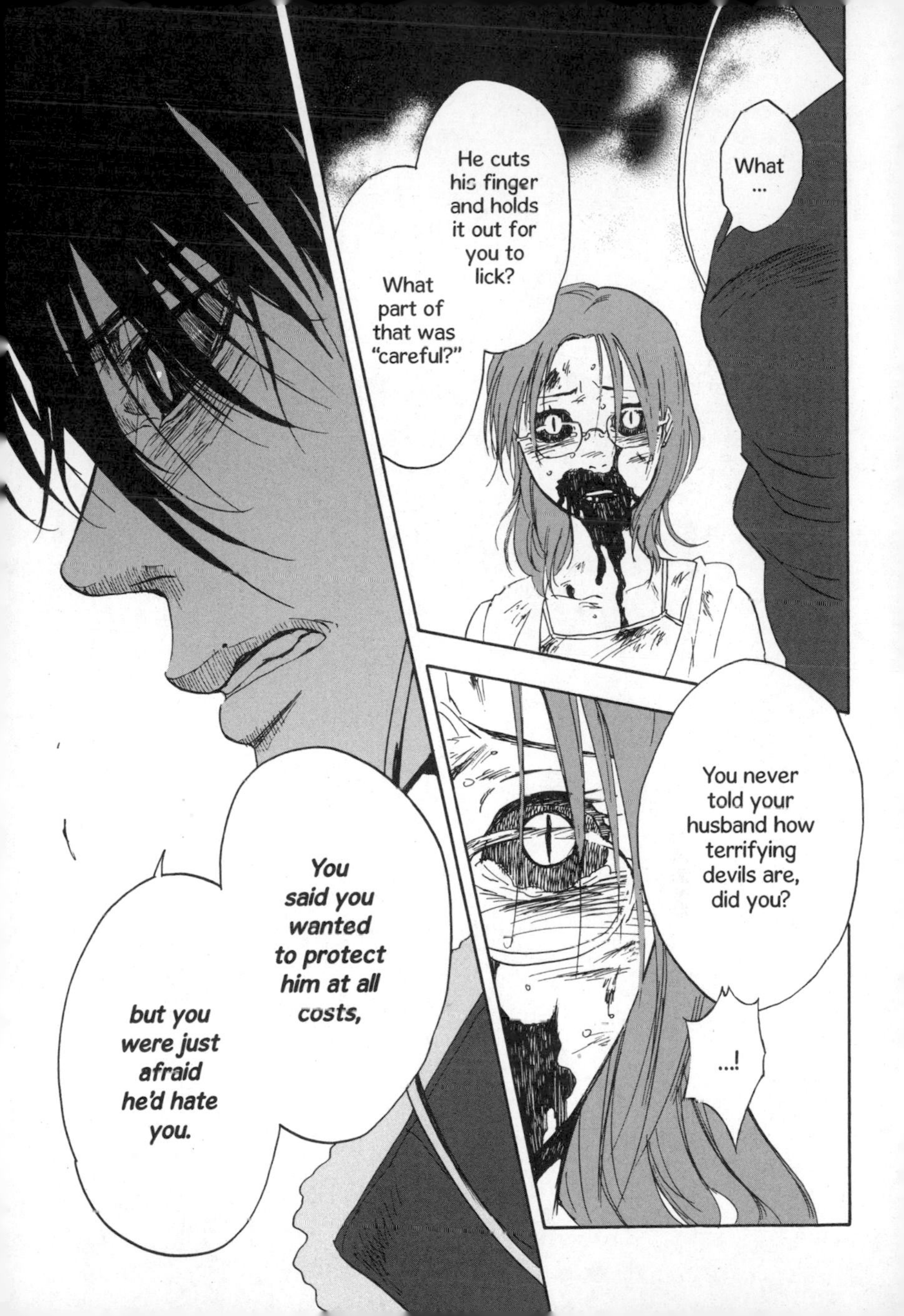
What ...
He cuts his finger and holds it out for you to lick?
What part of that was "careful?"
You never told your husband how terrifying devils are, did you?
...!
You said you wanted to protect him at all costs,
but you were just afraid he'd hate you.

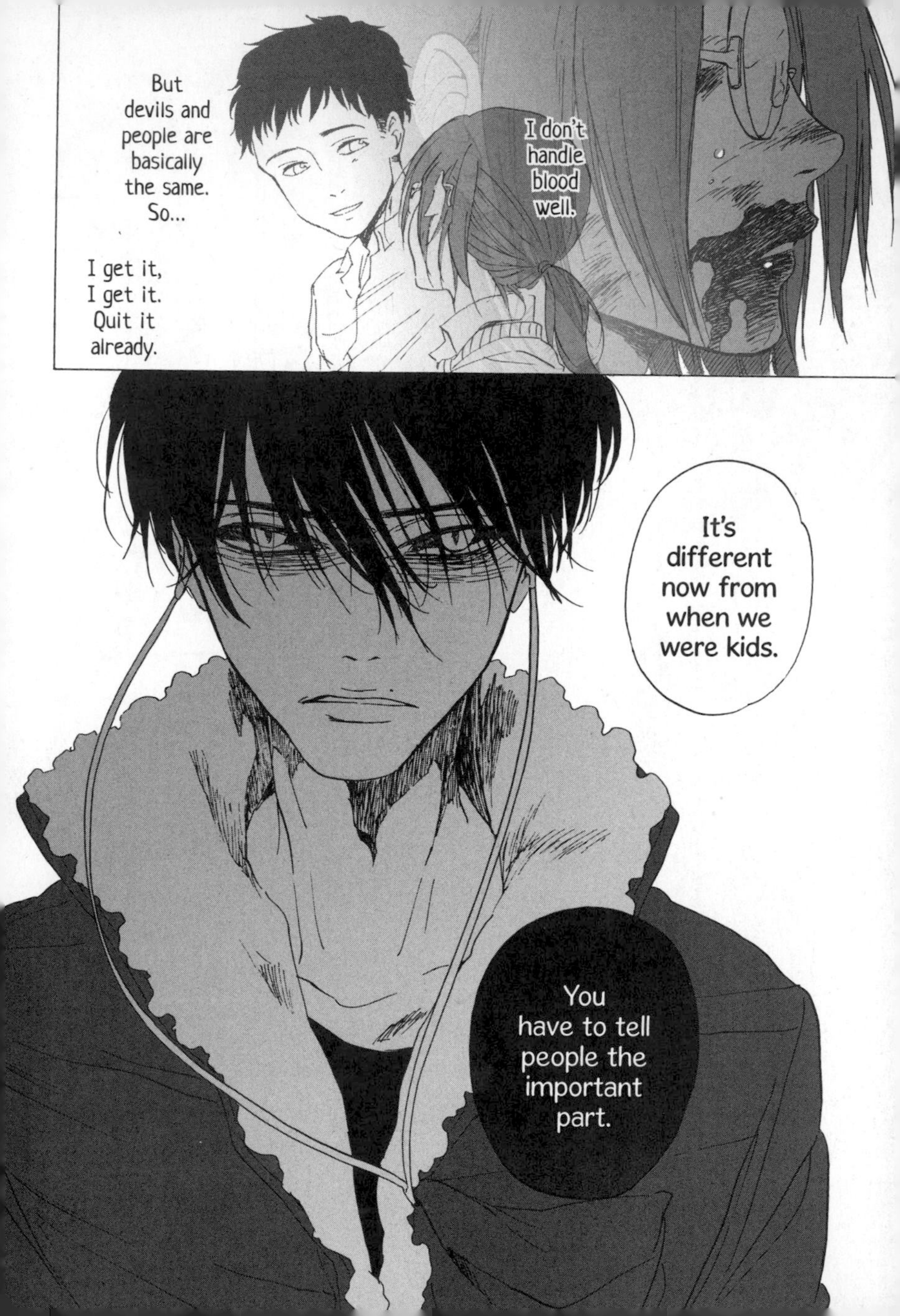
I don't handle blood well.
But devils and people are basically the same. So...
I get it, I get it. Quit it already.
It's different now from when we were kids.
You have to tell people the important part.

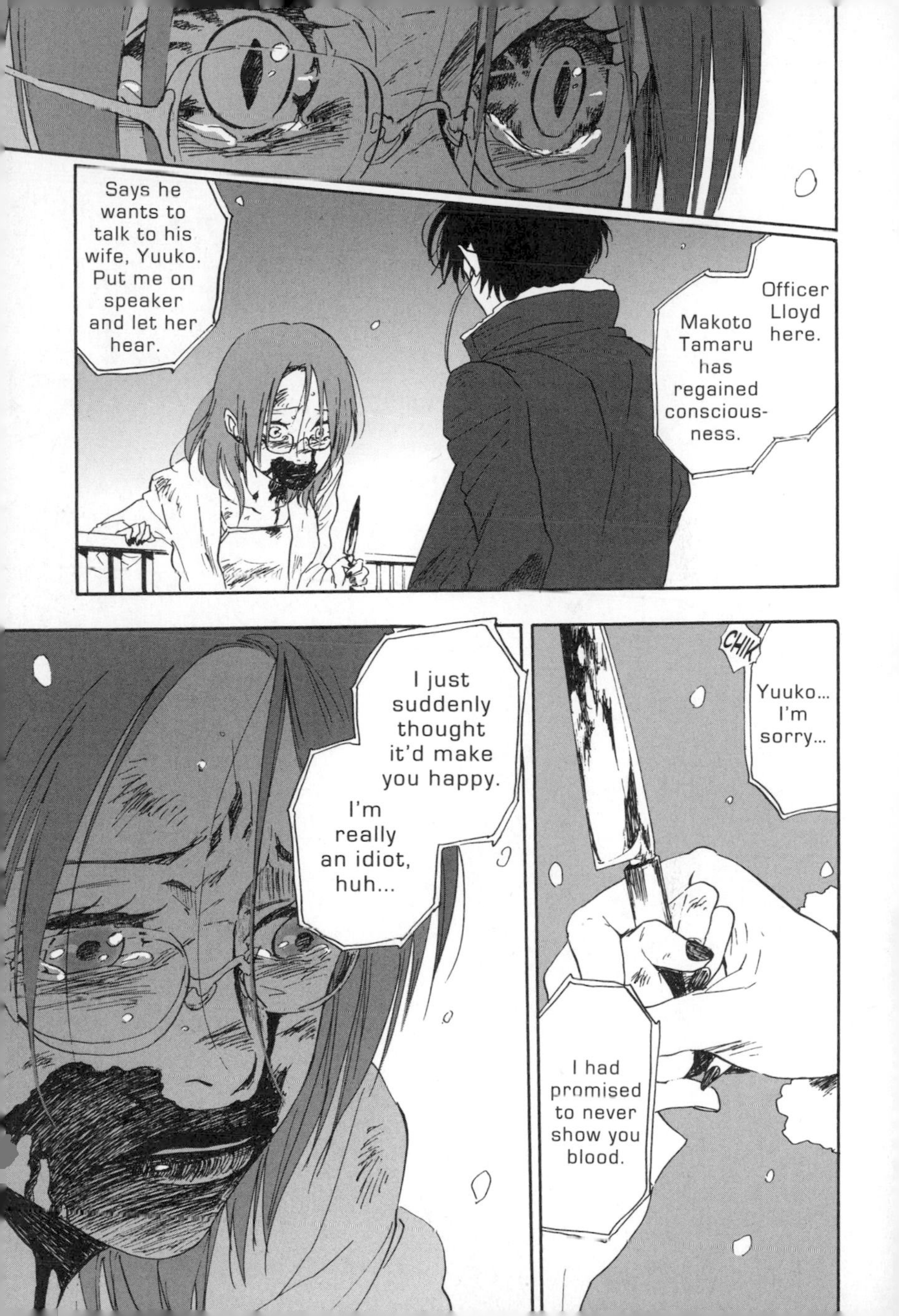
Officer Lloyd here. Makoto Tamaru has regained consciousness.
Says he wants to talk to his wife, Yuuko. Put me on speaker and let her hear.
CHIK
Yuuko... I'm sorry...
I had promised to never show you blood.
I just suddenly thought it'd make you happy.
I'm really an idiot, huh...

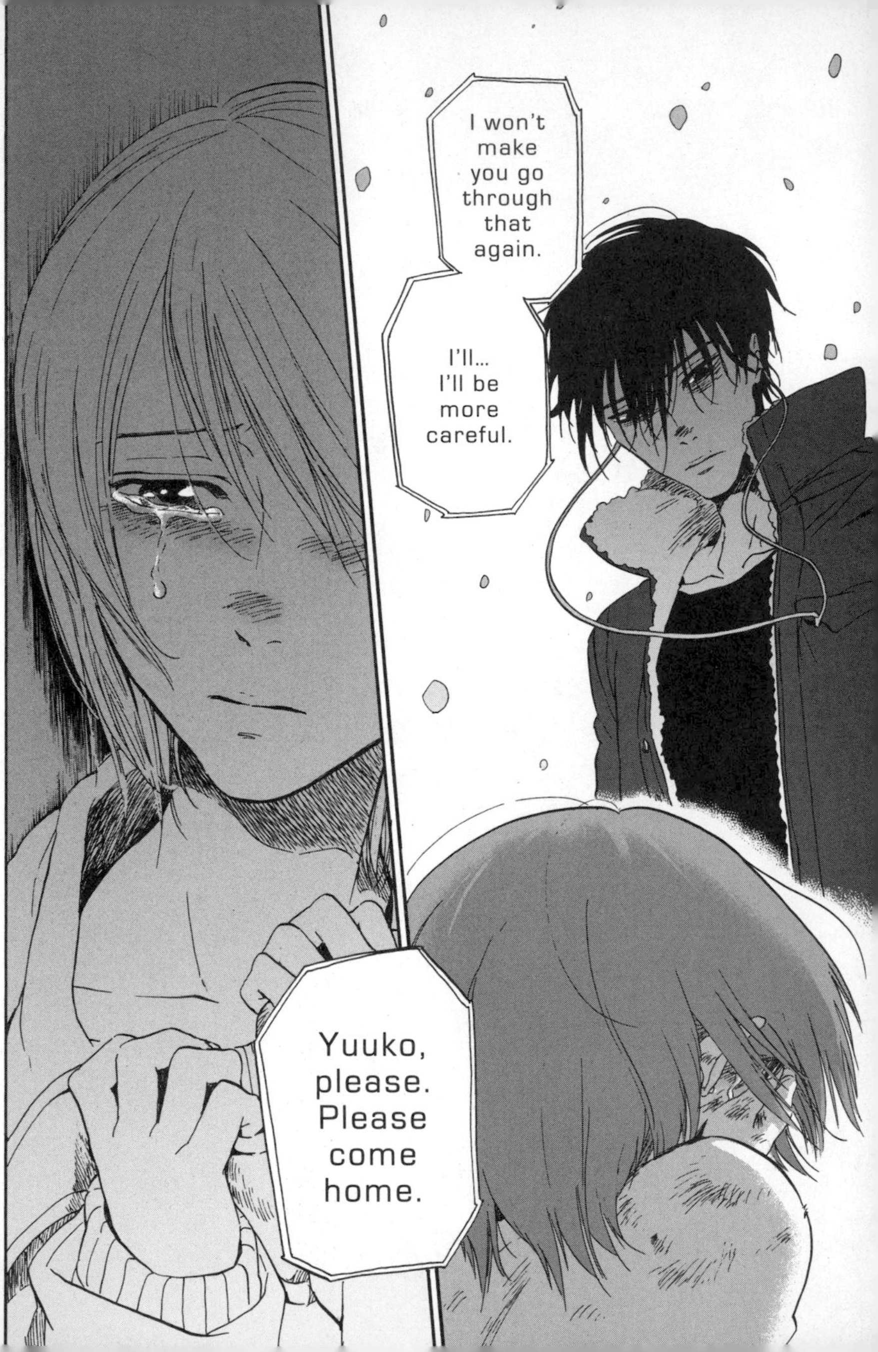
I won't make you go through that again.
I'll... I'll be more careful.
Yuuko, please. Please come home.

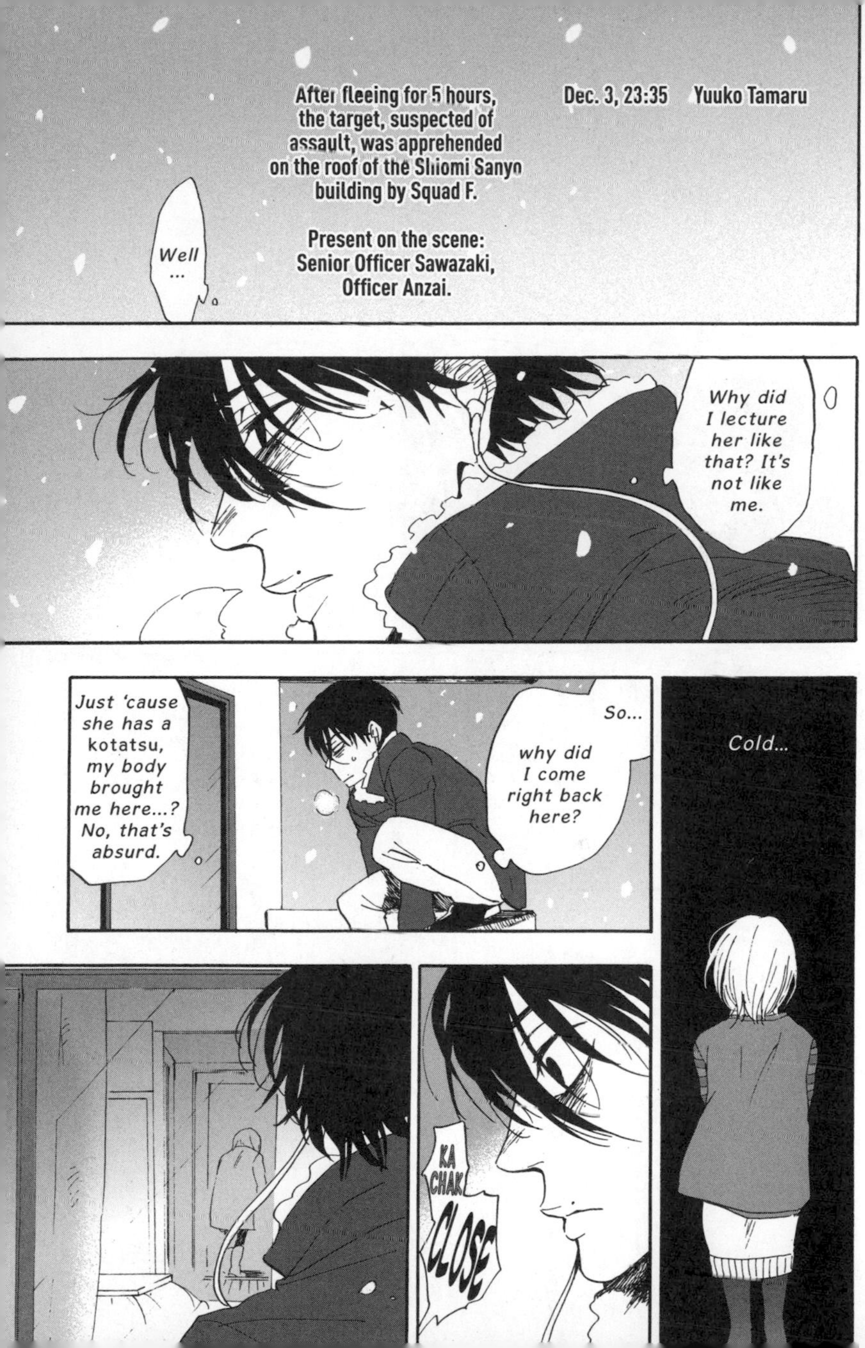
Dec. 3, 23:35 Yuuko Tamaru
After fleeing for 5 hours, the target, suspected of assault, was apprehended on the roof of the Shiomi Sanyo building by Squad F.
Present on the scene: Senior Officer Sawazaki, Officer Anzai.
Well ...
Why did I lecture her like that? It's not like me.
Cold...
So...
why did I come right back here?
Just 'cause she has a kotatsu, my body brought me here...? No, that's absurd.
KA CHAK
CLOSE

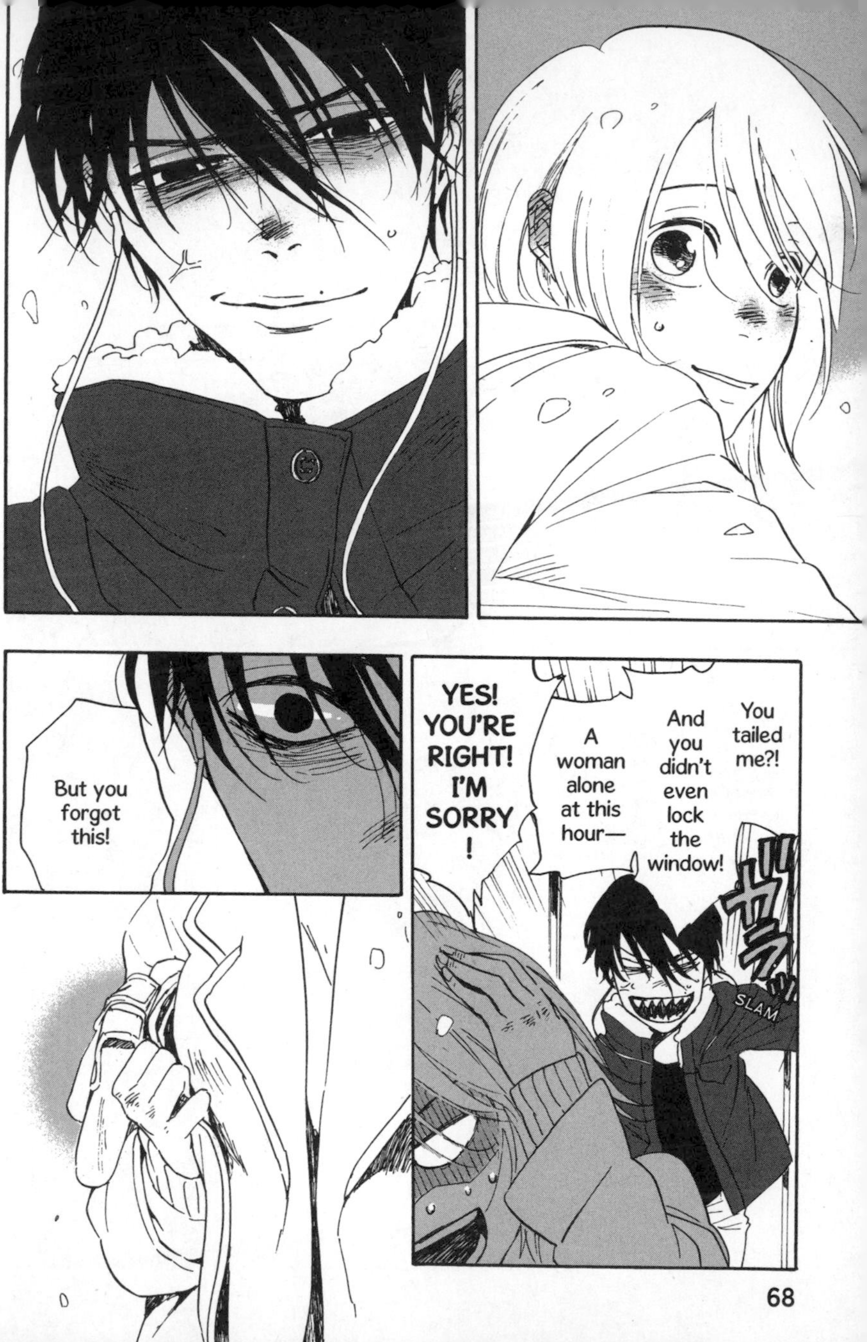
You tailed me?!
And you didn't even lock the window!
A woman alone at this hour—
YES! YOU'RE RIGHT! I'M SORRY!
SLAM
But you forgot this!

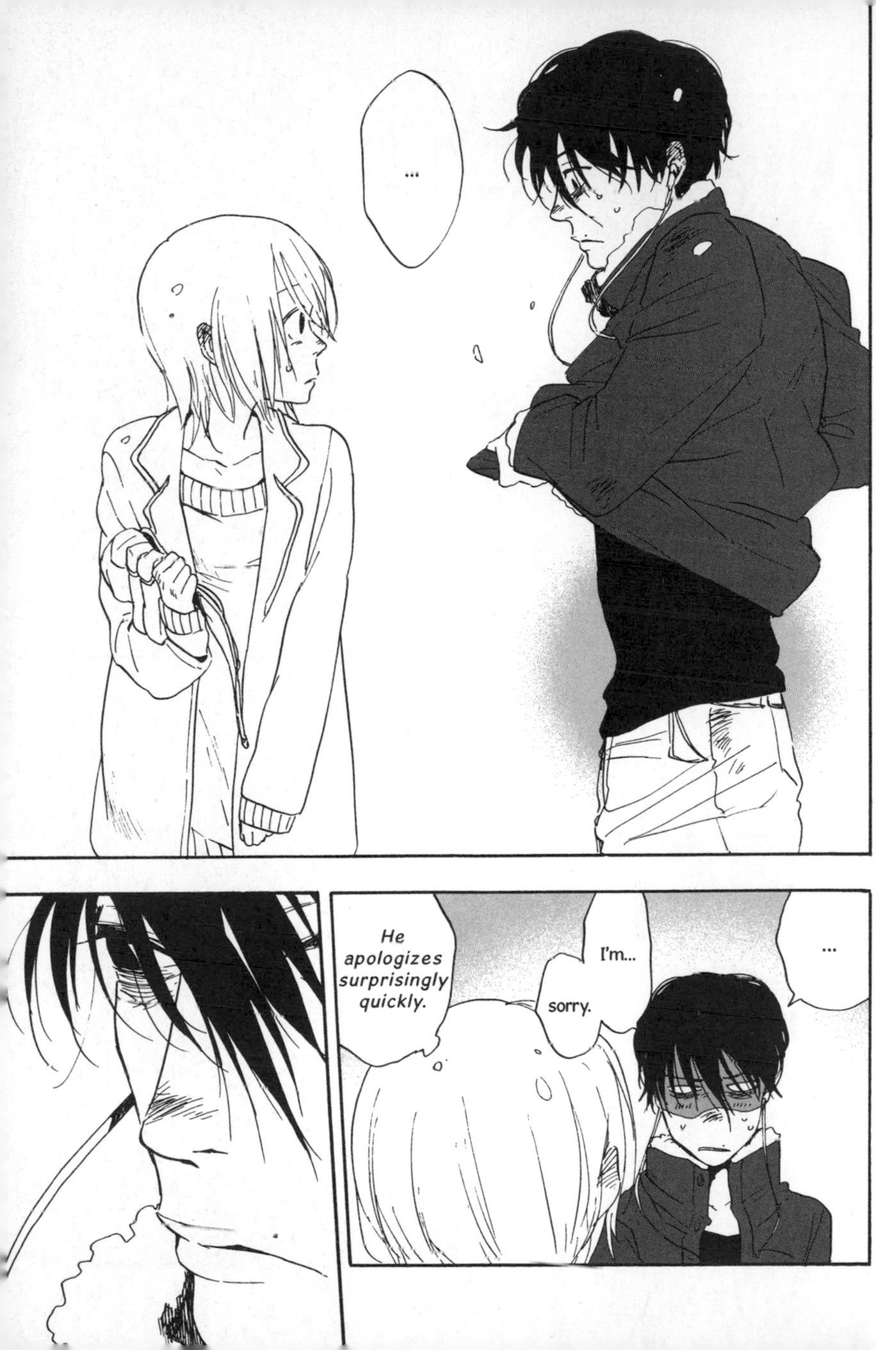
...
...
I'm...
sorry.
He apologizes surprisingly quickly.

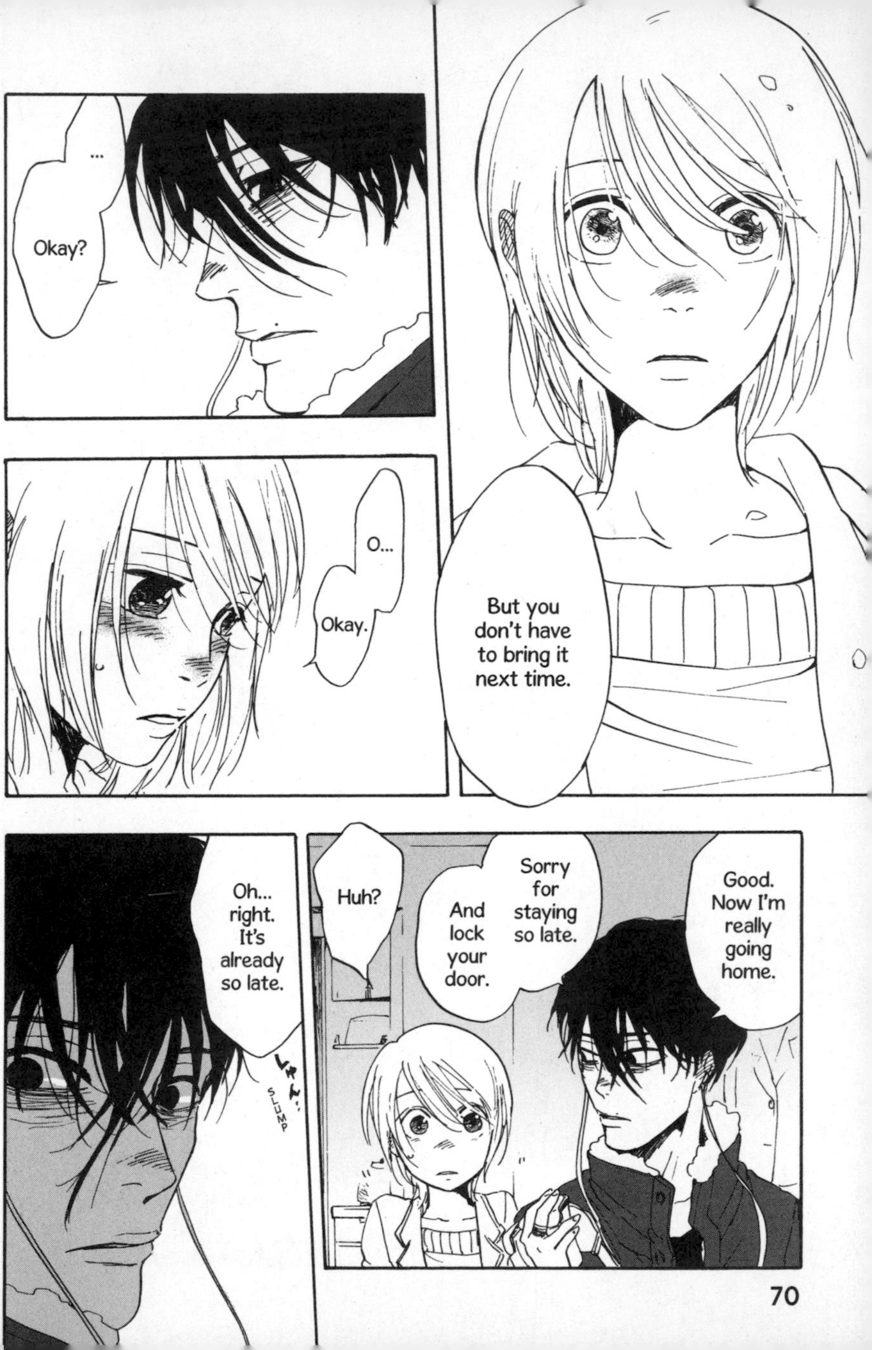
But you don't have to bring it next time.
...
Okay?
O...
Okay.
Good. Now I'm really going home.
Sorry for staying so late.
And lock your door.
Huh?
Oh... right. It's already so late.
SLUMP

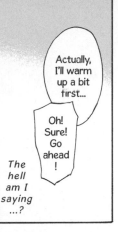

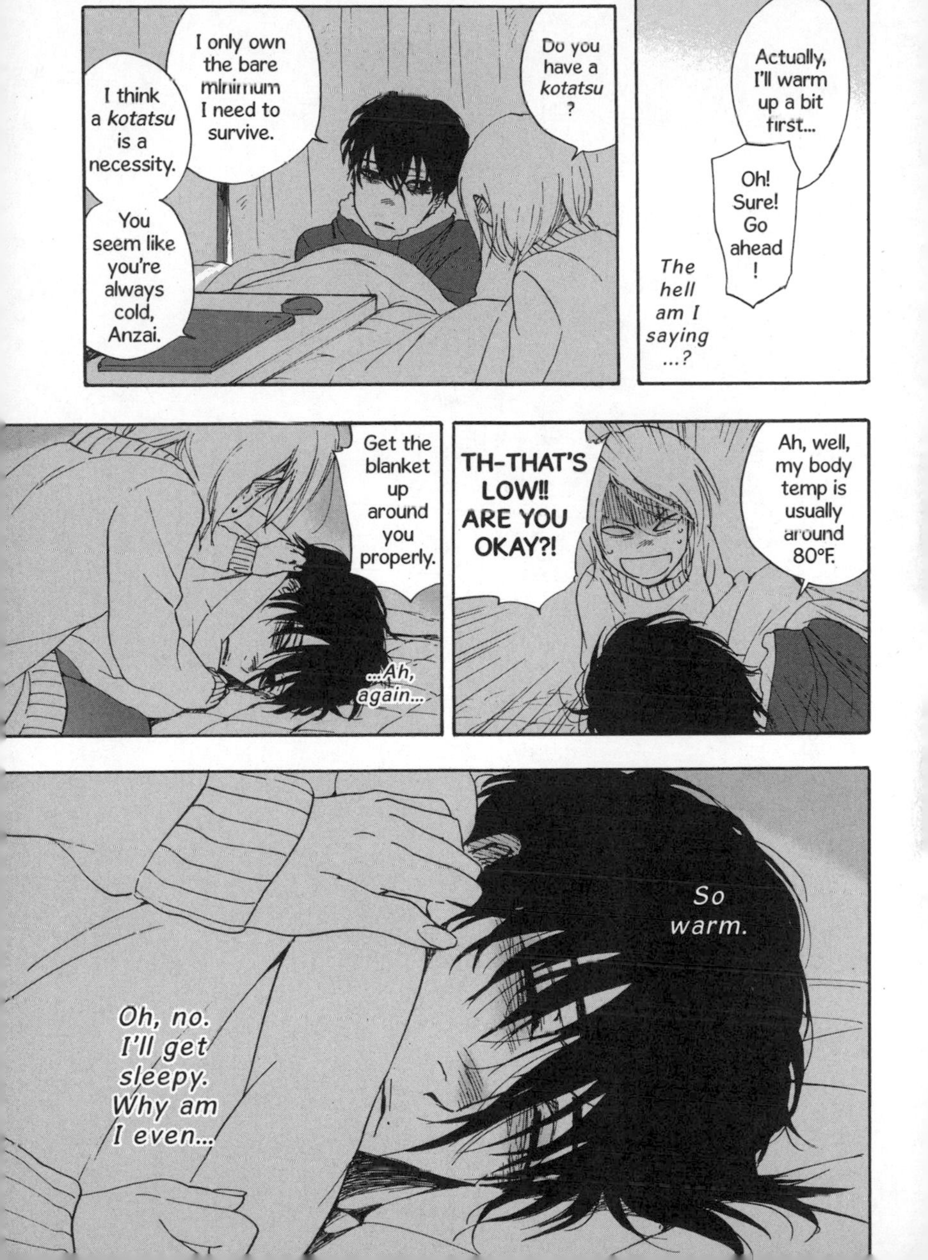
Actually, I'll warm up a bit first...
Oh! Sure! Go ahead!
The hell am I saying...?
Do you have a *kotatsu*?
I only own the bare minimum I need to survive.
I think a *kotatsu* is a necessity.
You seem like you're always cold, Anzai.
Ah, well, my body temp is usually around 80°F.
TH-THAT'S LOW!! ARE YOU OKAY?!
Get the blanket up around you properly.
...Ah, again...
So warm.
Oh, no. I'll get sleepy. Why am I even...

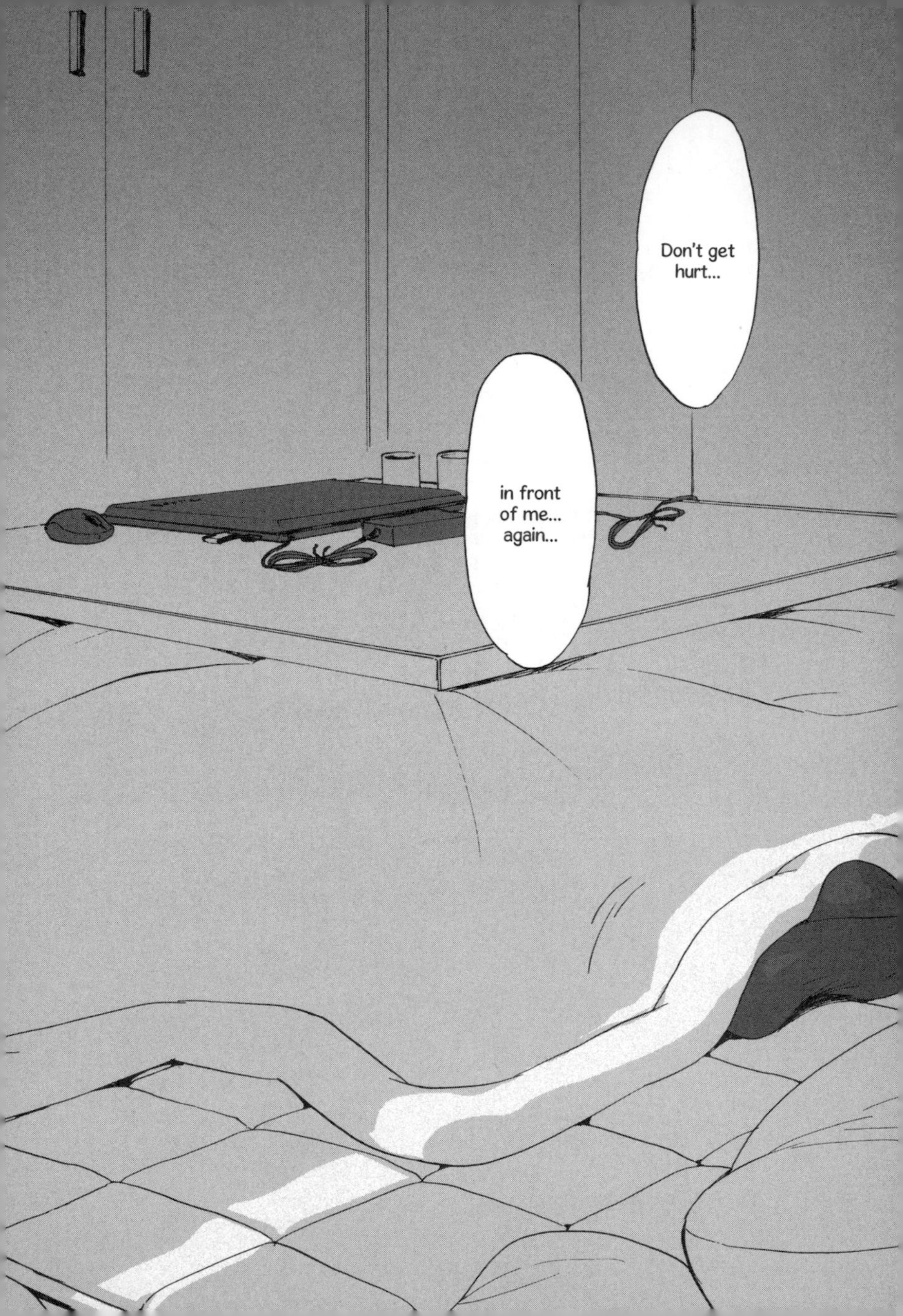
Don't get hurt...
in front of me... again...

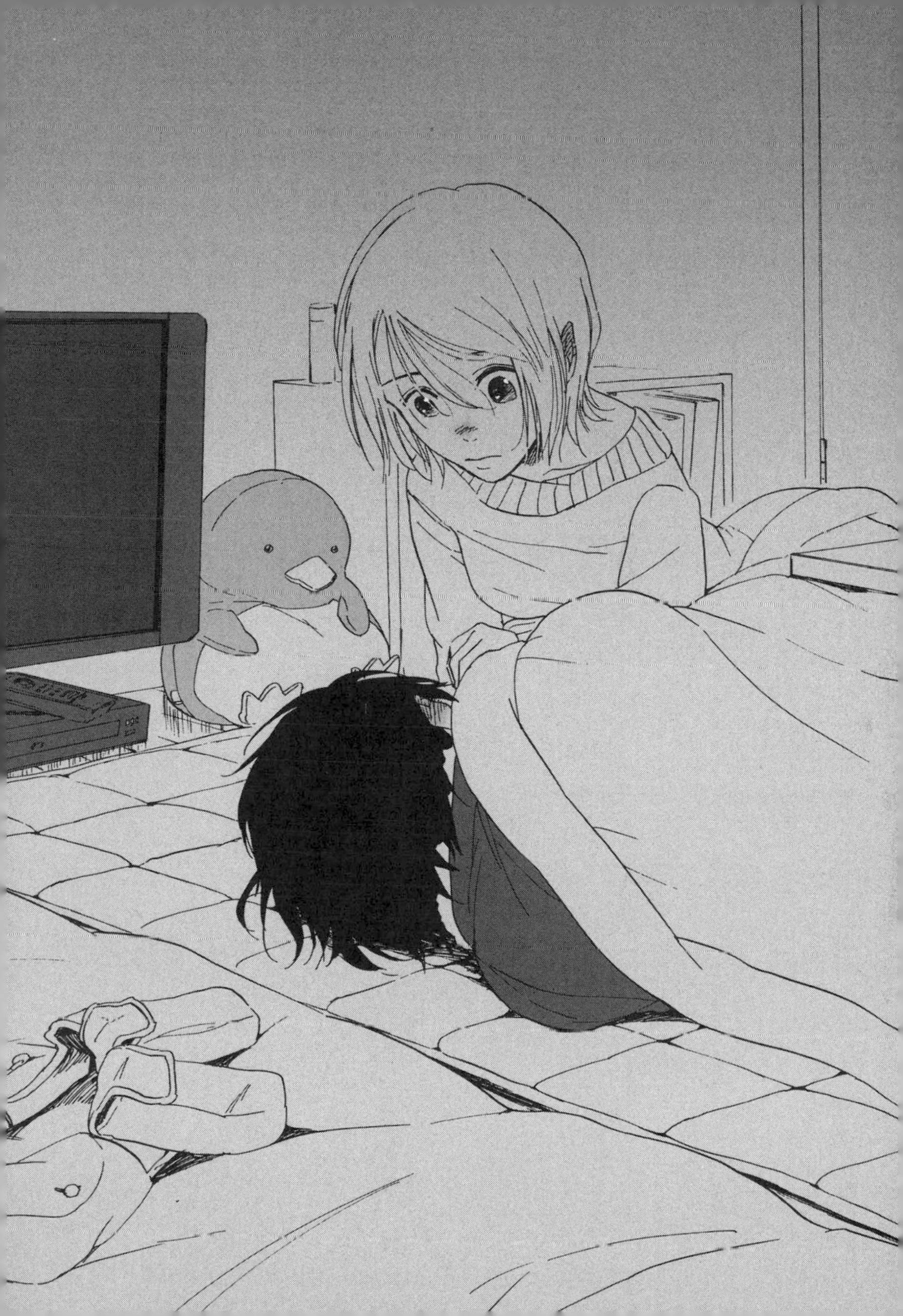

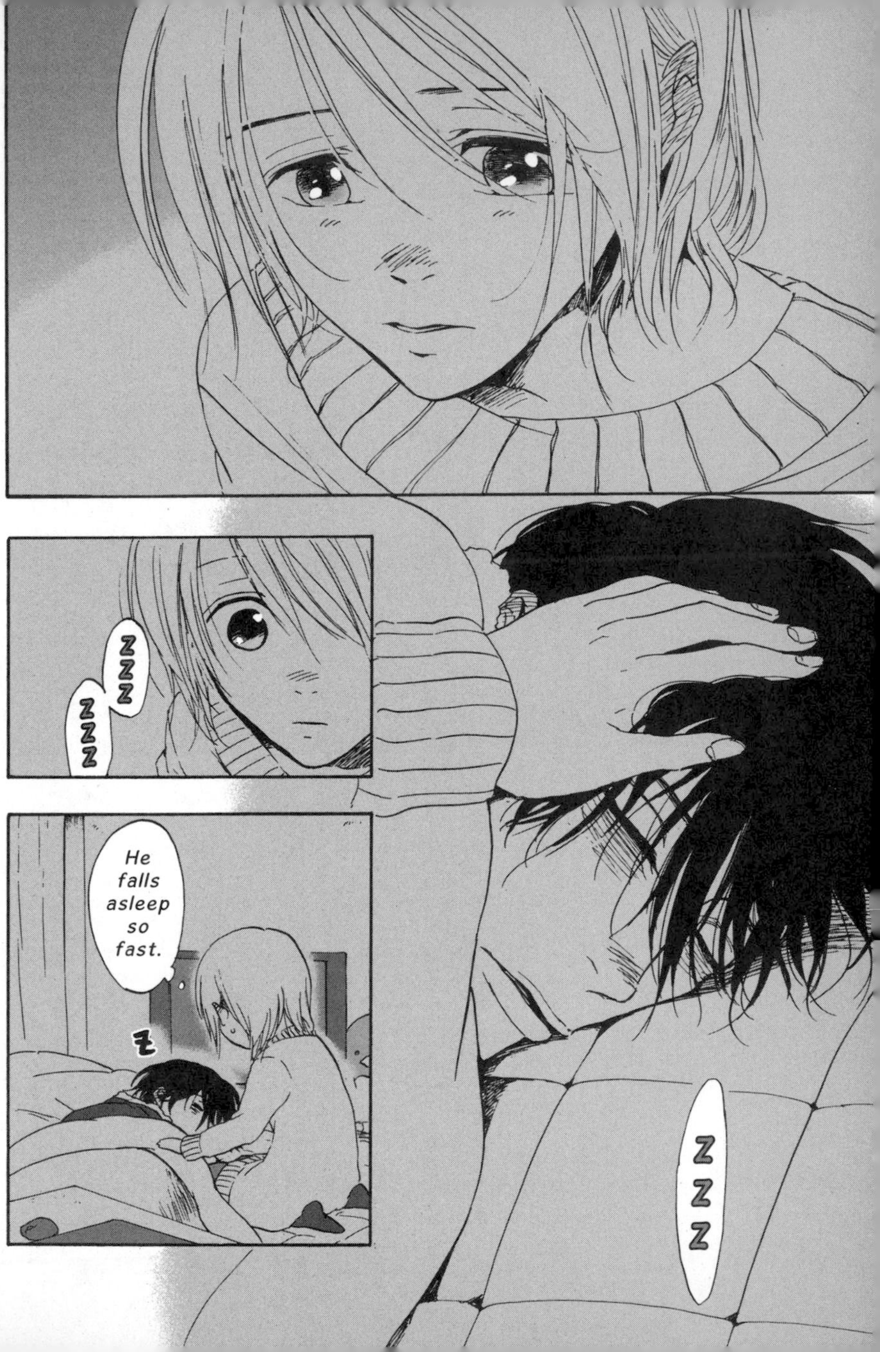
ZZZ
ZZZ
ZZZ
He falls asleep so fast.
Z

later
← Took a bath.
ほか warm
ほか warm
Is he really asleep?
Z
This is a pretty long nap!
Is he possibly staying the night?!
ドキドキドキ
BADUM BADUM BADUM
ムク
RISE
Aaah, I fell asleep...
Sorry. I'll go home.
Whaaaaaat?
...

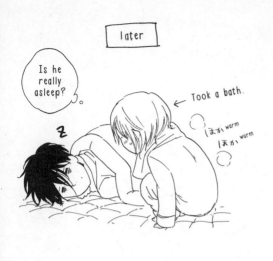

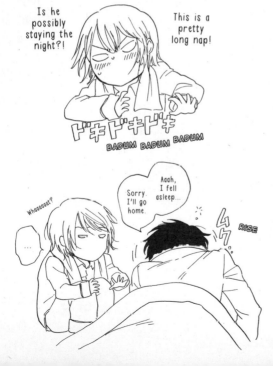

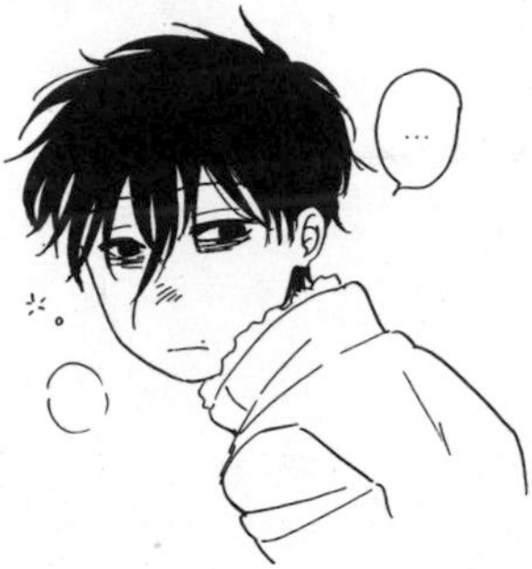
...

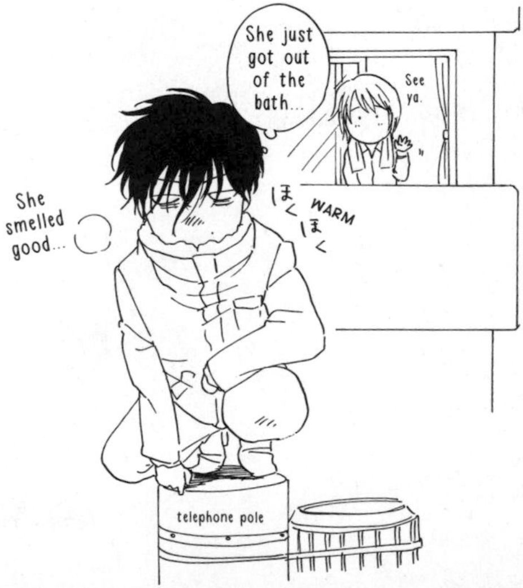
See ya.
She just got out of the bath...
ほくほく
WARM
She smelled good...
telephone pole

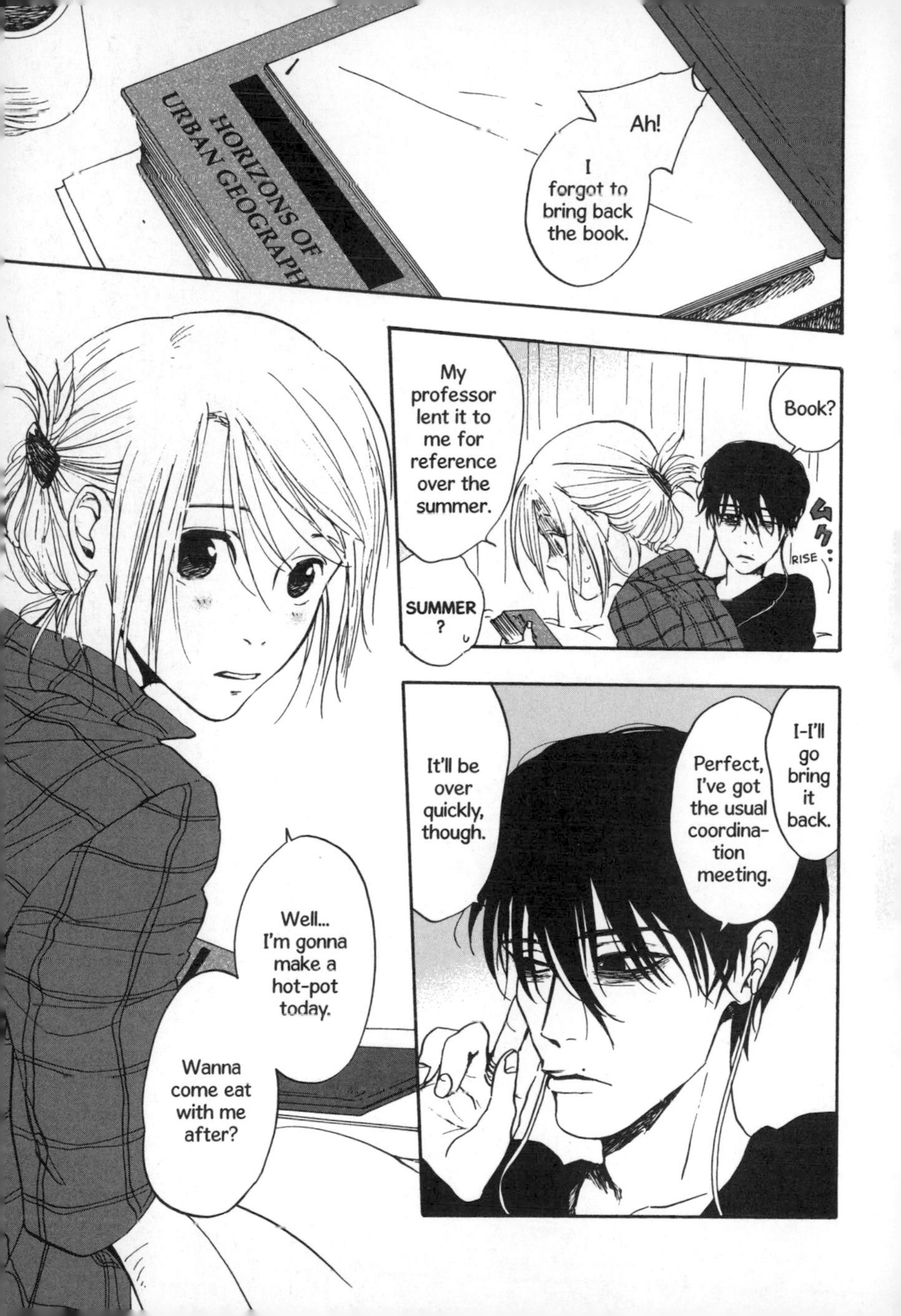
HORIZONS OF
URBAN GEOGRAPH
Ah!
I forgot to bring back the book.
Book?
RISE
My professor lent it to me for reference over the summer.
SUMMER?
I-I'll go bring it back.
Perfect, I've got the usual coordina-tion meeting.
It'll be over quickly, though.
Well... I'm gonna make a hot-pot today.
Wanna come eat with me after?

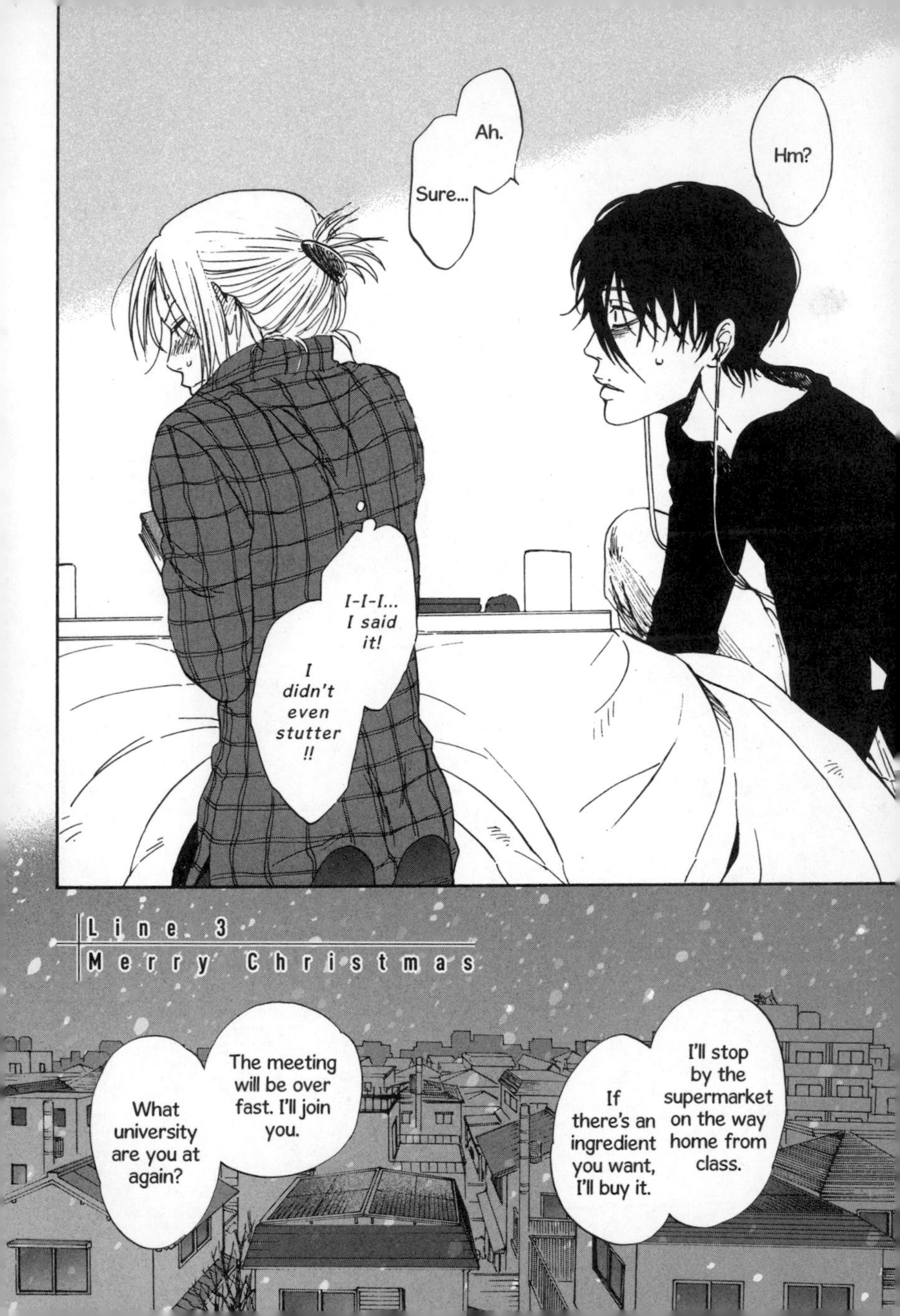
Hm?
Ah.
Sure...
I-I-I... I said it!
I didn't even stutter!!
Line 3
Merry Christmas
I'll stop by the supermarket on the way home from class.
If there's an ingredient you want, I'll buy it.
The meeting will be over fast. I'll join you.
What university are you at again?

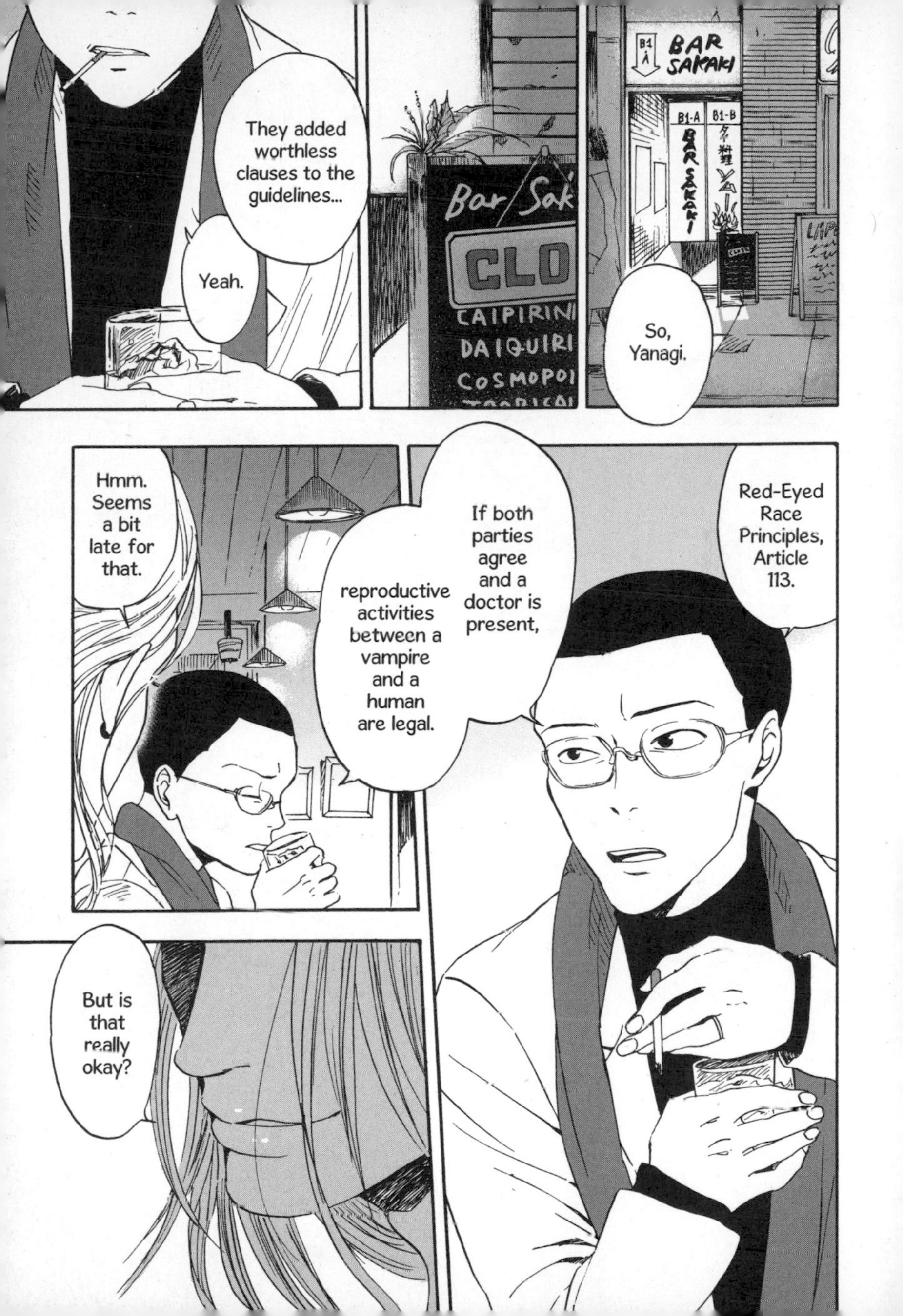
B1
BAR SAKAKI
B1-A
B1-B
BAR SAKAKI
So, Yanagi.
Bar Sak
CLO
DAIQUIRI
They added worthless clauses to the guidelines...
Yeah.
Red-Eyed Race Principles, Article 113.
If both parties agree and a doctor is present,
reproductive activities between a vampire and a human are legal.
Hmm. Seems a bit late for that.
But is that really okay?

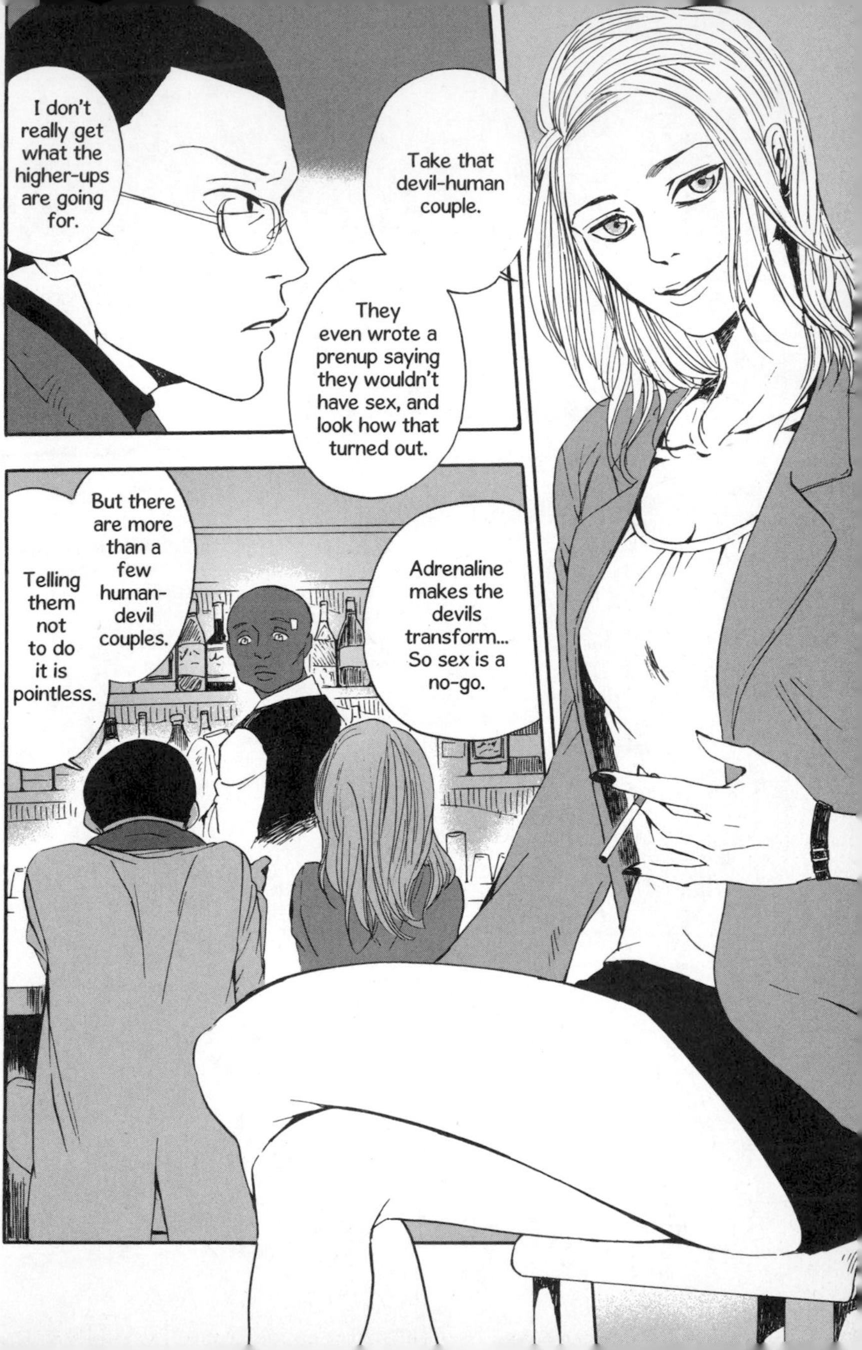
Take that devil-human couple.
They even wrote a prenup saying they wouldn't have sex, and look how that turned out.
Adrenaline makes the devils transform... So sex is a no-go.
I don't really get what the higher-ups are going for.
But there are more than a few human-devil couples.
Telling them not to do it is pointless.

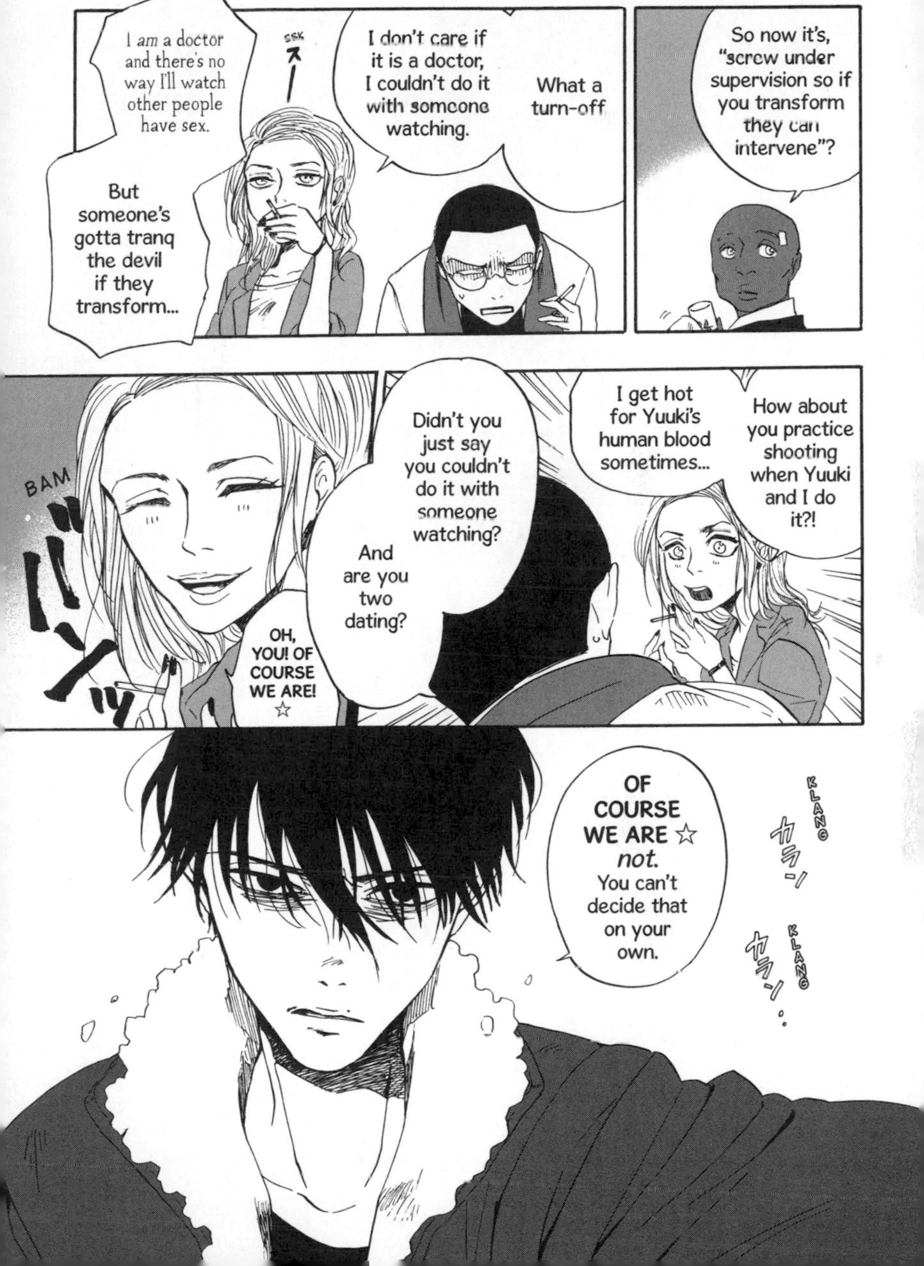
So now it's, "screw under supervision so if you transform they can intervene"?
What a turn-off
I don't care if it is a doctor, I couldn't do it with someone watching.
SSK
I *am* a doctor and there's no way I'll watch other people have sex.
But someone's gotta tranq the devil if they transform...
How about you practice shooting when Yuuki and I do it?!
I get hot for Yuuki's human blood sometimes...
Didn't you just say you couldn't do it with someone watching?
And are you two dating?
OH, YOU! OF COURSE WE ARE! ☆
BAM
KLANG
KLANG
OF COURSE WE ARE ☆ *not*. You can't decide that on your own.

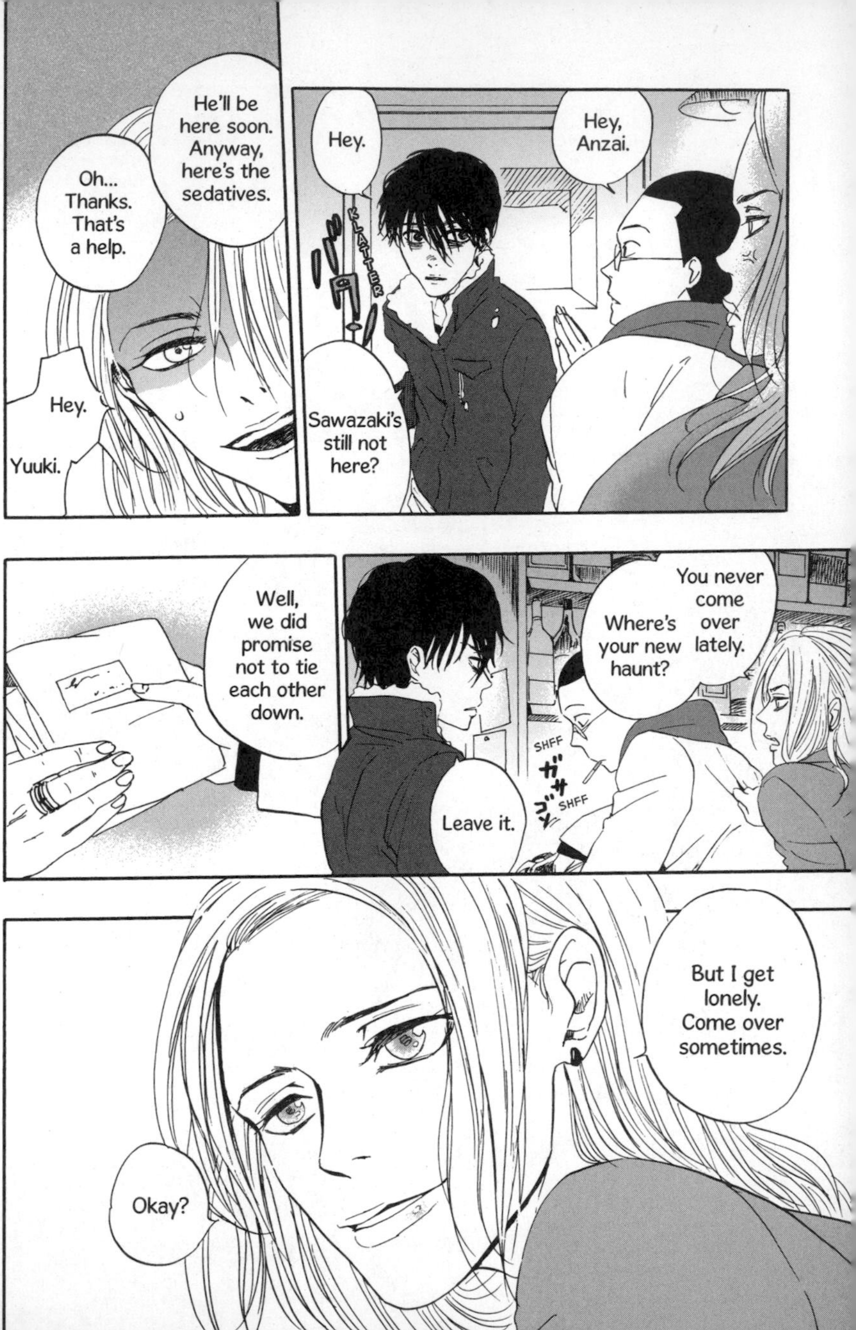
Hey, Anzai.
Hey.
KLATTER
Sawazaki's still not here?
He'll be here soon. Anyway, here's the sedatives.
Oh... Thanks. That's a help.
Hey.
Yuuki.
You never come over lately.
Where's your new haunt?
SHFF
SHFF
Leave it.
Well, we did promise not to tie each other down.
But I get lonely. Come over sometimes.
Okay?

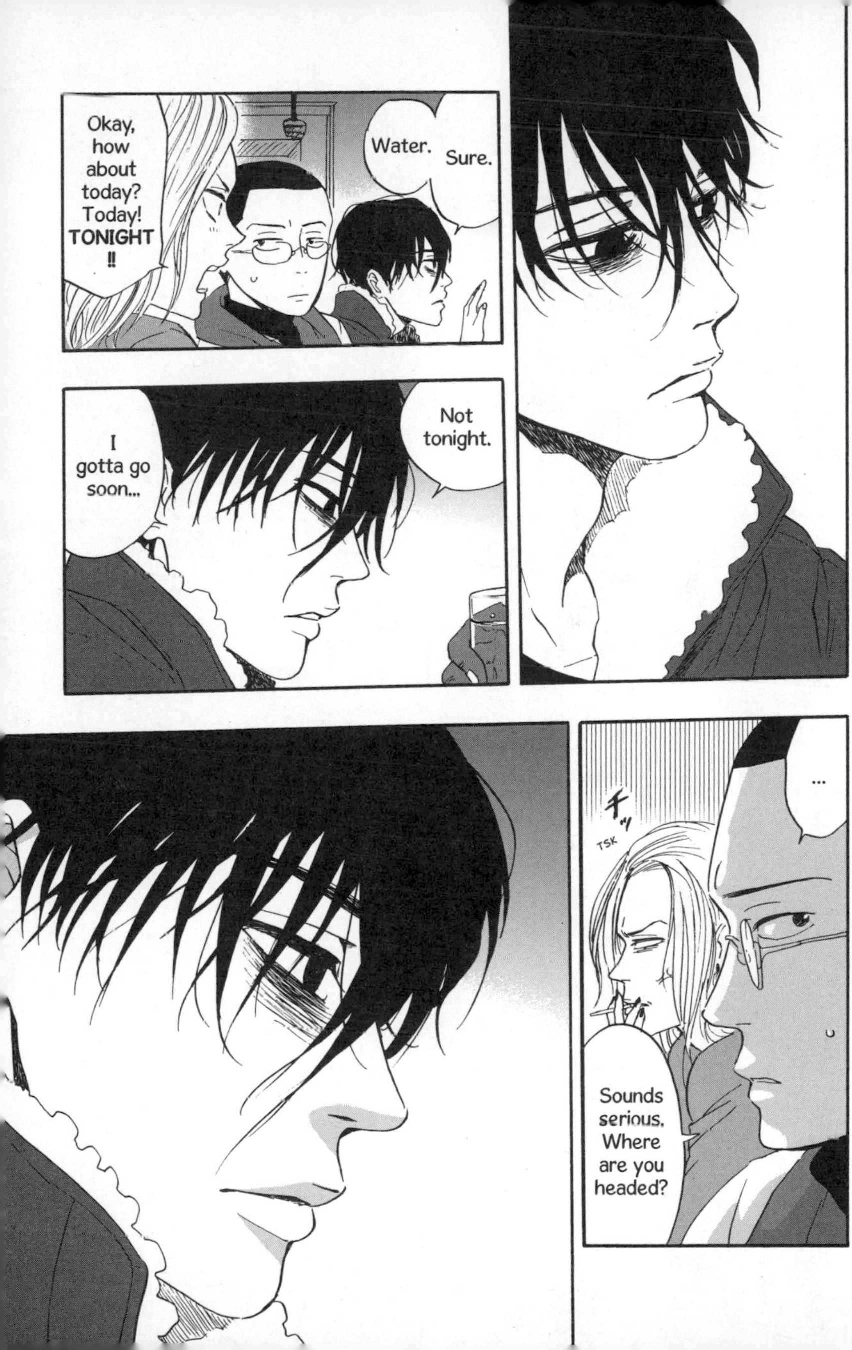

Water.
Sure.
Okay, how about today? Today! TONIGHT!!
Not tonight.
I gotta go soon...
...
チッ TSK
Sounds serious. Where are you headed?

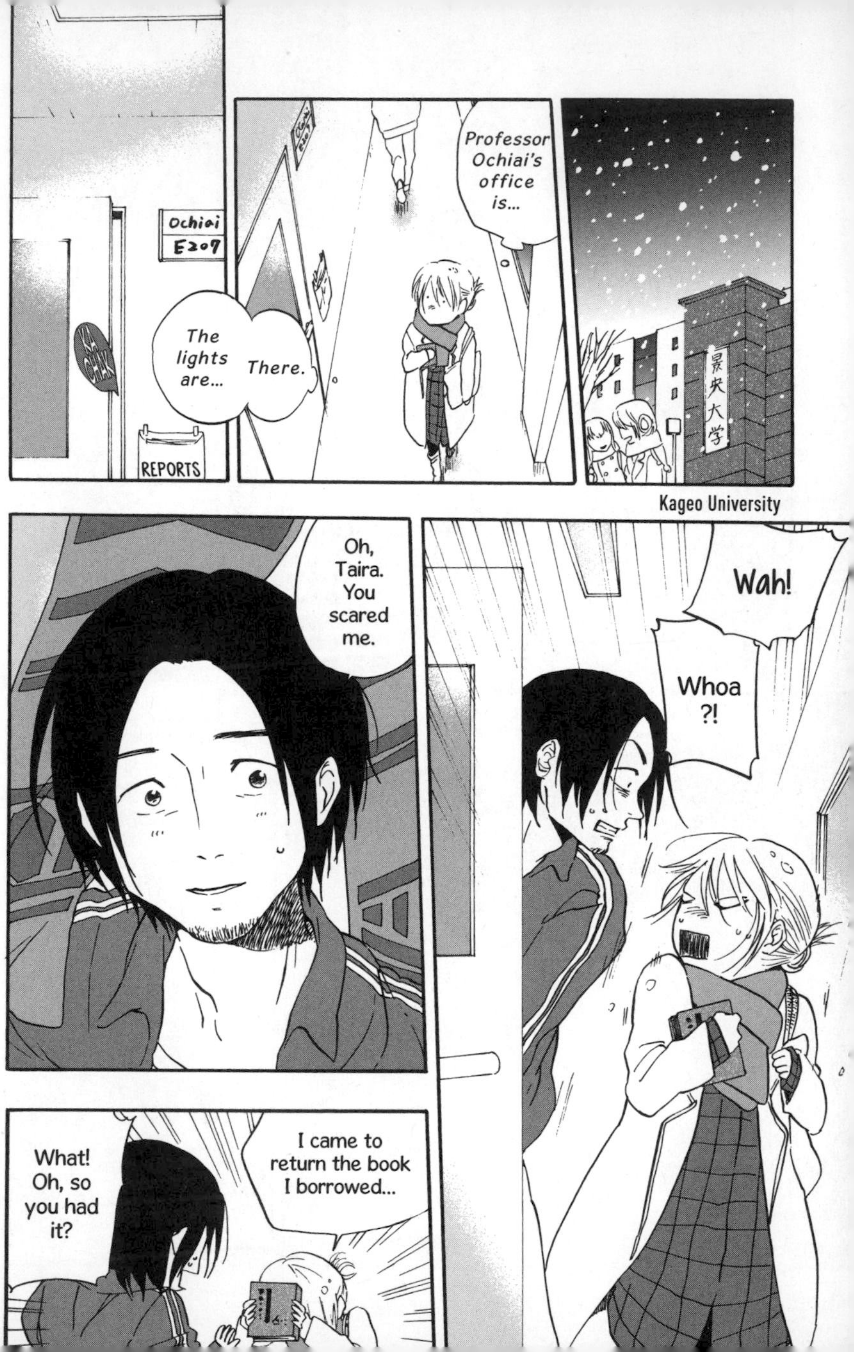
景央大学
Kageo University
Professor Ochiai's office is...
There.
Ochiai E207
The lights are...
KA CHAK
REPORTS
Wah!
Whoa ?!
Oh, Taira. You scared me.
I came to return the book I borrowed...
What! Oh, so you had it?

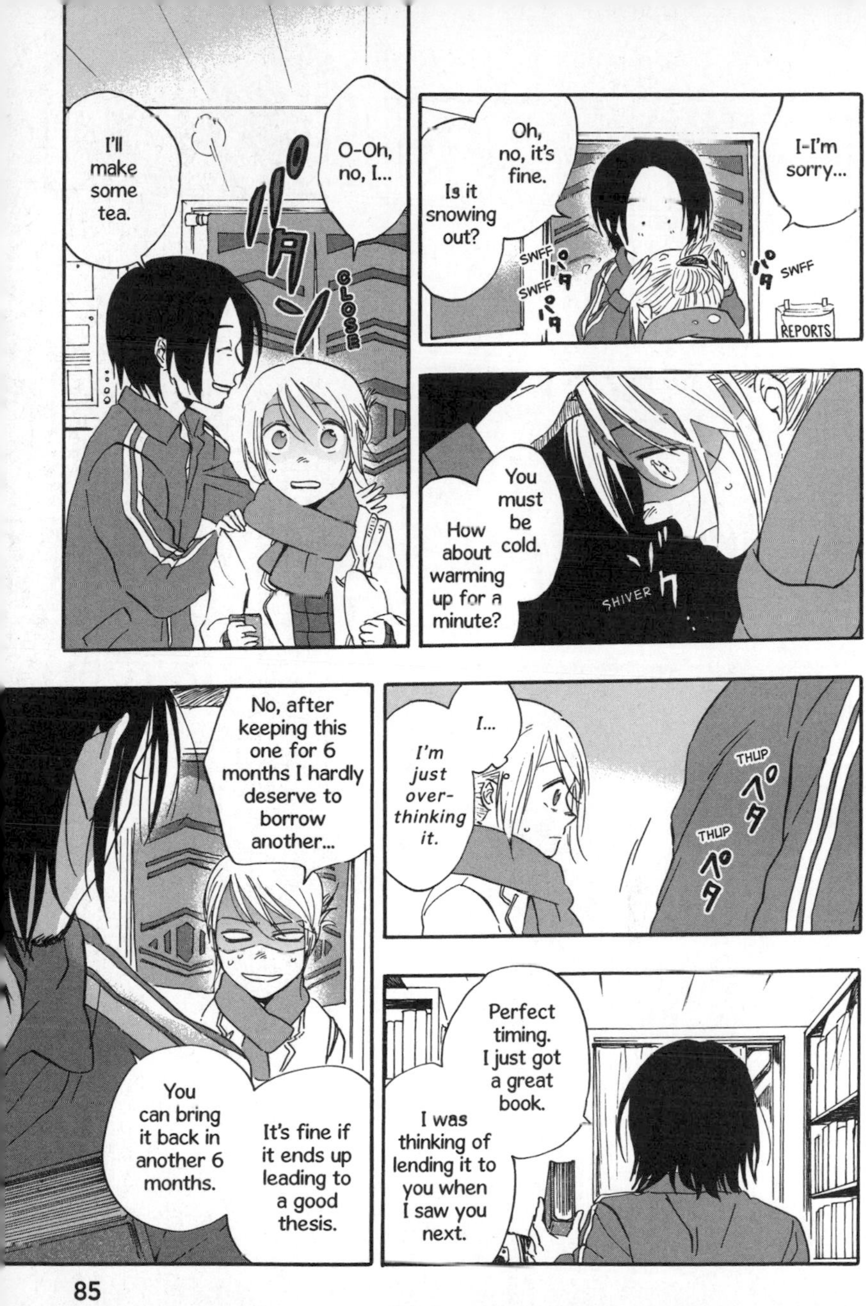
I-I'm sorry...
SWFF
Oh, no, it's fine.
Is it snowing out?
SWFF
SWFF
REPORTS
You must be cold.
How about warming up for a minute?
SHIVER
O-Oh, no, I...
I'll make some tea.
CLOSE
THUP
THUP
I...
I'm just over-thinking it.
Perfect timing. I just got a great book.
I was thinking of lending it to you when I saw you next.
No, after keeping this one for 6 months I hardly deserve to borrow another...
It's fine if it ends up leading to a good thesis.
You can bring it back in another 6 months.

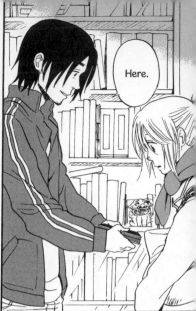

Here.

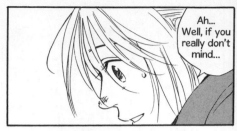

Ah...
Well, if you
really don't
mind...

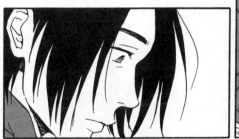

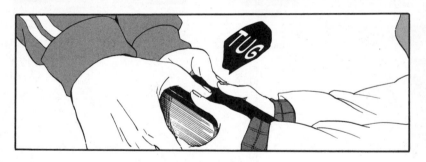

TUG

KISS

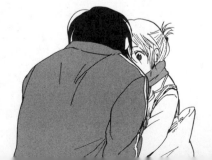

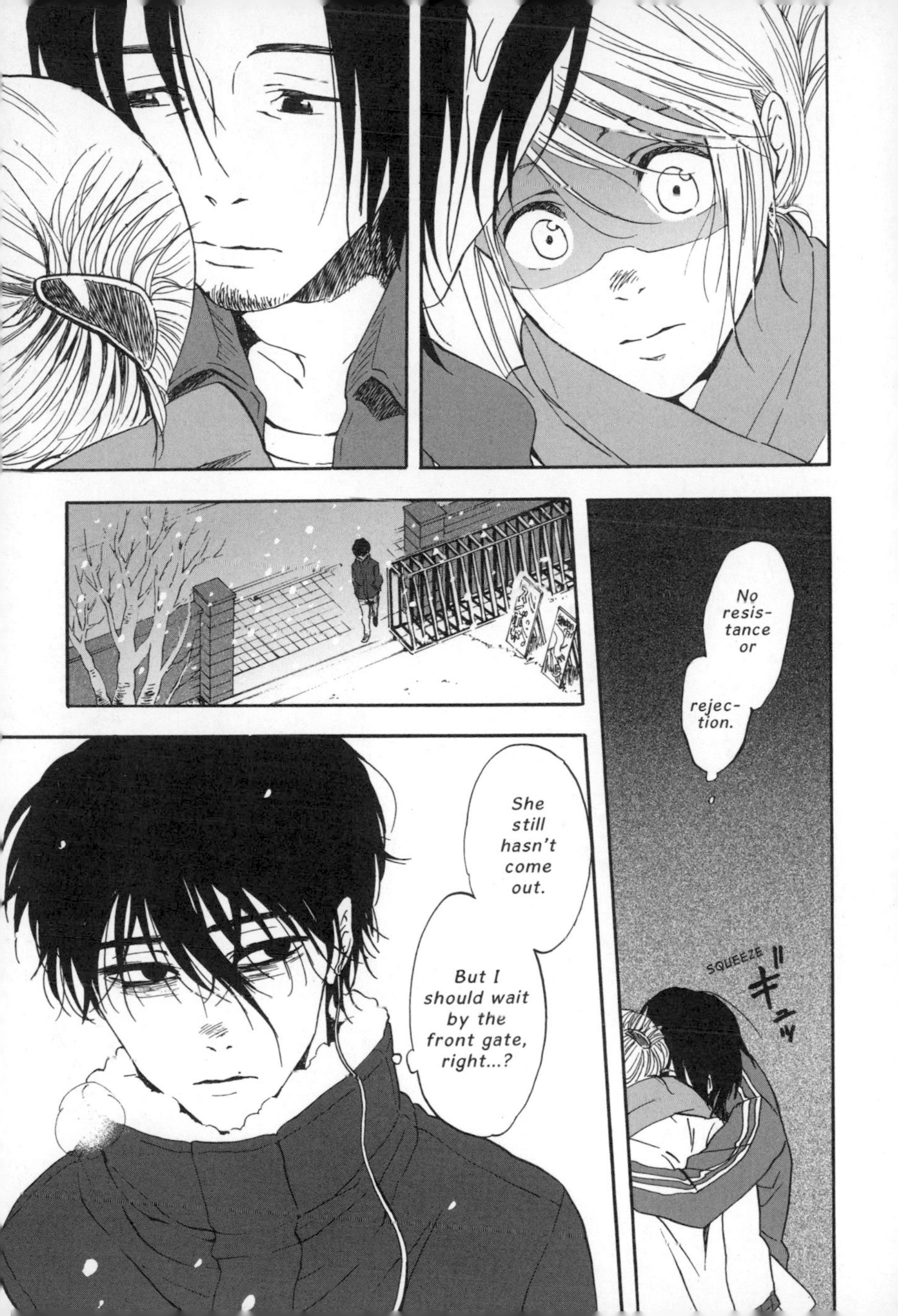
No resistance or rejection.
SQUEEZE
ギュッ
She still hasn't come out.
But I should wait by the front gate, right...?

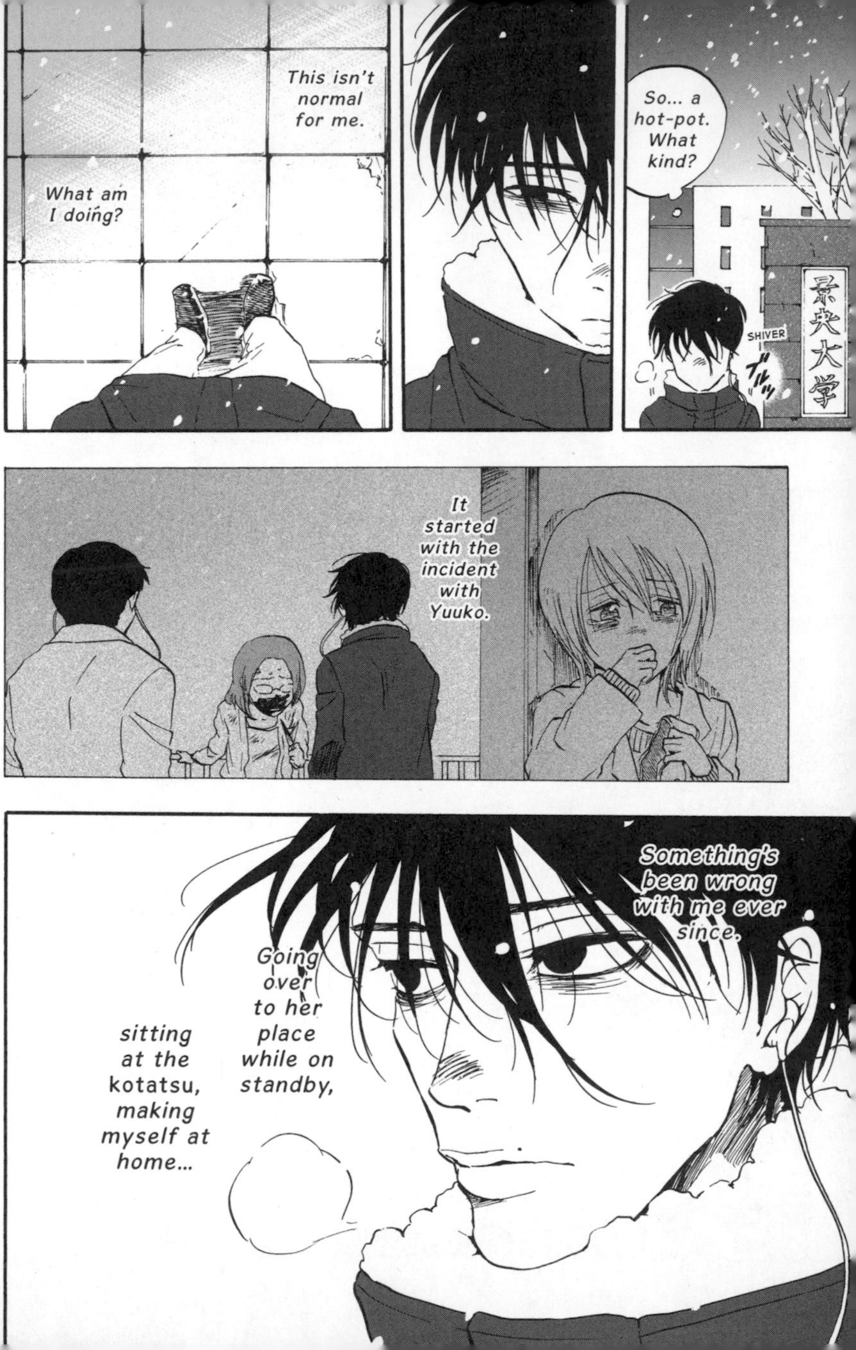
So... a hot-pot. What kind?
SHIVER
ブルッ
This isn't normal for me.
What am I doing?
It started with the incident with Yuuko.
Something's been wrong with me ever since.
Going over to her place while on standby,
sitting at the kotatsu, making myself at home...

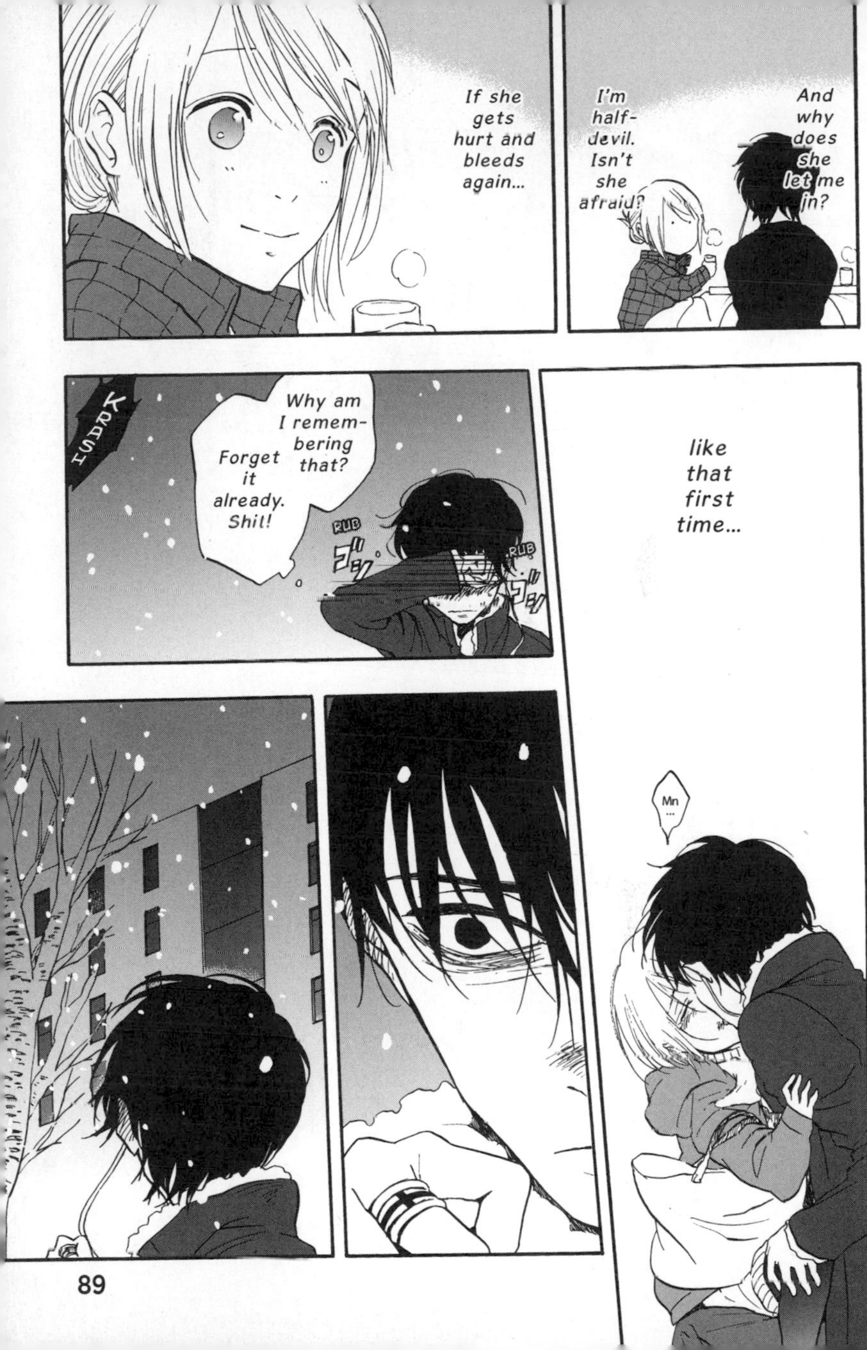

And why does she let me in?
I'm half-devil. Isn't she afraid?
If she gets hurt and bleeds again...
like that first time...
Mn...
KRASH
Why am I remembering that?
Forget it already. Shit!
RUB
RUB

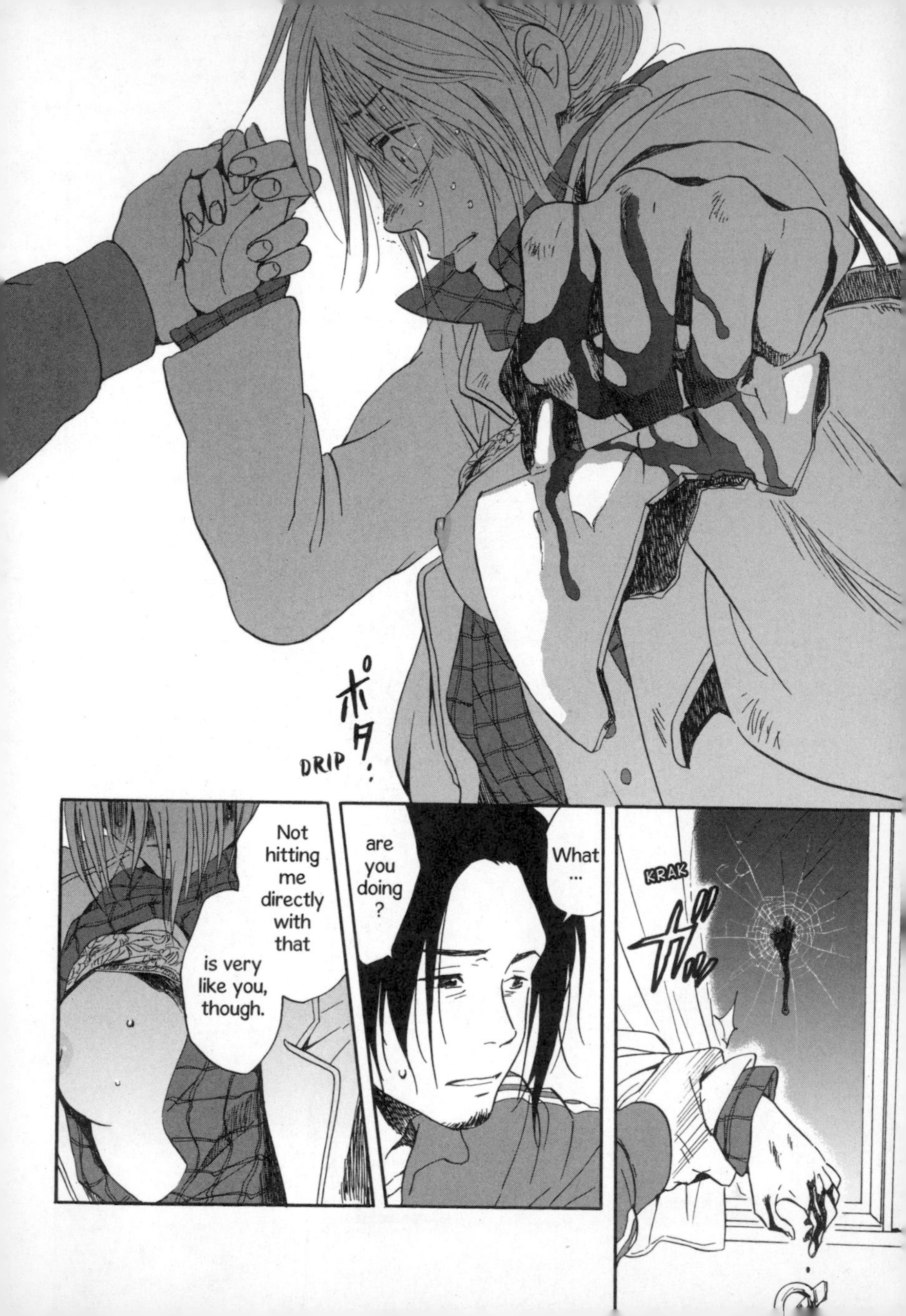
ポタ
DRIP
KRAK
ガッ
What ...
are you doing ?
Not hitting me directly with that
is very like you, though.

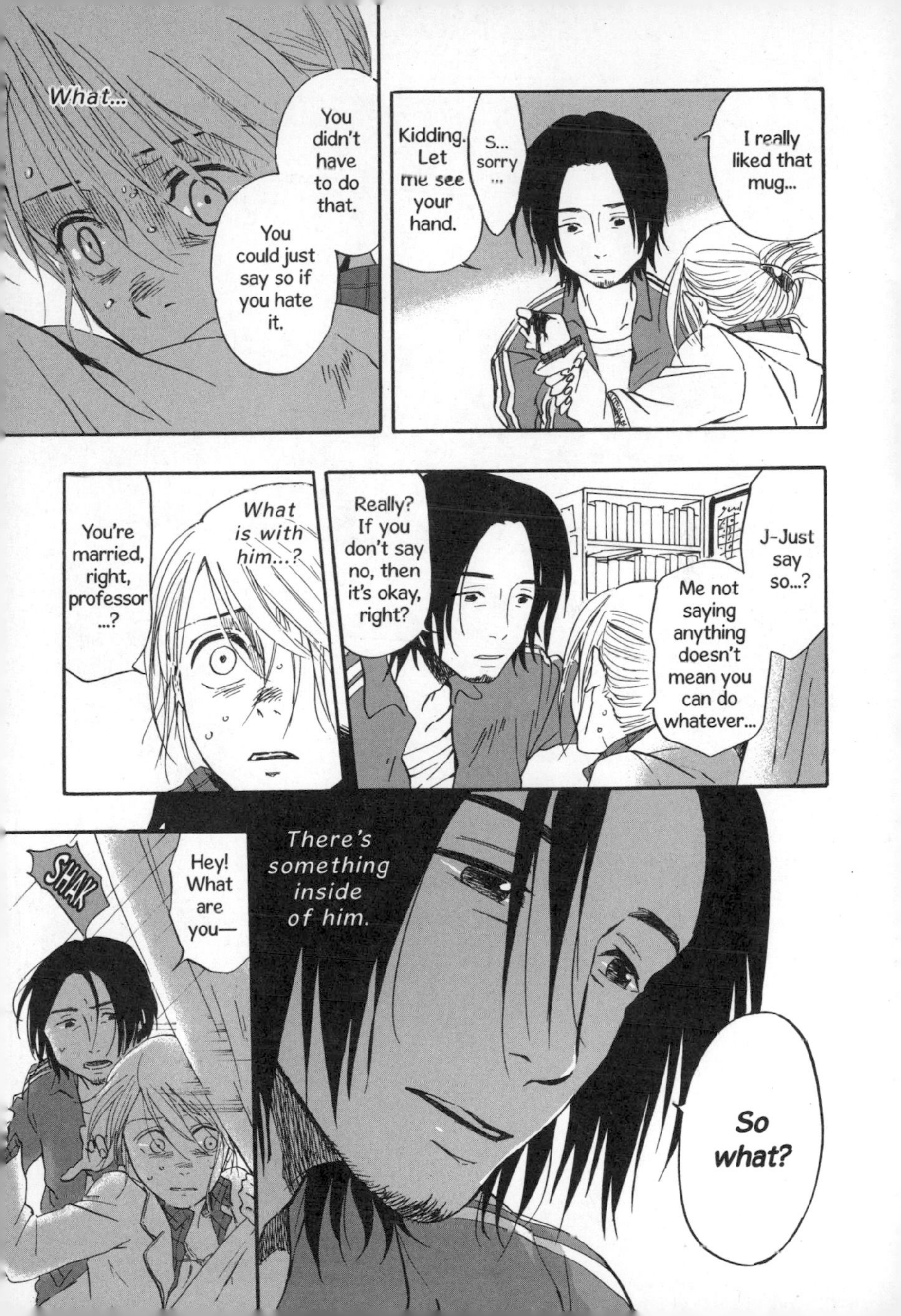
I really liked that mug...
S... sorry ...
Kidding. Let me see your hand.
You didn't have to do that.
You could just say so if you hate it.
What...
J-Just say so...?
Me not saying anything doesn't mean you can do whatever...
Really? If you don't say no, then it's okay, right?
What is with him...?
You're married, right, professor ...?
There's something inside of him.
So what?
SHAK
Hey! What are you—

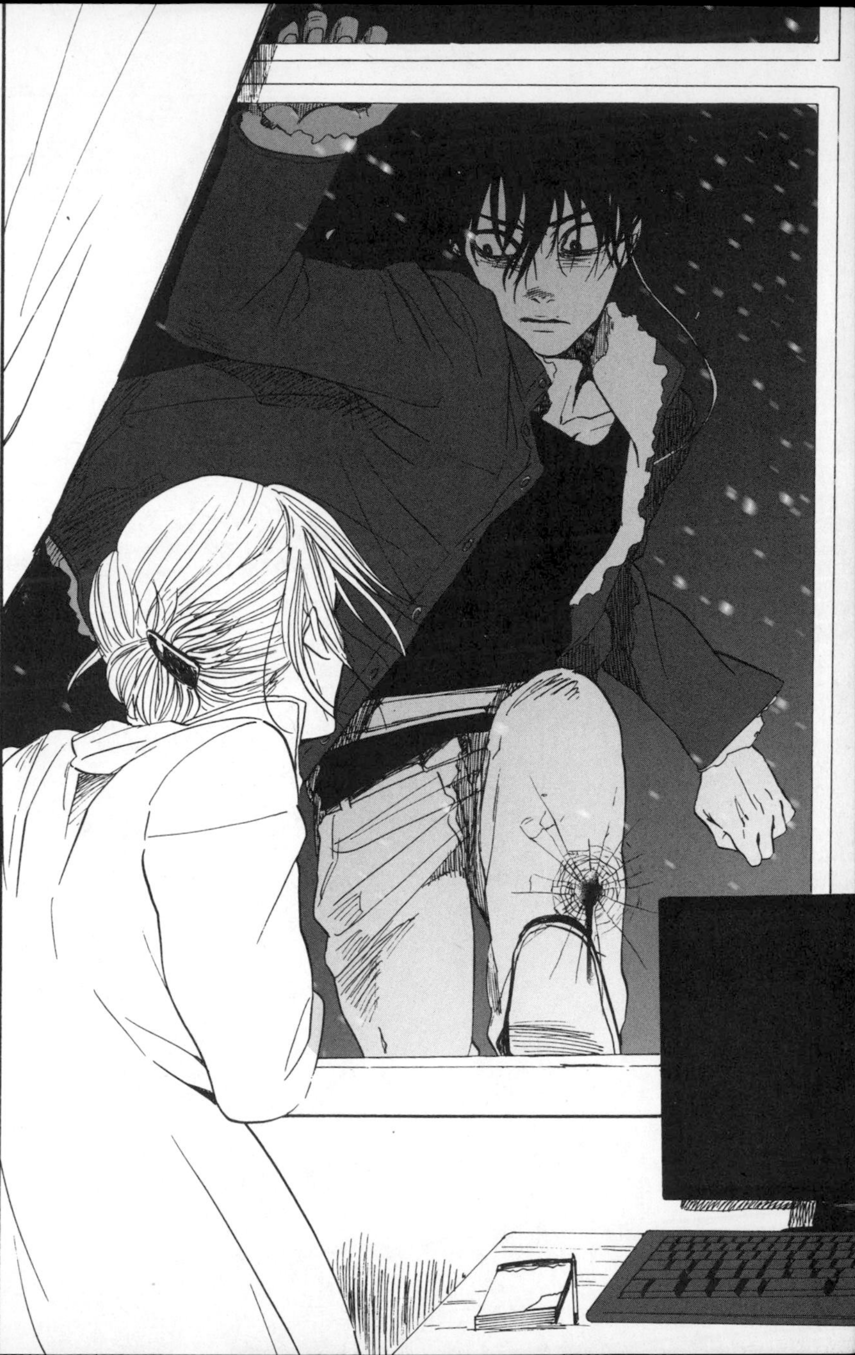

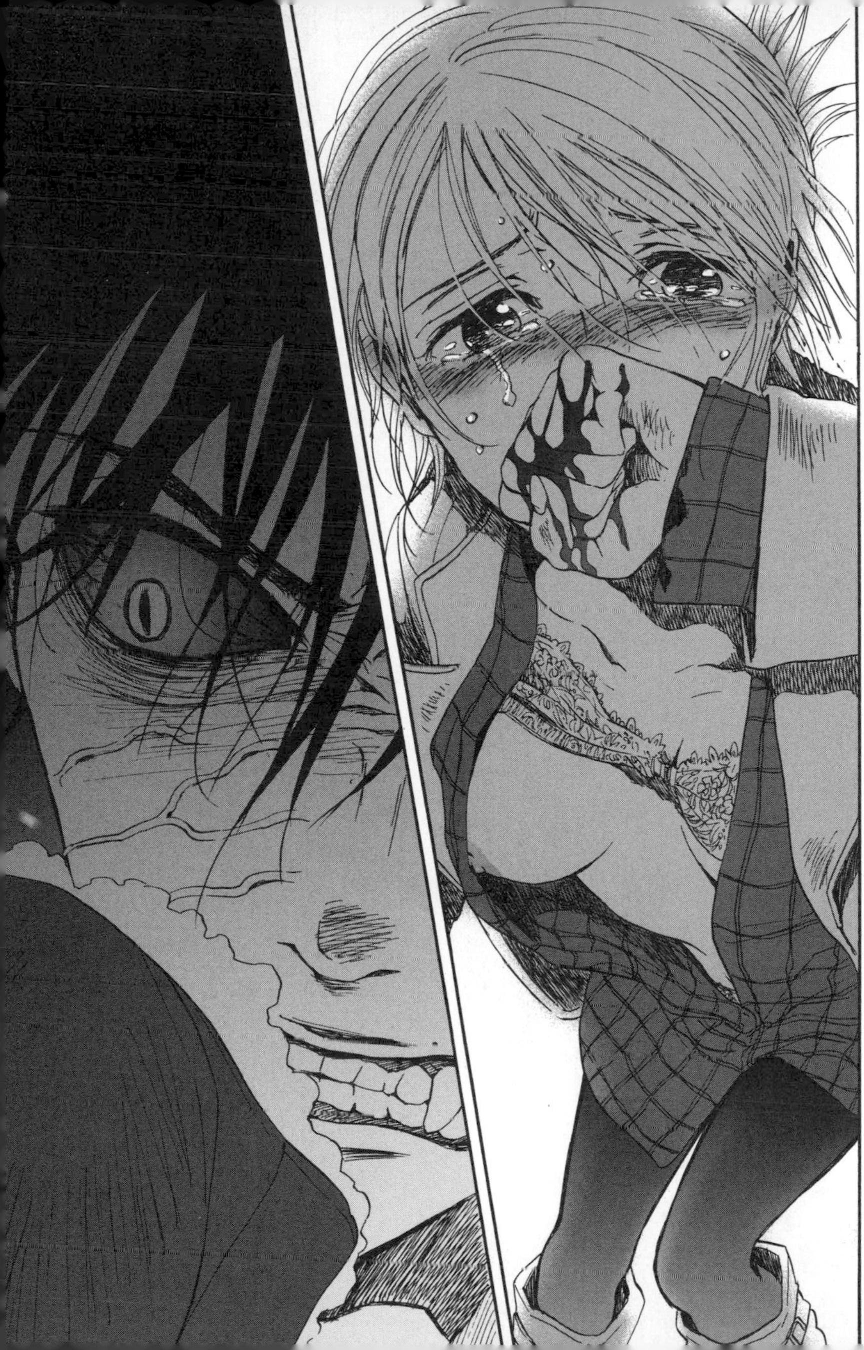

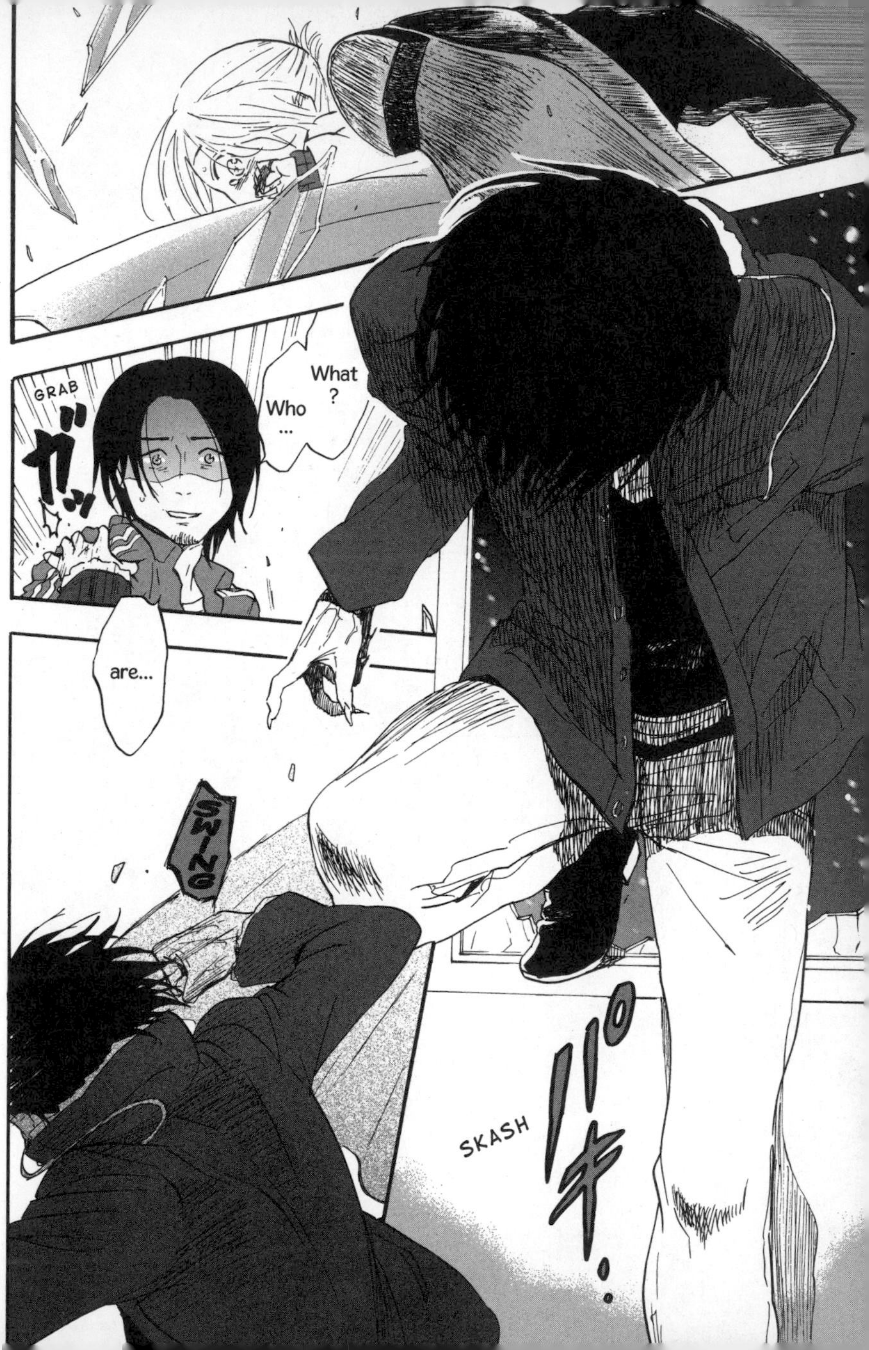
What? Who...
GRAB
ガッ
are...
SWING
SKASH
パキ・・

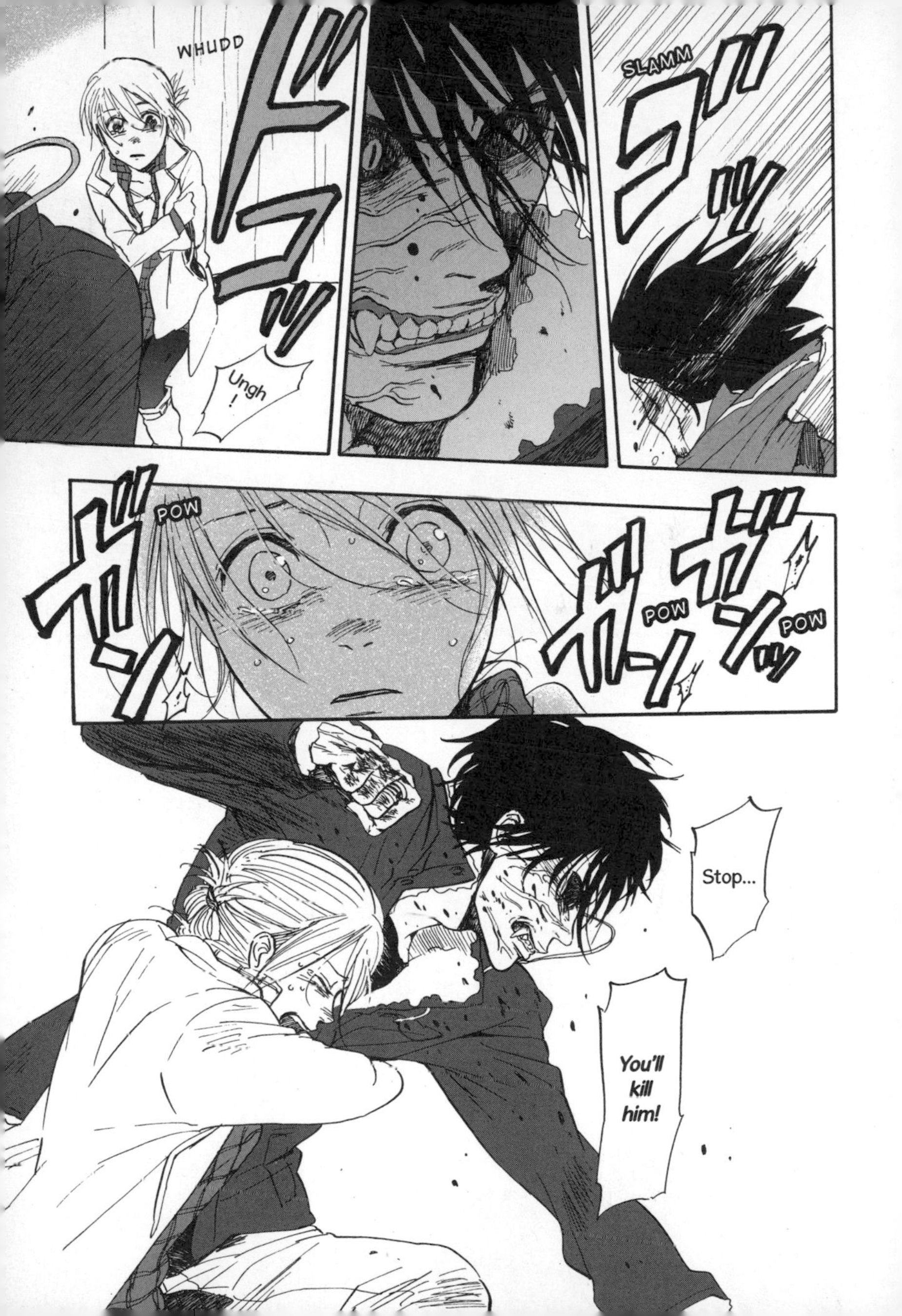
SLAMM
WHUDD
Ungh!
POW
POW
POW
Stop...
You'll kill him!

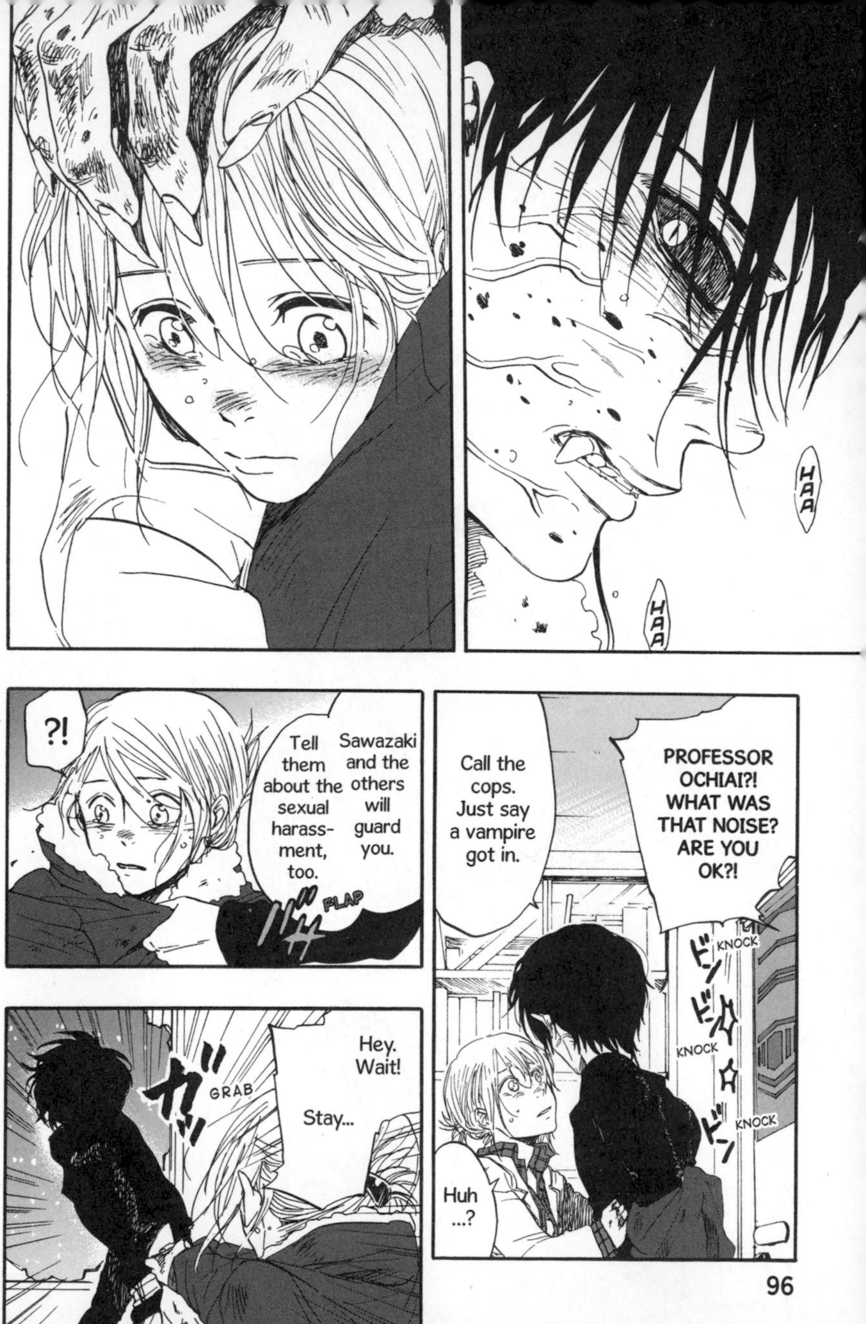
HAA
HAA
PROFESSOR OCHIAI?! WHAT WAS THAT NOISE? ARE YOU OK?!
Call the cops. Just say a vampire got in.
KNOCK
KNOCK
KNOCK
Huh ...?
Sawazaki and the others will guard you.
Tell them about the sexual harassment, too.
?!
FLAP
Hey. Wait!
Stay...
GRAB

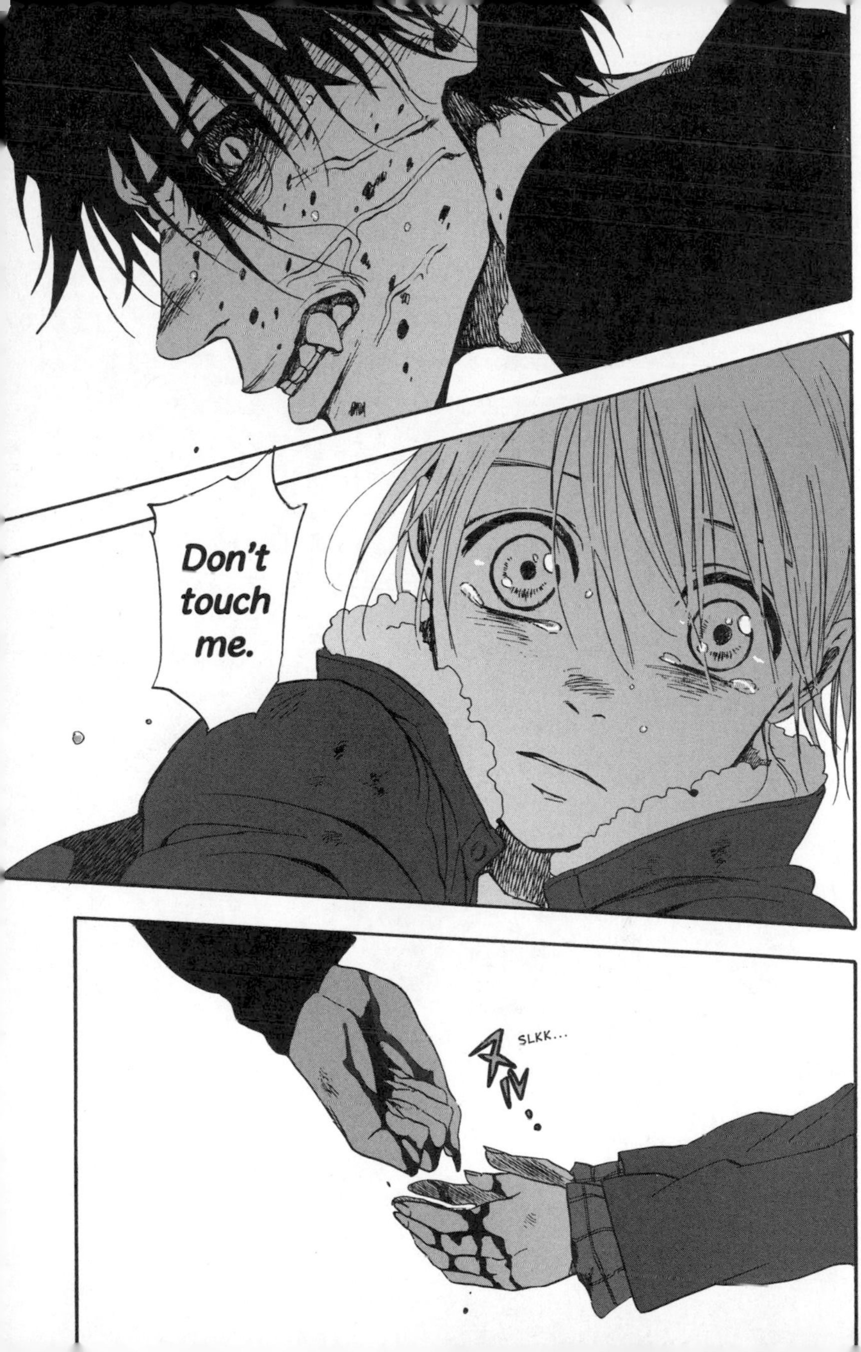
Don't touch me.
SLKK...

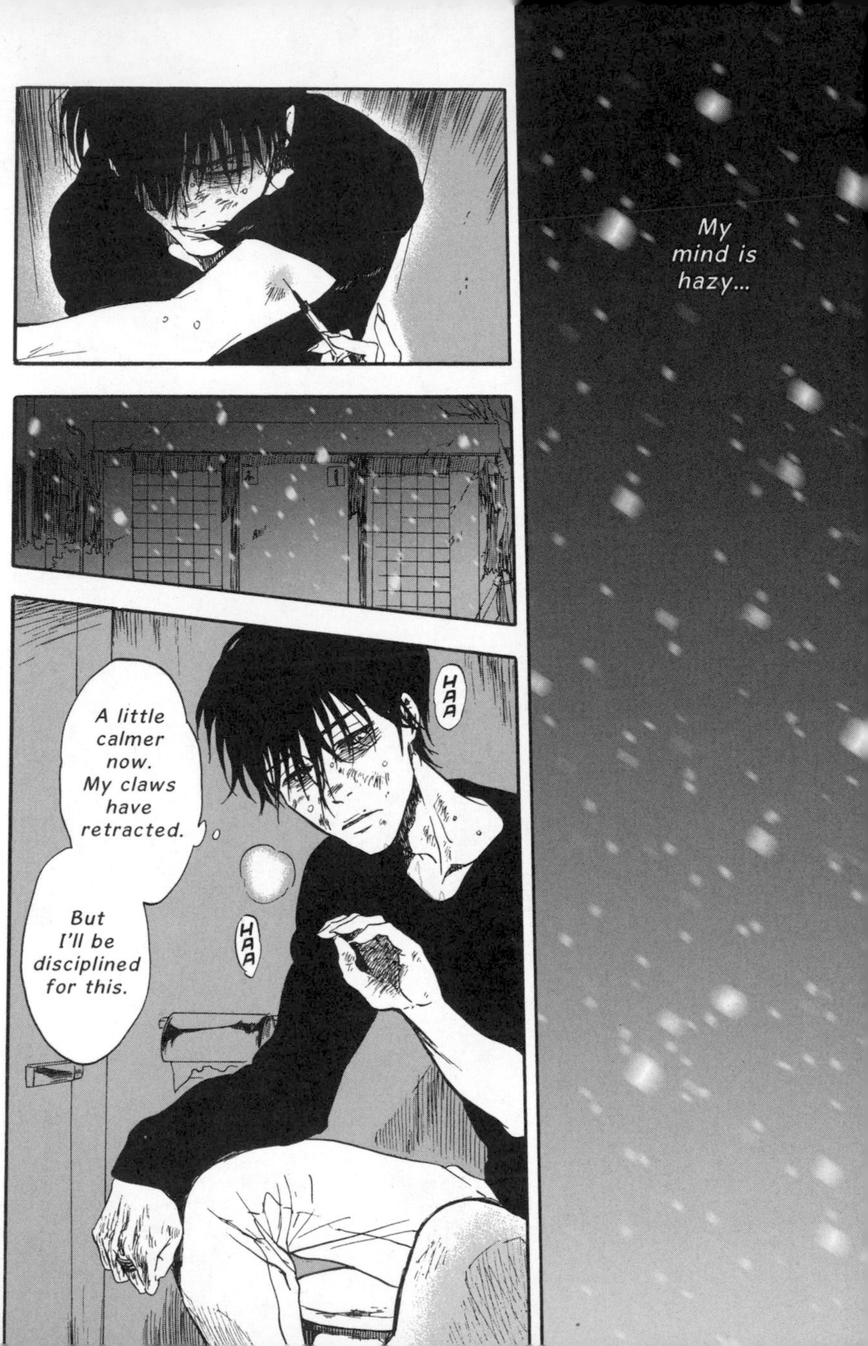
My mind is hazy...
HAA
A little calmer now. My claws have retracted.
HAA
But I'll be disciplined for this.

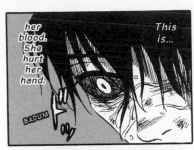

her blood. Sho hurt her hand.

This is...

BADUM

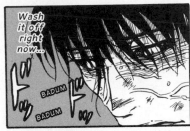

Wash it off right now...

BADUM BADUM BADUM

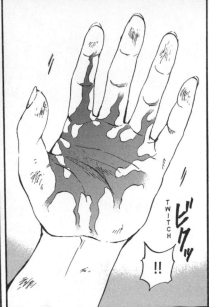

TWITCH

!!

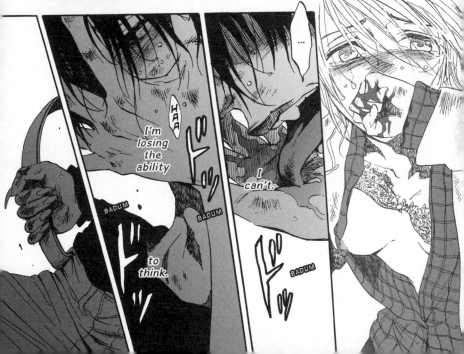

HAA

I'm losing the ability

BADUM

BADUM

to think.

...

I can't.

BADUM

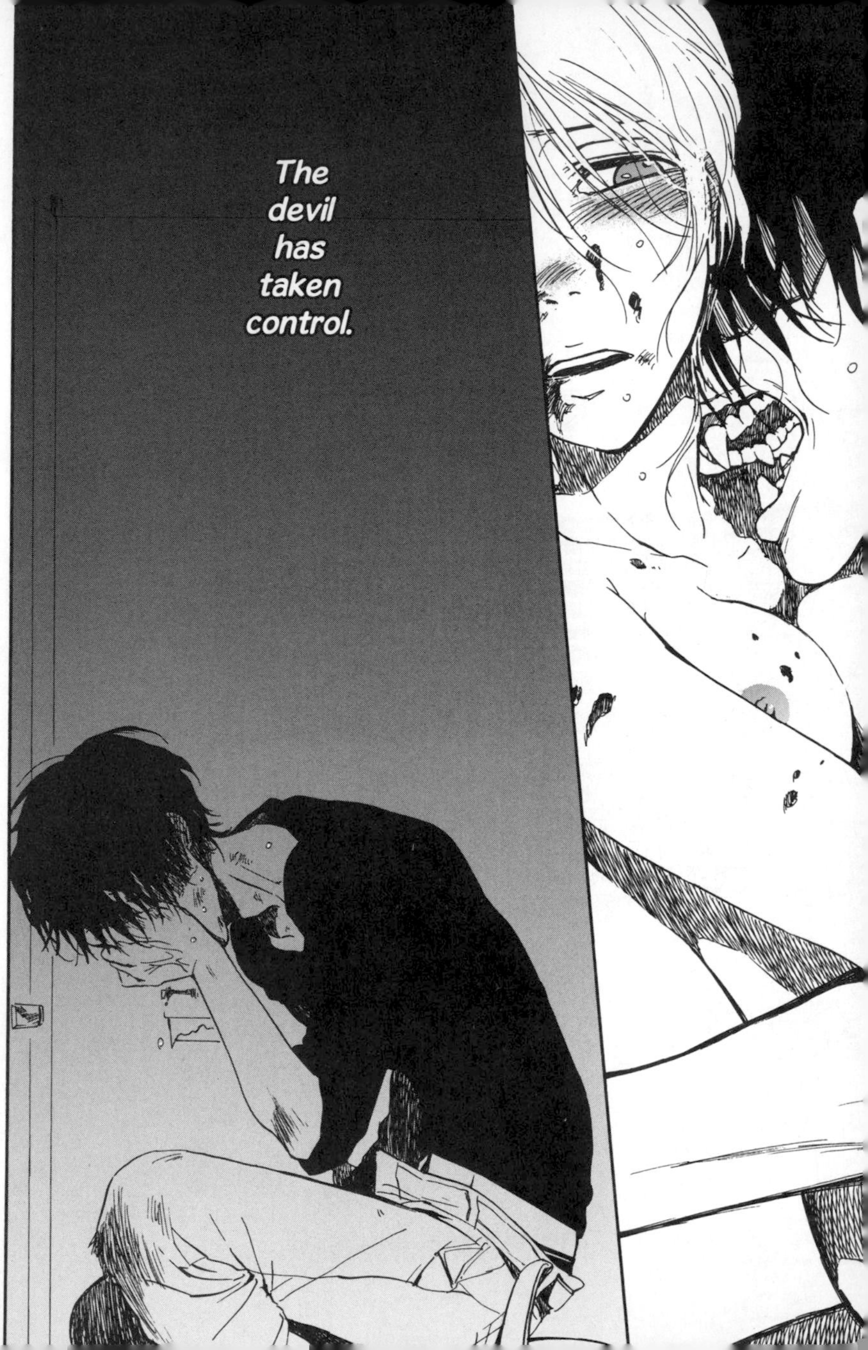
The devil has taken control.

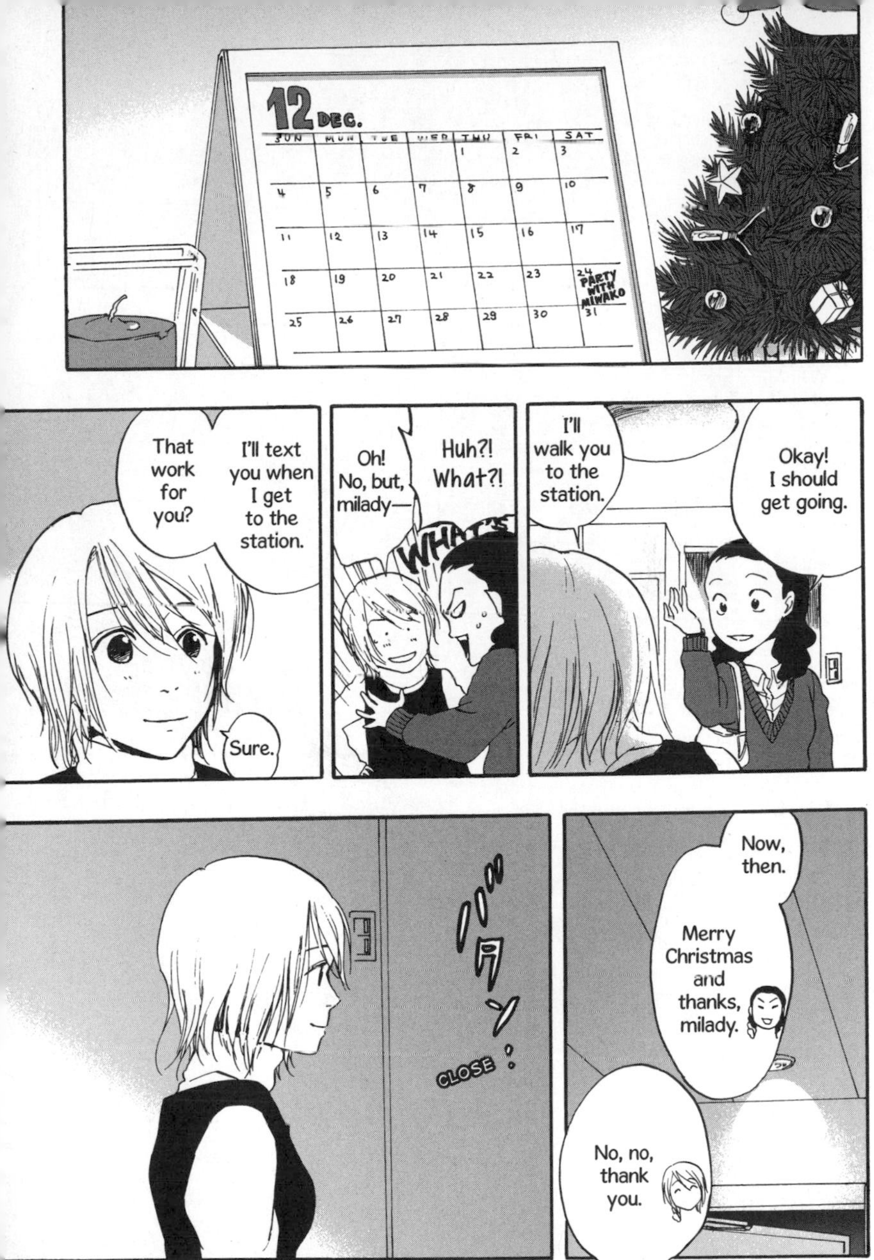
12 DEC.
SUN MON TUE WED THU FRI SAT
24 PARTY WITH MIWAKO
Okay! I should get going.
I'll walk you to the station.
Huh?! What?!
WHAT'S
Oh! No, but, milady—
I'll text you when I get to the station.
That work for you?
Sure.
Now, then.
Merry Christmas and thanks, milady.
No, no, thank you.
CLOSE

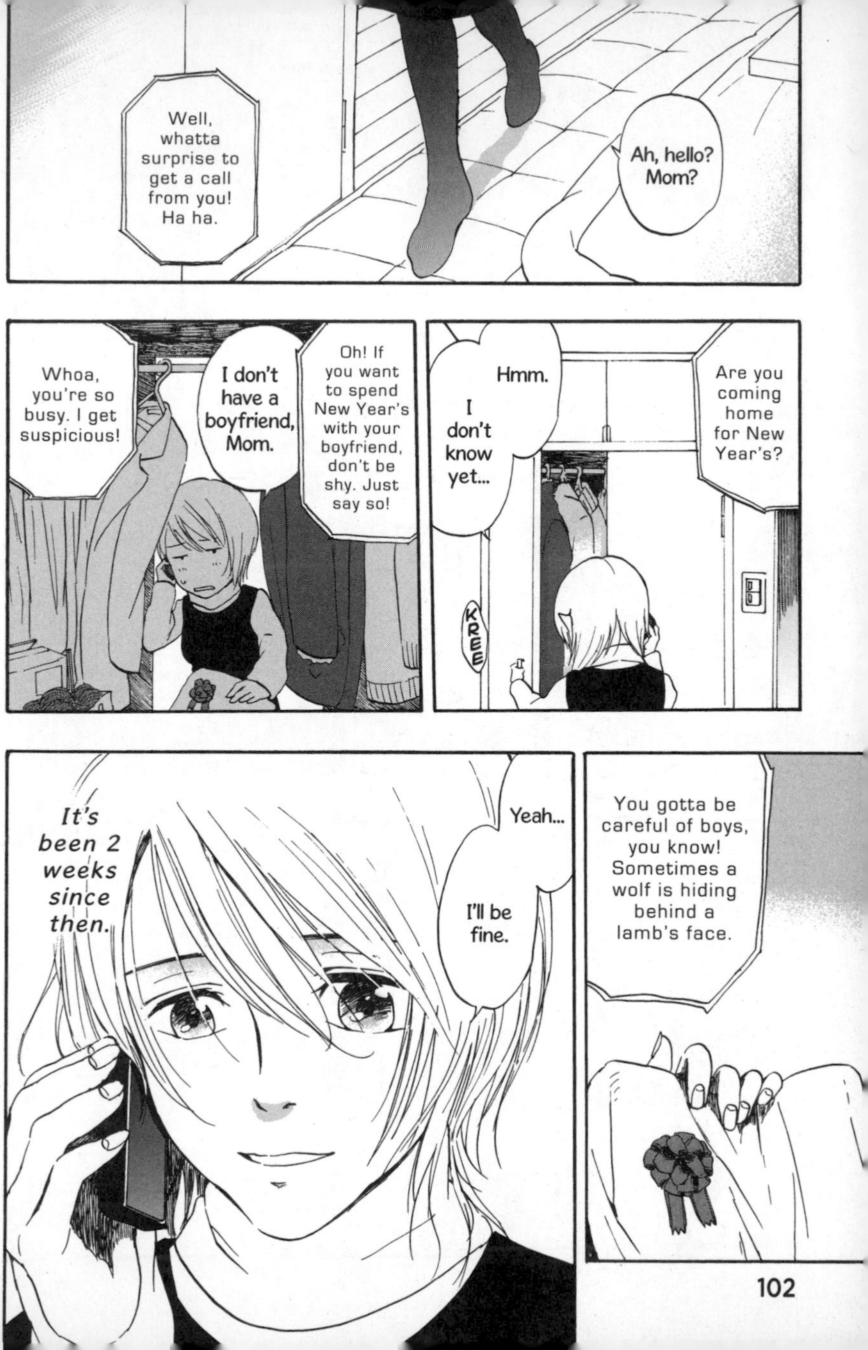
Ah, hello? Mom?
Well, whatta surprise to get a call from you! Ha ha.
Are you coming home for New Year's?
Hmm.
I don't know yet...
KREE
Oh! If you want to spend New Year's with your boyfriend, don't be shy. Just say so!
I don't have a boyfriend, Mom.
Whoa, you're so busy. I get suspicious!
You gotta be careful of boys, you know! Sometimes a wolf is hiding behind a lamb's face.
Yeah...
I'll be fine.
It's been 2 weeks since then.

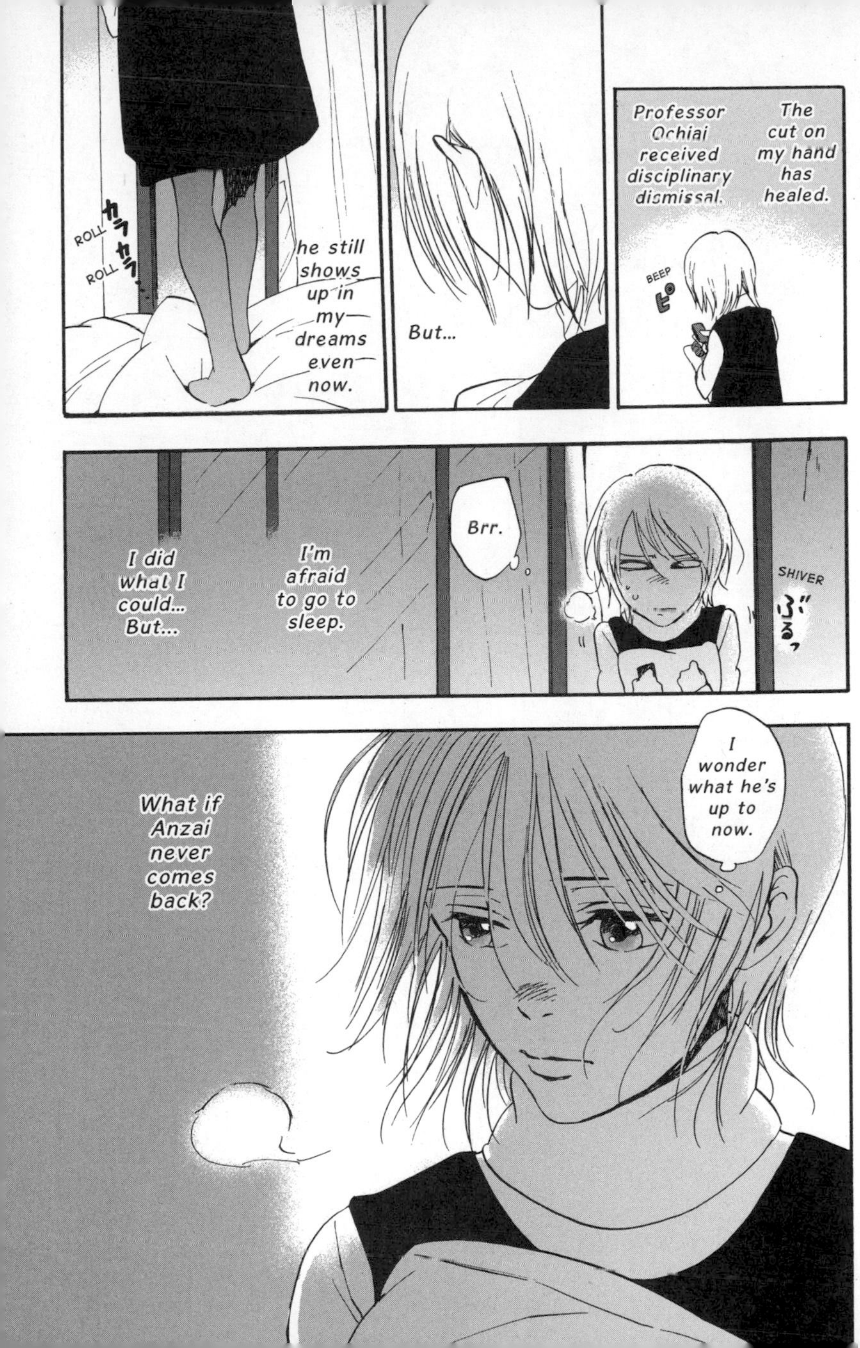
The cut on my hand has healed.
Professor Ochiai received disciplinary dismissal.
BEEP
ピ
But...
he still shows up in my dreams even now.
ROLL
カラ
ROLL
カラ
SHIVER
ぶるっ
Brr.
I'm afraid to go to sleep.
I did what I could... But...
I wonder what he's up to now.
What if Anzai never comes back?

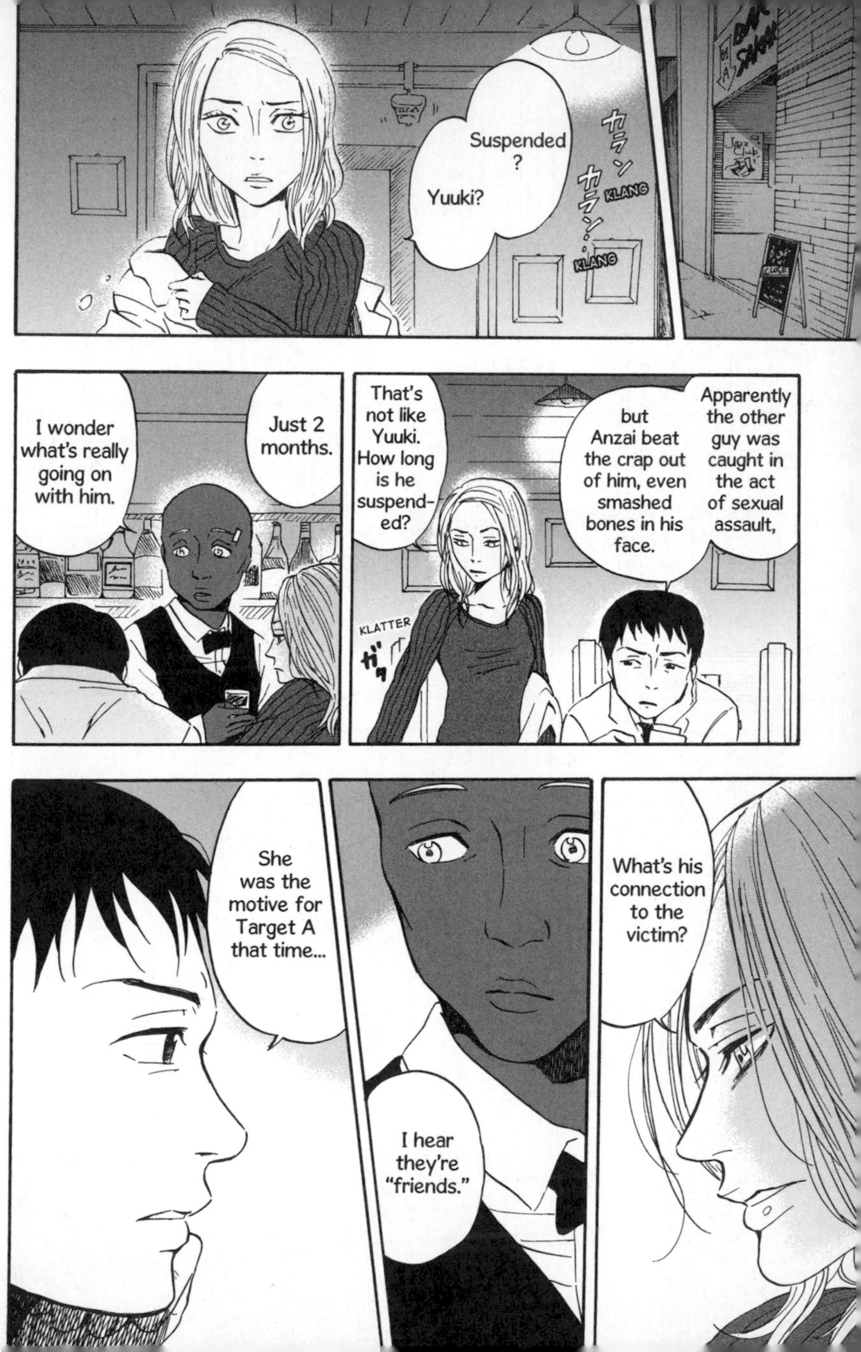
カラン
KLANG
カラン
KLANG
Suspended?
Yuuki?
Apparently the other guy was caught in the act of sexual assault,
but Anzai beat the crap out of him, even smashed bones in his face.
That's not like Yuuki. How long is he suspend-ed?
KLATTER
ガタ
Just 2 months.
I wonder what's really going on with him.
What's his connection to the victim?
I hear they're "friends."
She was the motive for Target A that time...

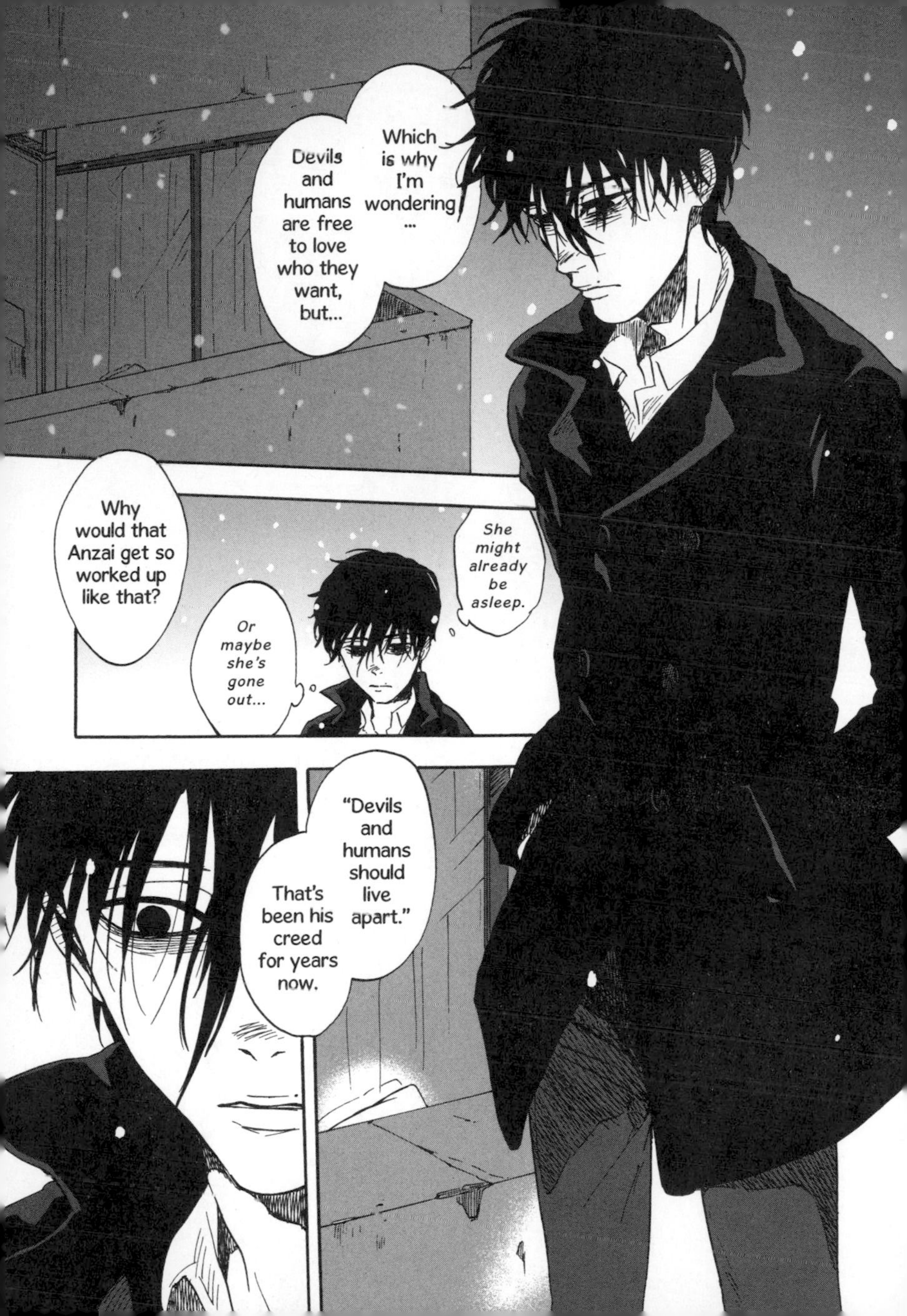
Which is why I'm wondering ...
Devils and humans are free to love who they want, but...
She might already be asleep.
Or maybe she's gone out...
Why would that Anzai get so worked up like that?
"Devils and humans should live apart."
That's been his creed for years now.

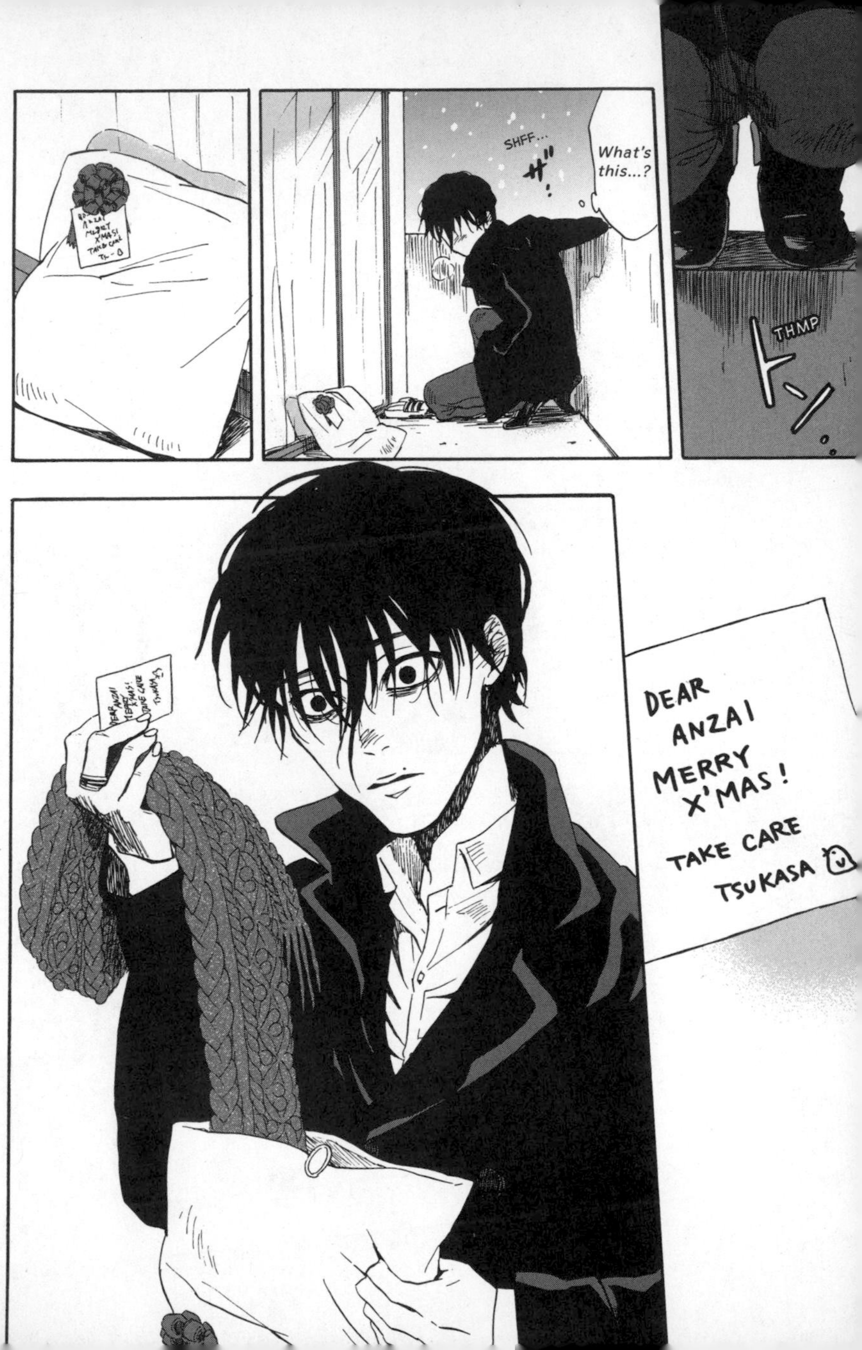
THMP
SHFF...
What's this...?
DEAR ANZAI
MERRY X'MAS!
TAKE CARE
TSUKASA

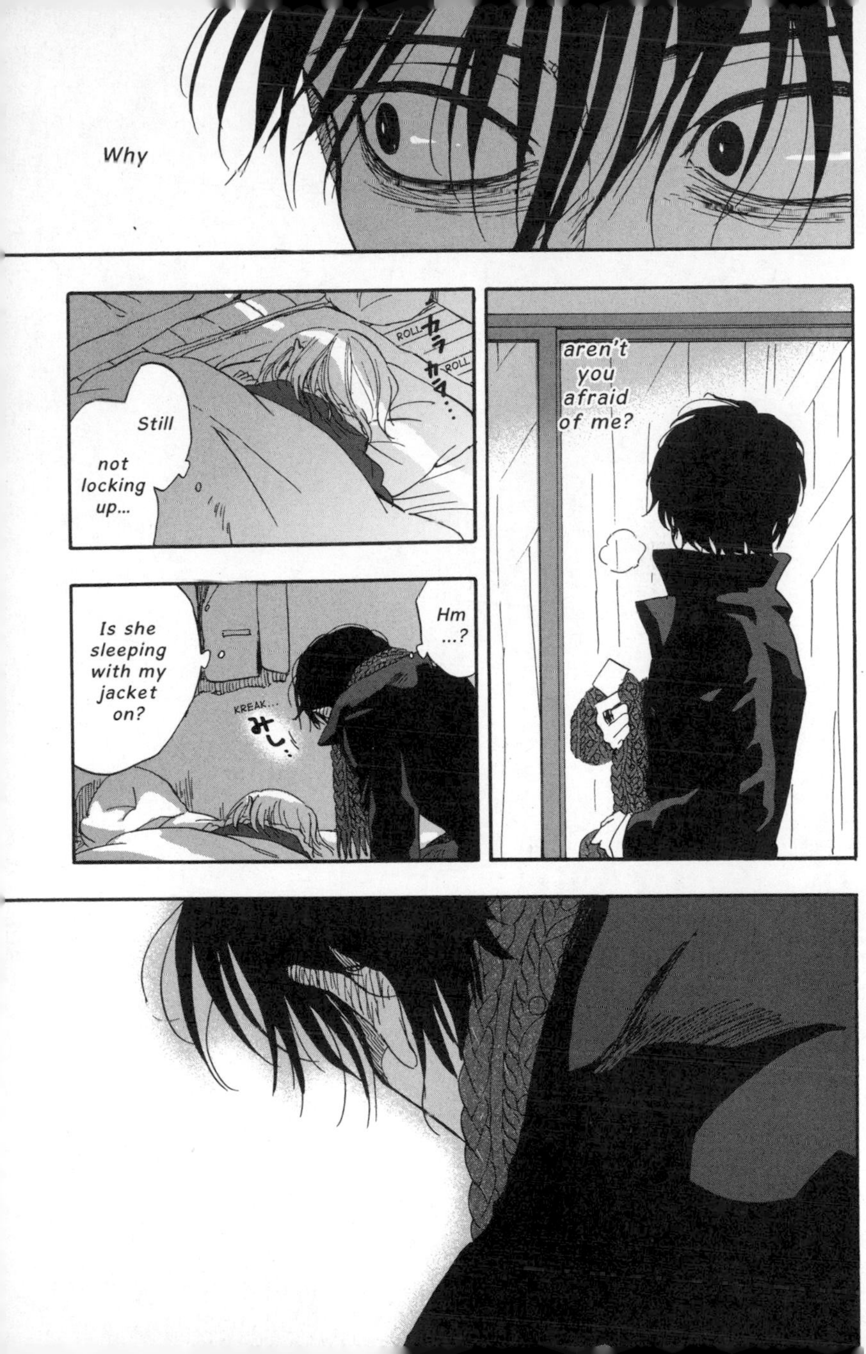
Why
aren't you afraid of me?
ROLL カラ ROLL カラ…
Still
not locking up…
Hm …?
Is she sleeping with my jacket on?
KREAK… みし…

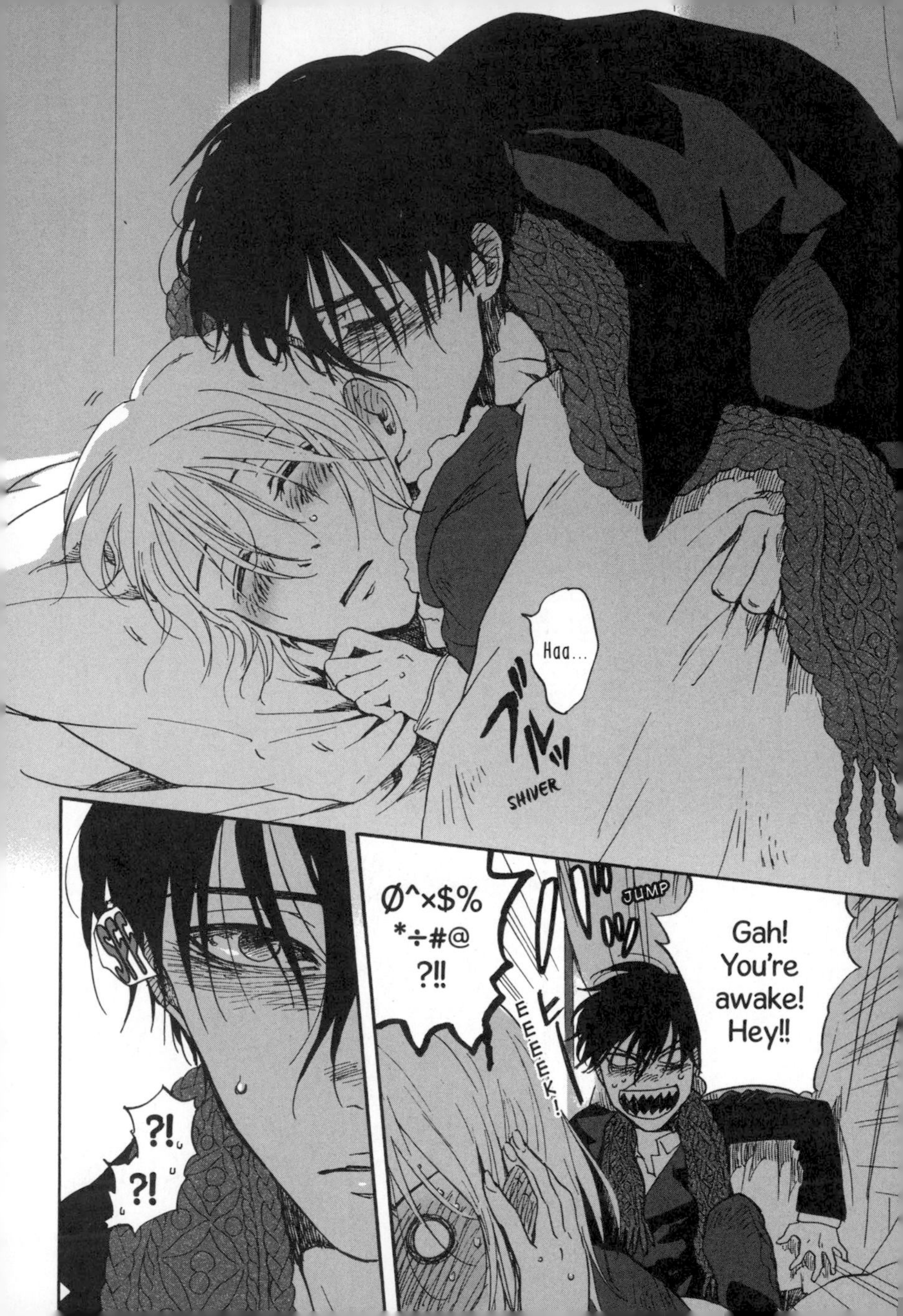
Haa...
ブルッ
SHIVER
Gah! You're awake! Hey!!
JUMP
Ø^×$% *÷#@ ?!!
EEEEEK!
?!
?!

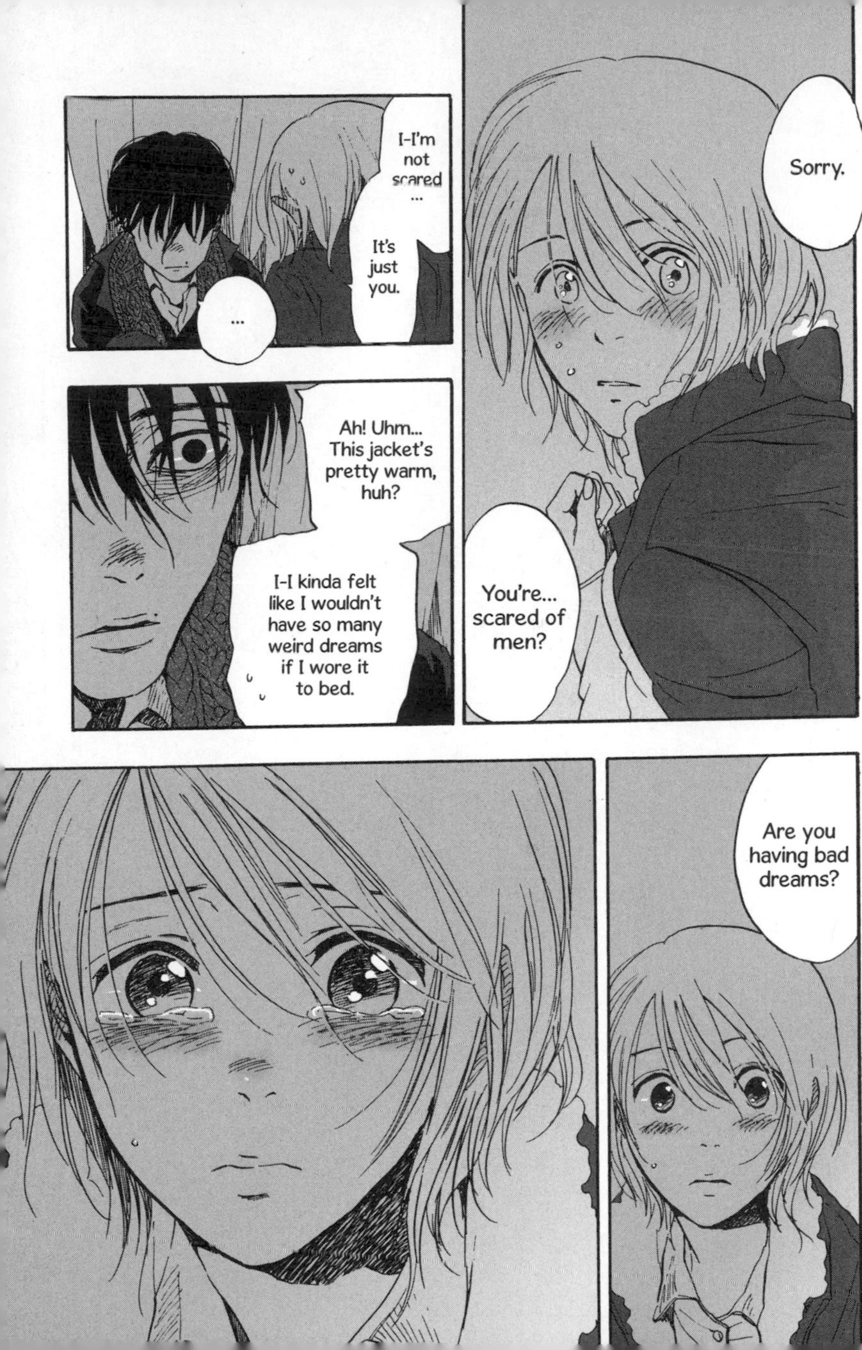
Sorry.
You're... scared of men?
I-I'm not scared ... It's just you.
...
Ah! Uhm... This jacket's pretty warm, huh?
I-I kinda felt like I wouldn't have so many weird dreams if I wore it to bed.
Are you having bad dreams?

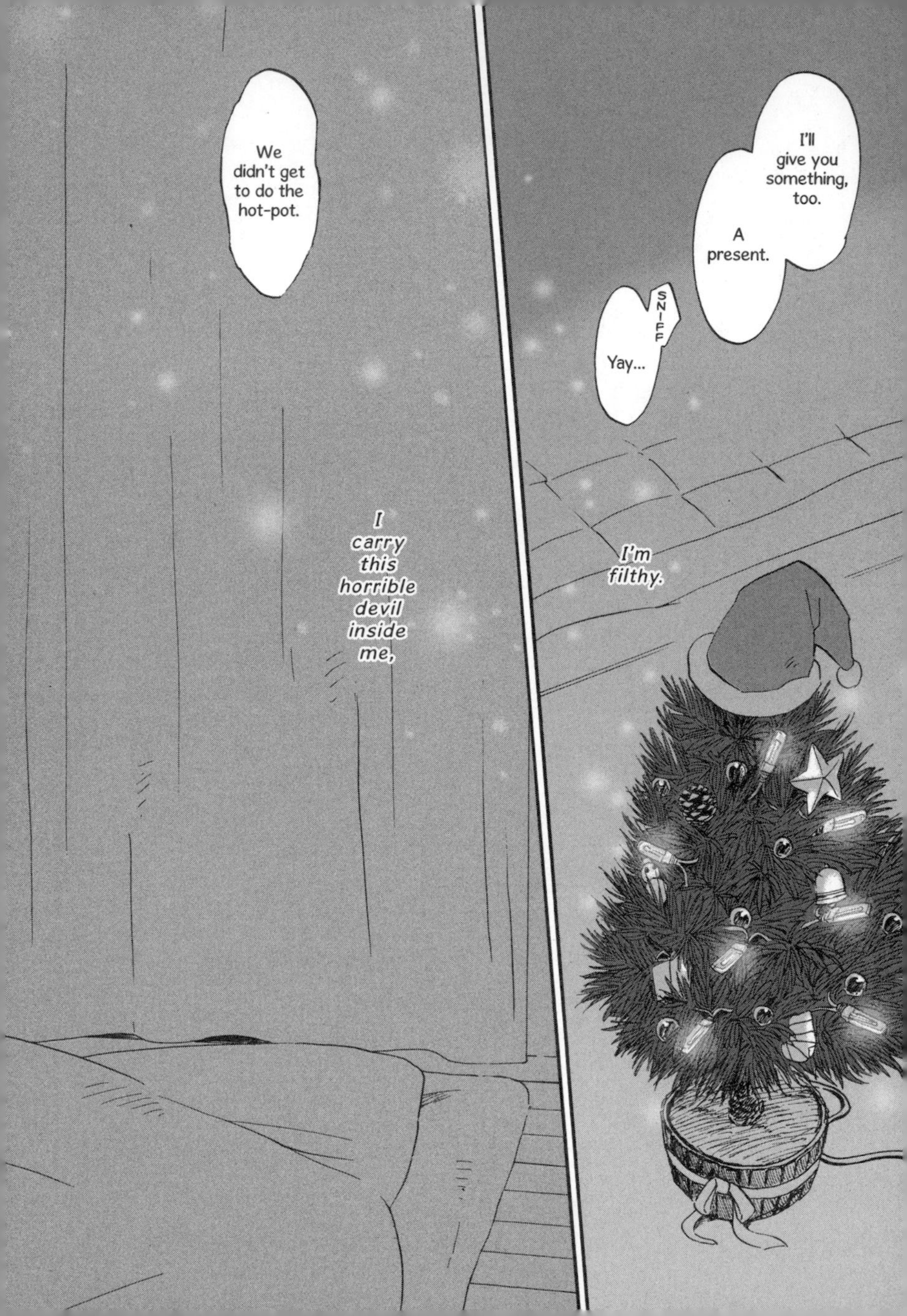
I'll give you something, too.
A present.
SNIFF
Yay...
I'm filthy.
We didn't get to do the hot-pot.
I carry this horrible devil inside me,

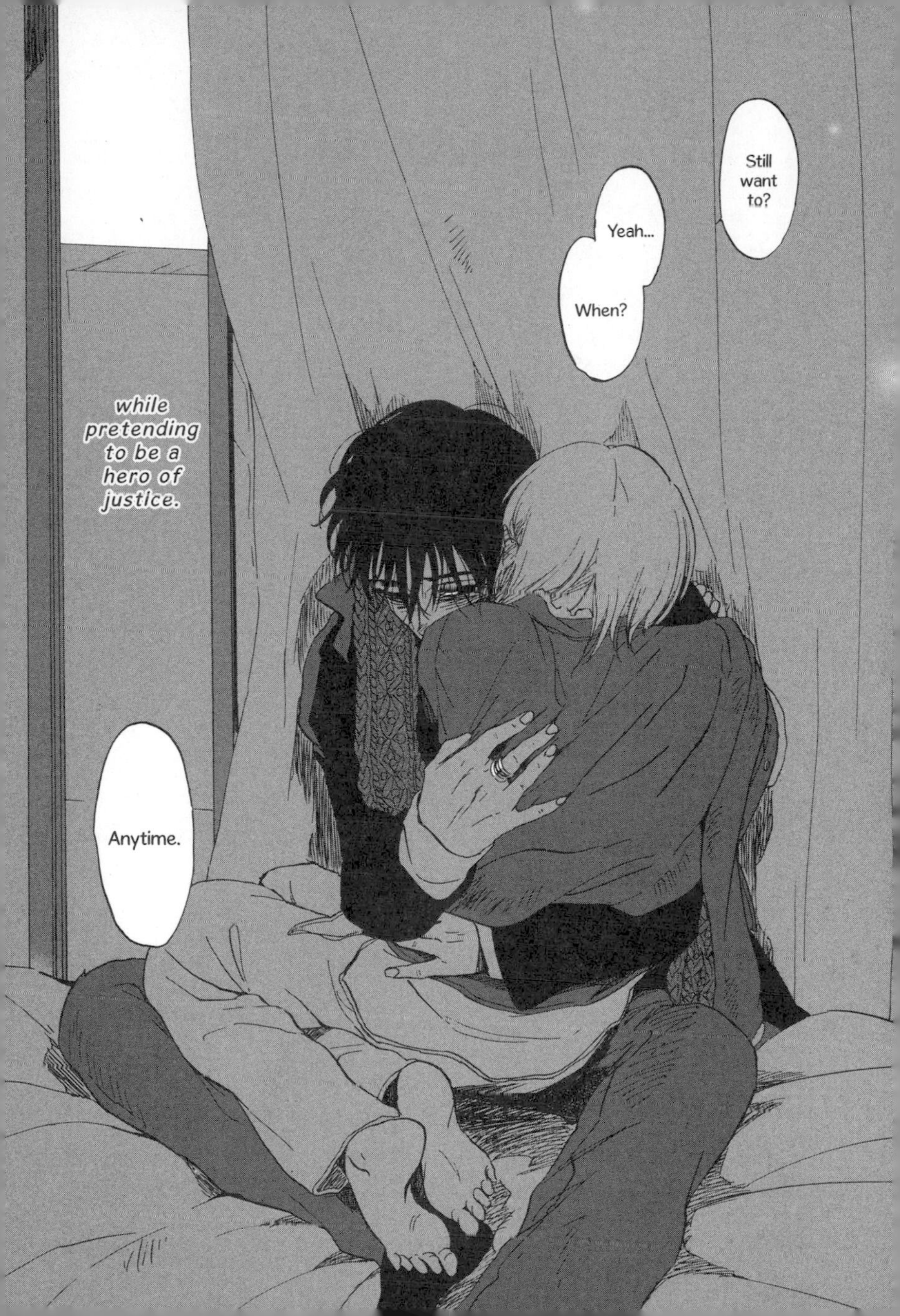
Still want to?
Yeah...
When?
while pretending to be a hero of justice.
Anytime.

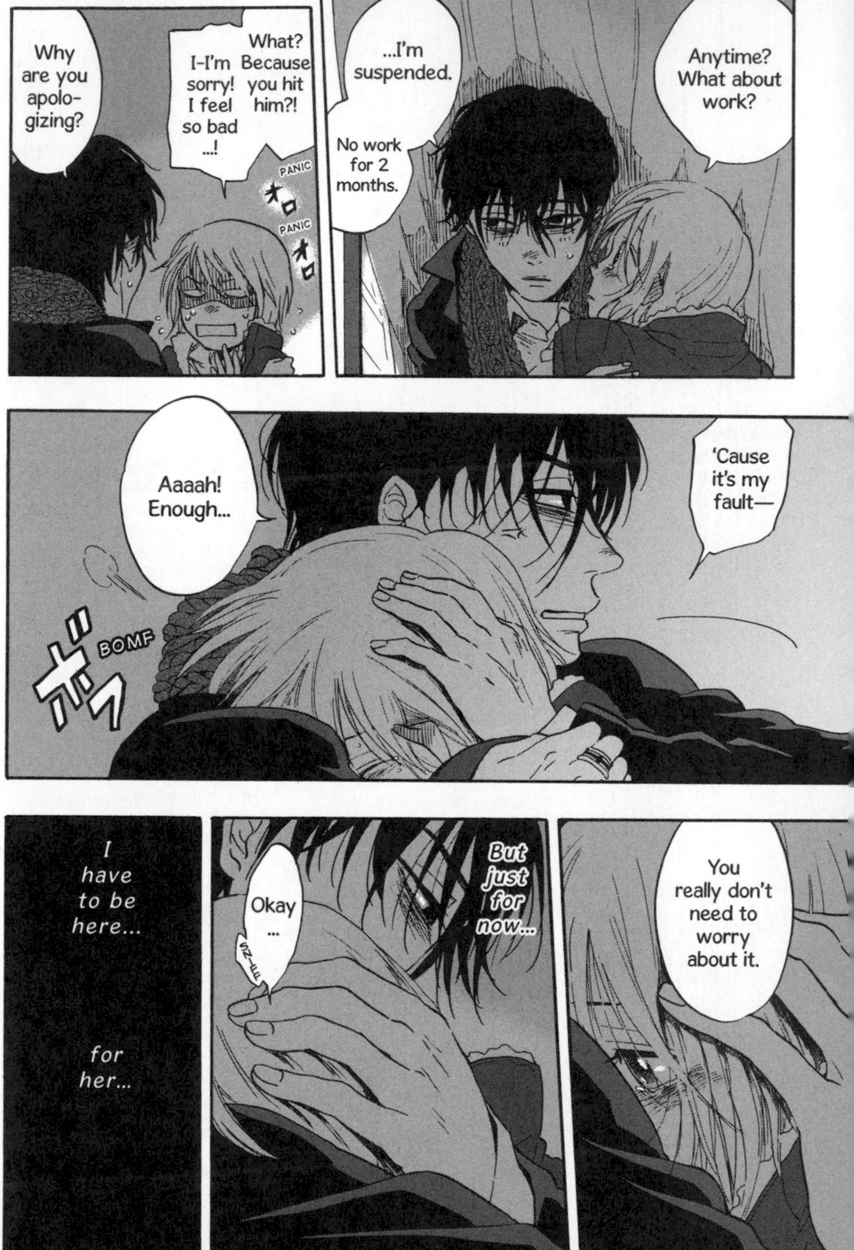
Anytime? What about work?
...I'm suspended.
No work for 2 months.
What? Because you hit him?!
PANIC
PANIC
I-I'm sorry! I feel so bad ...!
Why are you apologizing?
'Cause it's my fault—
Aaaah! Enough...
BOMF
You really don't need to worry about it.
But just for now...
Okay ...
SNIFF
I have to be here...
for her...

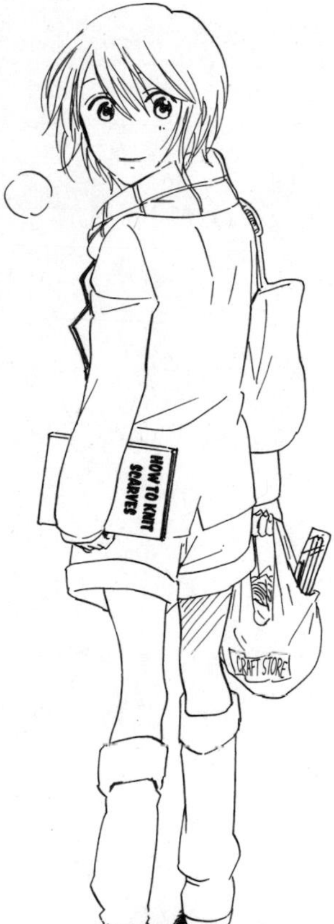
HOW TO KNIT SCARVES
CRAFT STORE

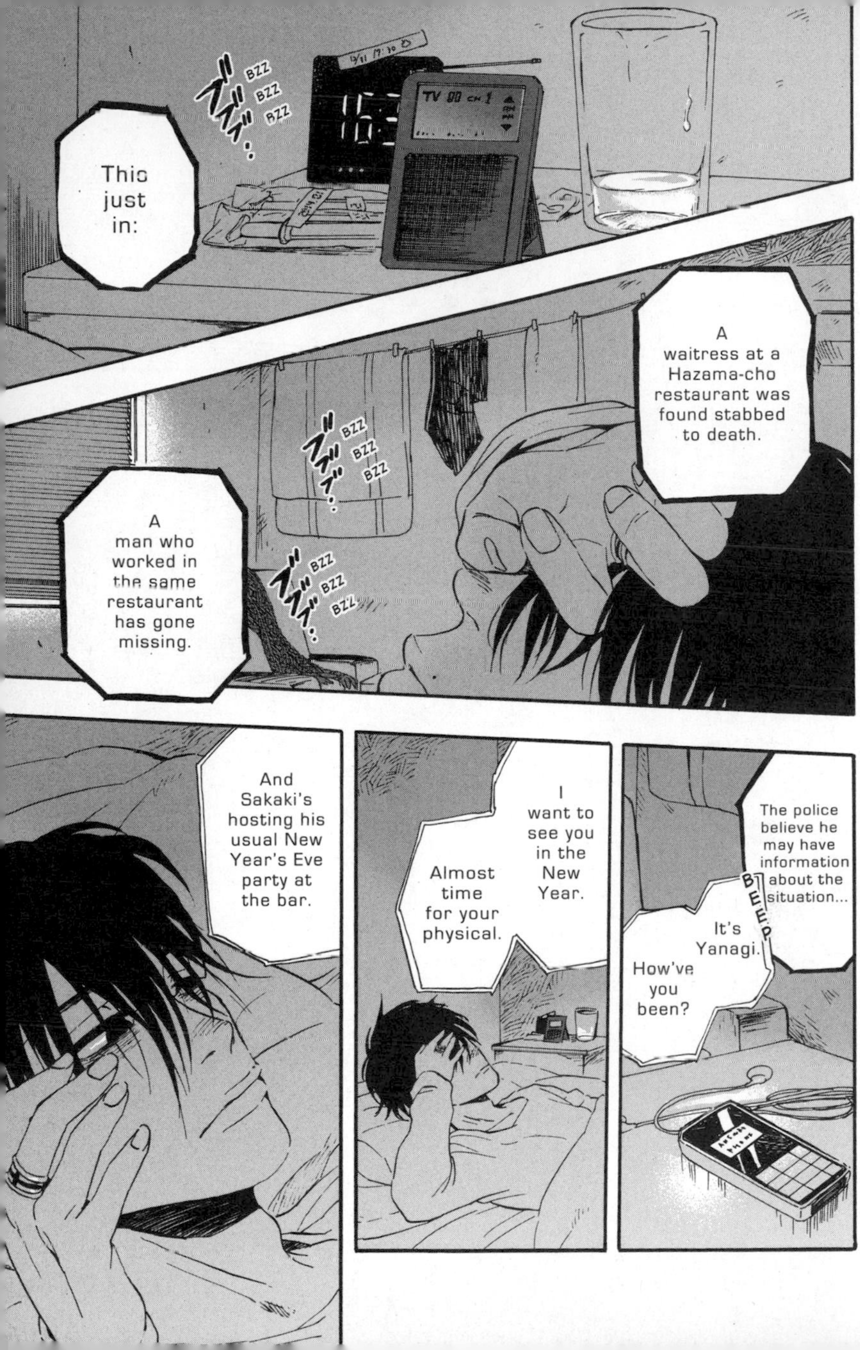
BZZ BZZ BZZ
This just in:
A waitress at a Hazama-cho restaurant was found stabbed to death.
BZZ BZZ BZZ
BZZ BZZ BZZ
A man who worked in the same restaurant has gone missing.
The police believe he may have information about the situation...
BEEP
It's Yanagi.
How've you been?
I want to see you in the New Year.
Almost time for your physical.
And Sakaki's hosting his usual New Year's Eve party at the bar.

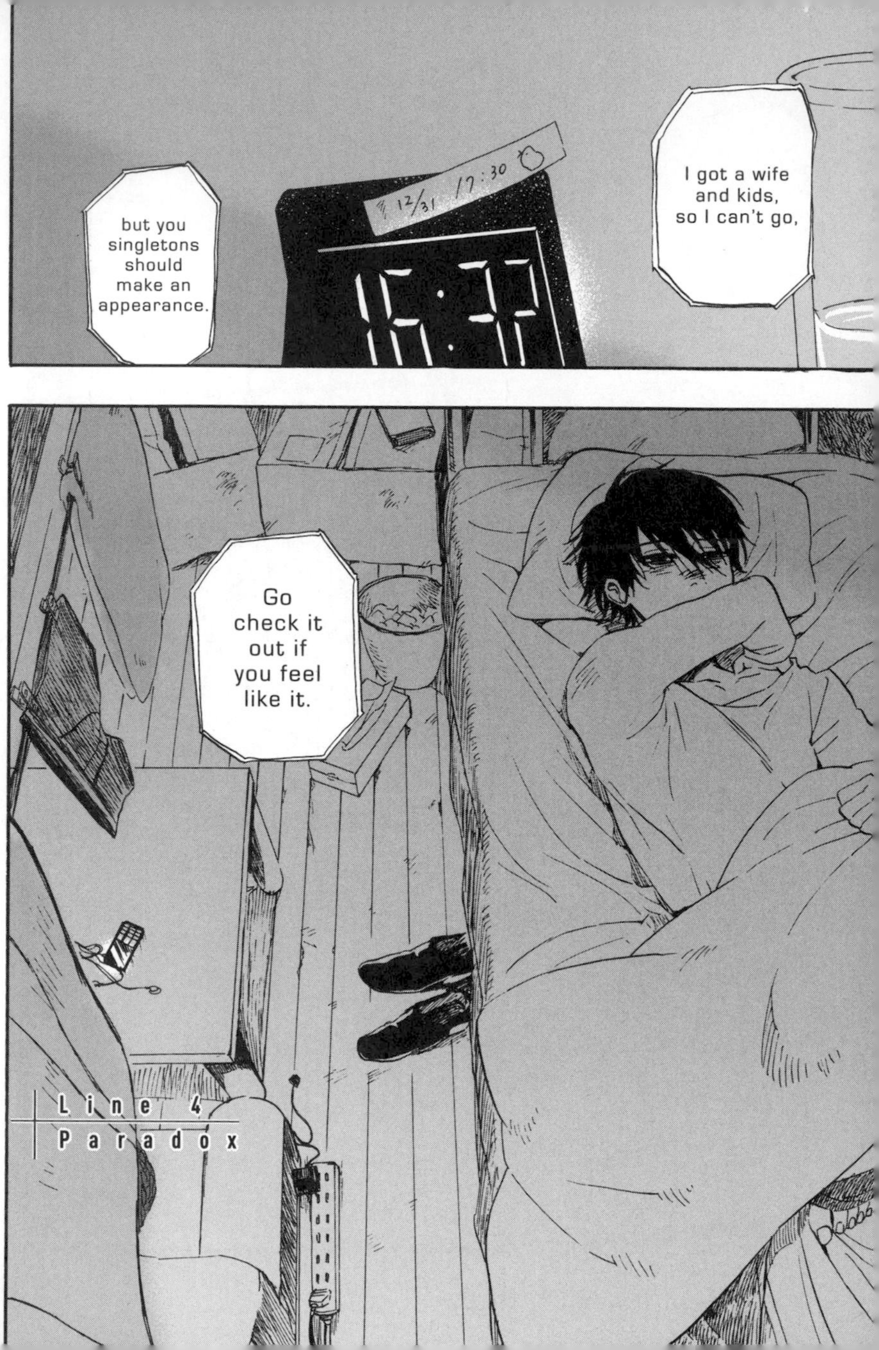
I got a wife and kids, so I can't go,
but you singletons should make an appearance.
Go check it out if you feel like it.
Line 4
Paradox

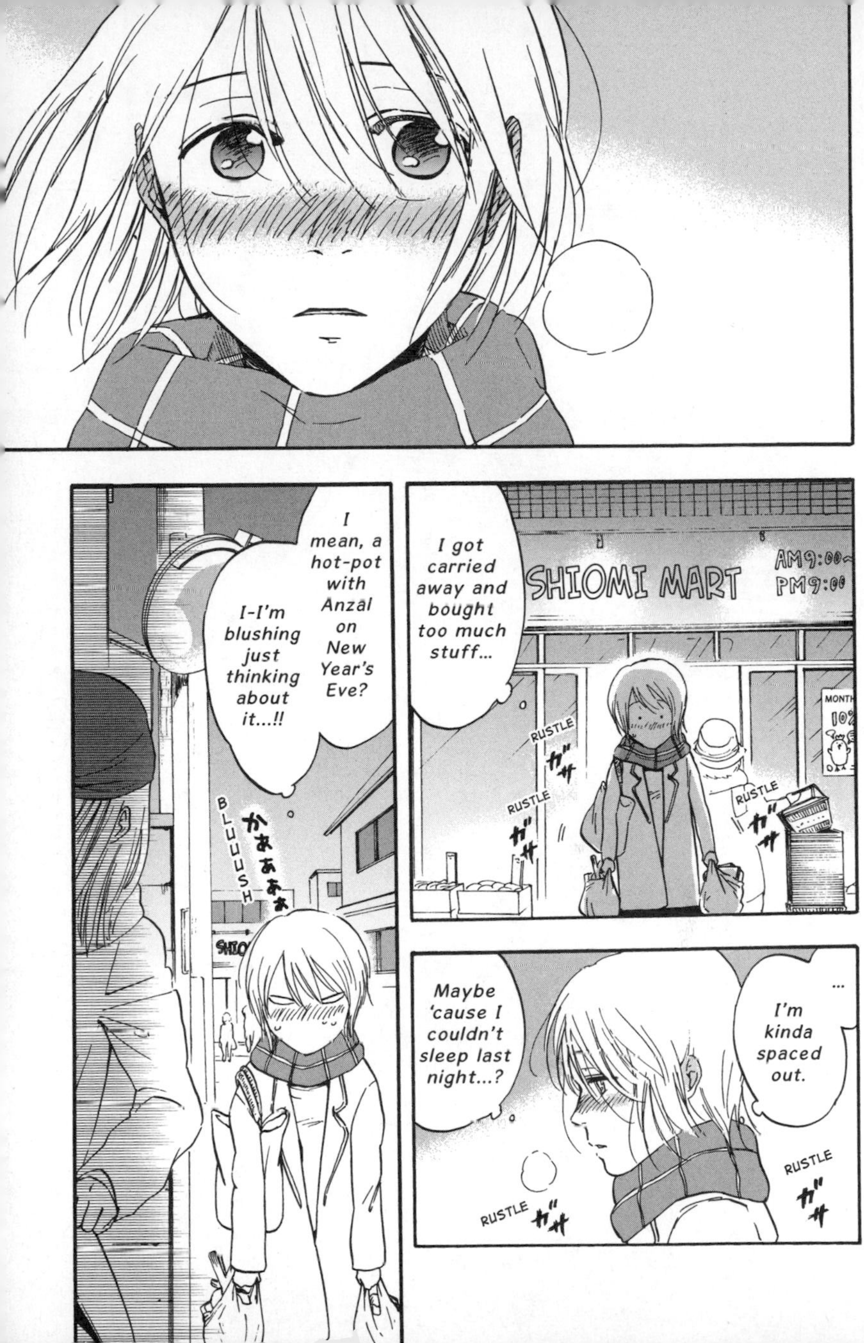
SHIOMI MART
AM9:00~ PM9:00
I got carried away and bought too much stuff...
RUSTLE
RUSTLE
RUSTLE
... I'm kinda spaced out.
Maybe 'cause I couldn't sleep last night...?
RUSTLE
RUSTLE
I mean, a hot-pot with Anzai on New Year's Eve?
I-I'm blushing just thinking about it...!!
BLUUUSH

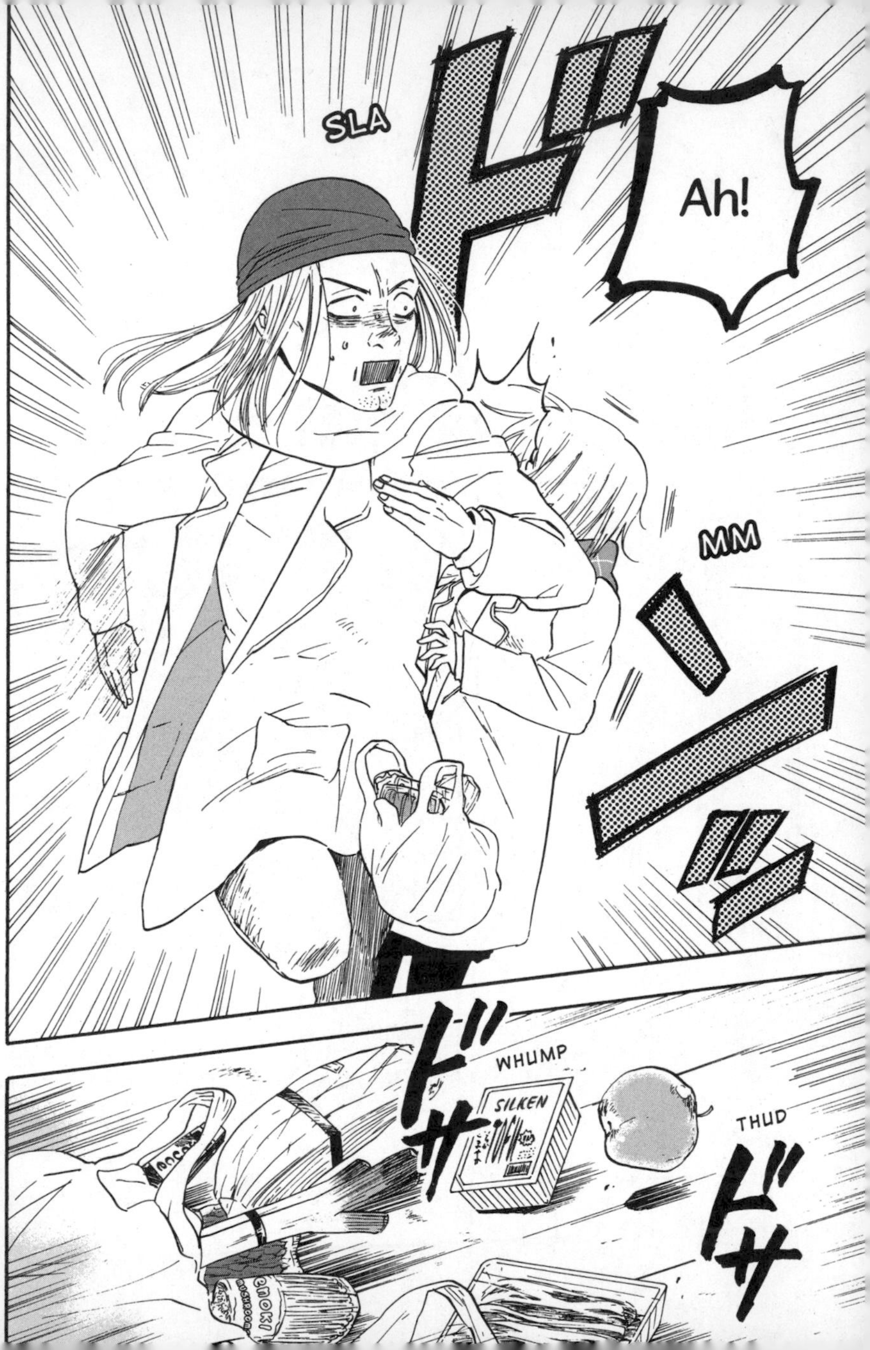
Ah!
SLA
MM
THUD
WHUMP
SILKEN
enoki

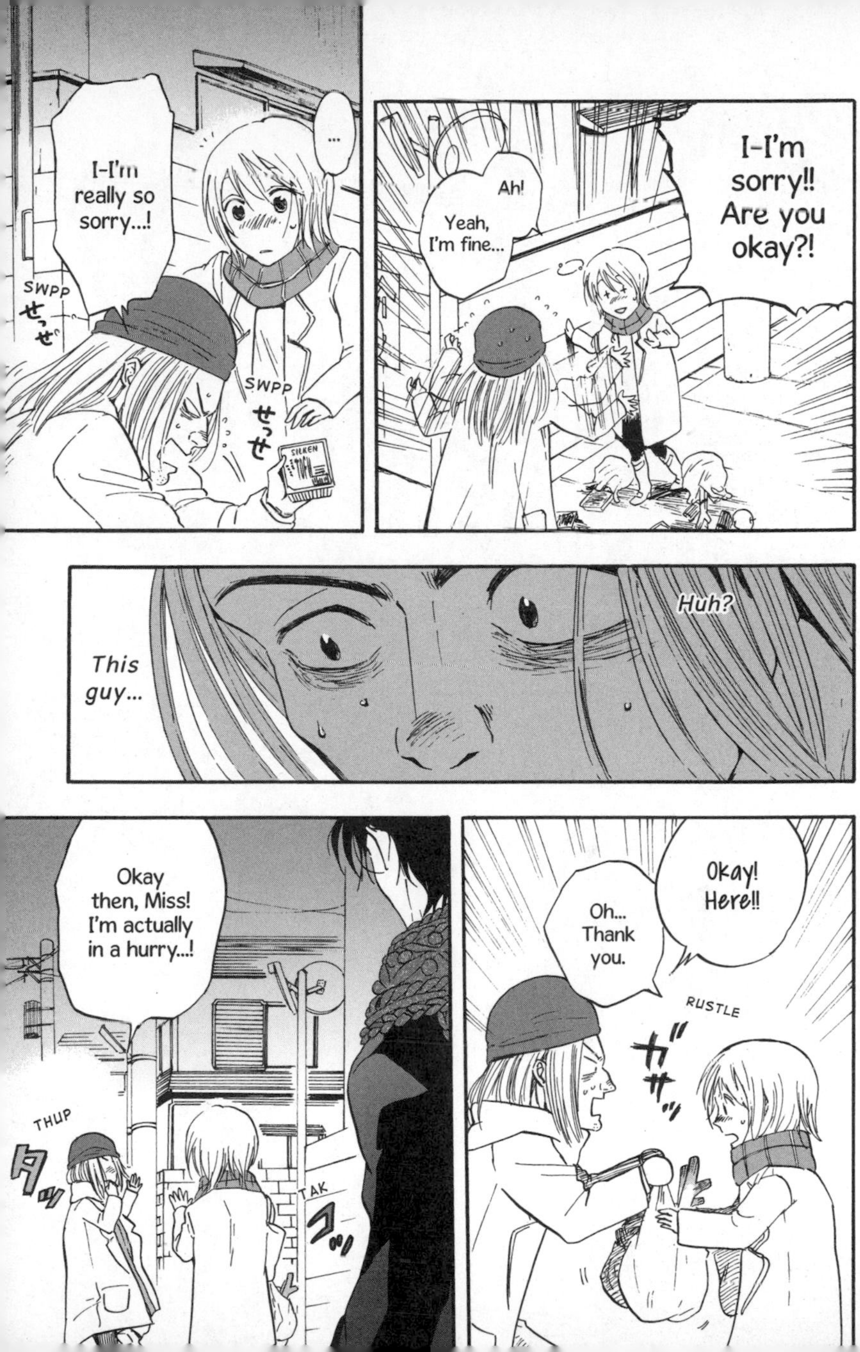
I-I'm sorry!! Are you okay?!
Ah! Yeah, I'm fine...
...
I-I'm really so sorry...!
SWPP
せっせ
SWPP
せっせ
SILKEN
Huh?
This guy...
Okay! Here!!
Oh... Thank you.
RUSTLE
ガサッ
Okay then, Miss! I'm actually in a hurry...!
THUP
タッ
TAK
コツ

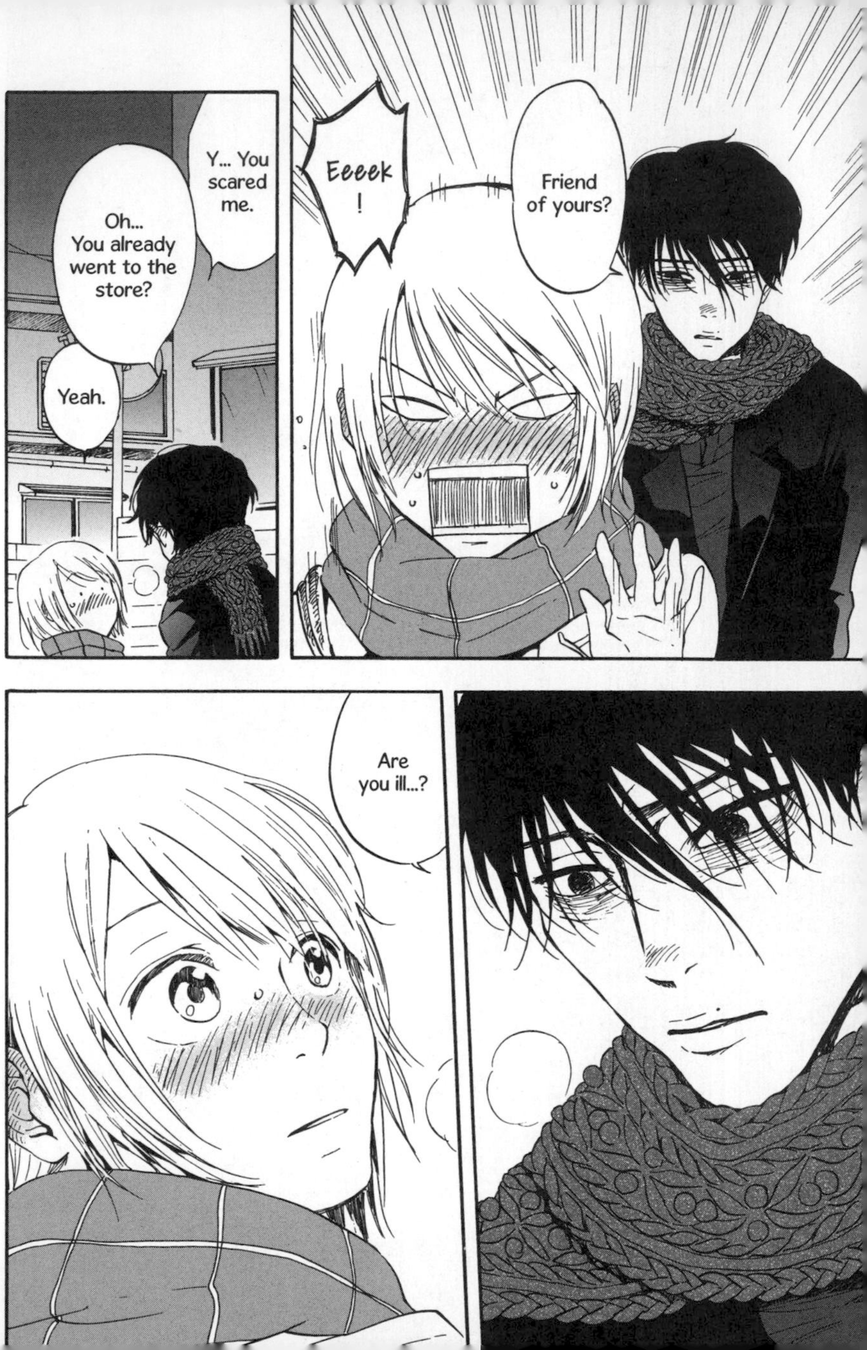
Friend of yours?
Eeeek !
Y... You scared me.
Oh... You already went to the store?
Yeah.
Are you ill...?

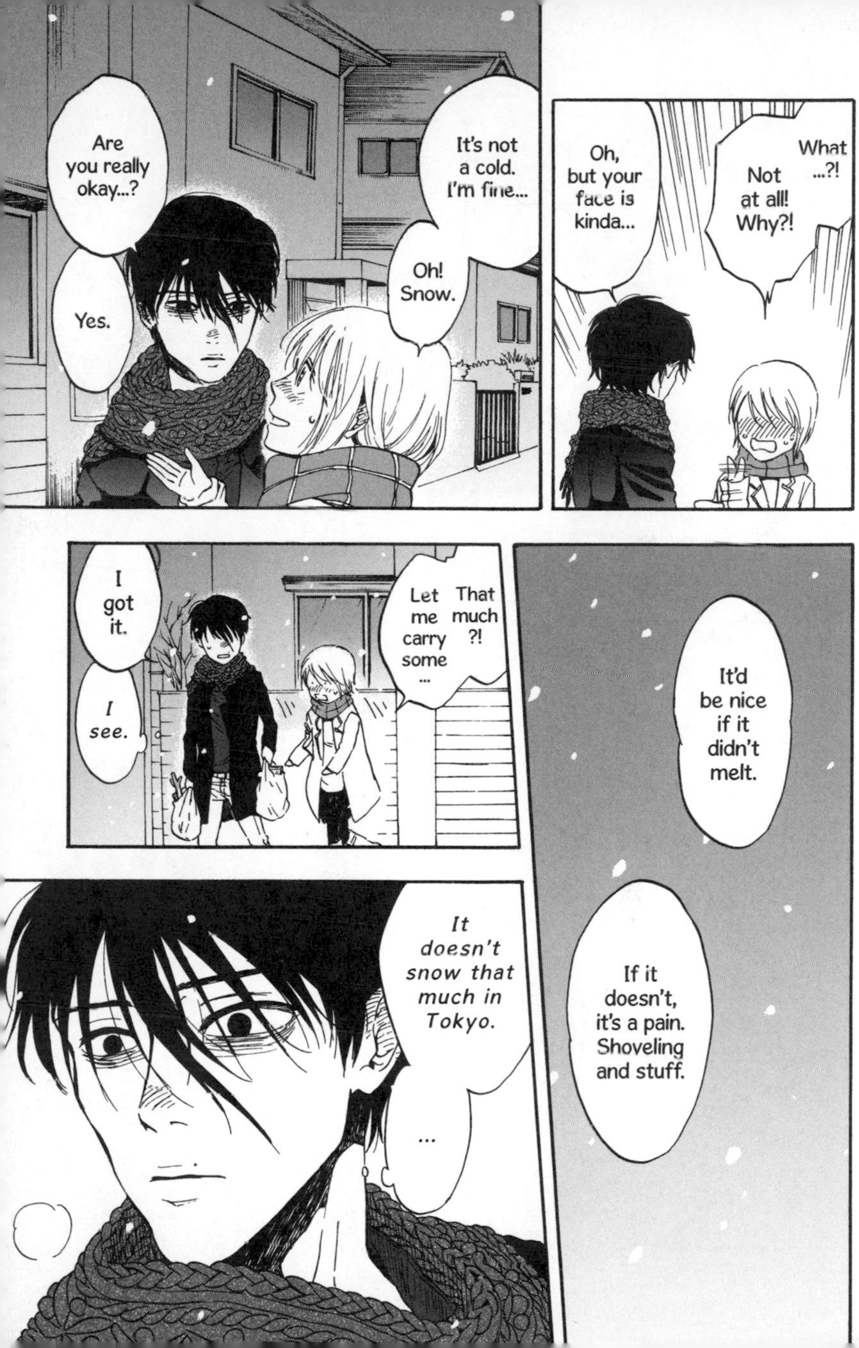
What ...?!
Not at all! Why?!
Oh, but your face is kinda...
It's not a cold. I'm fine...
Oh! Snow.
Are you really okay...?
Yes.
It'd be nice if it didn't melt.
If it doesn't, it's a pain. Shoveling and stuff.
That much ?!
Let me carry some ...
I got it.
I see.
It doesn't snow that much in Tokyo.
...

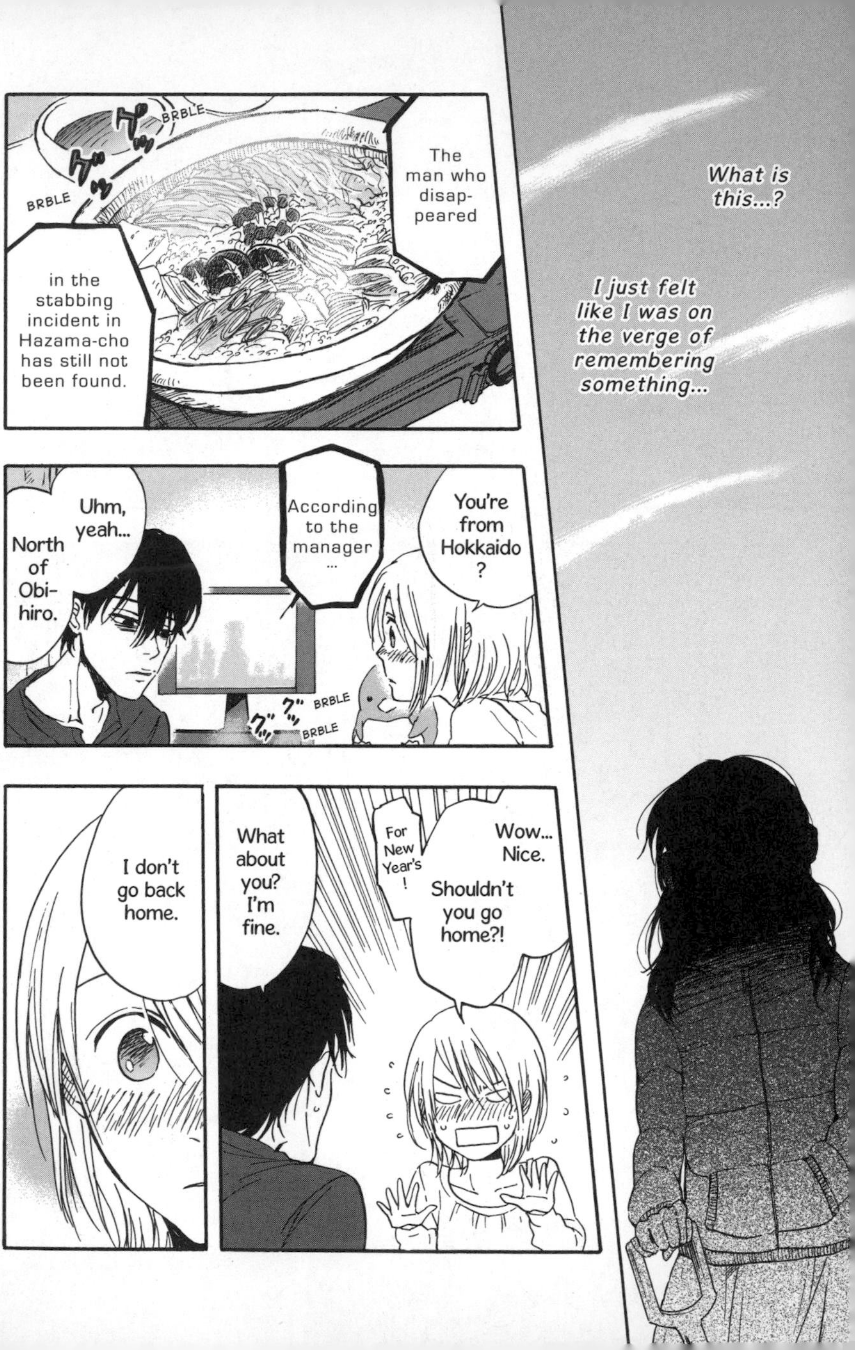
What is this...?
I just felt like I was on the verge of remembering something...
BRBLE
BRBLE
The man who disappeared
in the stabbing incident in Hazama-cho has still not been found.
You're from Hokkaido?
According to the manager...
Uhm, yeah...
North of Obihiro.
BRBLE
BRBLE
Wow... Nice.
Shouldn't you go home?!
For New Year's!
What about you? I'm fine.
I don't go back home.

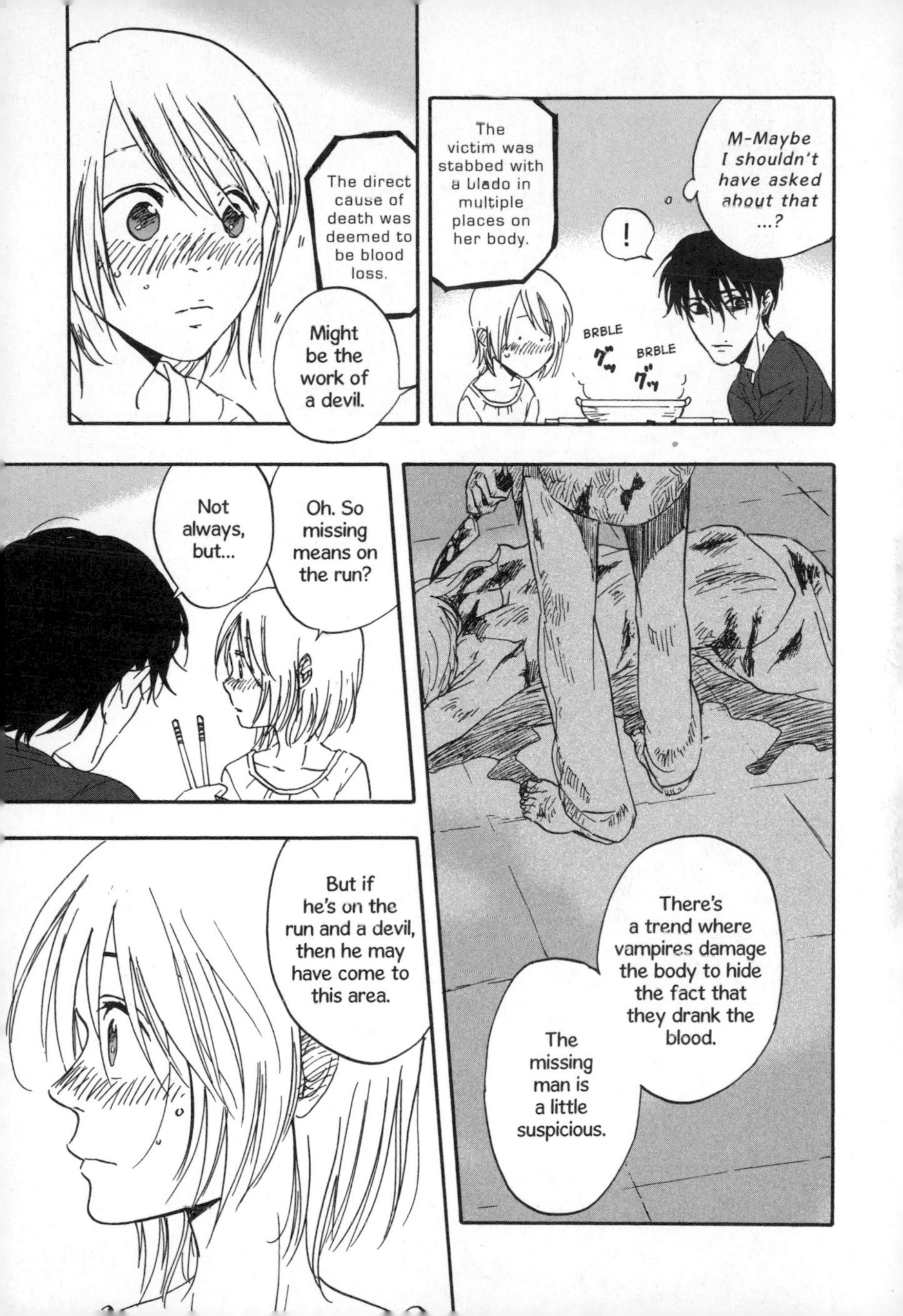
M-Maybe I shouldn't have asked about that ...?
The victim was stabbed with a blado in multiple places on her body.
!
BRBLE
BRBLE
The direct cause of death was deemed to be blood loss.
Might be the work of a devil.
There's a trend where vampires damage the body to hide the fact that they drank the blood.
The missing man is a little suspicious.
Oh. So missing means on the run?
Not always, but...
But if he's on the run and a devil, then he may have come to this area.

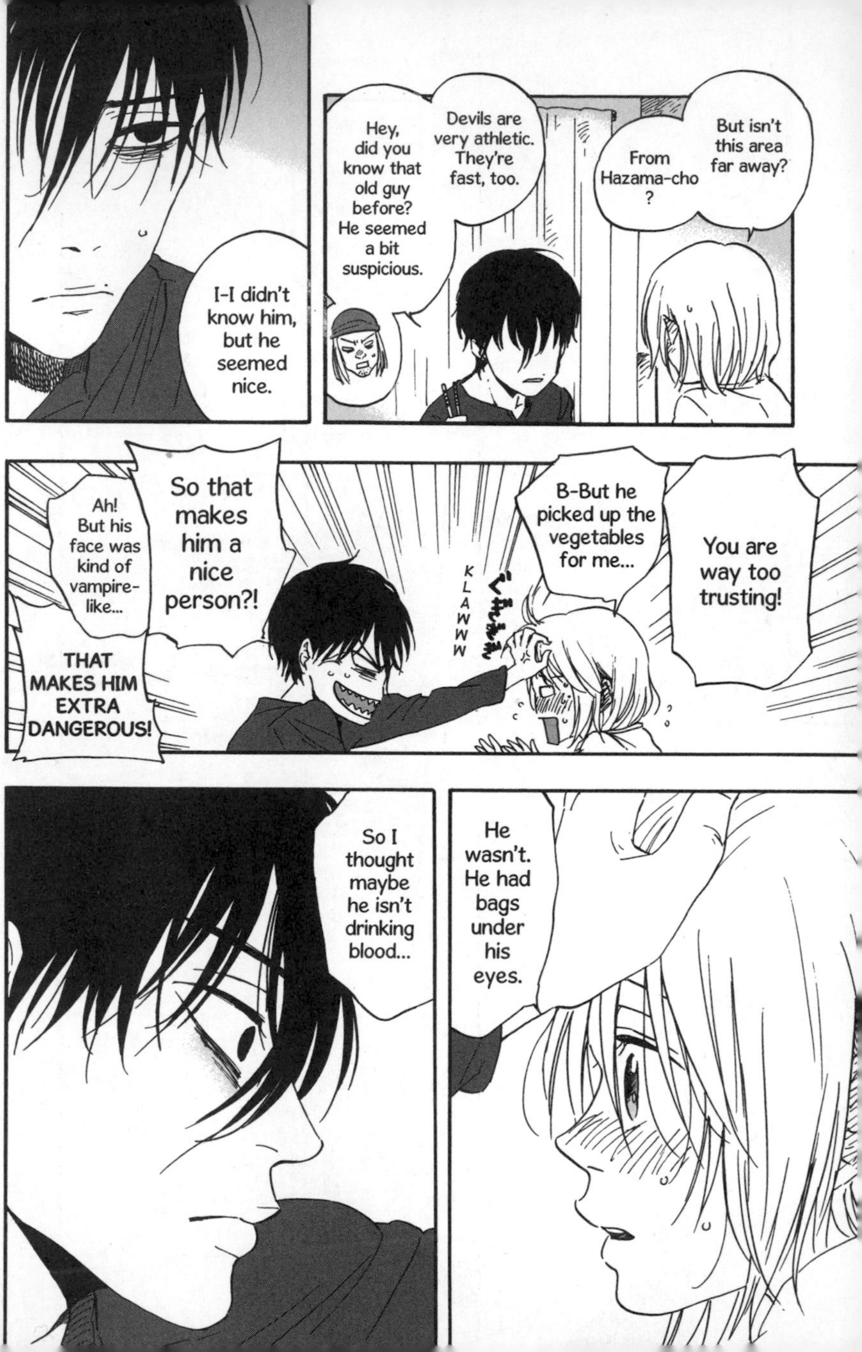
But isn't this area far away?
From Hazama-cho?
Devils are very athletic. They're fast, too.
Hey, did you know that old guy before? He seemed a bit suspicious.
I-I didn't know him, but he seemed nice.
You are way too trusting!
B-But he picked up the vegetables for me...
KLAWWW
So that makes him a nice person?!
Ah! But his face was kind of vampire-like...
THAT MAKES HIM EXTRA DANGEROUS!
He wasn't. He had bags under his eyes.
So I thought maybe he isn't drinking blood...

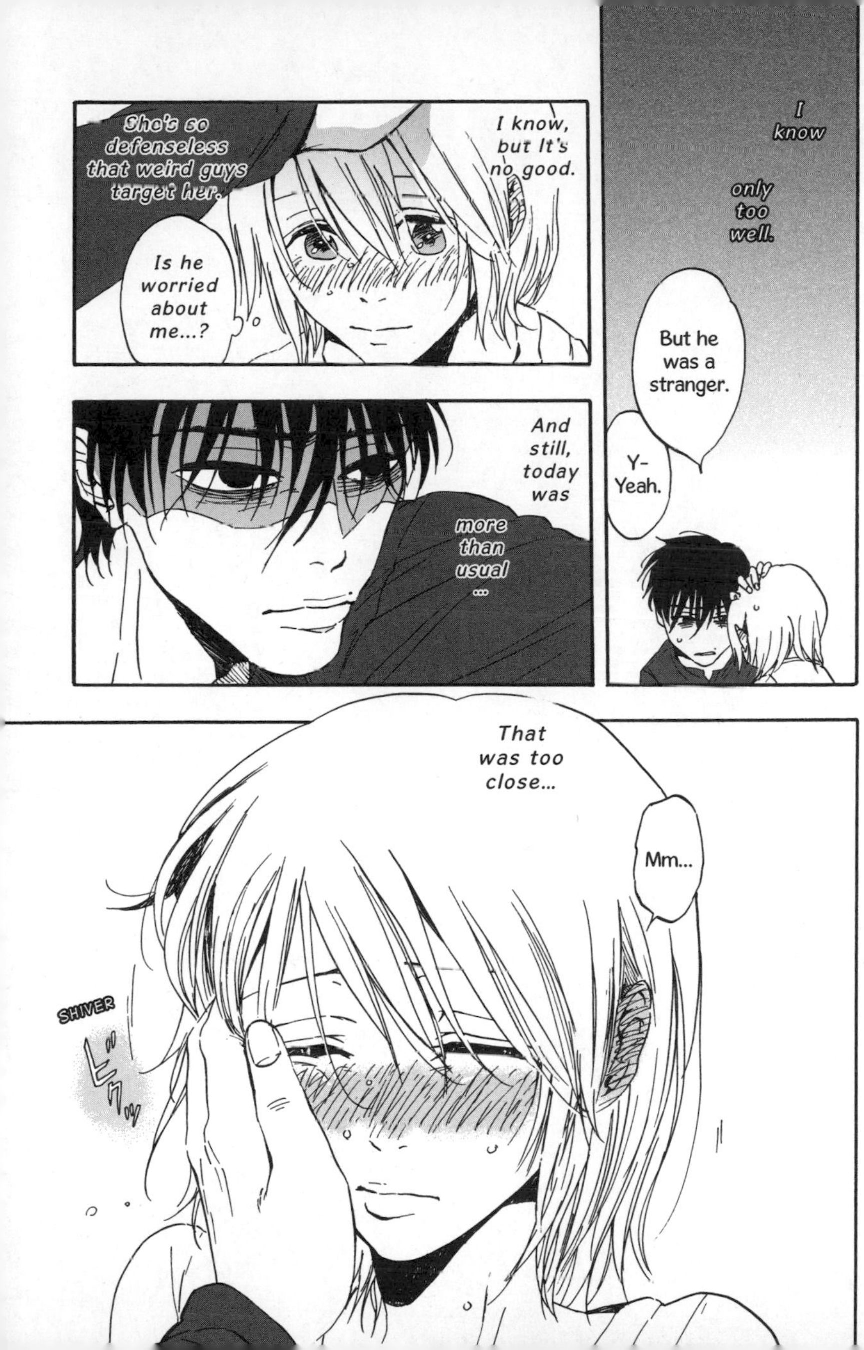
I know only too well.
But he was a stranger.
Y-Yeah.
I know, but It's no good.
She's so defenseless that weird guys target her.
Is he worried about me...?
And still, today was
more than usual...
That was too close...
Mm...
SHIVER
ビクッ

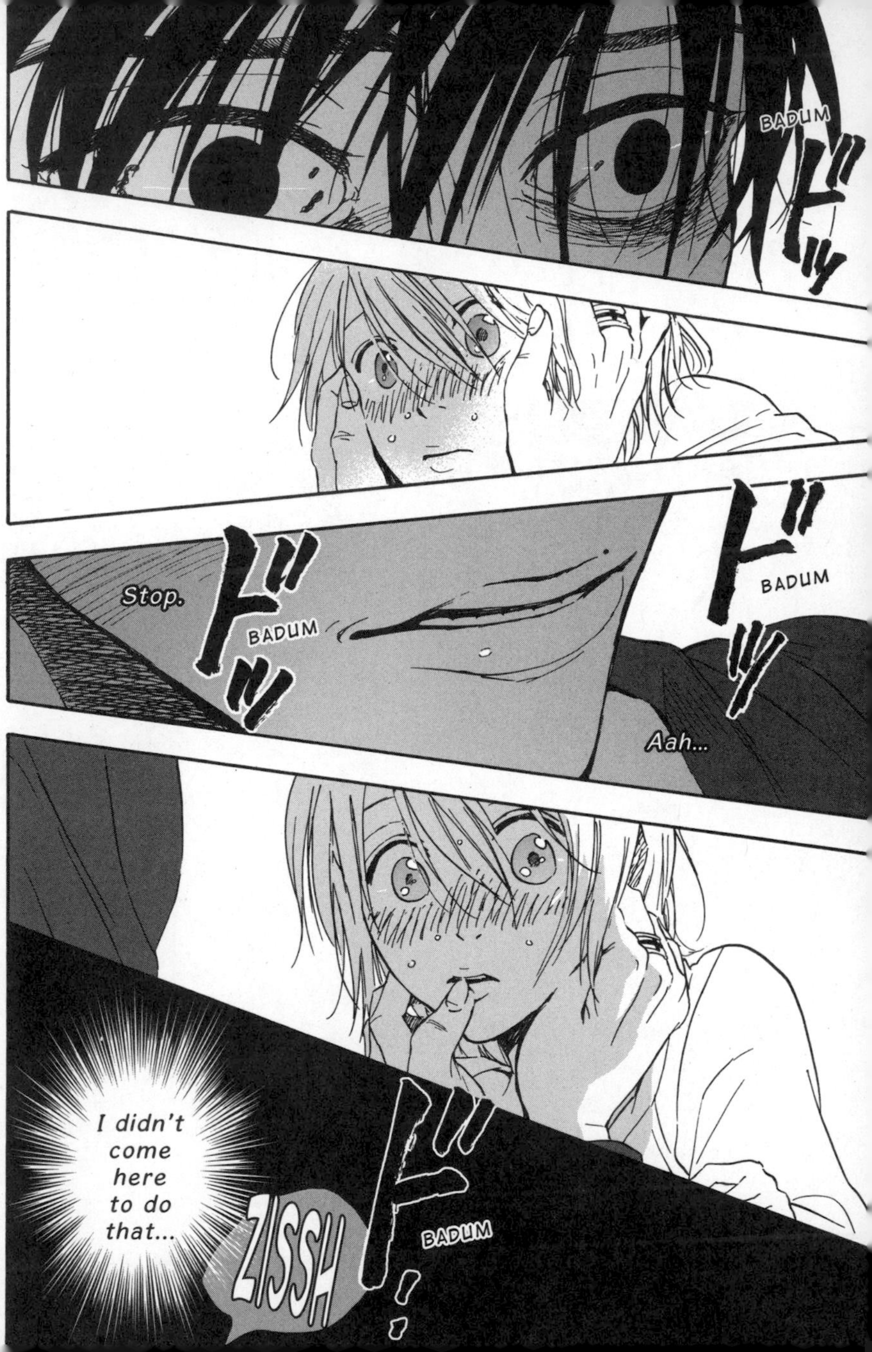
BADUM
ドッ
BADUM
ドッ
Aah...
BADUM
ドッ
Stop.
BADUM
ドッ
ZISSH
I didn't come here to do that...

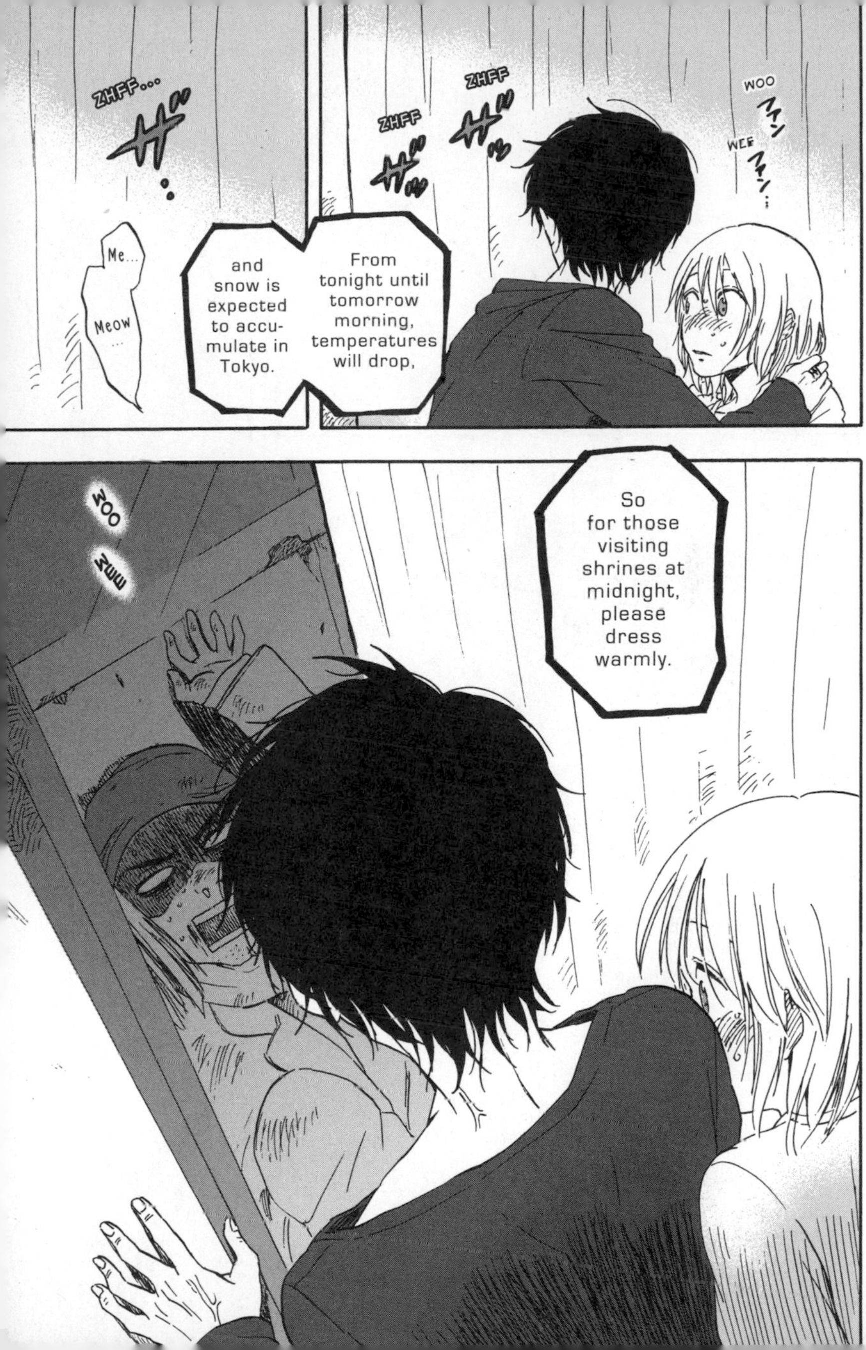

ZHFF
ZHFF
WOO
ファン
WEE
ファン…
From tonight until tomorrow morning, temperatures will drop,
and snow is expected to accu-mulate in Tokyo.
ZHFF...
Me...
Meow...
So for those visiting shrines at midnight, please dress warmly.
WOO
WEE

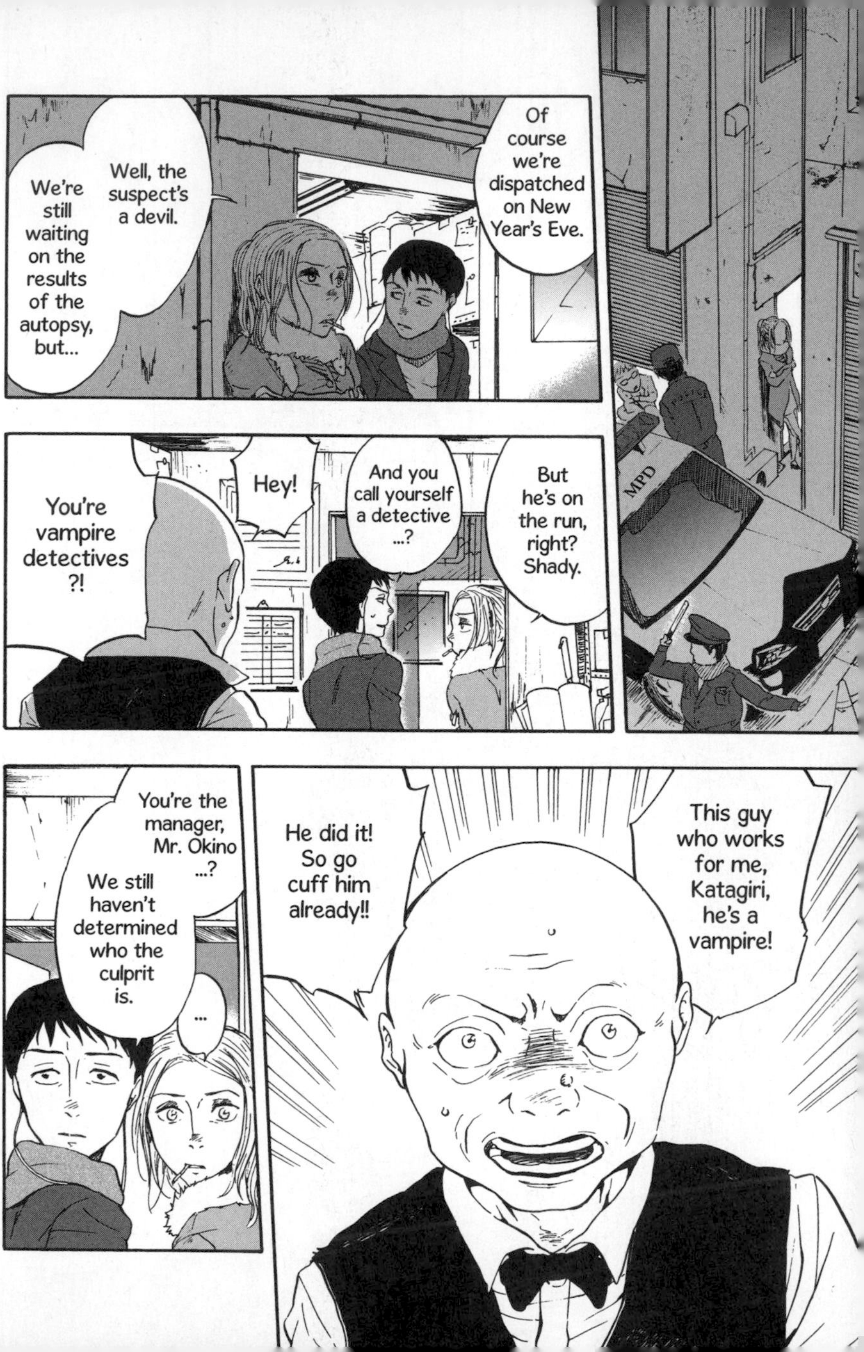
Of course we're dispatched on New Year's Eve.
Well, the suspect's a devil.
We're still waiting on the results of the autopsy, but...
But he's on the run, right? Shady.
And you call yourself a detective ...?
Hey!
You're vampire detectives ?!
MPD
This guy who works for me, Katagiri, he's a vampire!
He did it! So go cuff him already!!
You're the manager, Mr. Okino ...?
We still haven't determined who the culprit is.
...

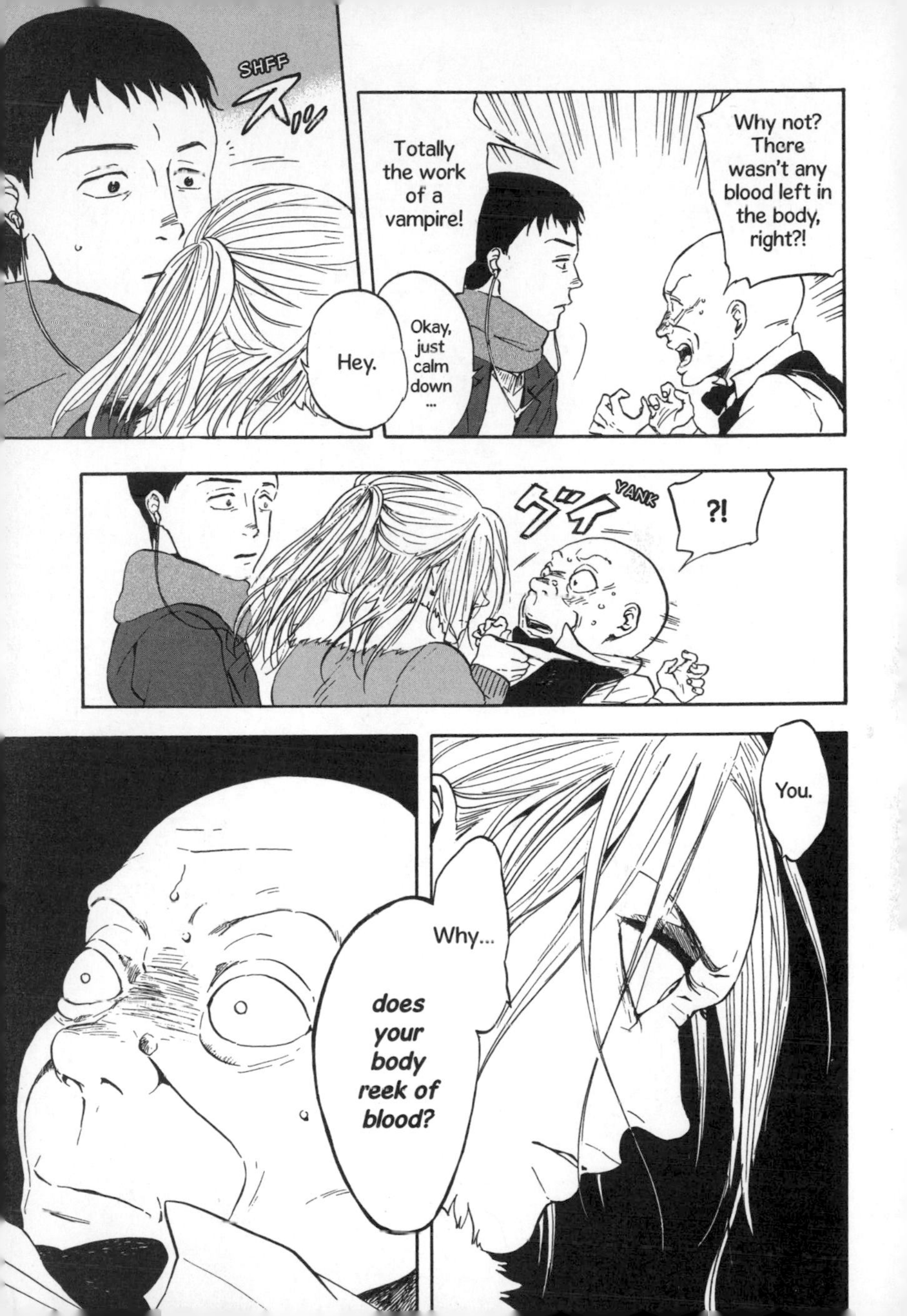
Why not? There wasn't any blood left in the body, right?!
Totally the work of a vampire!
Okay, just calm down ...
Hey.
SHFF
?!
YANK
You.
Why...
does your body reek of blood?

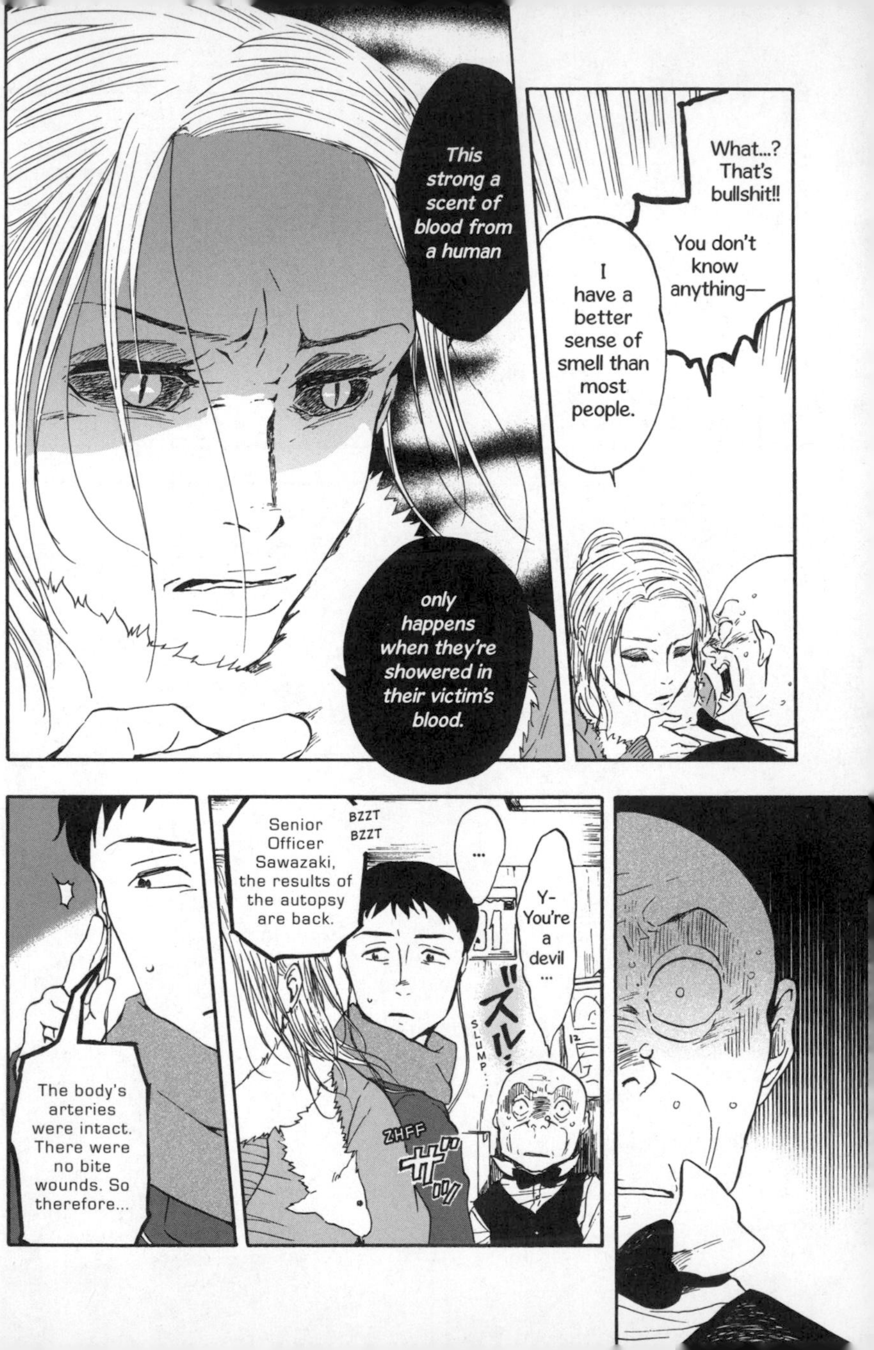
What...? That's bullshit!!
You don't know anything—
I have a better sense of smell than most people.
This strong a scent of blood from a human
only happens when they're showered in their victim's blood.
...
Y- You're a devil ...
ズル SLUMP...
BZZT BZZT
Senior Officer Sawazaki, the results of the autopsy are back.
ザッ ZHFF
The body's arteries were intact. There were no bite wounds. So therefore...

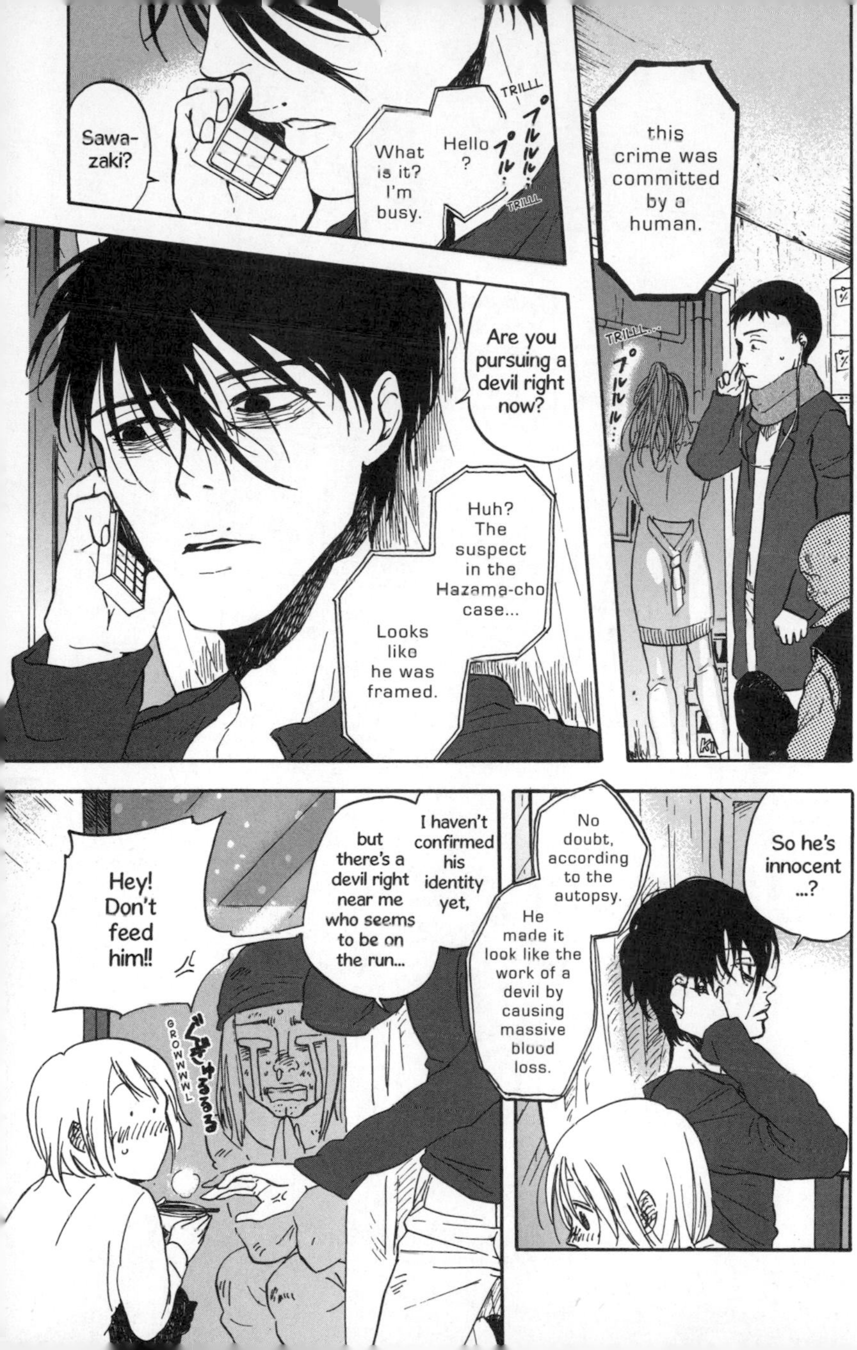
this crime was committed by a human.
TRILLL...
TRILLL
Hello?
TRILLL
What is it? I'm busy.
Sawa-zaki?
Are you pursuing a devil right now?
Huh? The suspect in the Hazama-cho case...
Looks like he was framed.
So he's innocent...?
No doubt, according to the autopsy.
He made it look like the work of a devil by causing massive blood loss.
I haven't confirmed his identity yet,
but there's a devil right near me who seems to be on the run...
Hey! Don't feed him!!
GROWWWL

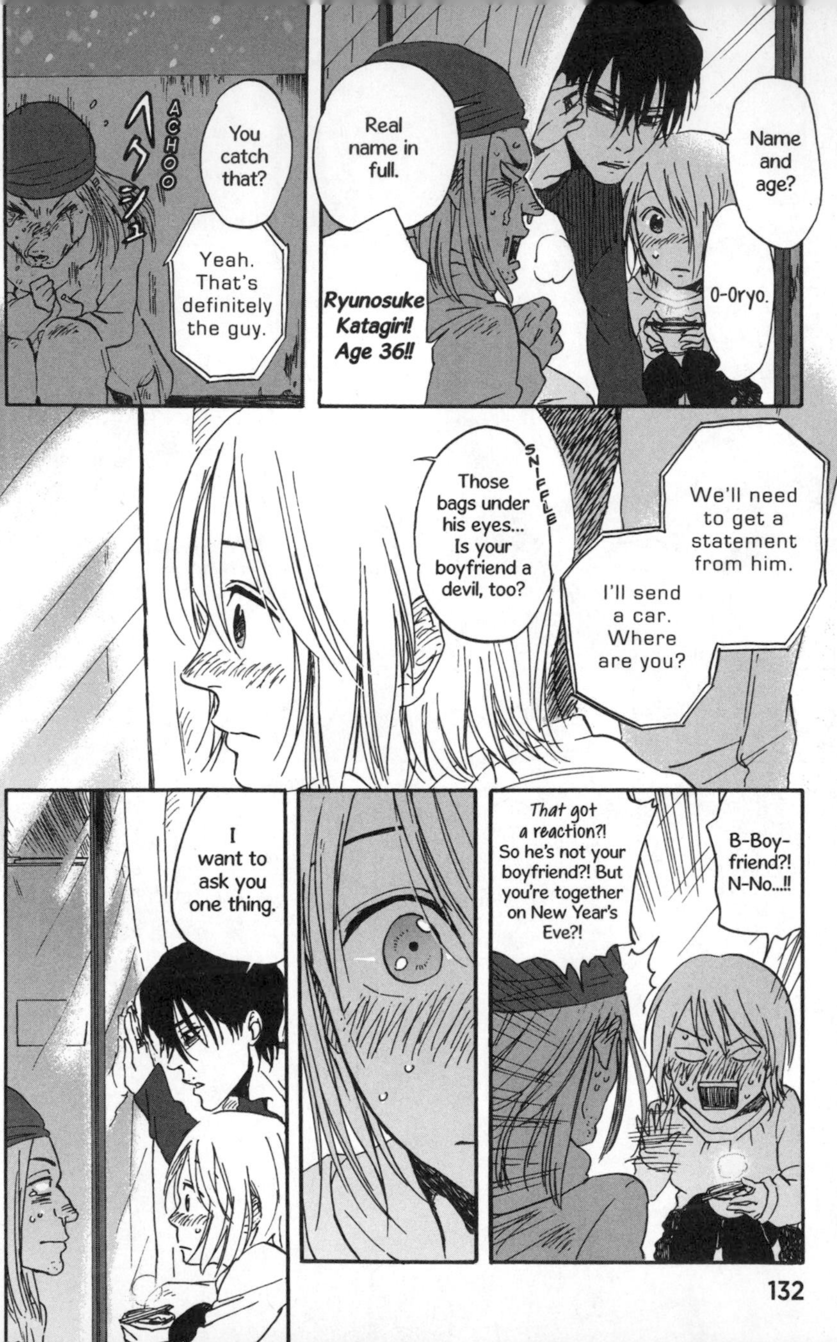
Name and age?
O-Oryo.
Real name in full.
Ryunosuke Katagiri! Age 36!!
You catch that?
ACHOO
Yeah. That's definitely the guy.
We'll need to get a statement from him.
I'll send a car. Where are you?
SNIFFLE
Those bags under his eyes... Is your boyfriend a devil, too?
B-Boy-friend?! N-No...!!
That got a reaction?! So he's not your boyfriend?! But you're together on New Year's Eve?!
I want to ask you one thing.

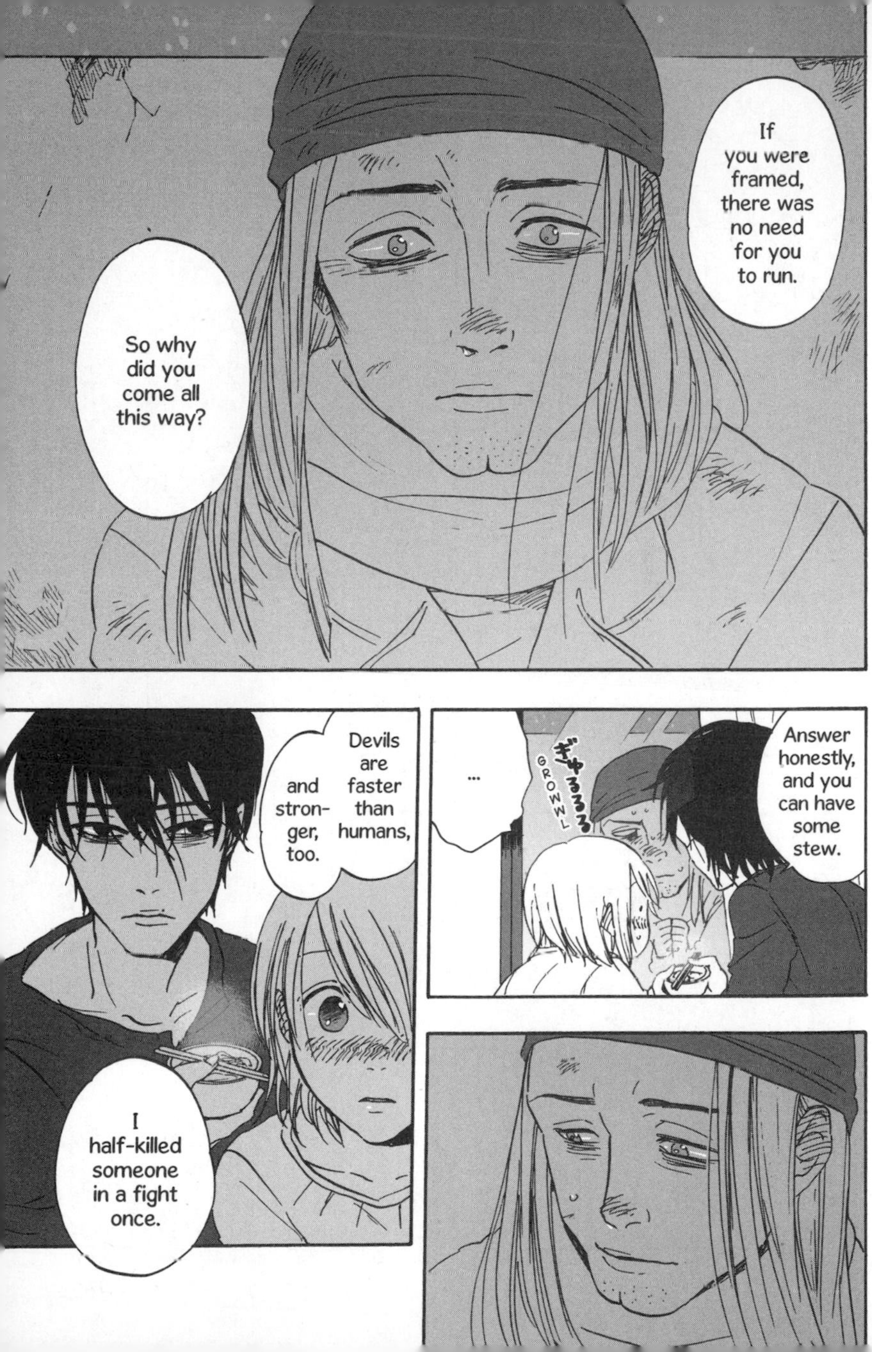
If you were framed, there was no need for you to run.
So why did you come all this way?
Answer honestly, and you can have some stew.
ぎゃるるる
GROWL
...
Devils are faster than humans,
and stronger, too.
I half-killed someone in a fight once.

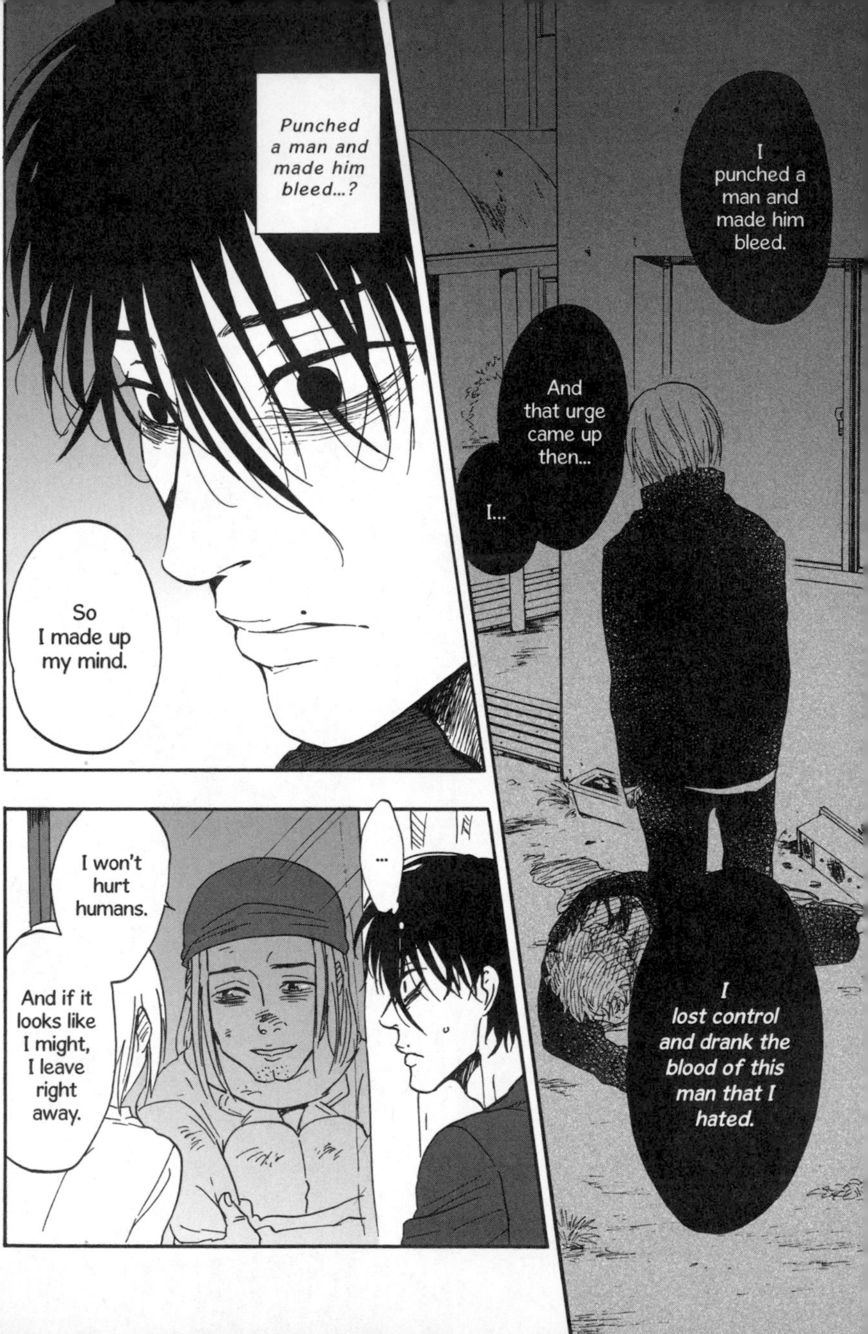
I punched a man and made him bleed.
And that urge came up then...
I...
I lost control and drank the blood of this man that I hated.
Punched a man and made him bleed...?
So I made up my mind.
...
I won't hurt humans.
And if it looks like I might, I leave right away.

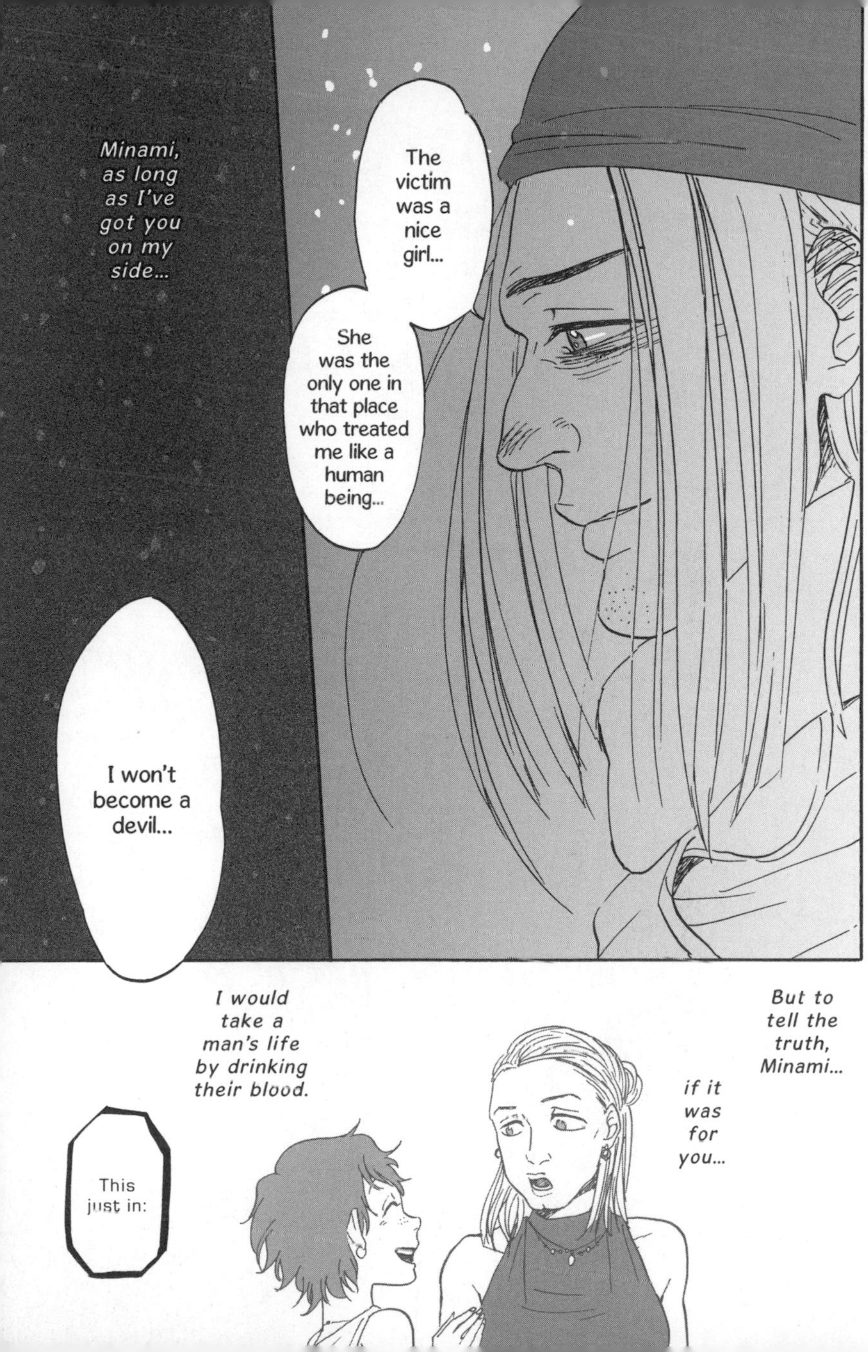
The victim was a nice girl...
She was the only one in that place who treated me like a human being...
Minami, as long as I've got you on my side...
I won't become a devil...
But to tell the truth, Minami...
if it was for you...
I would take a man's life by drinking their blood.
This just in:

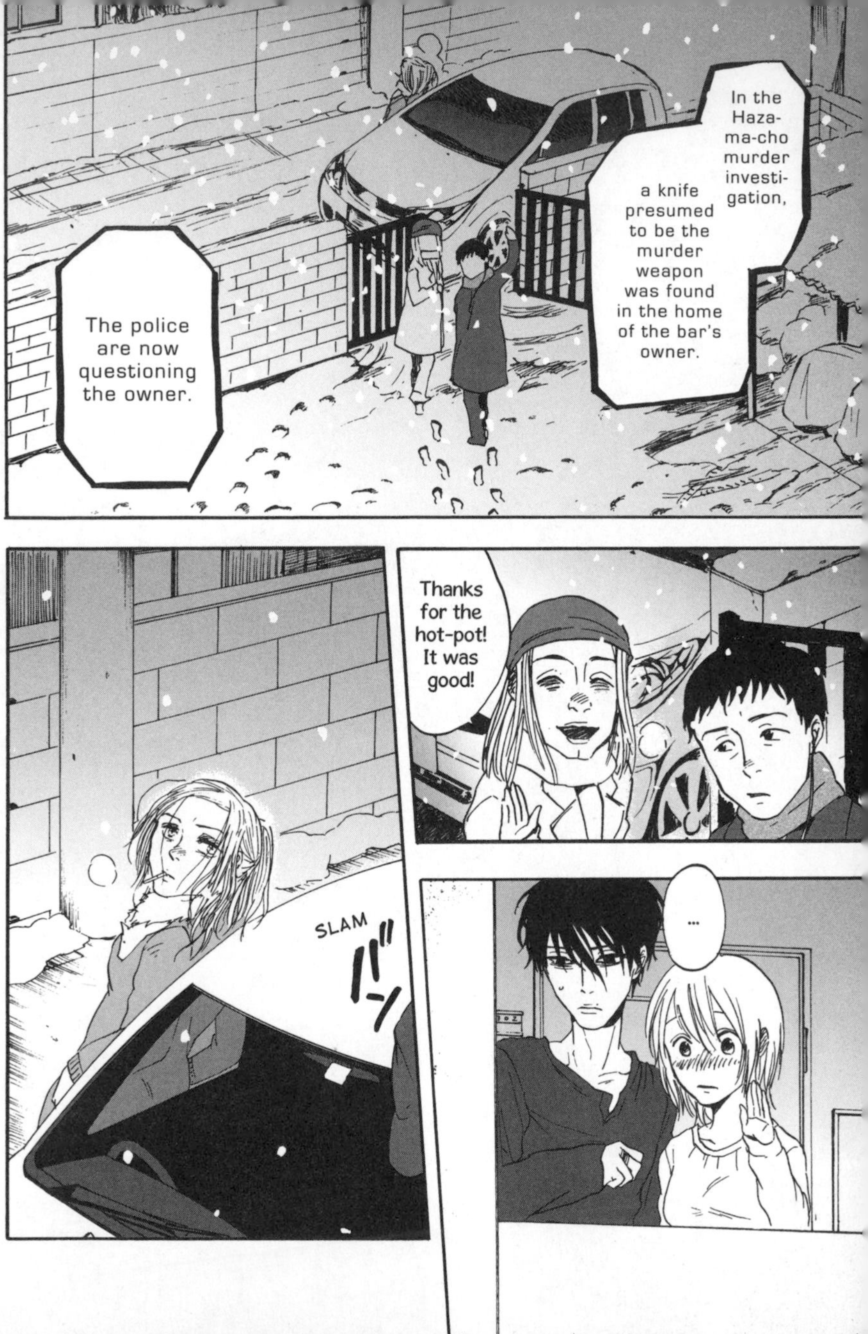
In the Hazama-cho murder investigation, a knife presumed to be the murder weapon was found in the home of the bar's owner.
The police are now questioning the owner.
Thanks for the hot-pot! It was good!
...
SLAM

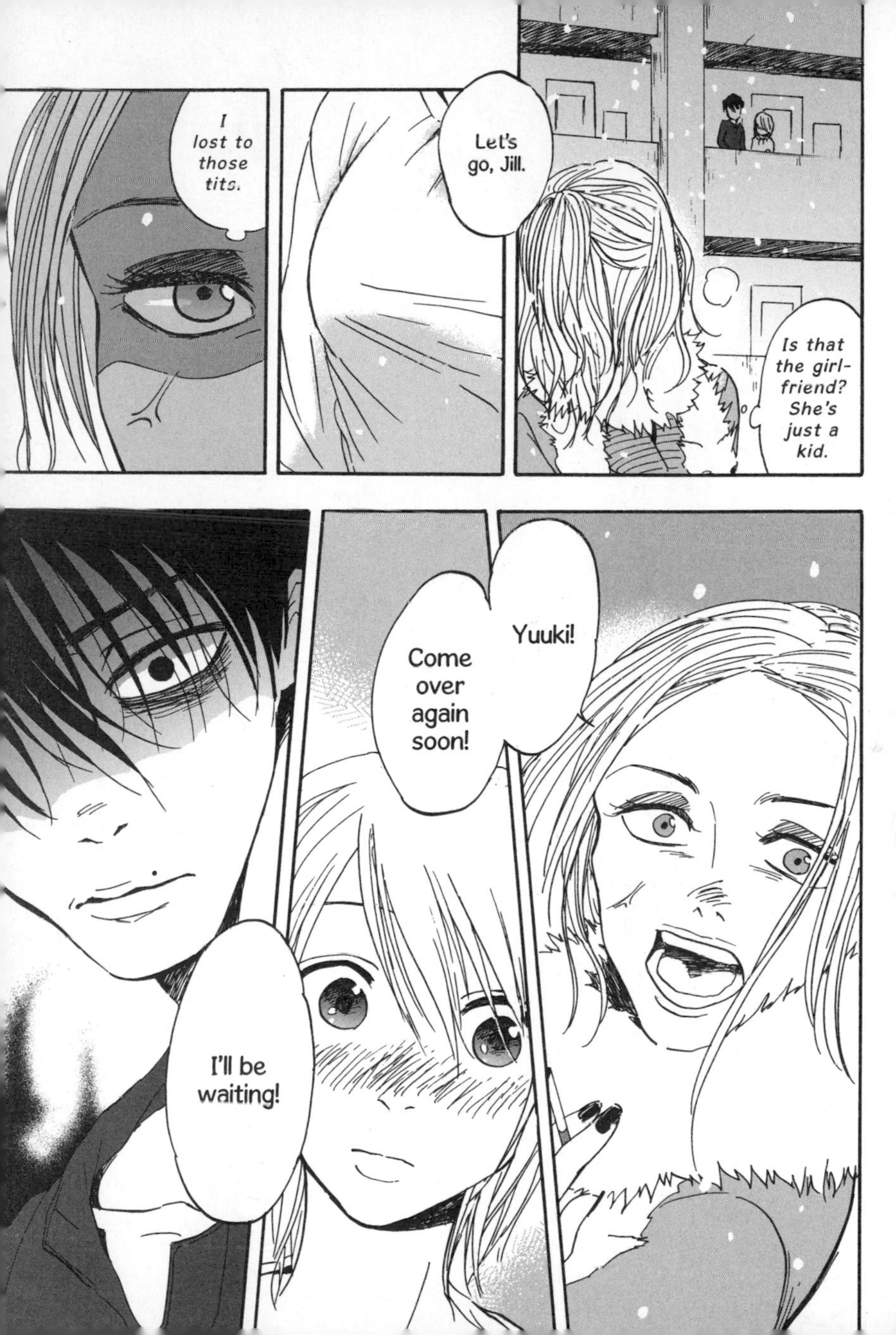
Is that the girlfriend? She's just a kid.
Let's go, Jill.
I lost to those tits.
Yuuki!
Come over again soon!
I'll be waiting!

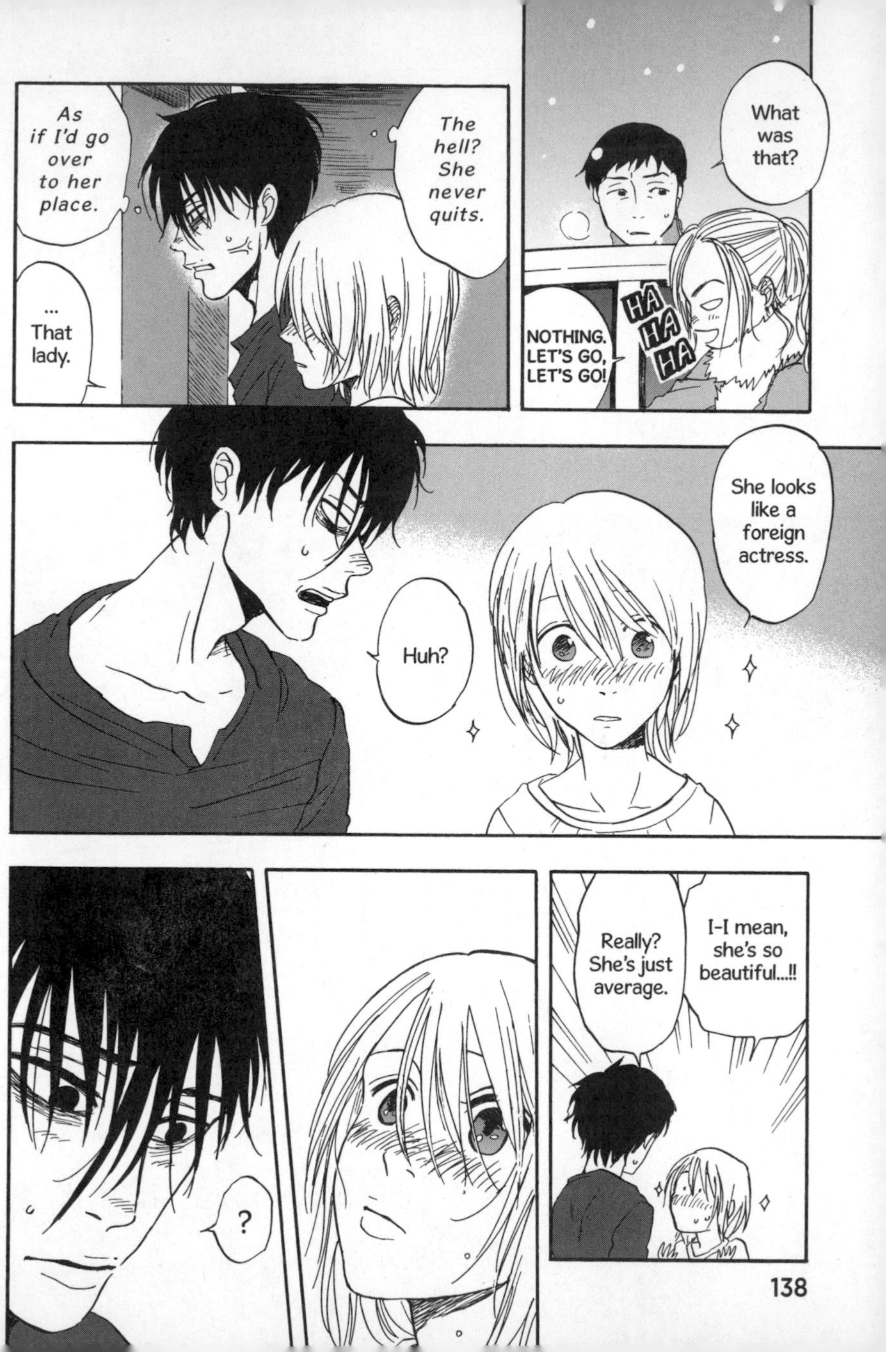
What was that?
NOTHING. LET'S GO, LET'S GO!
HA HA HA
The hell? She never quits.
As if I'd go over to her place.
... That lady.
She looks like a foreign actress.
Huh?
I-I mean, she's so beautiful...!!
Really? She's just average.
?

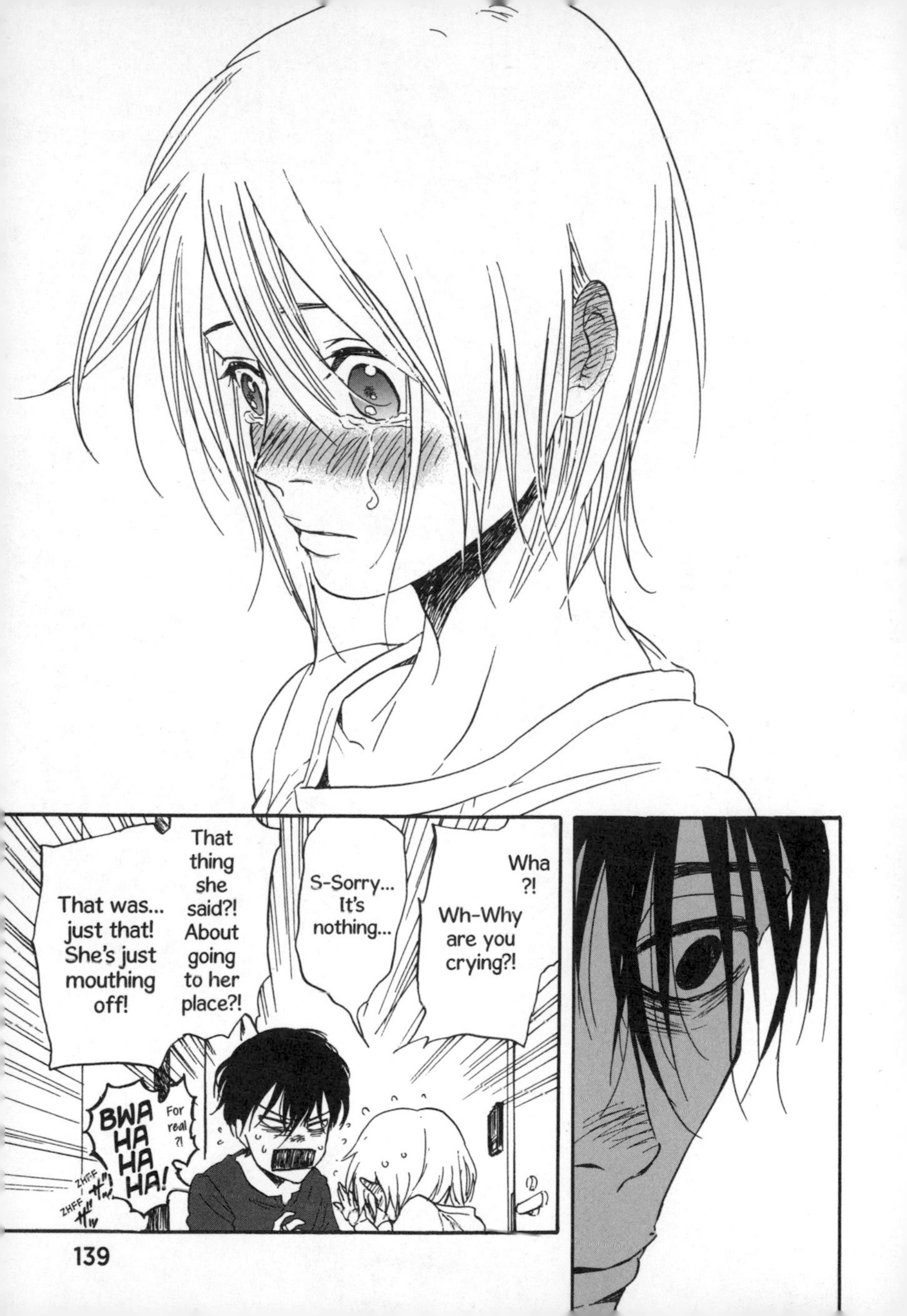
Wha ?!
Wh-Why are you crying?!
S-Sorry... It's nothing...
That thing she said?! About going to her place?!
That was... just that! She's just mouthing off!
For real ?!
BWA HA HA HA!
ZHFF ZHFF

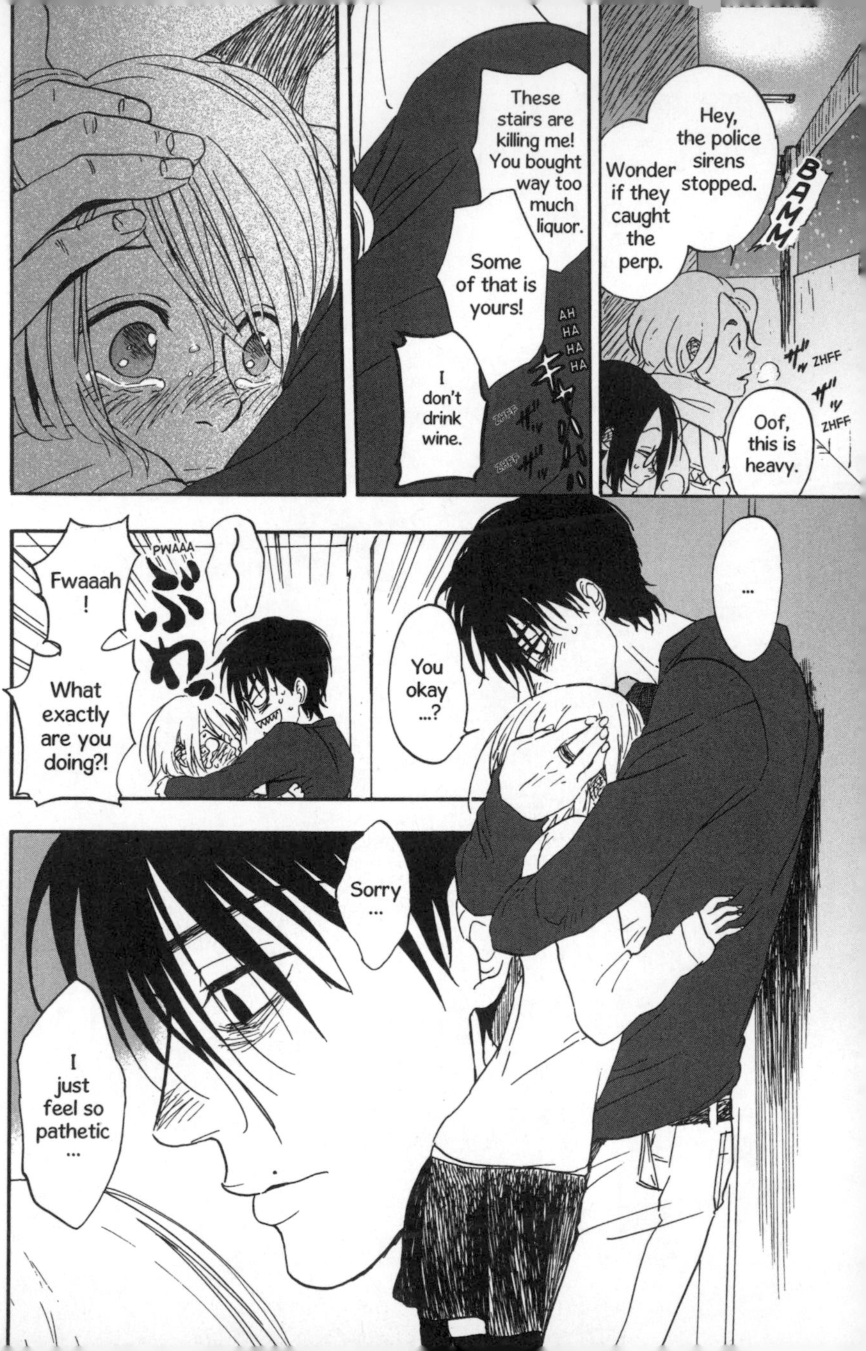
Hey, the police sirens stopped.
Wonder if they caught the perp.
BAMM
ZHFF
ZHFF
Oof, this is heavy.
These stairs are killing me! You bought way too much liquor.
Some of that is yours!
AH HA HA HA
I don't drink wine.
ZHFF
ZHFF
...
You okay ...?
Fwaaah!
PWAAA
What exactly are you doing?!
Sorry ...
I just feel so pathetic ...

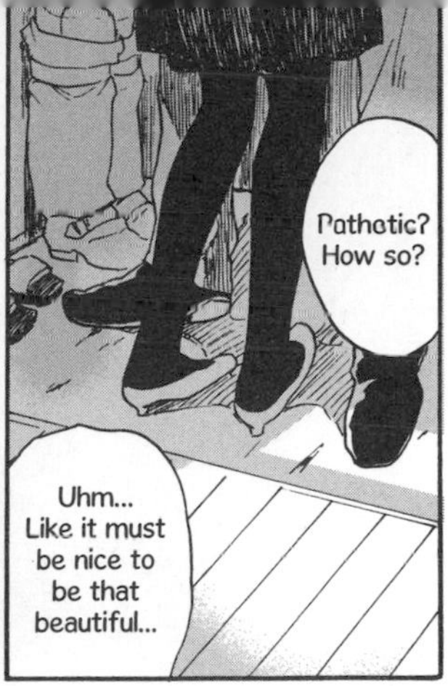
Pathetic? How so?
Uhm... Like it must be nice to be that beautiful...
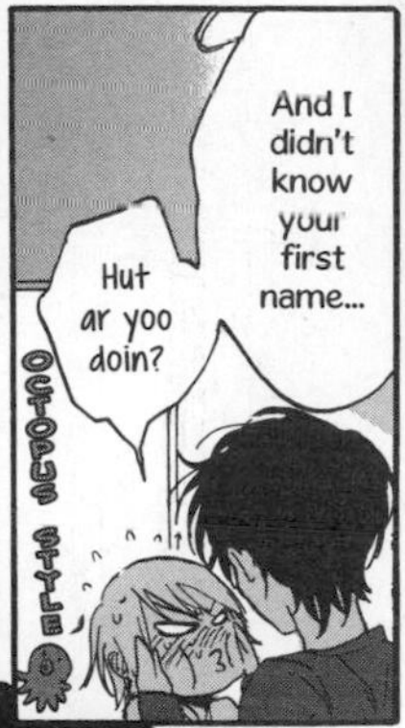
And I didn't know your first name...
Hut ar yoo doin?
OCTOPUS STYLE
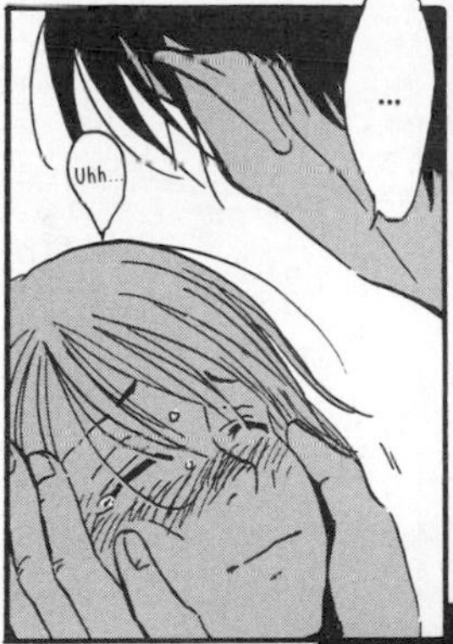
...
Uhh...
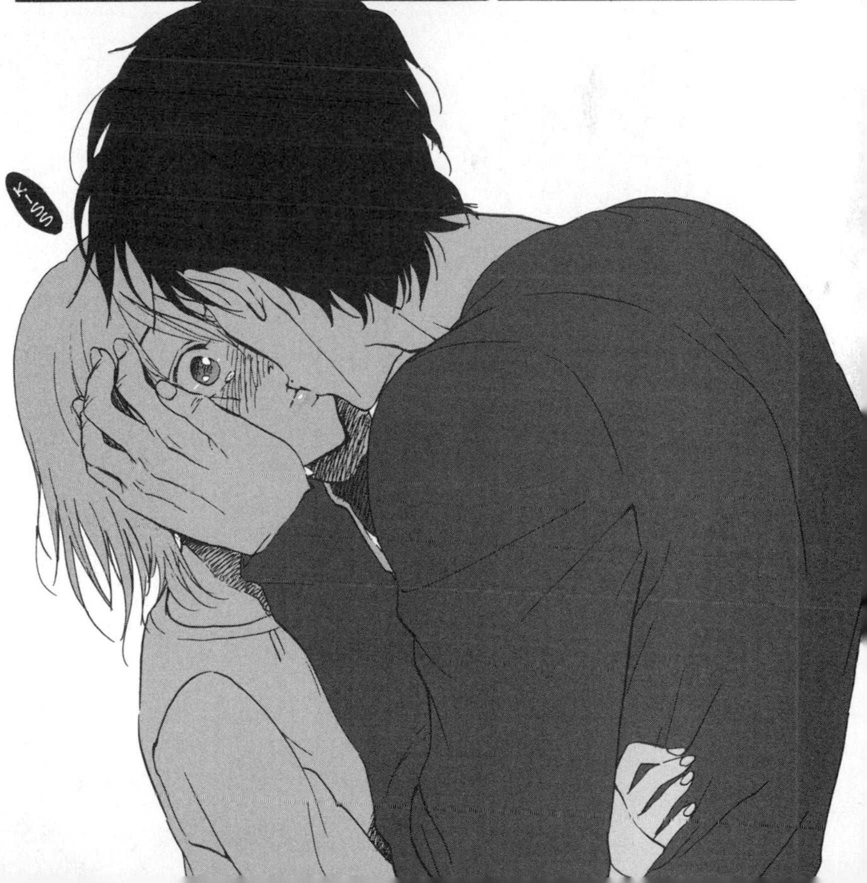
K-SS

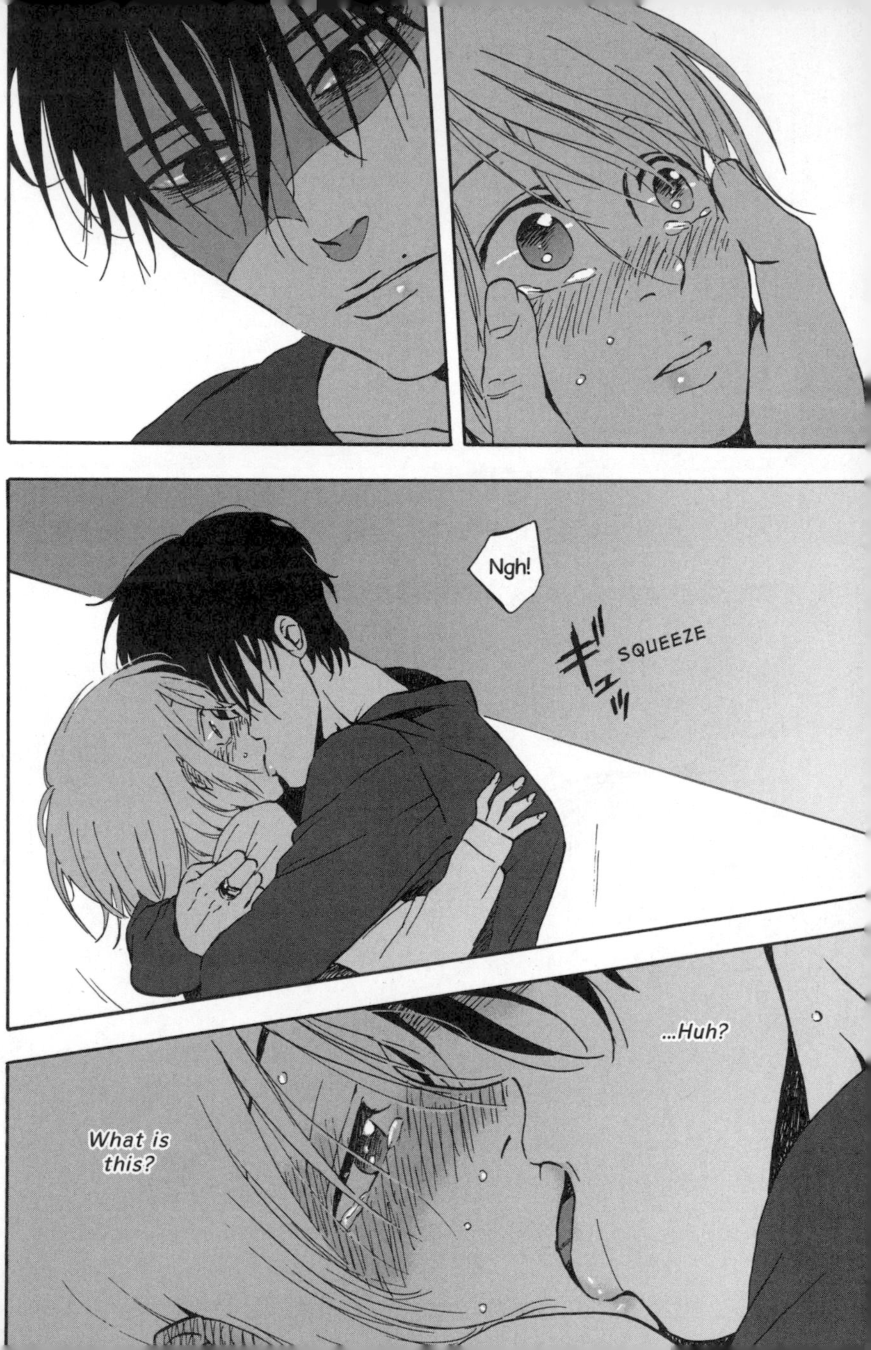
Ngh!
ギュッ SQUEEZE
...Huh?
What is this?

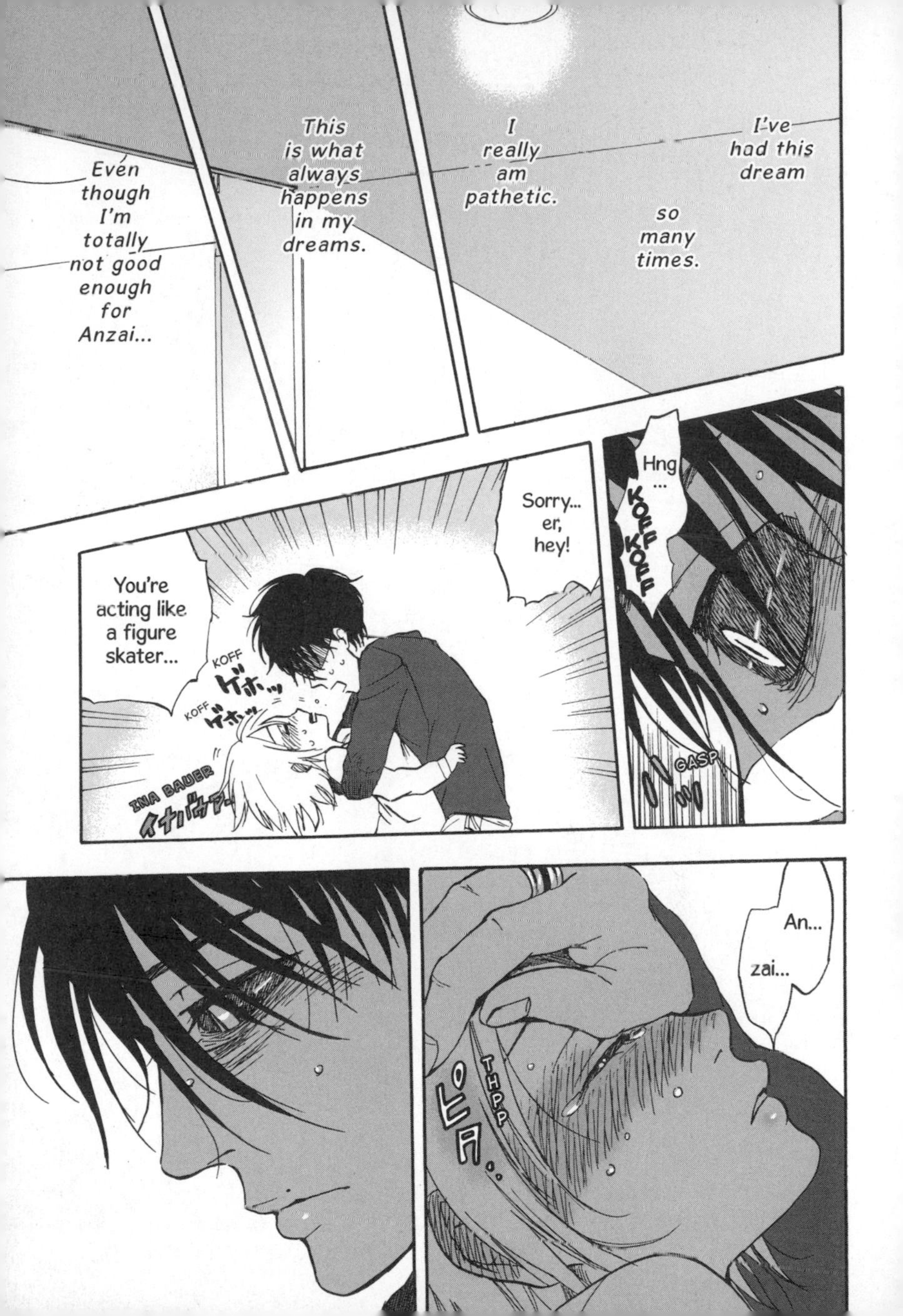

I've had this dream
so many times.
I really am pathetic.
This is what always happens in my dreams.
Even though I'm totally not good enough for Anzai...
Hng...
KOFF KOFF
GASP
Sorry... er, hey!
You're acting like a figure skater...
KOFF ゲホッ
KOFF ゲホッ
INA BAUER イナバウアー
An...
zai...
THPP ピタ...

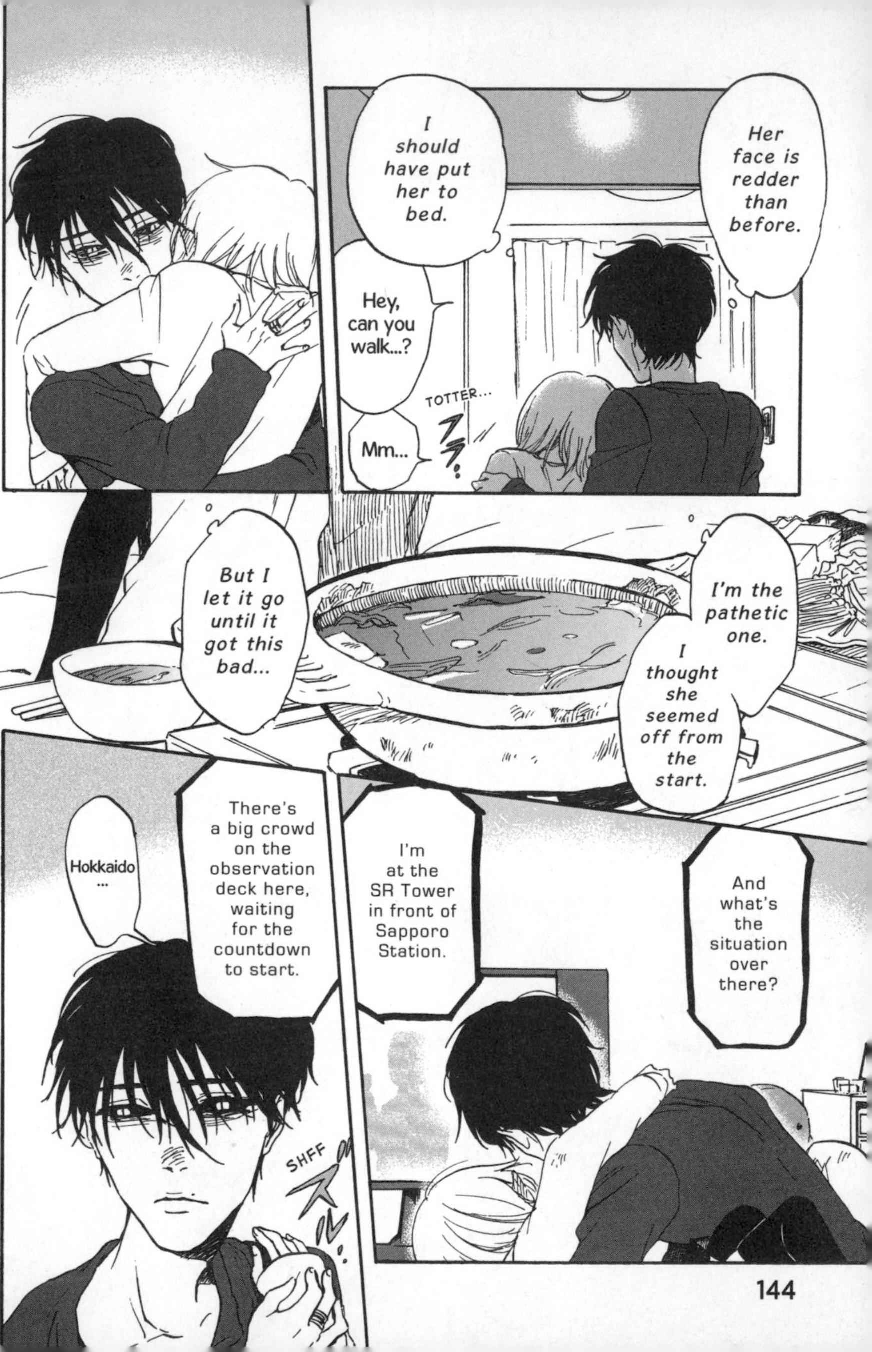
Her face is redder than before.
I should have put her to bed.
Hey, can you walk...?
TOTTER...
Mm...
I'm the pathetic one.
I thought she seemed off from the start.
But I let it go until it got this bad...
And what's the situation over there?
I'm at the SR Tower in front of Sapporo Station.
There's a big crowd on the observation deck here, waiting for the countdown to start.
Hokkaido...
SHFF

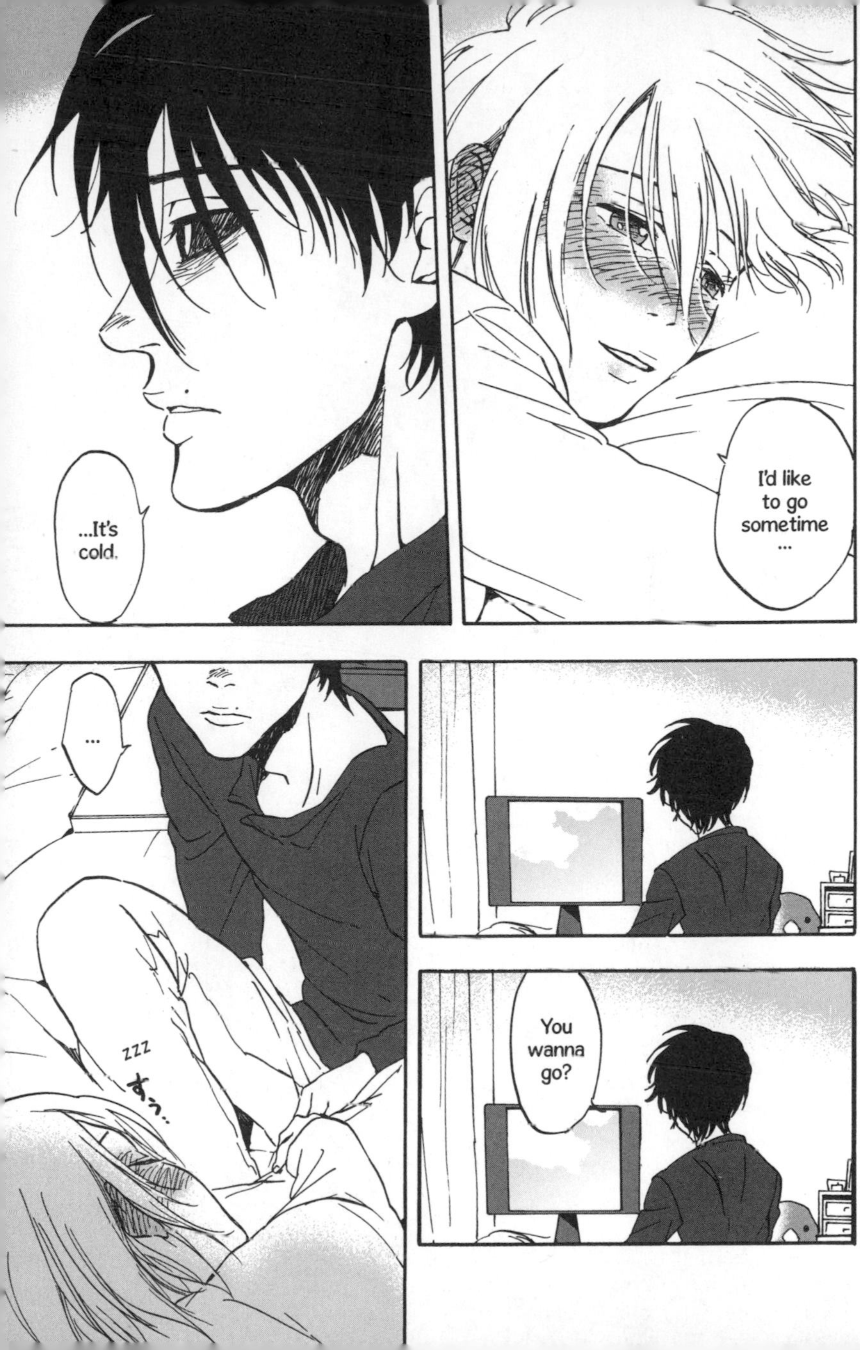
I'd like to go sometime ...
...It's cold.
You wanna go?
...
ZZZ
すぅ..

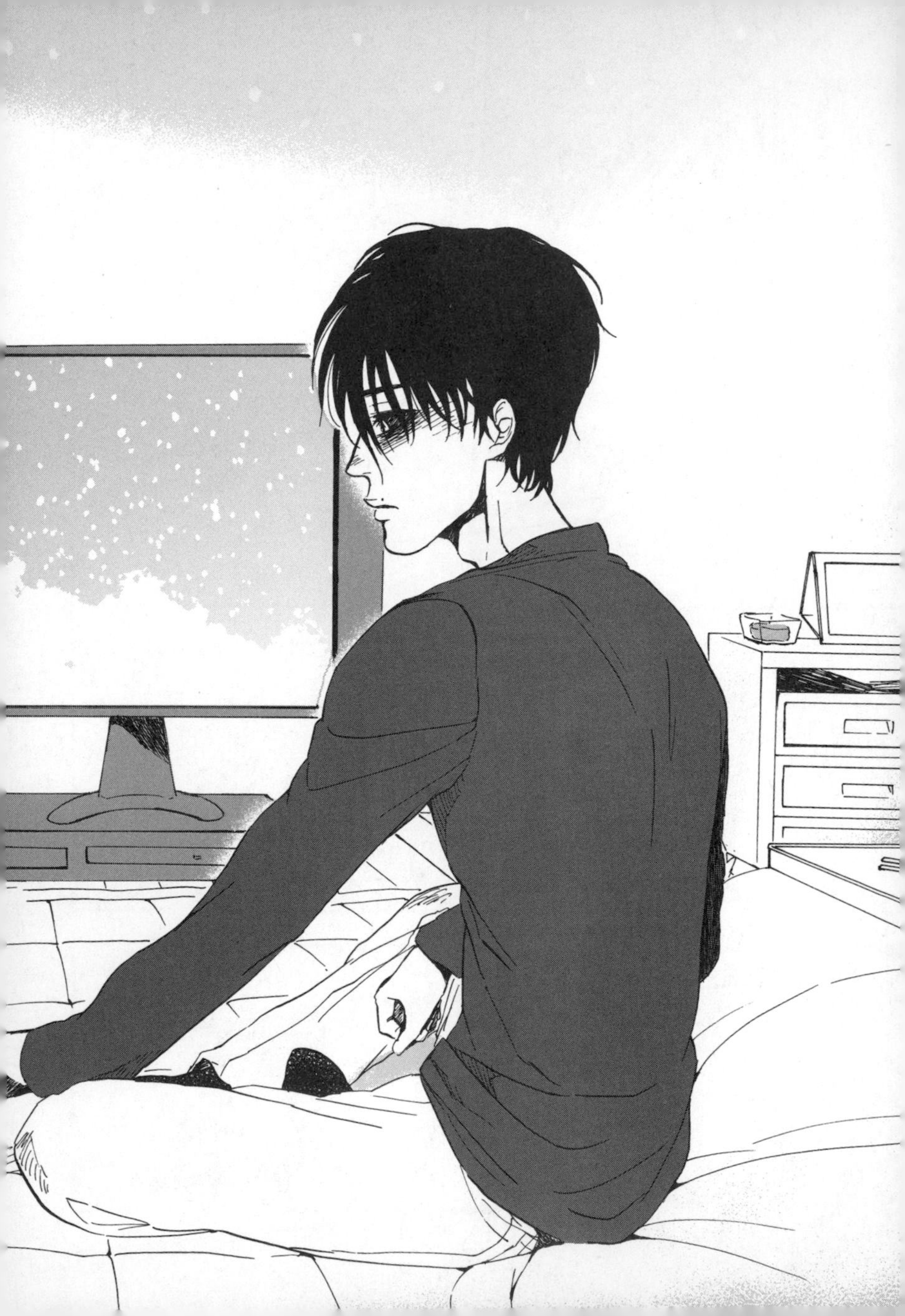

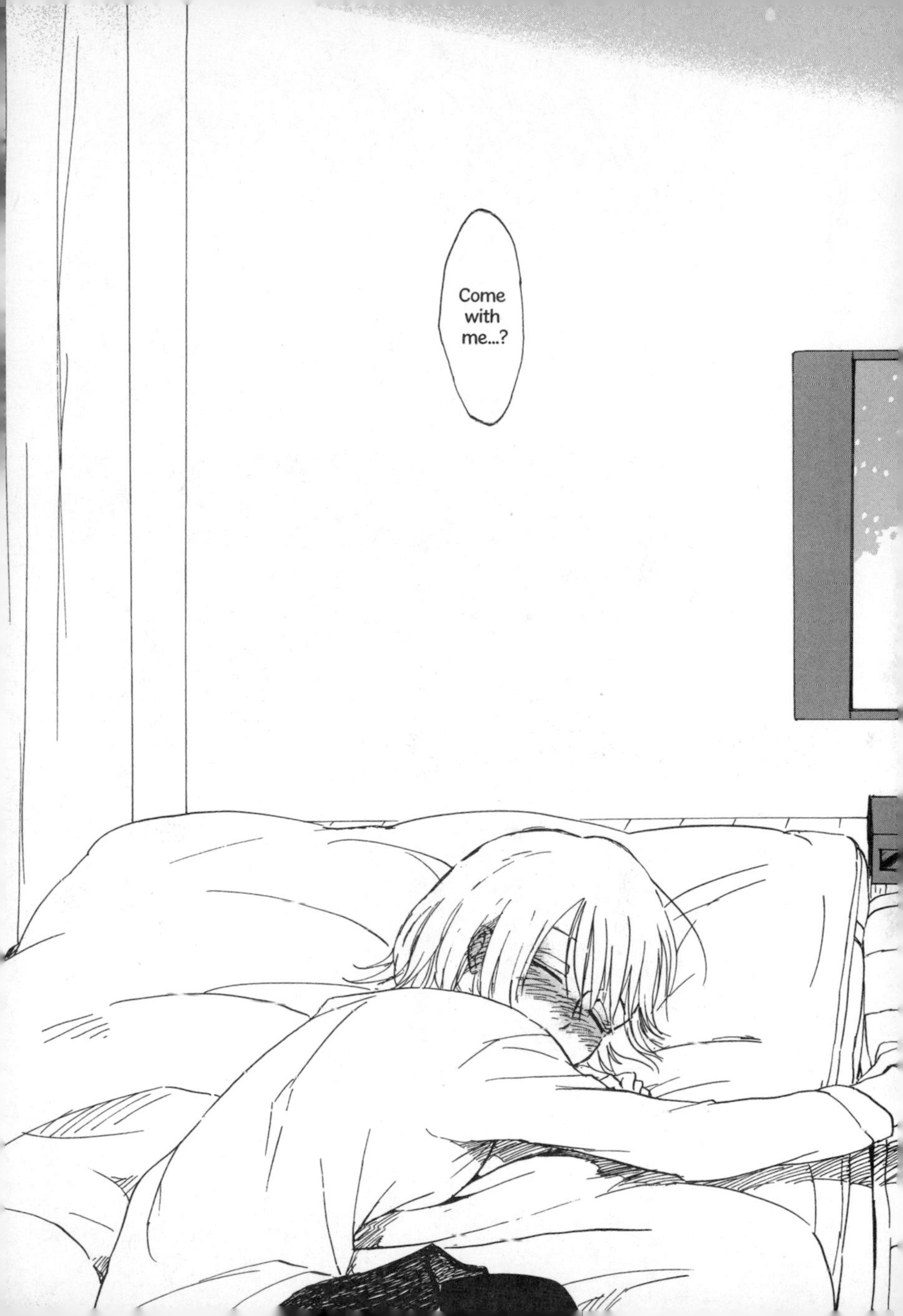
Come with me...?

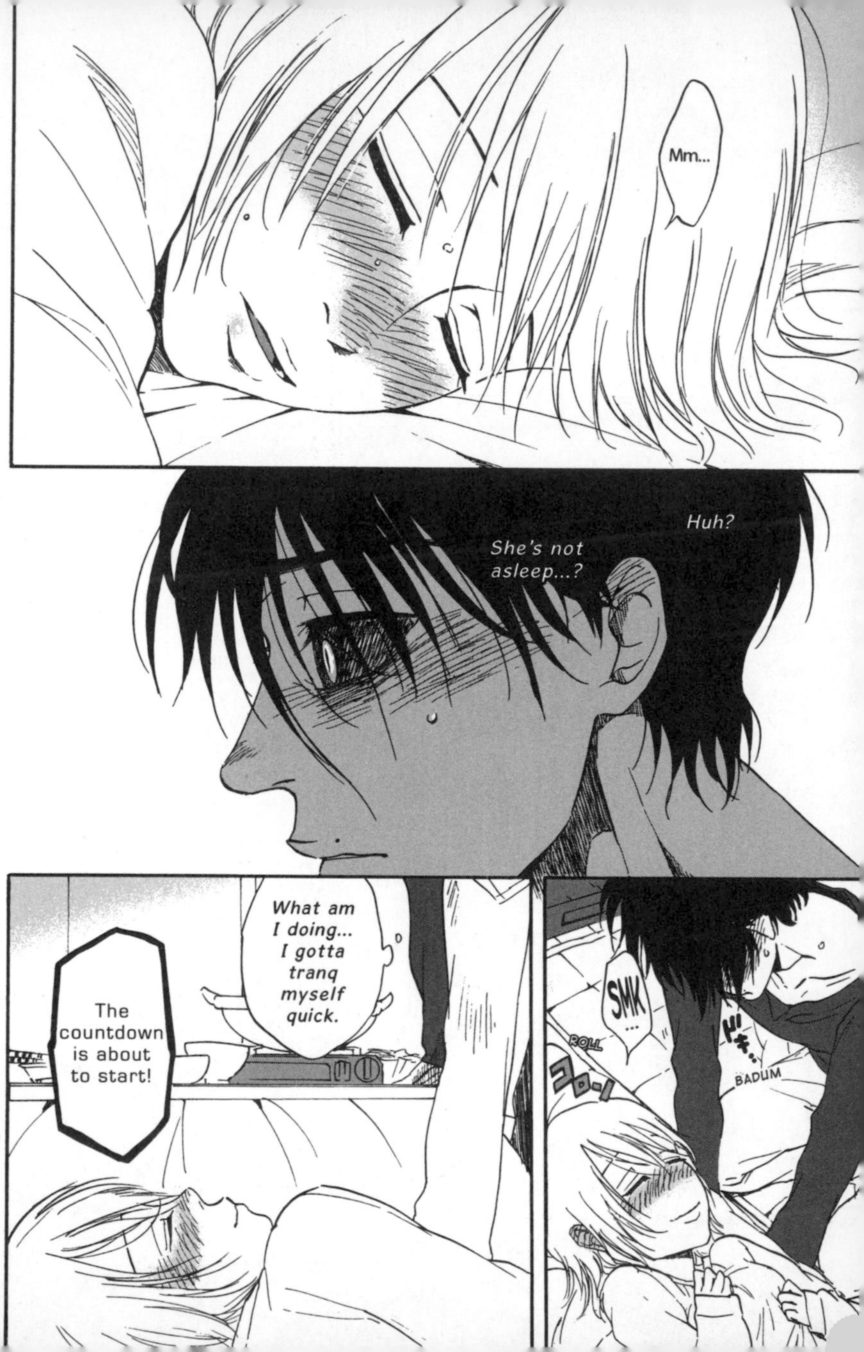
Mm...
Huh?
She's not asleep...?
SMK ...
ROLL
BADUM
What am I doing... I gotta tranq myself quick.
The countdown is about to start!

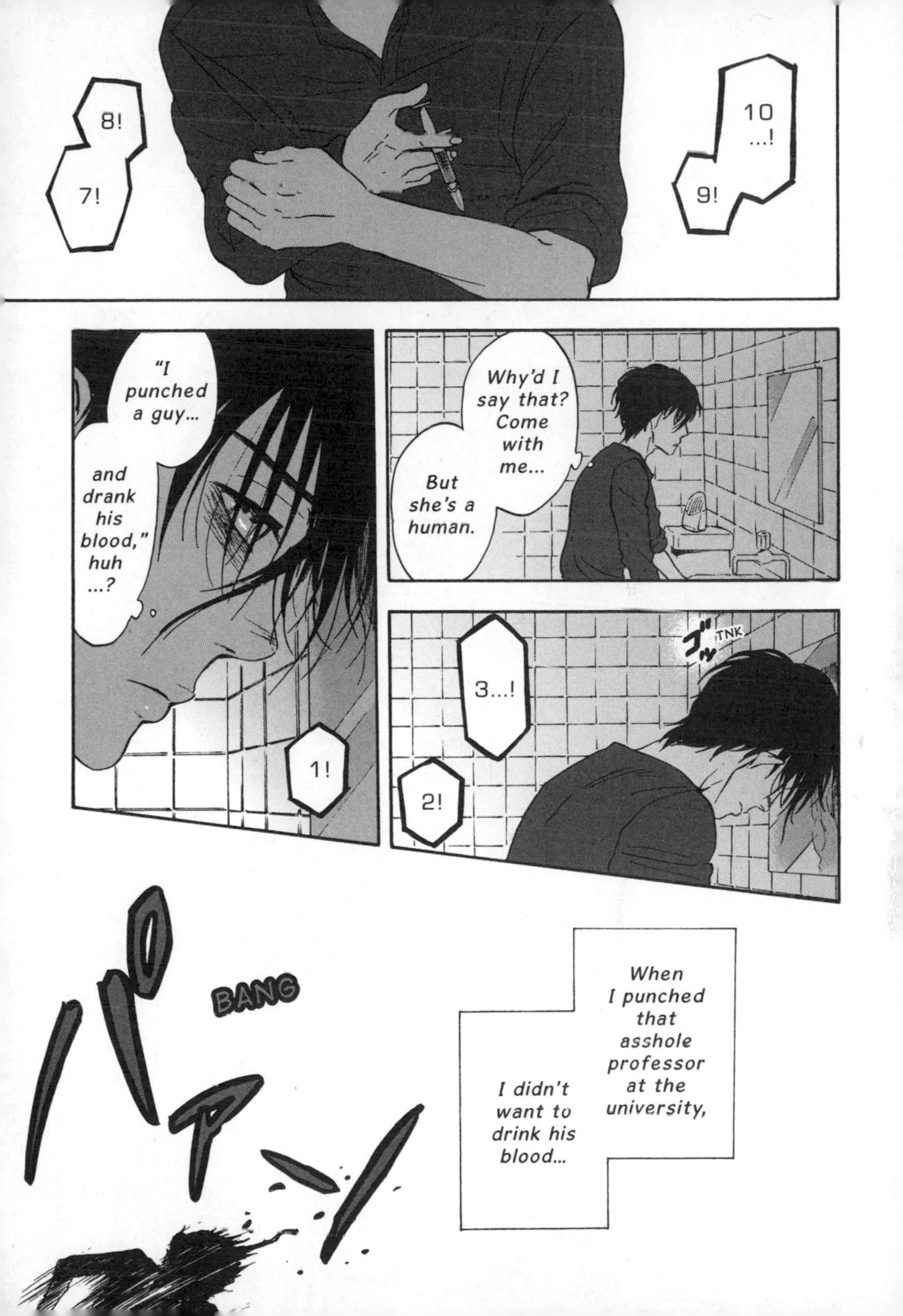
10 ...!
9!
8!
7!
Why'd I say that? Come with me...
But she's a human.
TNK
3...!
2!
"I punched a guy...
and drank his blood," huh ...?
1!
When I punched that asshole professor at the university,
I didn't want to drink his blood...
BANG

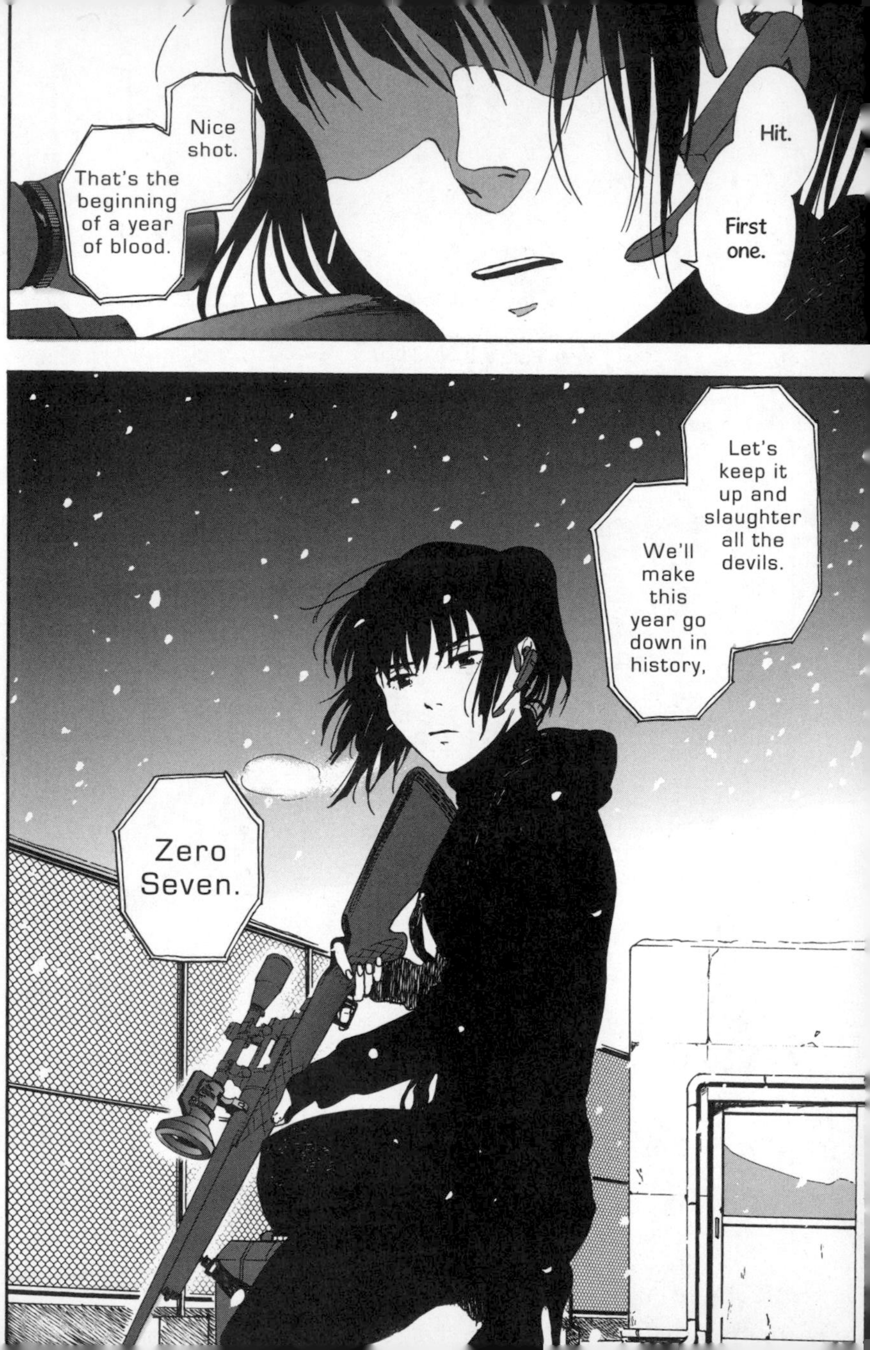
Hit.
First one.
Nice shot.
That's the beginning of a year of blood.
Let's keep it up and slaughter all the devils.
We'll make this year go down in history,
Zero Seven.

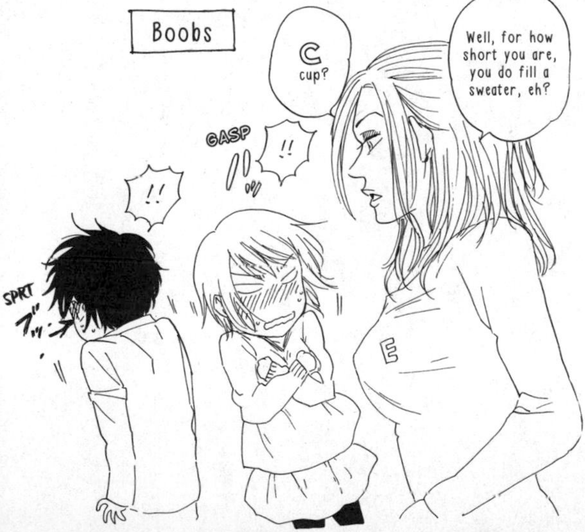
Boobs
Well, for how short you are, you do fill a sweater, eh?
C cup?
GASP
!!
!!
E
SPRT

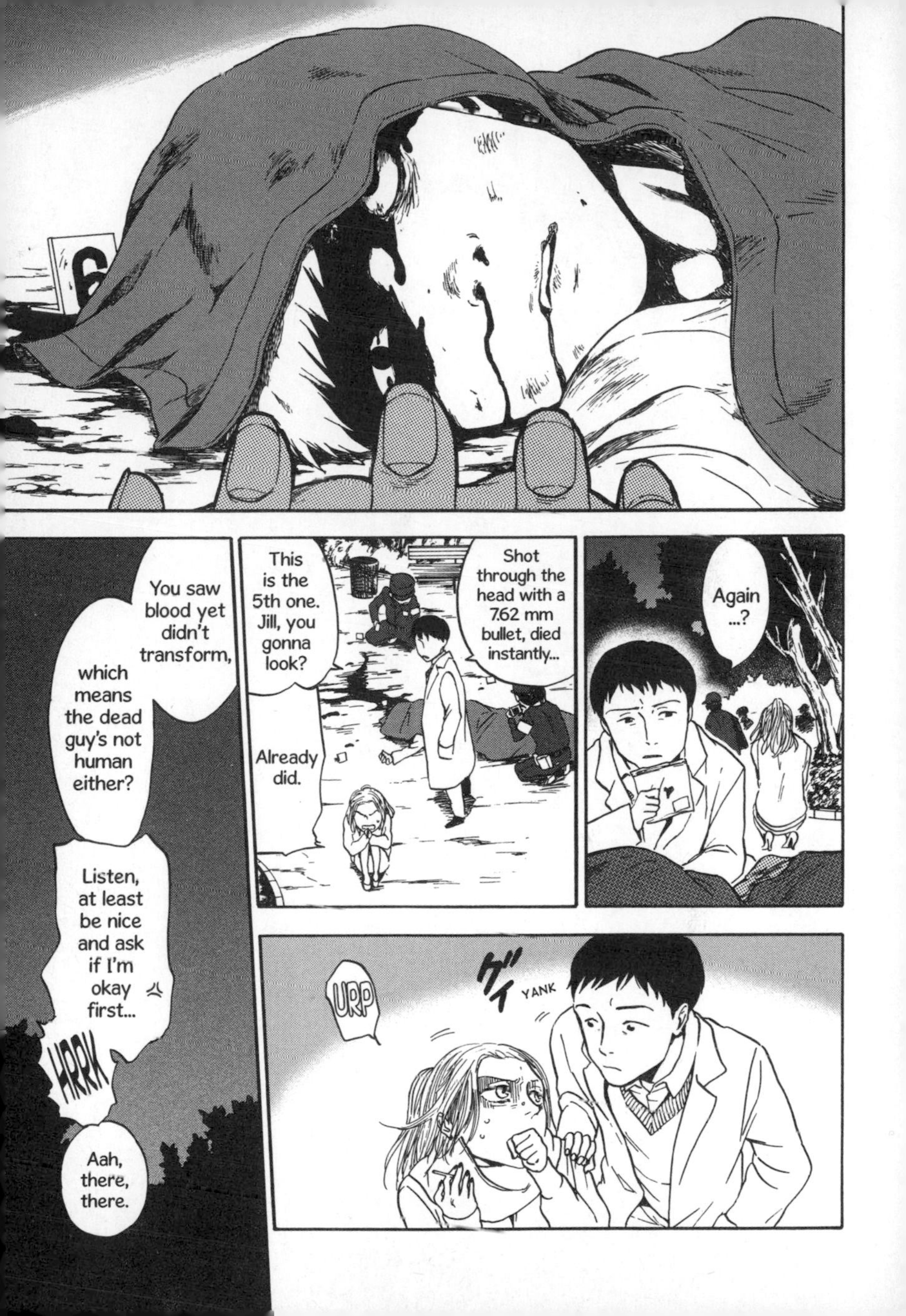
Again ...?
Shot through the head with a 7.62 mm bullet, died instantly...
This is the 5th one. Jill, you gonna look?
Already did.
URP
YANK
You saw blood yet didn't transform,
which means the dead guy's not human either?
Listen, at least be nice and ask if I'm okay first...
HRRK
Aah, there, there.

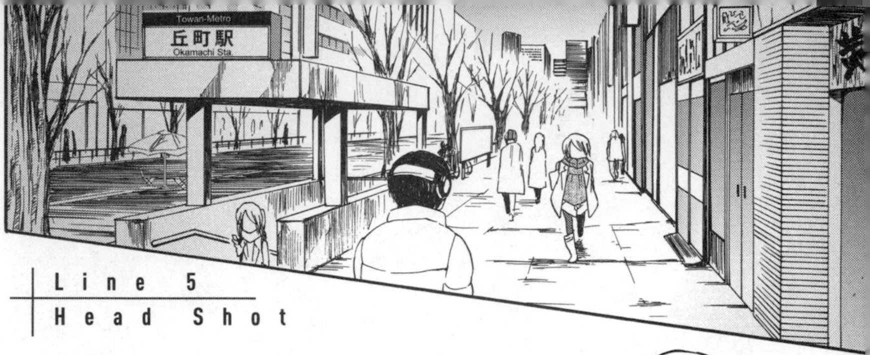
Towan-Metro
丘町駅
Okamachi Sta.

Line 5
Head Shot

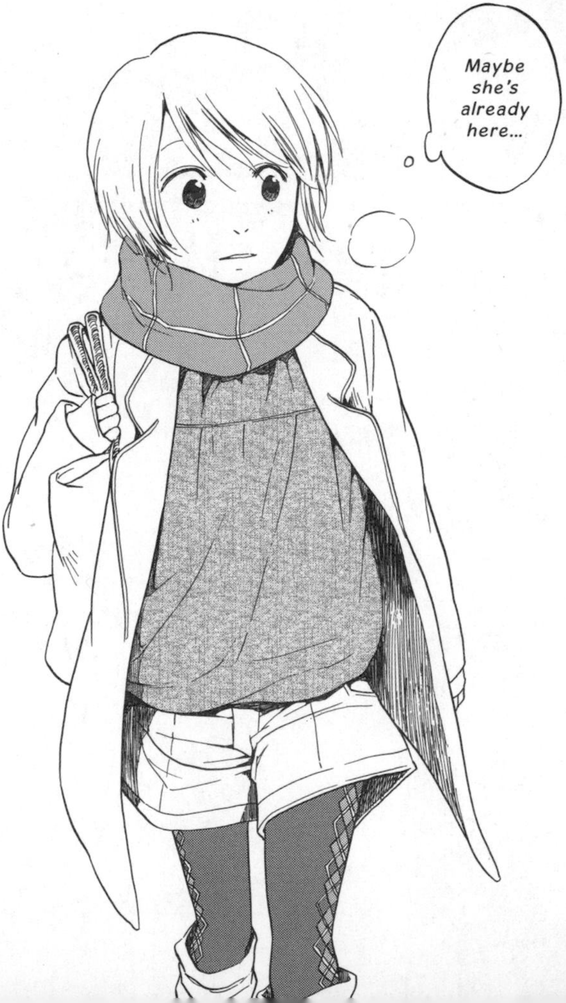
Maybe she's already here...

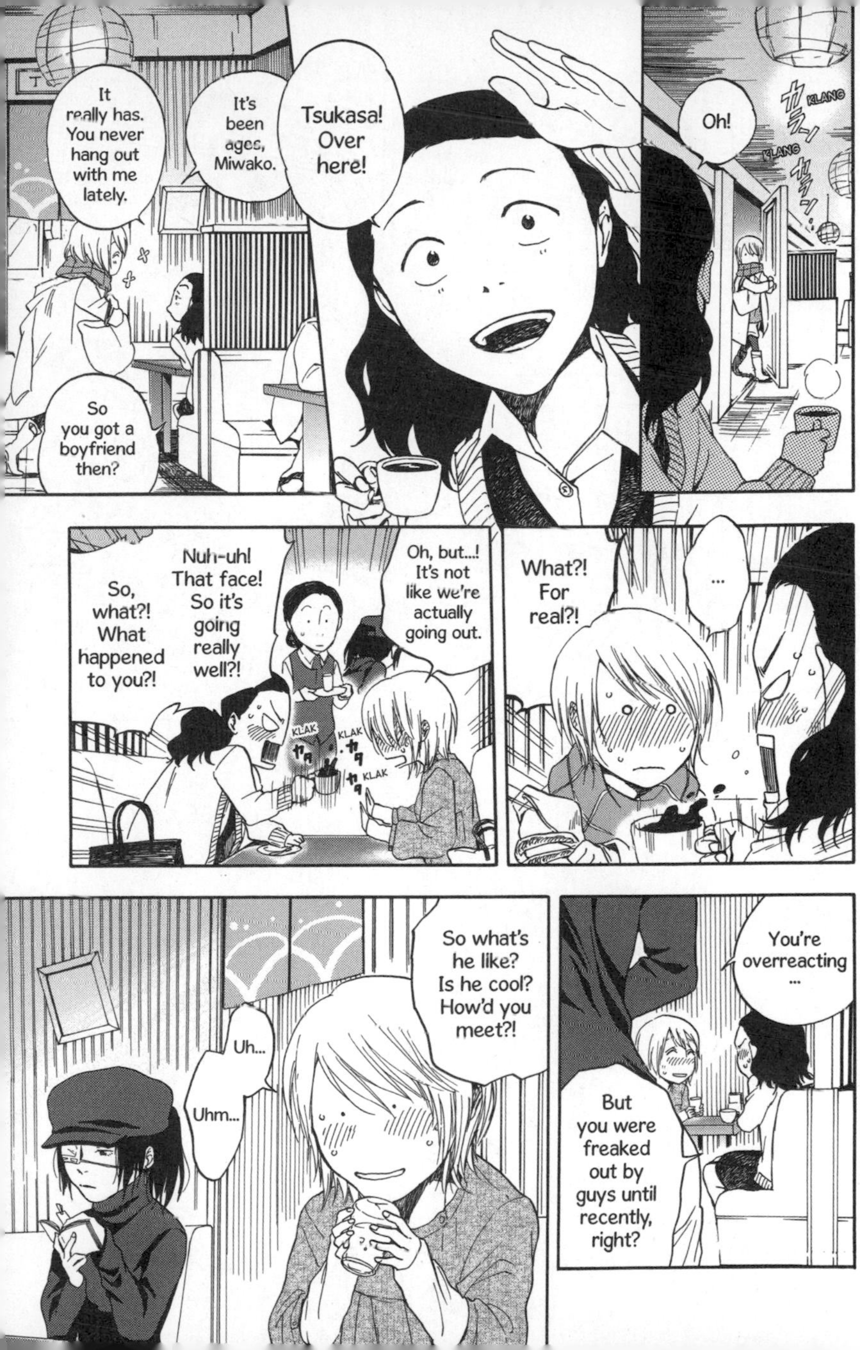
Oh!
KLANG
KLANG
Tsukasa! Over here!
It's been ages, Miwako.
It really has. You never hang out with me lately.
So you got a boyfriend then?
What?! For real?!
...
Oh, but...! It's not like we're actually going out.
Nuh-uh! That face! So it's going really well?!
So, what?! What happened to you?!
KLAK
KLAK
KLAK
You're overreacting ...
But you were freaked out by guys until recently, right?
So what's he like? Is he cool? How'd you meet?!
Uh...
Uhm...

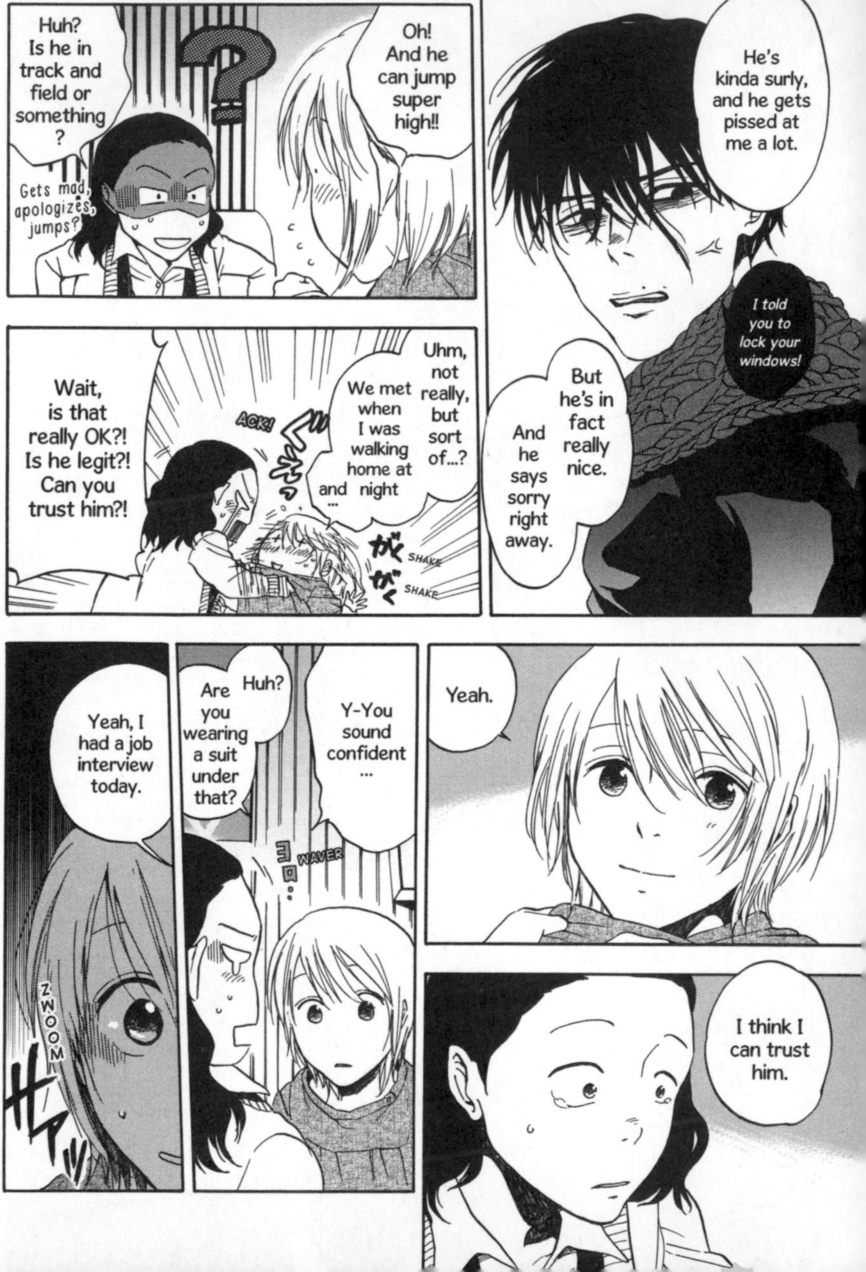
He's kinda surly, and he gets pissed at me a lot.
I told you to lock your windows!
But he's in fact really nice.
And he says sorry right away.
Oh! And he can jump super high!!
Huh? Is he in track and field or something?
Gets mad, apologizes, jumps?
Uhm, not really, but sort of...?
We met when I was walking home at night and ...
ACK!
Wait, is that really OK?! Is he legit?! Can you trust him?!
SHAKE
SHAKE
Yeah.
I think I can trust him.
Y-You sound confident ...
Huh?
Are you wearing a suit under that?
WAVER
Yeah, I had a job interview today.
ZWOOM

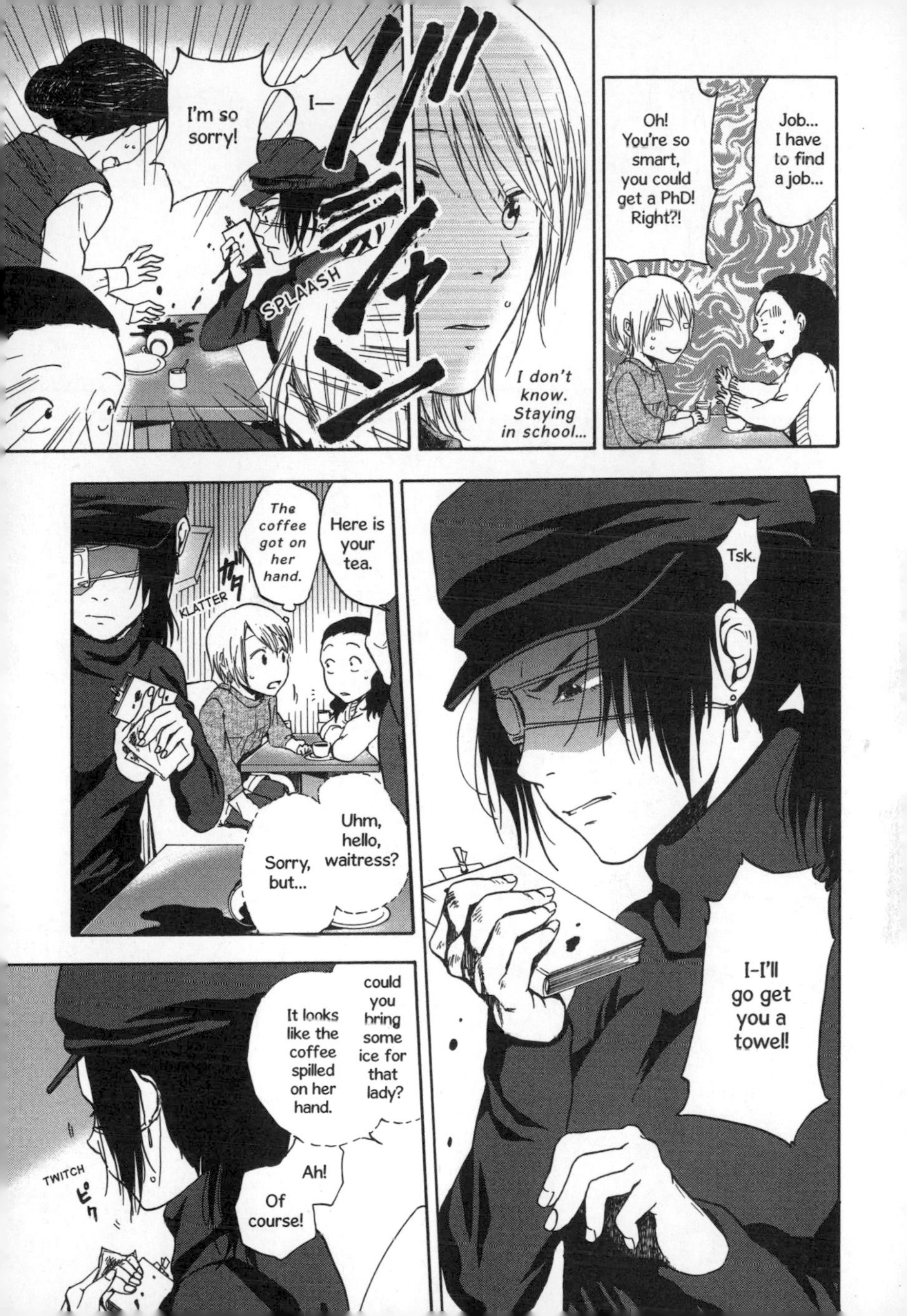
Job... I have to find a job...
Oh! You're so smart, you could get a PhD! Right?!
I don't know. Staying in school...
I—
I'm so sorry!
SPLAASH
Tsk.
I-I'll go get you a towel!
Here is your tea.
The coffee got on her hand.
KLATTER
Uhm, hello, waitress?
Sorry, but...
could you bring some ice for that lady?
It looks like the coffee spilled on her hand.
Ah!
Of course!
TWITCH

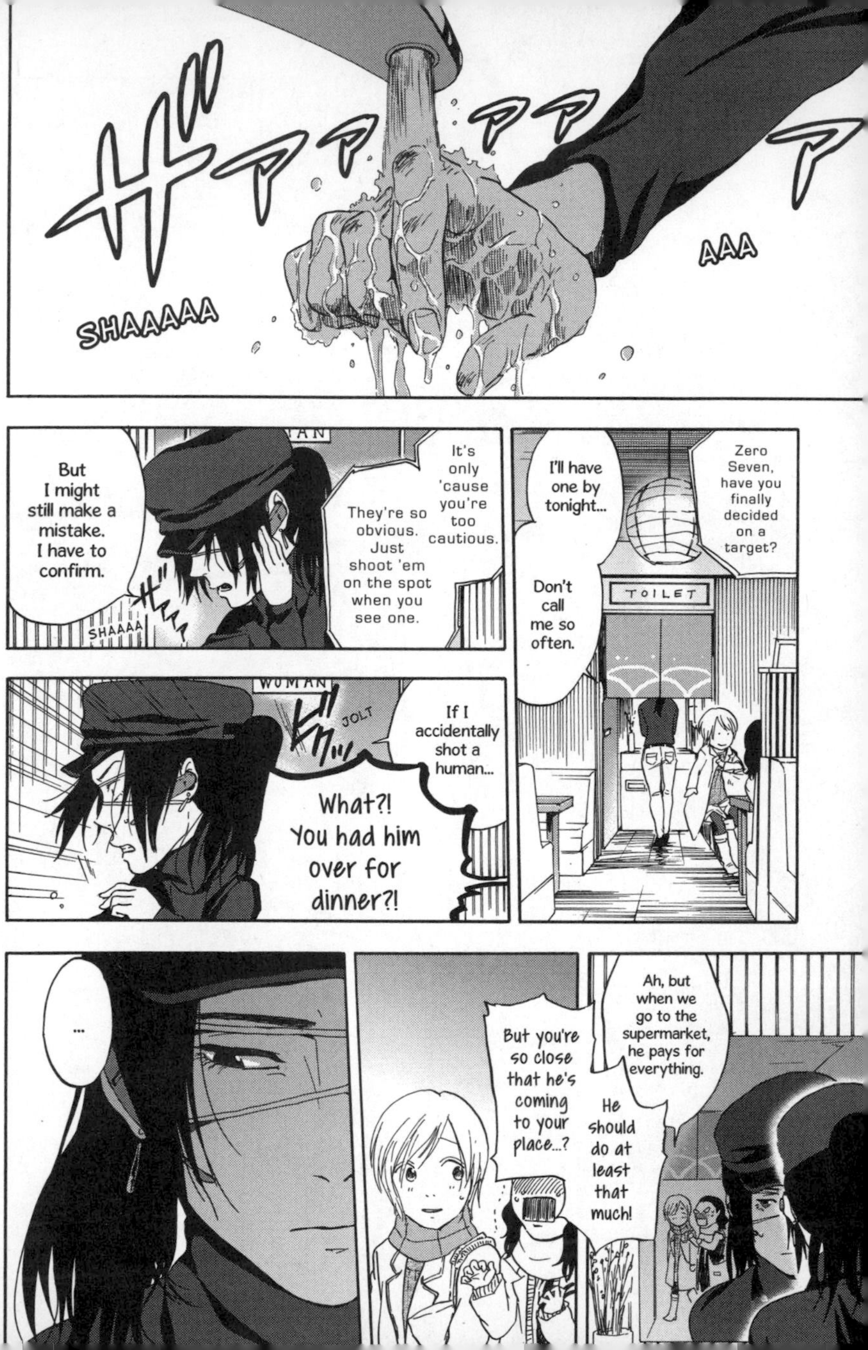
SHAAAAA
AAA
Zero Seven, have you finally decided on a target?
I'll have one by tonight...
Don't call me so often.
TOILET
It's only 'cause you're too cautious.
They're so obvious. Just shoot 'em on the spot when you see one.
But I might still make a mistake. I have to confirm.
SHAAAA
JOLT
If I accidentally shot a human...
What?! You had him over for dinner?!
Ah, but when we go to the supermarket, he pays for everything.
But you're so close that he's coming to your place...?
He should do at least that much!
...

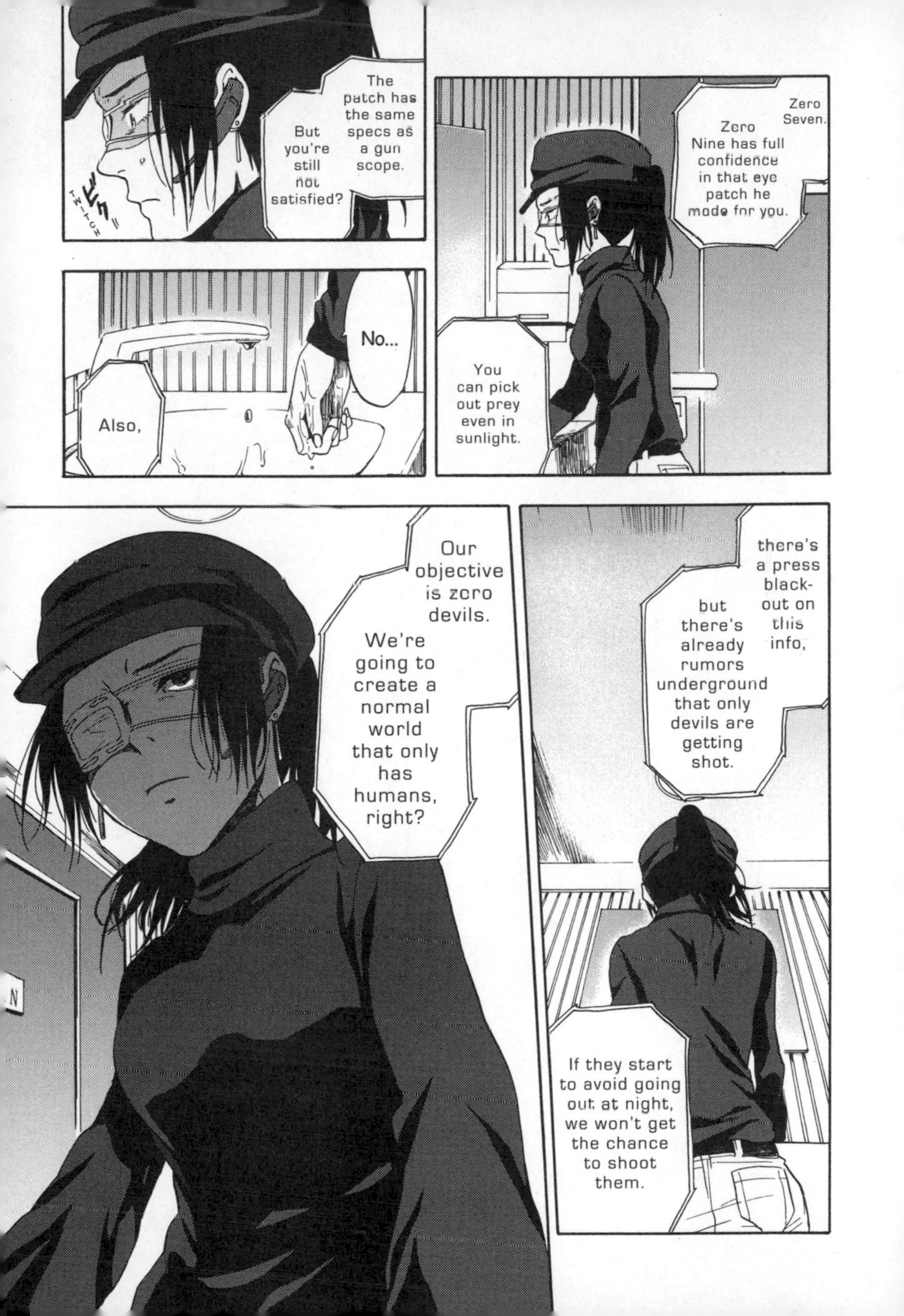
Zero Seven.
Zero Nine has full confidence in that eye patch he made for you.
You can pick out prey even in sunlight.
The patch has the same specs as a gun scope.
But you're still not satisfied?
ビク
TWITCH
No...
Also,
there's a press black-out on this info,
but there's already rumors underground that only devils are getting shot.
If they start to avoid going out at night, we won't get the chance to shoot them.
Our objective is zero devils.
We're going to create a normal world that only has humans, right?

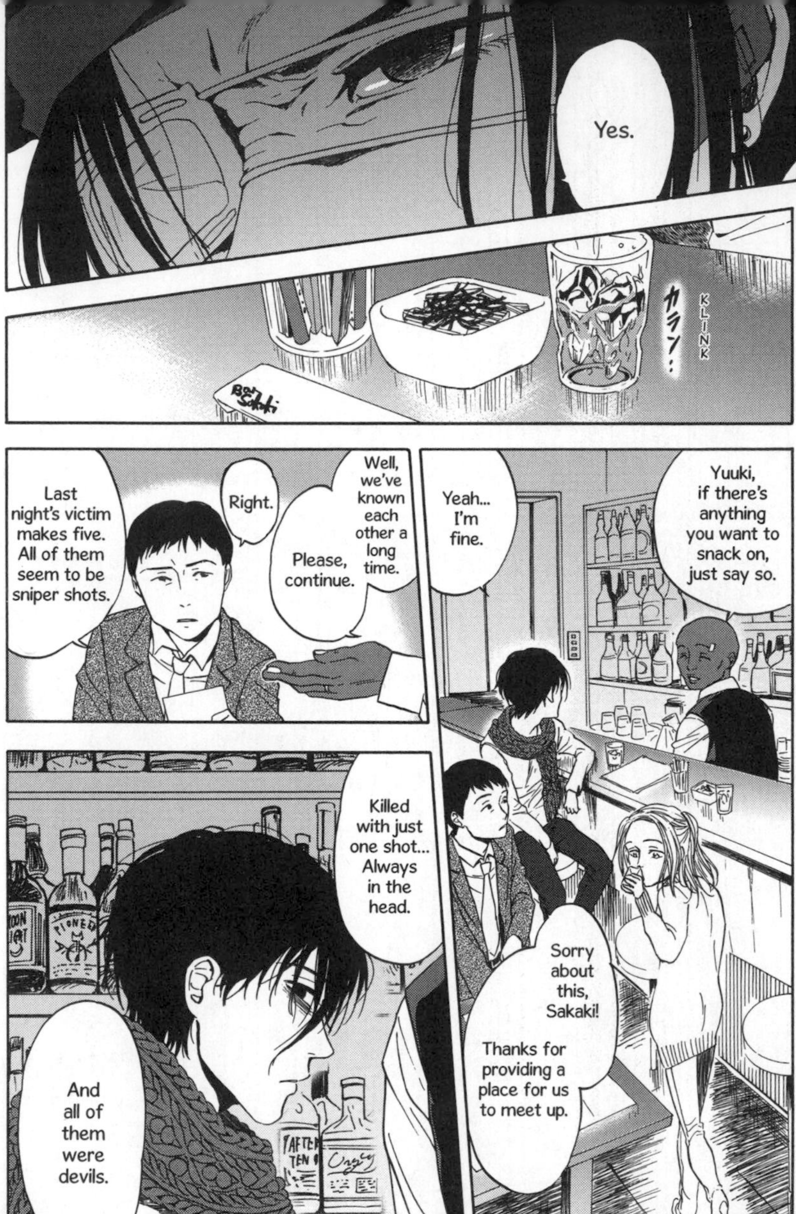
Yes.
カラン…
KLINK
Bar Sakaki
Yuuki, if there's anything you want to snack on, just say so.
Yeah... I'm fine.
Sorry about this, Sakaki!
Thanks for providing a place for us to meet up.
Well, we've known each other a long time.
Right.
Please, continue.
Last night's victim makes five. All of them seem to be sniper shots.
Killed with just one shot... Always in the head.
And all of them were devils.

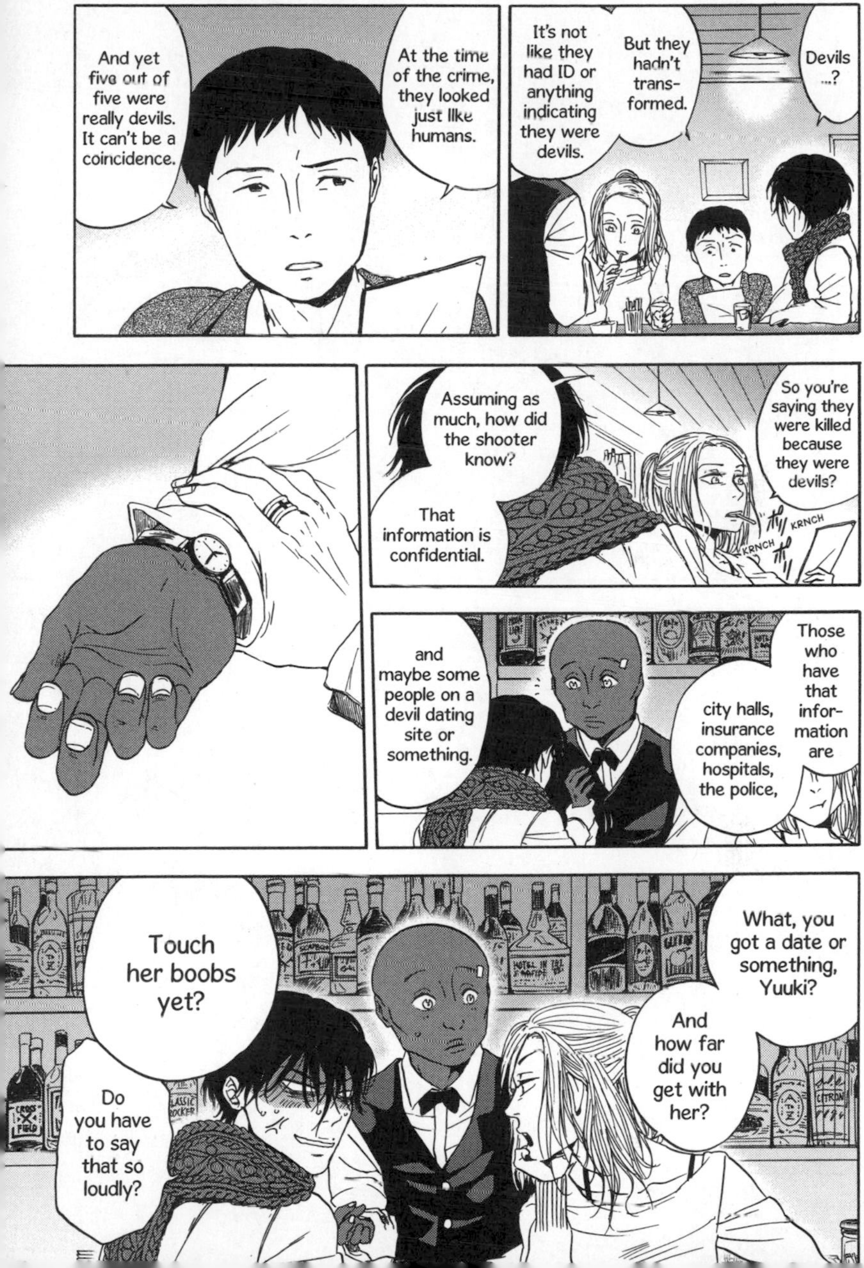
Devils ...?
But they hadn't trans-formed.
It's not like they had ID or anything indicating they were devils.
At the time of the crime, they looked just like humans.
And yet five out of five were really devils. It can't be a coincidence.
So you're saying they were killed because they were devils?
KRNCH
KRNCH
Assuming as much, how did the shooter know?
That information is confidential.
Those who have that infor-mation are
city halls, insurance companies, hospitals, the police,
and maybe some people on a devil dating site or something.
What, you got a date or something, Yuuki?
And how far did you get with her?
Touch her boobs yet?
Do you have to say that so loudly?

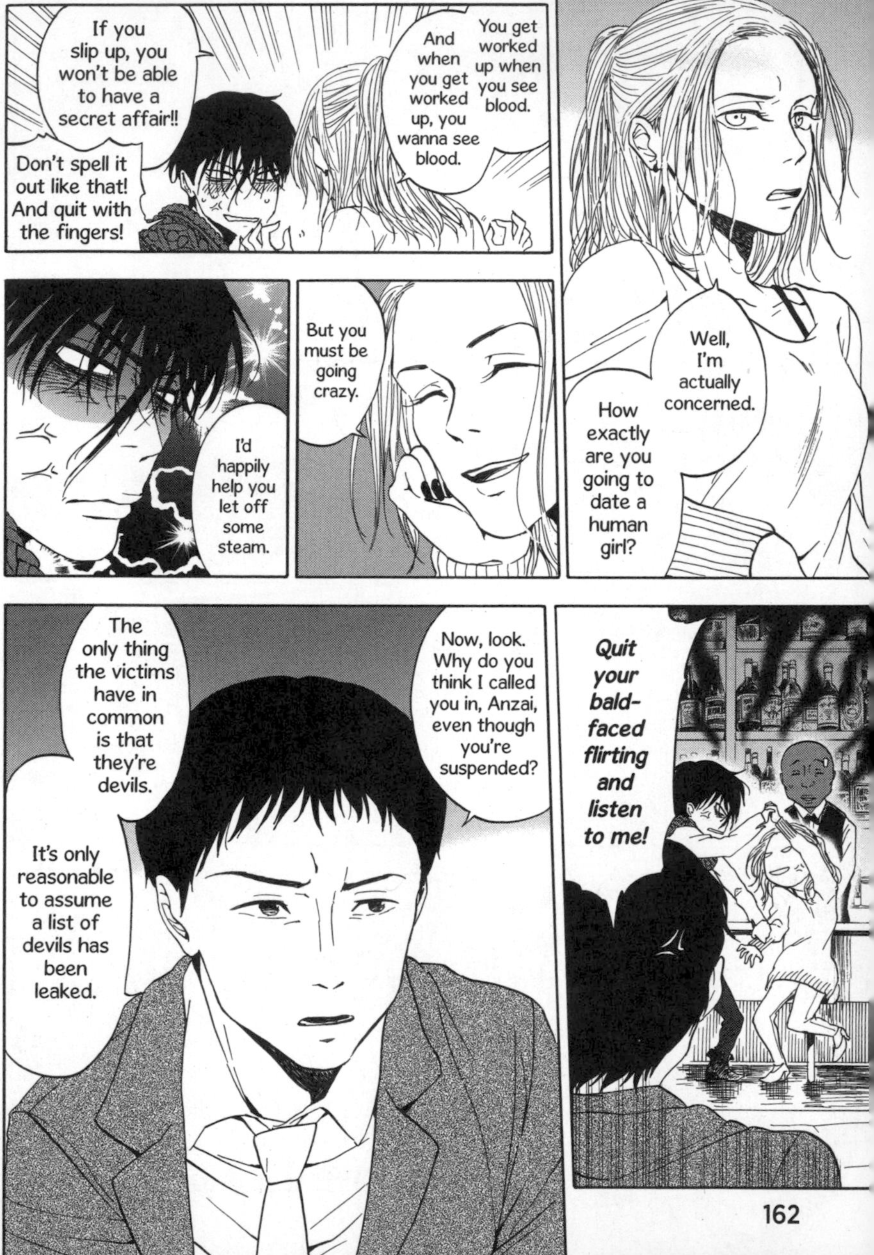
Well, I'm actually concerned.
How exactly are you going to date a human girl?
You get worked up when you see blood.
And when you get worked up, you wanna see blood.
If you slip up, you won't be able to have a secret affair!!
Don't spell it out like that! And quit with the fingers!
But you must be going crazy.
I'd happily help you let off some steam.
Quit your bald-faced flirting and listen to me!
Now, look. Why do you think I called you in, Anzai, even though you're suspended?
The only thing the victims have in common is that they're devils.
It's only reasonable to assume a list of devils has been leaked.

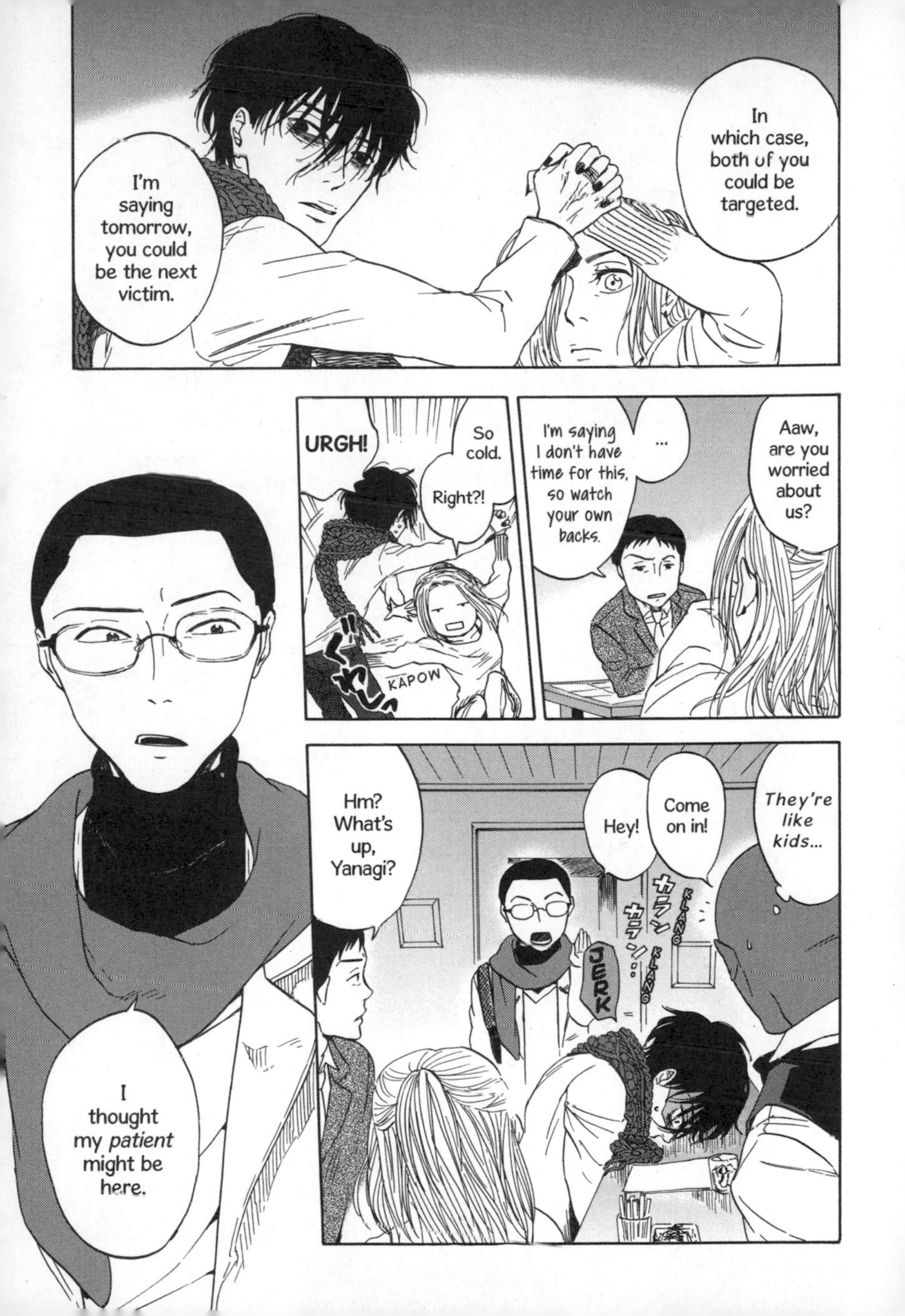
In which case, both of you could be targeted.
I'm saying tomorrow, you could be the next victim.
Aaw, are you worried about us?
...
I'm saying I don't have time for this, so watch your own backs.
So cold.
Right?!
URGH!
KAPOW
They're like kids...
Come on in!
Hey!
カラン
KLANG
カラン
KLANG
Hm? What's up, Yanagi?
JERK
I thought my *patient* might be here.

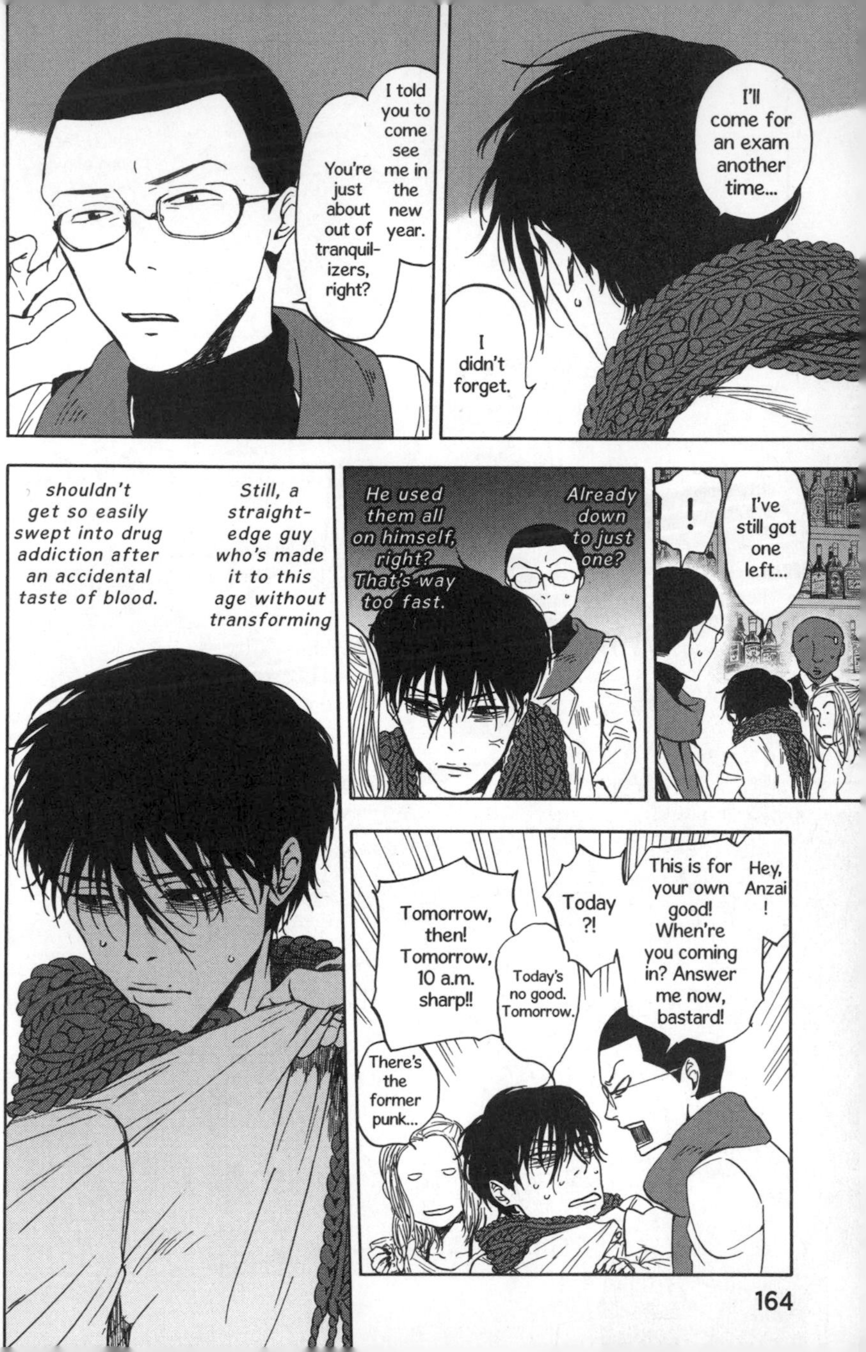

I'll come for an exam another time...
I didn't forget.
I told you to come see me in the new year.
You're just about out of tranquilizers, right?
!
I've still got one left...
Already down to just one?
He used them all on himself, right? That's way too fast.
Hey, Anzai!
This is for your own good! When're you coming in? Answer me now, bastard!
Today?!
Today's no good. Tomorrow.
Tomorrow, then! Tomorrow, 10 a.m. sharp!!
There's the former punk...
Still, a straight-edge guy who's made it to this age without transforming
shouldn't get so easily swept into drug addiction after an accidental taste of blood.

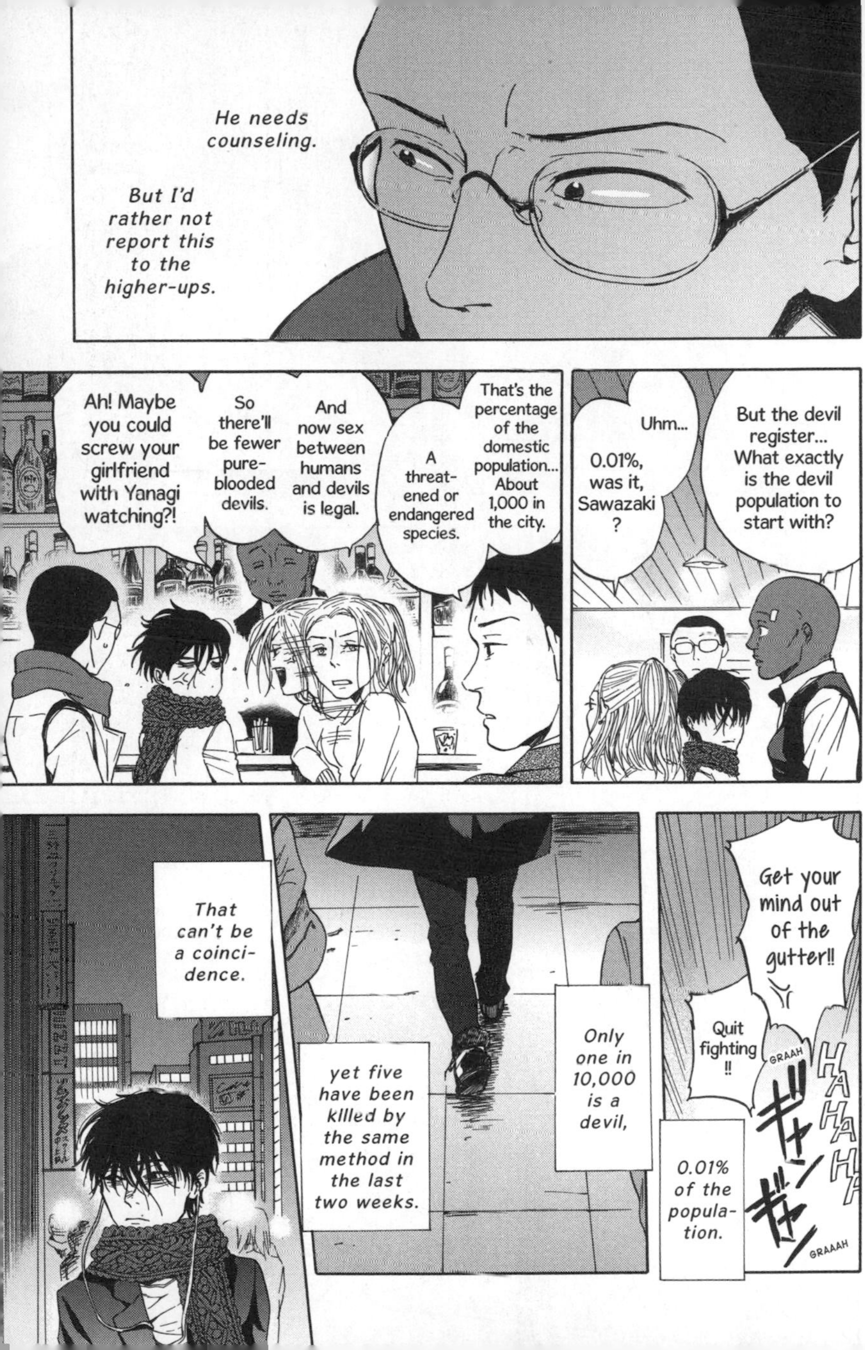
He needs counseling.
But I'd rather not report this to the higher-ups.
But the devil register... What exactly is the devil population to start with?
Uhm...
0.01%, was it, Sawazaki?
That's the percentage of the domestic population... About 1,000 in the city.
A threatened or endangered species.
And now sex between humans and devils is legal.
So there'll be fewer pure-blooded devils.
Ah! Maybe you could screw your girlfriend with Yanagi watching?!
Get your mind out of the gutter!!
Quit fighting!!
GRAAH
HAHAHAHA
GRAAAH
0.01% of the population.
Only one in 10,000 is a devil,
yet five have been killed by the same method in the last two weeks.
That can't be a coincidence.

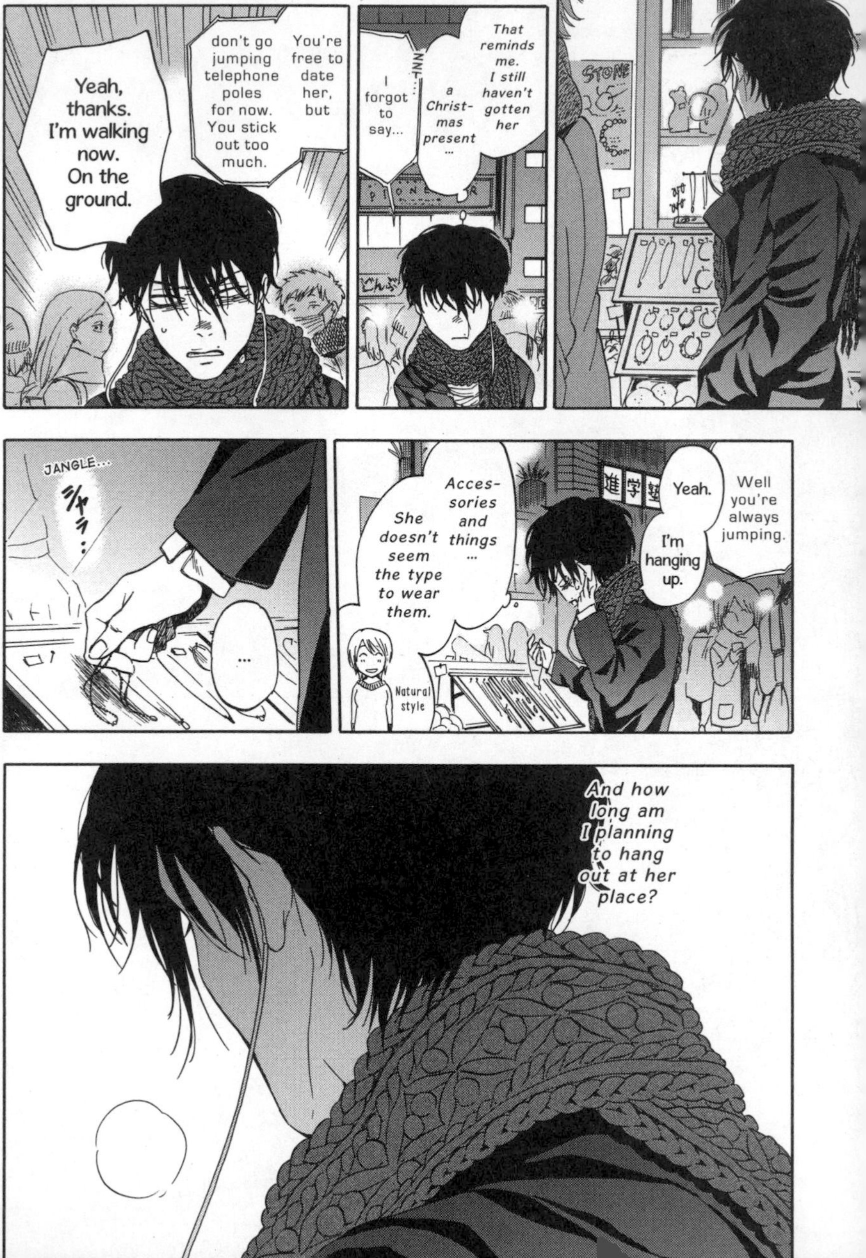

STONE
That reminds me. I still haven't gotten her
a Christmas present ...
I forgot to say...
You're free to date her, but
don't go jumping telephone poles for now. You stick out too much.
Yeah, thanks. I'm walking now. On the ground.
Well you're always jumping.
Yeah.
I'm hanging up.
Accessories and things ...
She doesn't seem the type to wear them.
Natural style
JANGLE...
シャラ・・
...
And how long am I planning to hang out at her place?

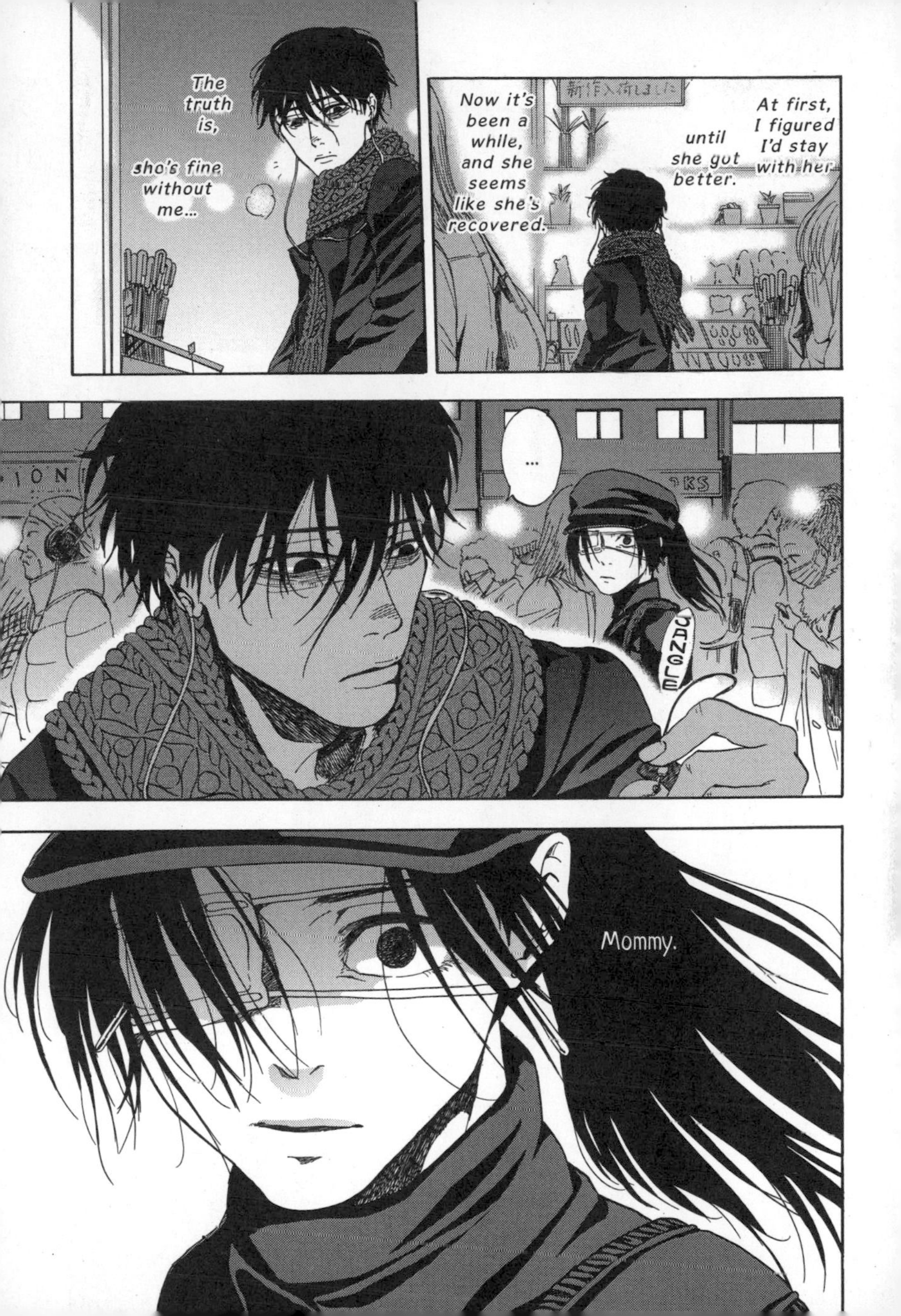
At first, I figured I'd stay with her
until she got better.
新作入荷しました
Now it's been a while, and she seems like she's recovered.
The truth is,
she's fine without me...
...
JANGLE
Mommy.

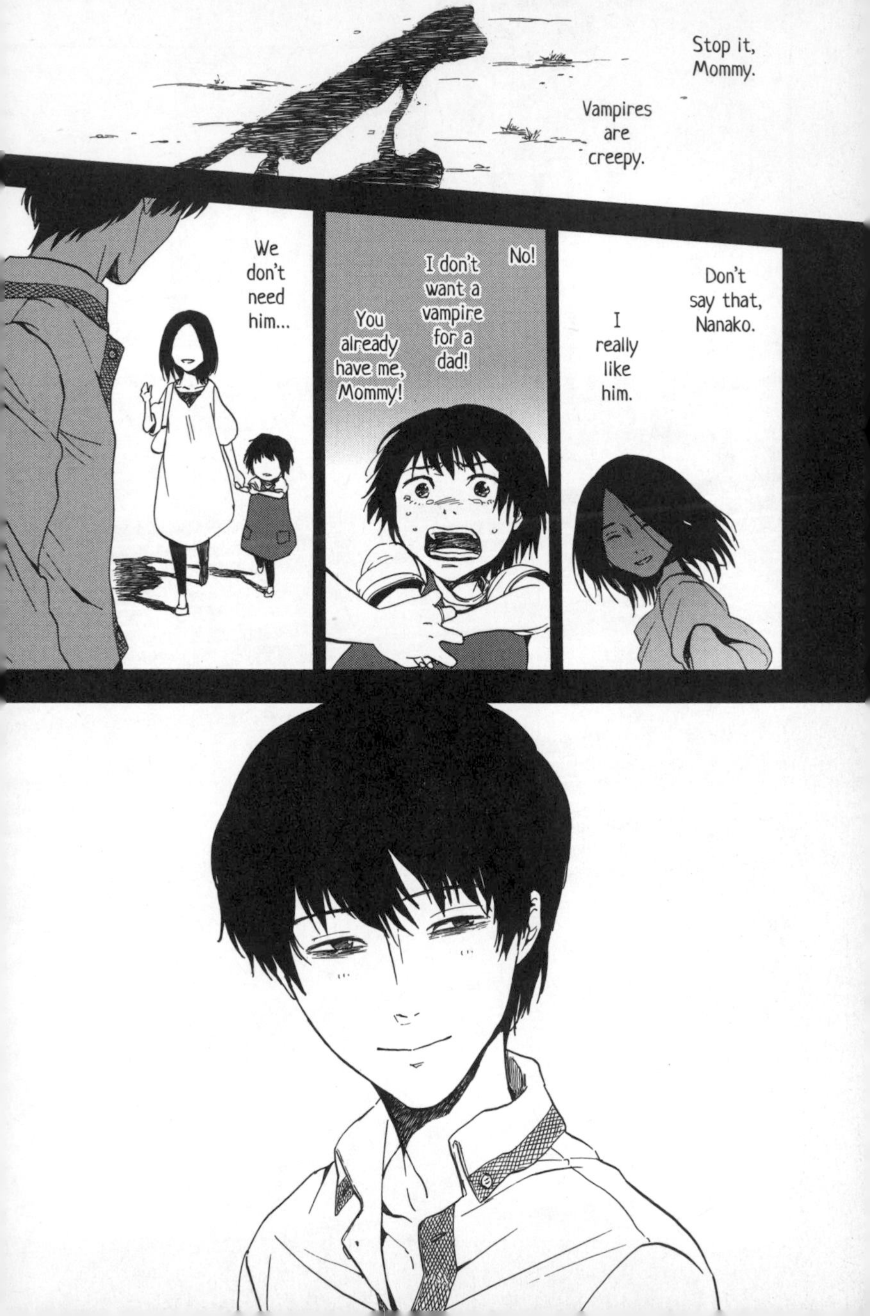
Stop it, Mommy.
Vampires are creepy.
Don't say that, Nanako.
I really like him.
No!
I don't want a vampire for a dad!
You already have me, Mommy!
We don't need him...

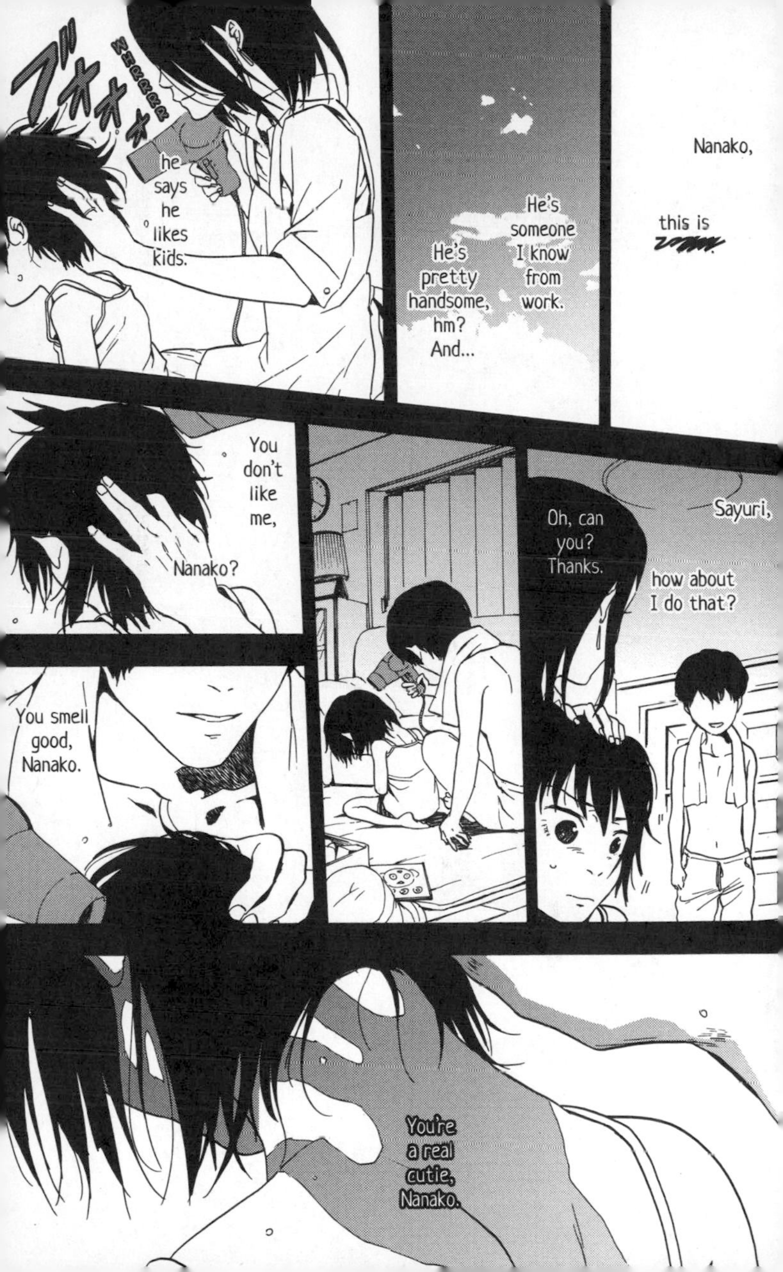
Nanako,
this is
He's someone I know from work.
He's pretty handsome, hm? And...
ブオオオ
WHRRRR
he says he likes kids.
Sayuri,
how about I do that?
Oh, can you? Thanks.
You don't like me,
Nanako?
You smell good, Nanako.
You're a real cutie, Nanako.

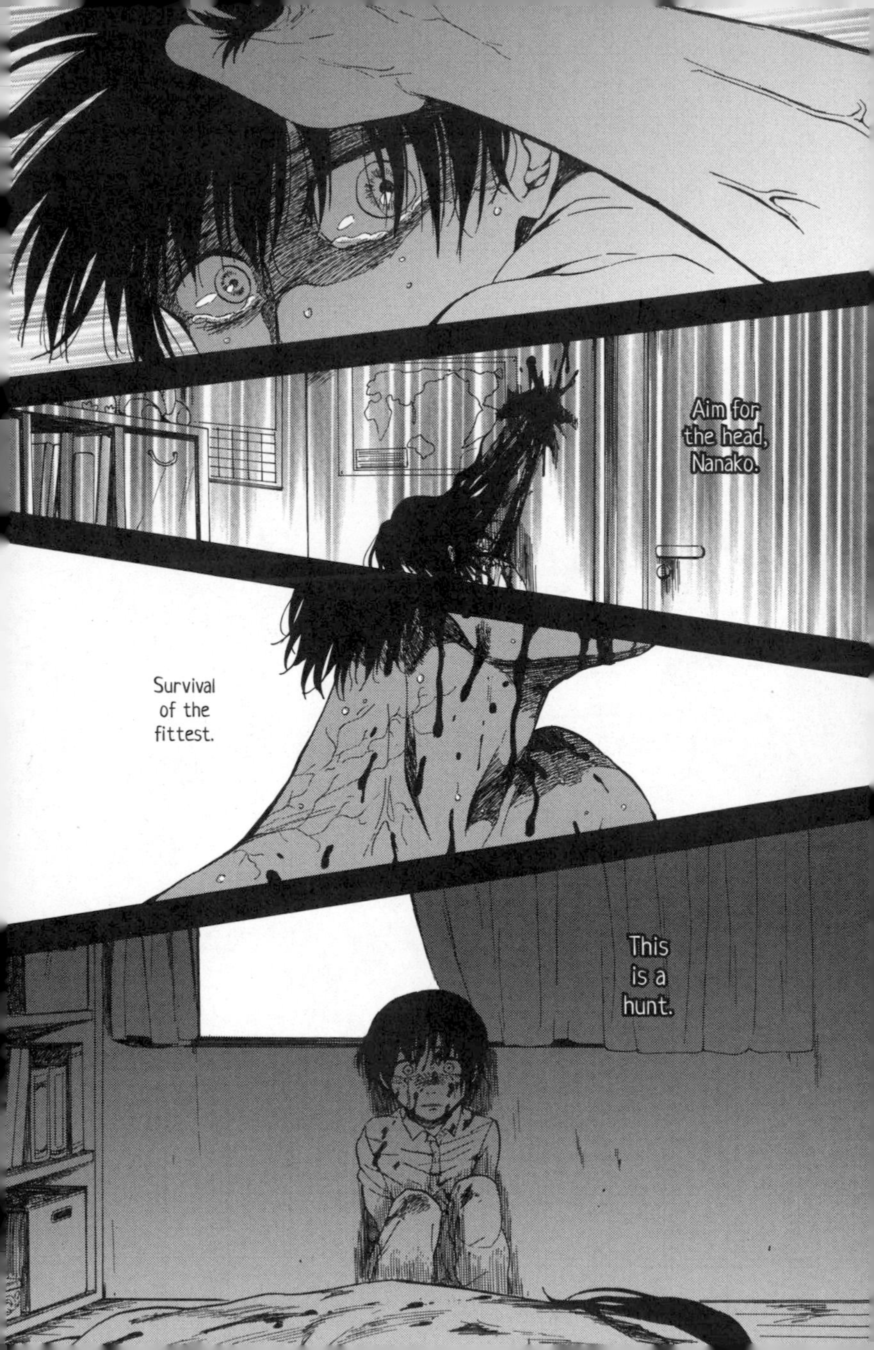
Aim for the head, Nanako.
Survival of the fittest.
This is a hunt.

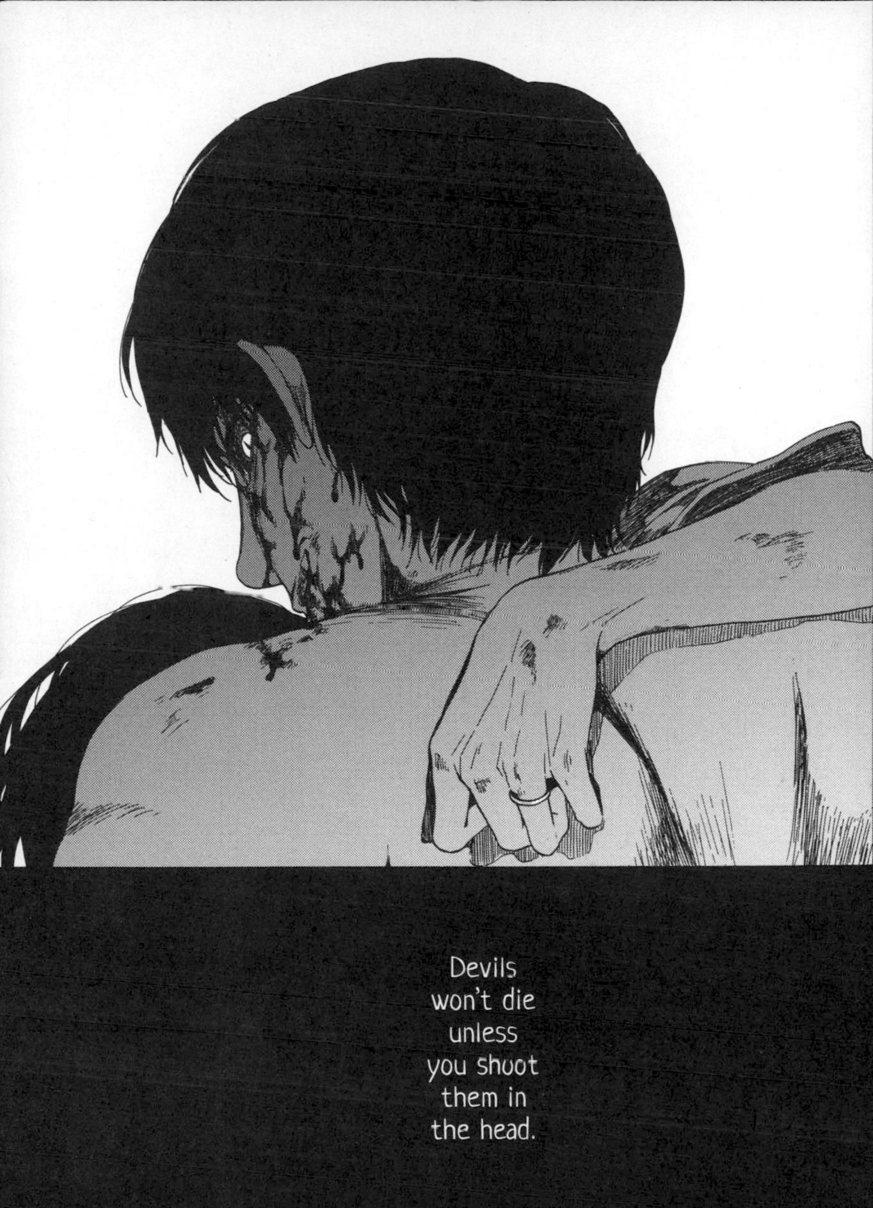
Devils won't die unless you shoot them in the head.

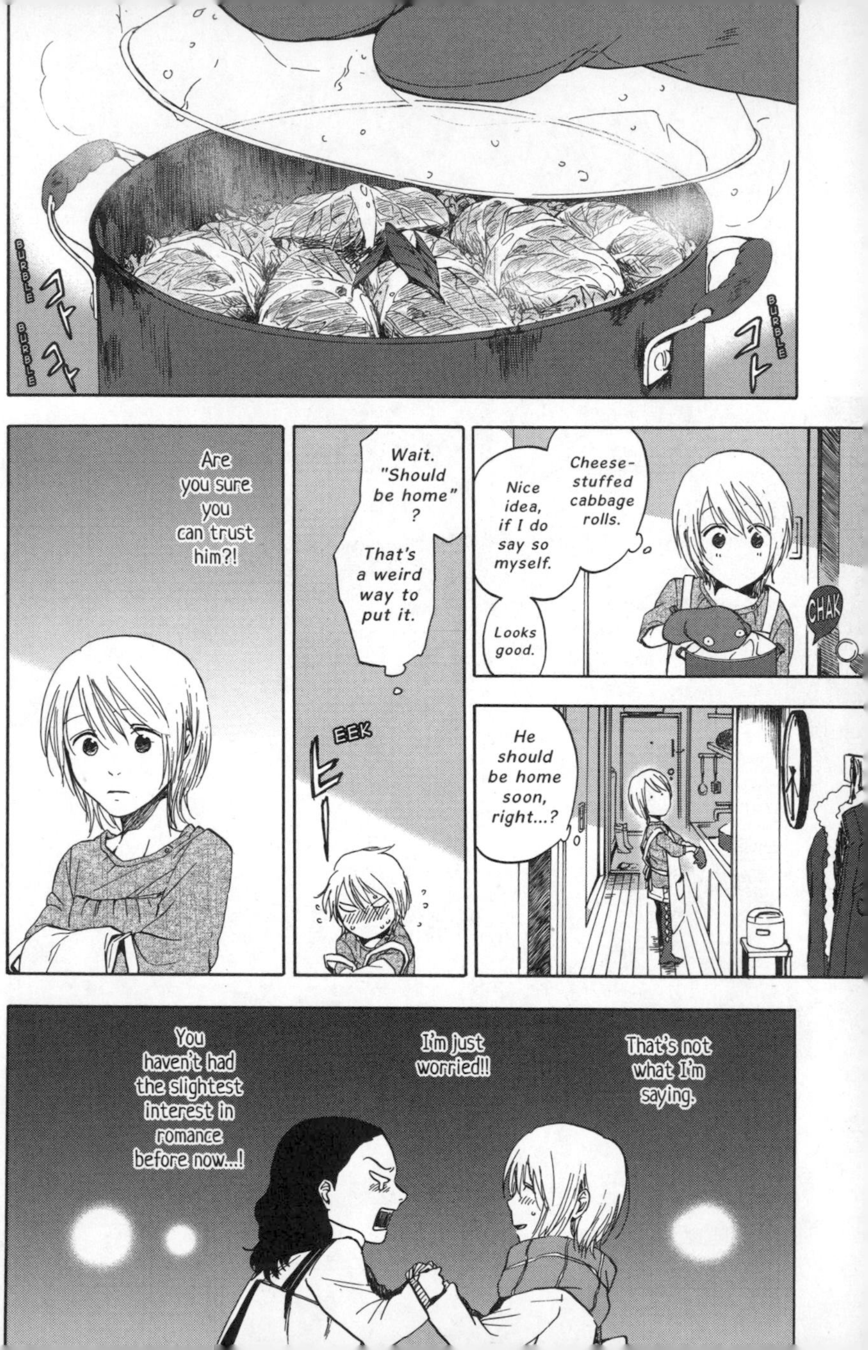
BURBLE
コト
BURBLE
BURBLE
コトコト
CHAK
Cheese-stuffed cabbage rolls.
Nice idea, if I do say so myself.
Looks good.
He should be home soon, right...?
Wait. "Should be home"?
That's a weird way to put it.
EEK
Are you sure you can trust him?!
That's not what I'm saying.
I'm just worried!!
You haven't had the slightest interest in romance before now...!

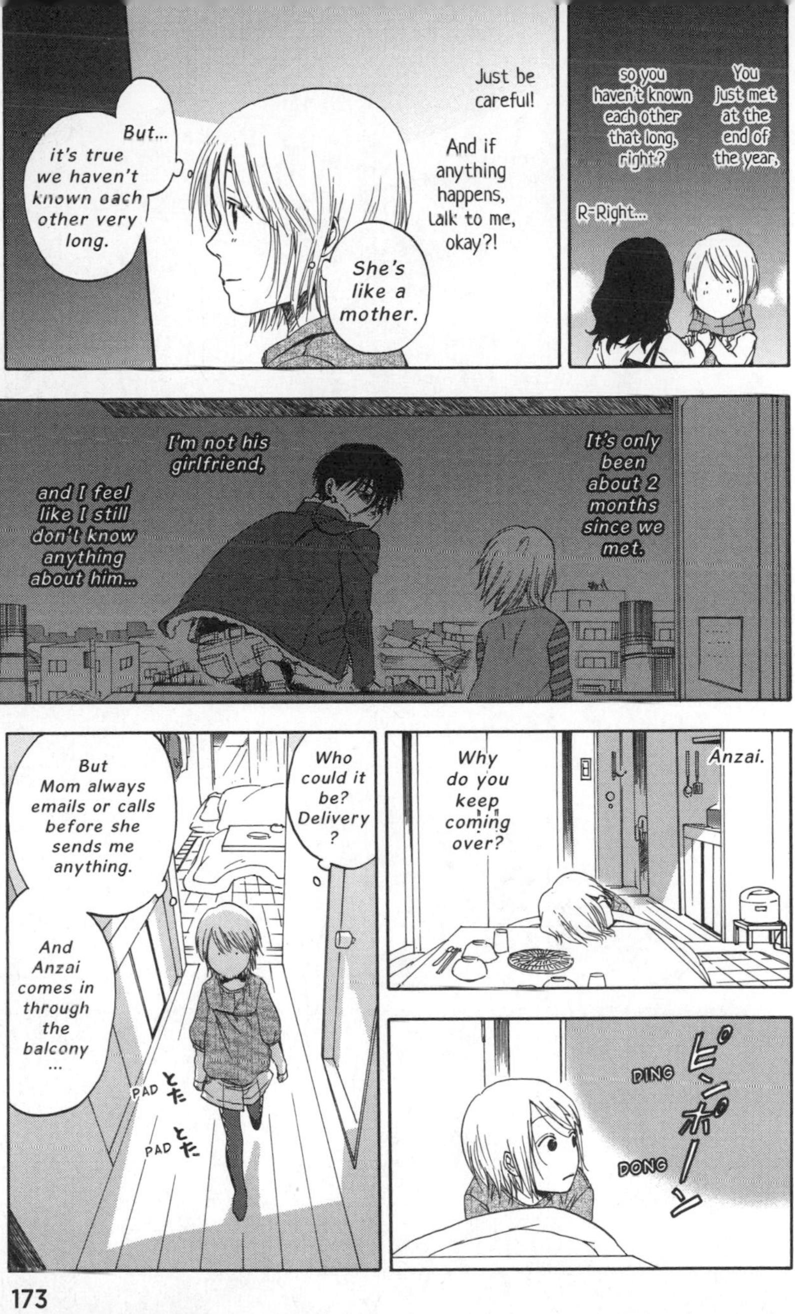
You just met at the end of the year,
so you haven't known each other that long, right?
R-Right...
Just be careful!
And if anything happens, talk to me, okay?!
But... it's true we haven't known each other very long.
She's like a mother.
It's only been about 2 months since we met.
I'm not his girlfriend,
and I feel like I still don't know anything about him...
Anzai.
Why do you keep coming over?
DING
ピンポーン
DONG
Who could it be? Delivery?
But Mom always emails or calls before she sends me anything.
And Anzai comes in through the balcony...
PAD とた
PAD とた

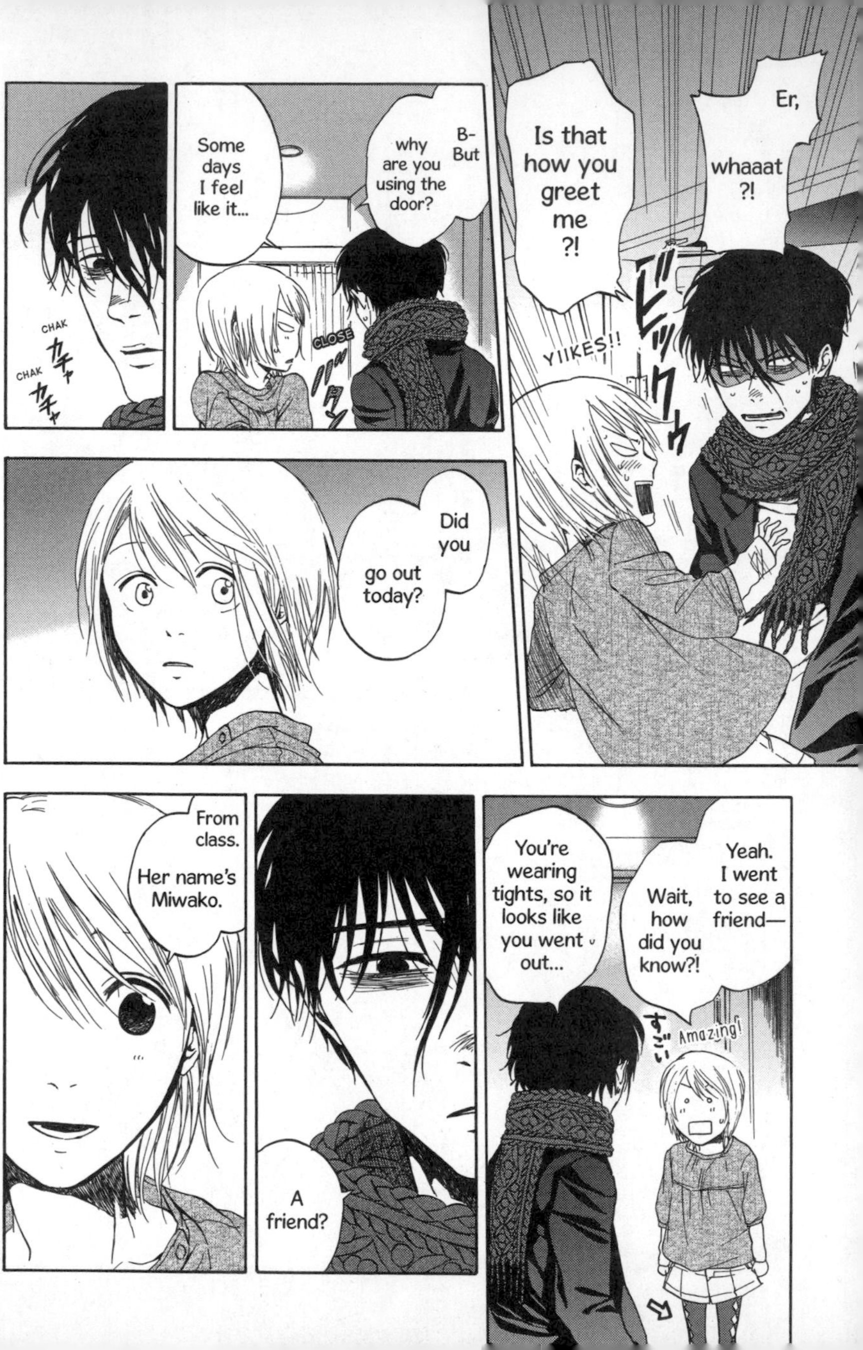
Er, whaaat?!
Is that how you greet me?!
ビックゥ
YIIKES!!
B-But why are you using the door?
CLOSE
Some days I feel like it...
CHAK カチャ
CHAK カチャ
Did you go out today?
Yeah. I went to see a friend—
Wait, how did you know?!
You're wearing tights, so it looks like you went out...
すごい
Amazing!
A friend?
From class.
Her name's Miwako.

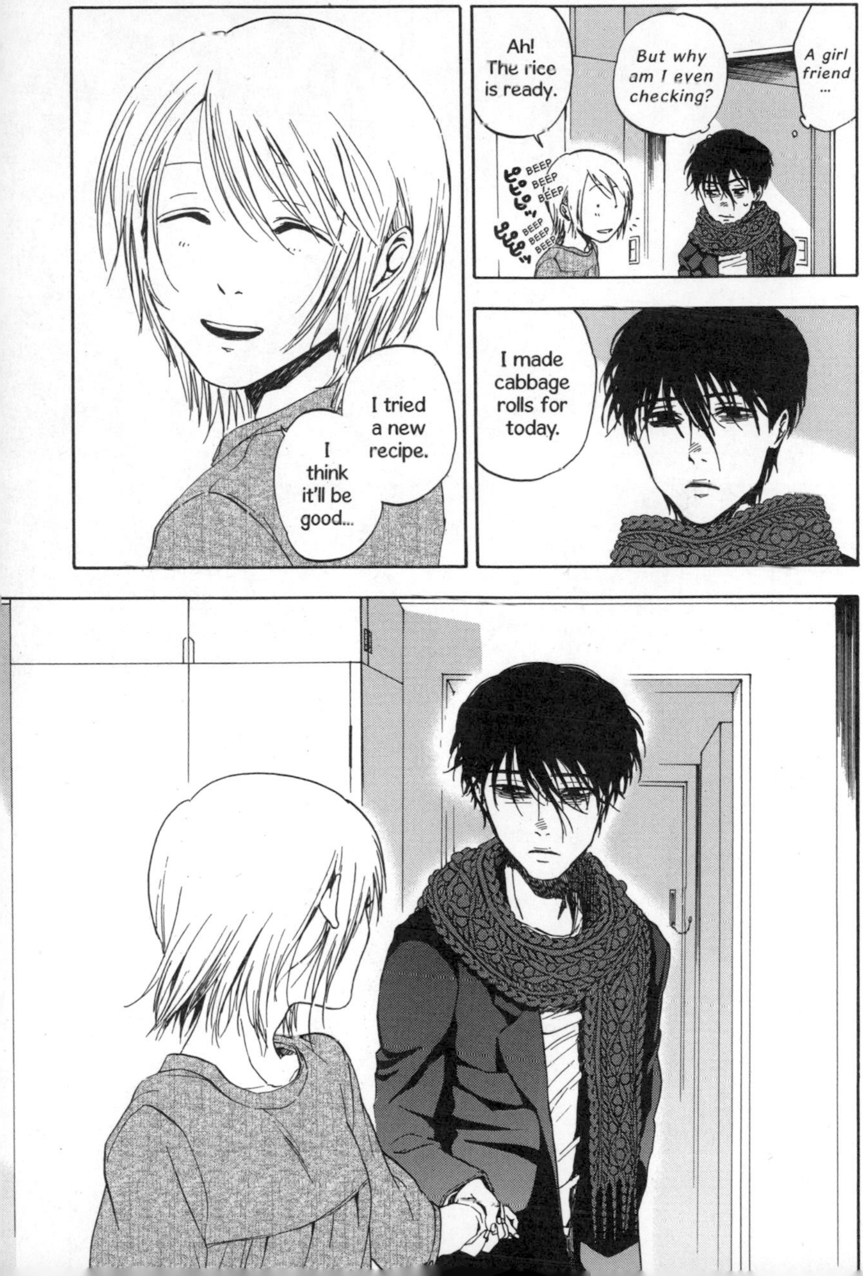
A girl friend ...
But why am I even checking?
Ah! The rice is ready.
BEEP BEEP BEEP
BEEP BEEP BEEP
I made cabbage rolls for today.
I tried a new recipe.
I think it'll be good...

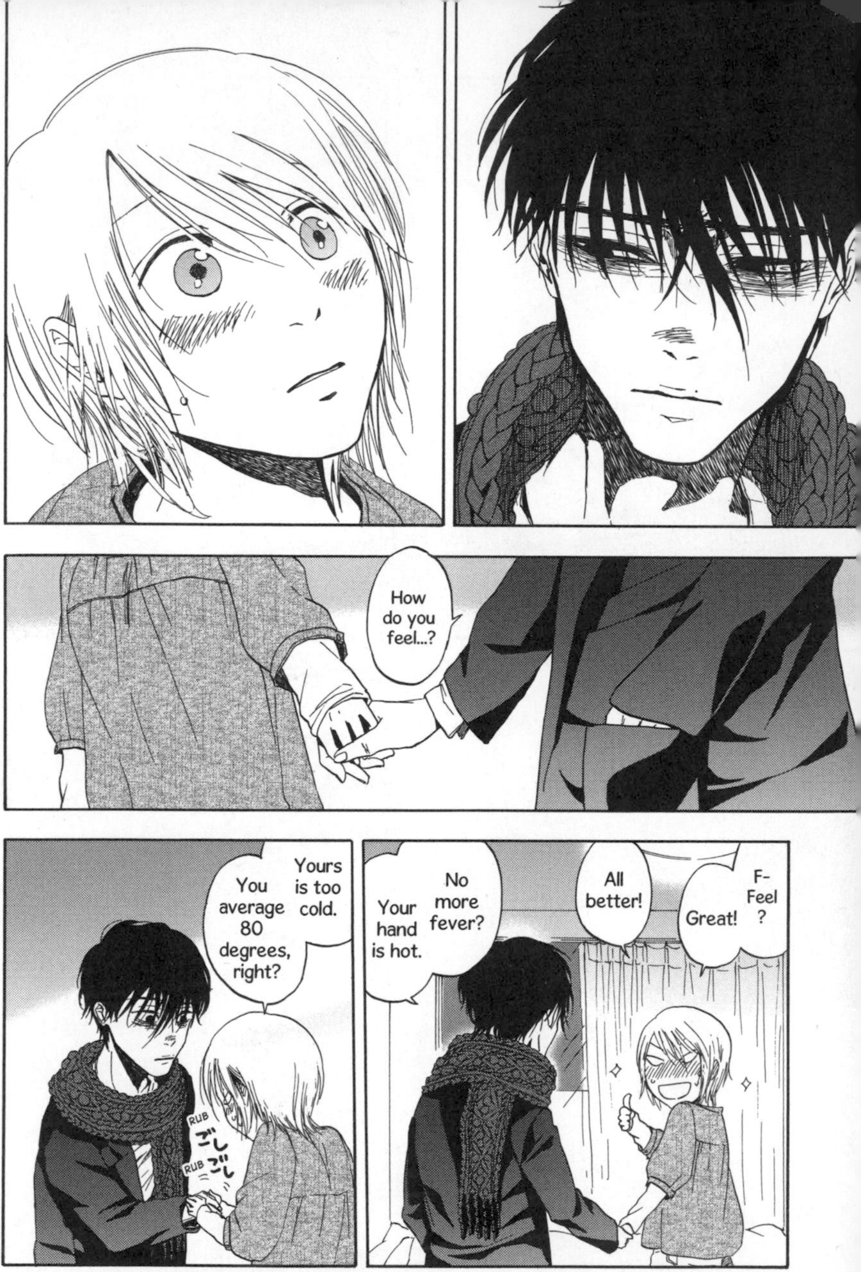
How do you feel...?
F- Feel ?
Great!
All better!
No more fever?
Your hand is hot.
Yours is too cold.
You average 80 degrees, right?
RUB ごし
RUB ごし

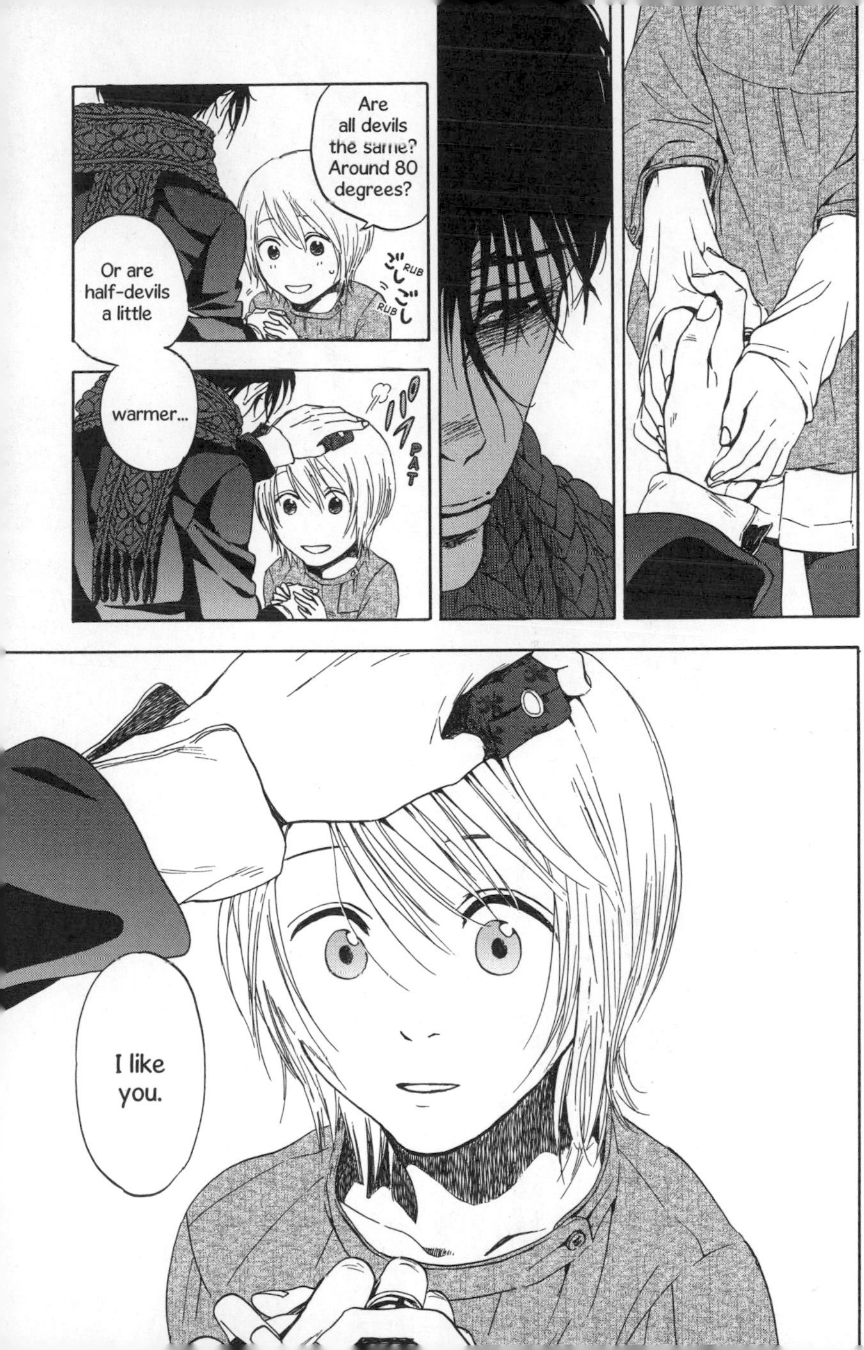
Are all devils the same? Around 80 degrees?
Or are half-devils a little
ごしごし
RUB RUB
warmer...
PAT
I like you.

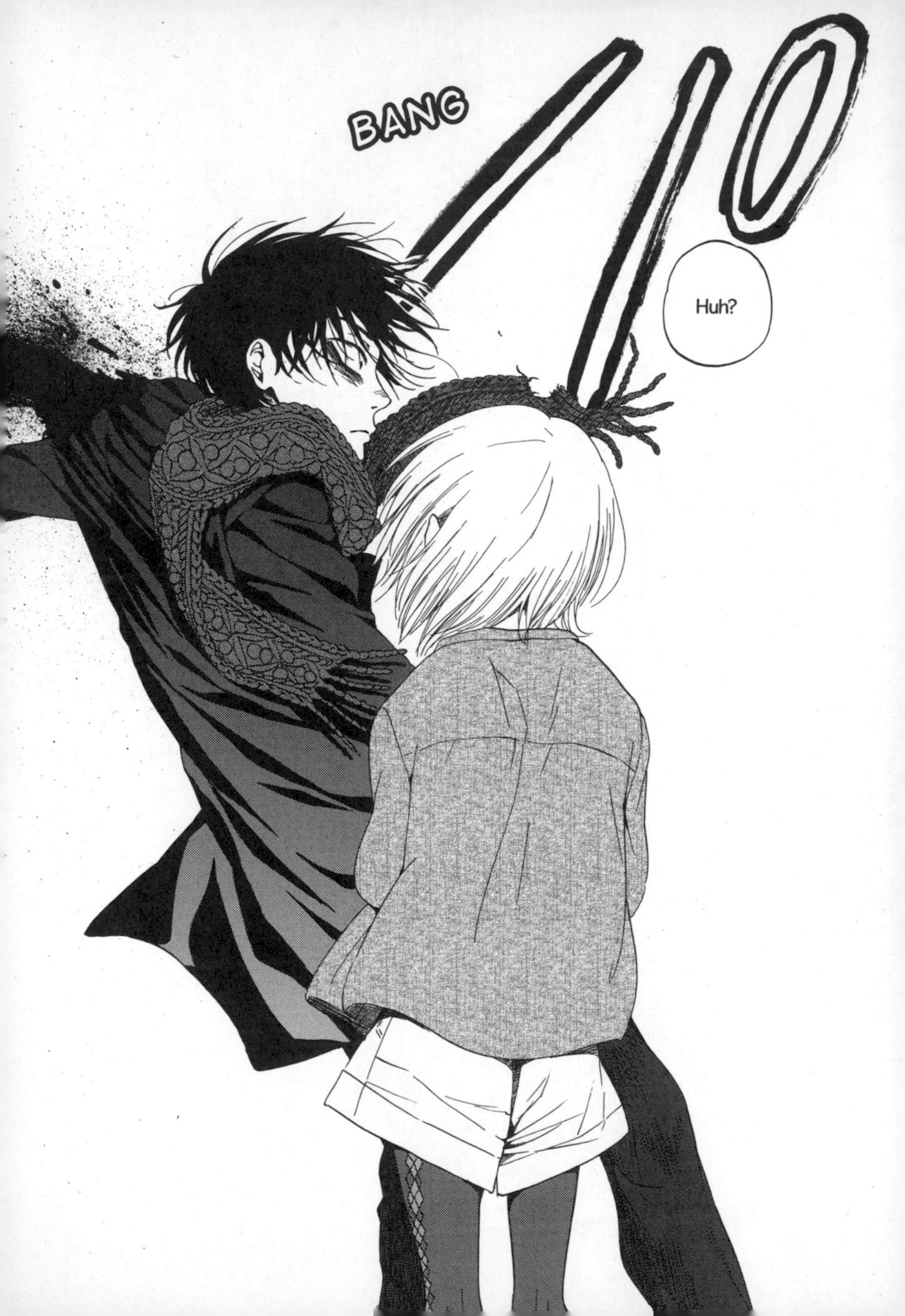
BANG
Huh?

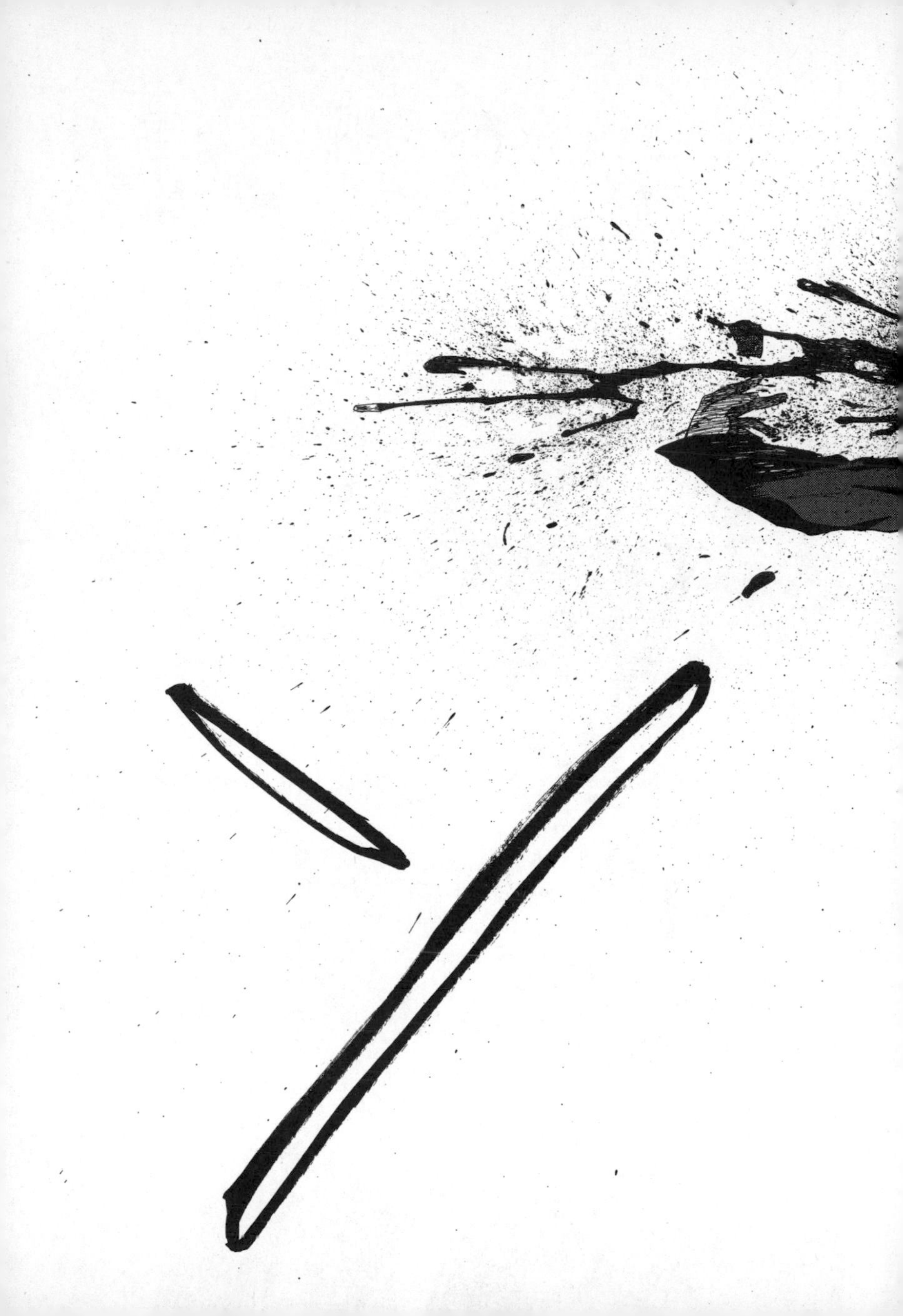
ソ

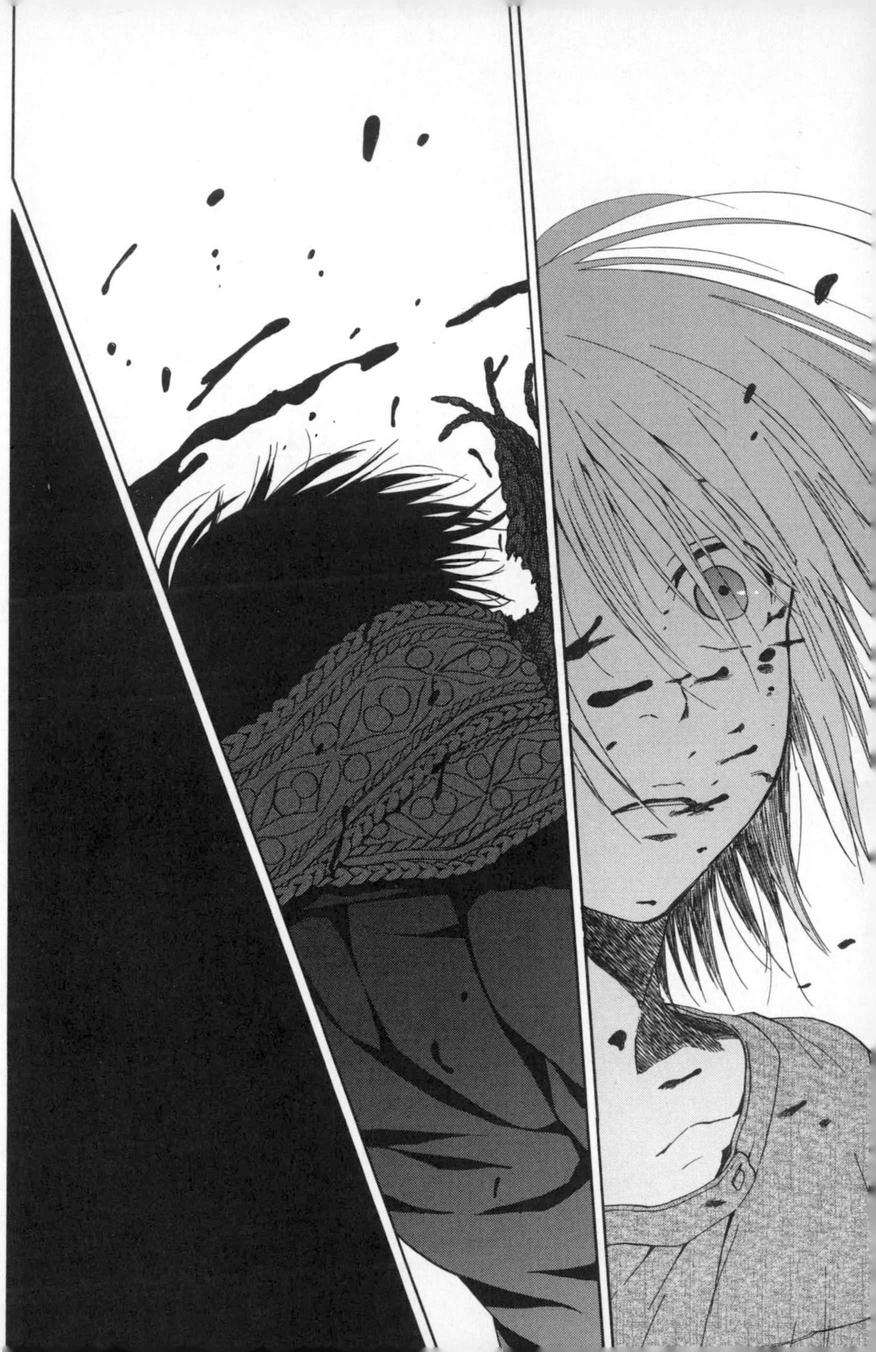

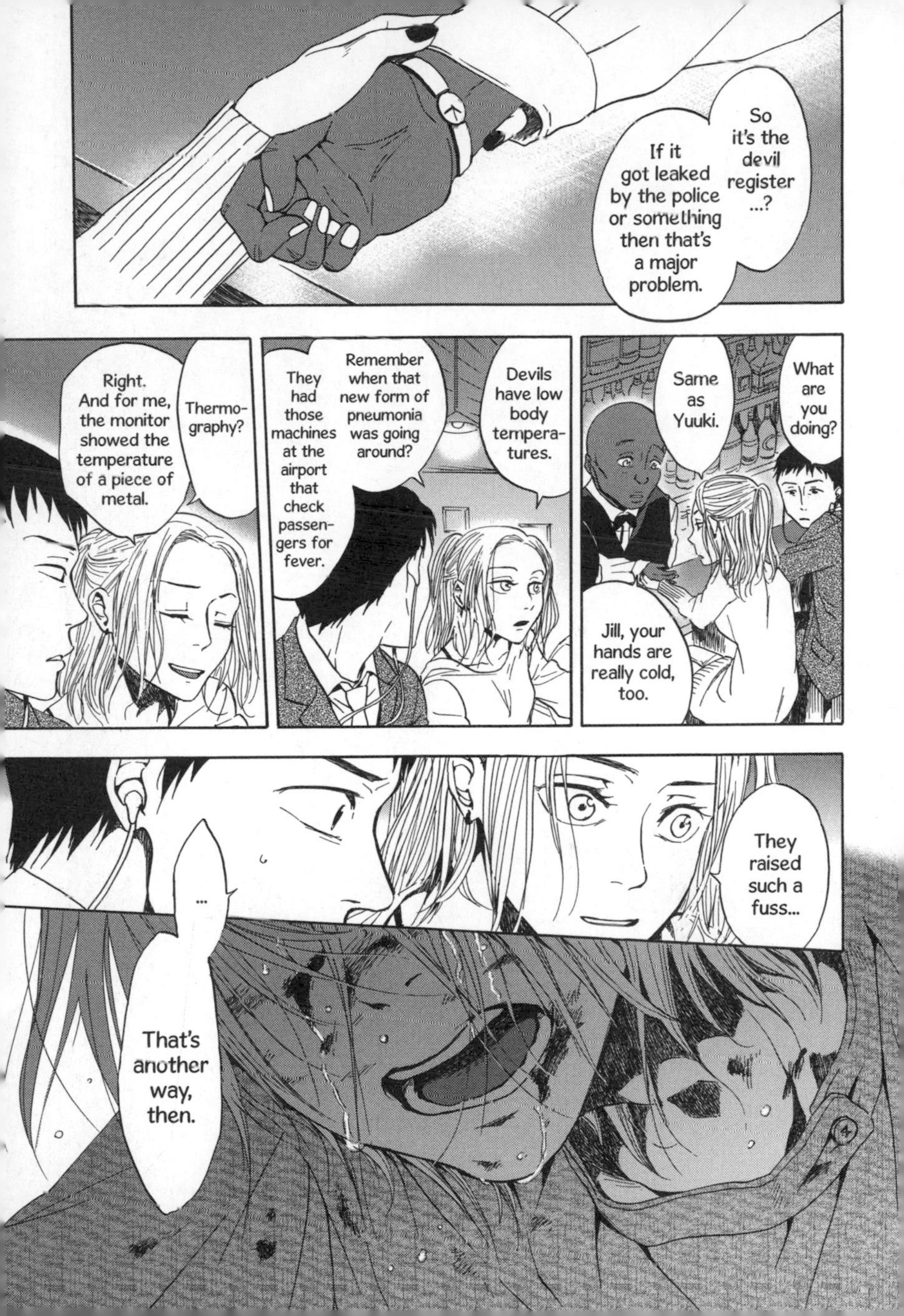
So it's the devil register ...?
If it got leaked by the police or something then that's a major problem.
What are you doing?
Same as Yuuki.
Jill, your hands are really cold, too.
Devils have low body tempera-tures.
Remember when that new form of pneumonia was going around?
They had those machines at the airport that check passen-gers for fever.
Thermo-graphy?
Right. And for me, the monitor showed the temperature of a piece of metal.
They raised such a fuss...
...
That's another way, then.

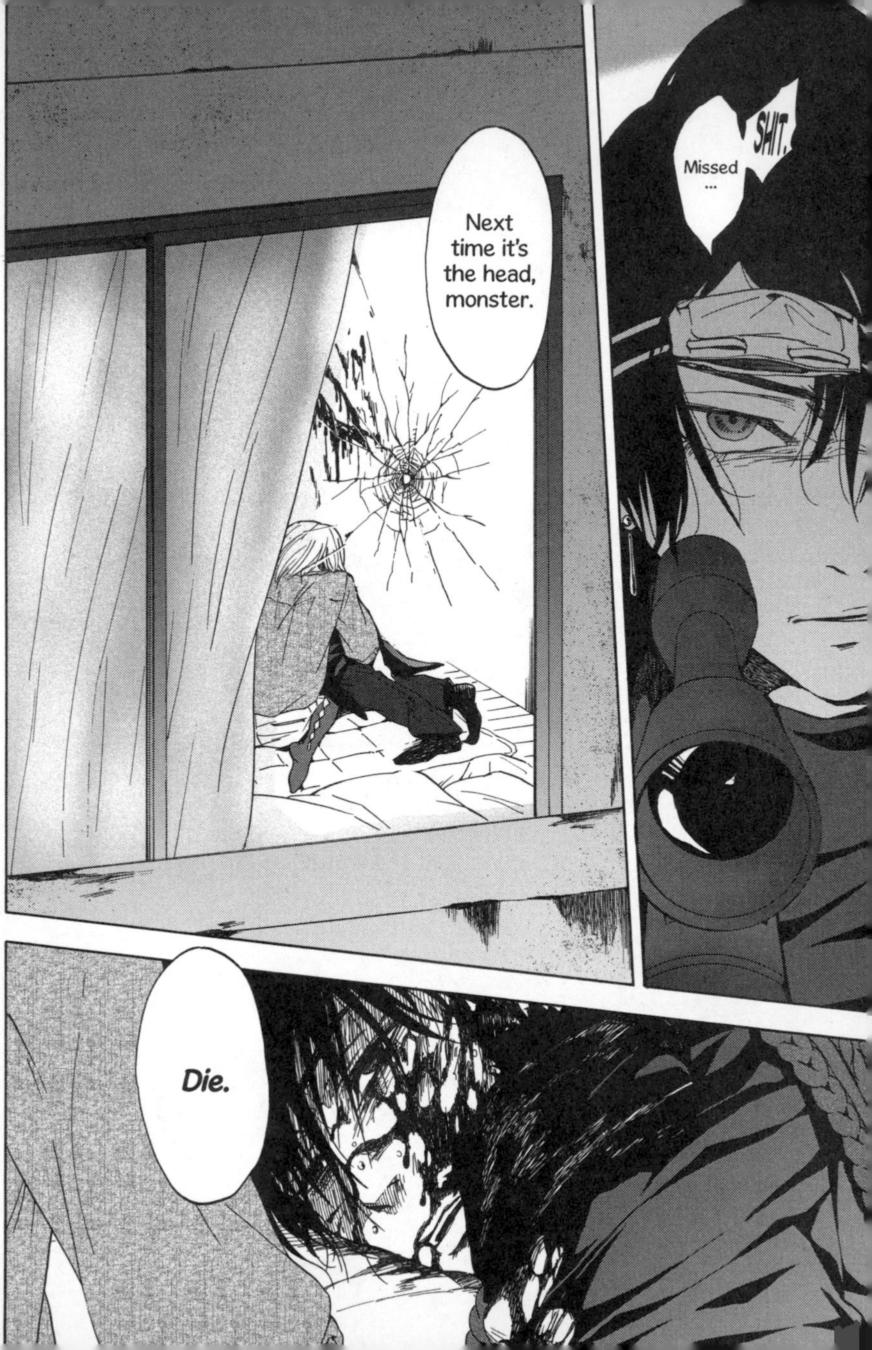
SHIT.
Missed ...
Next time it's the head, monster.
Die.

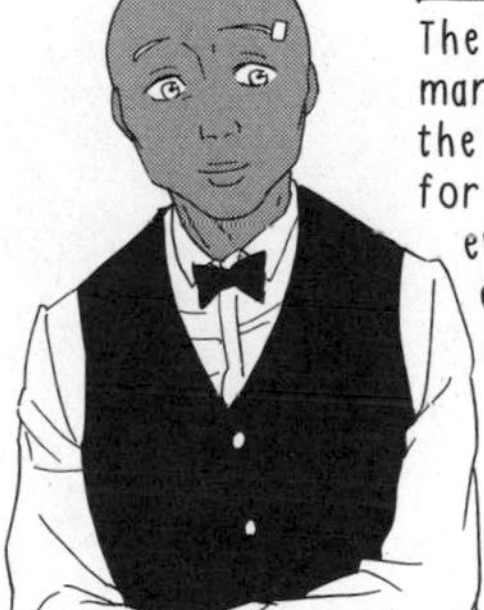

Toshiro Sakaki

The owner of Bar Sakaki, he also manages a real estate business in the same building. He runs the bar for fun, so he closes up whenever he pleases, and uses it to entertain Anzai and the others. His mother is American, his father is Japanese. He came up with the nickname Sat using the first letters of his name, but it was easily confused with the SAT so it was nixed.

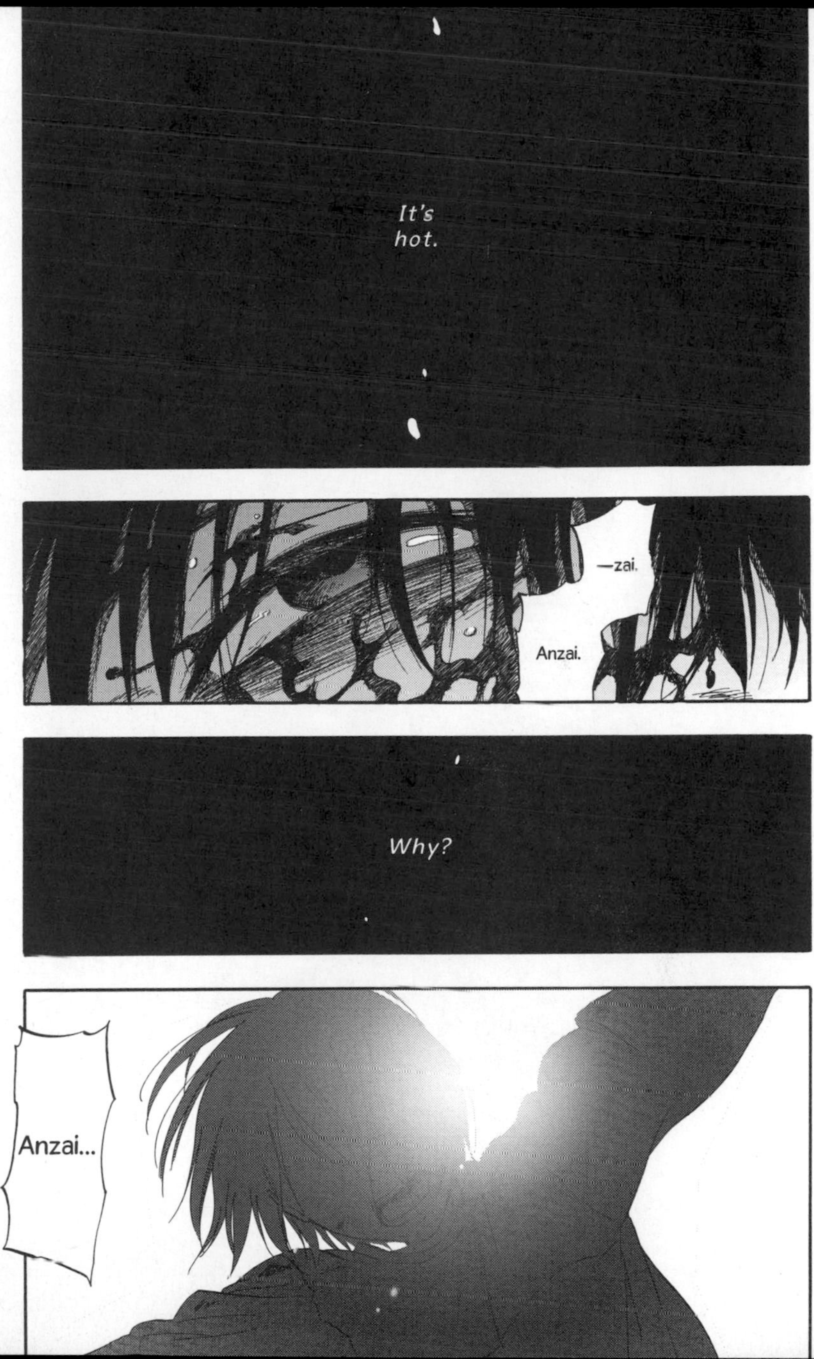
It's hot.
—zai.
Anzai.
Why?
Anzai...

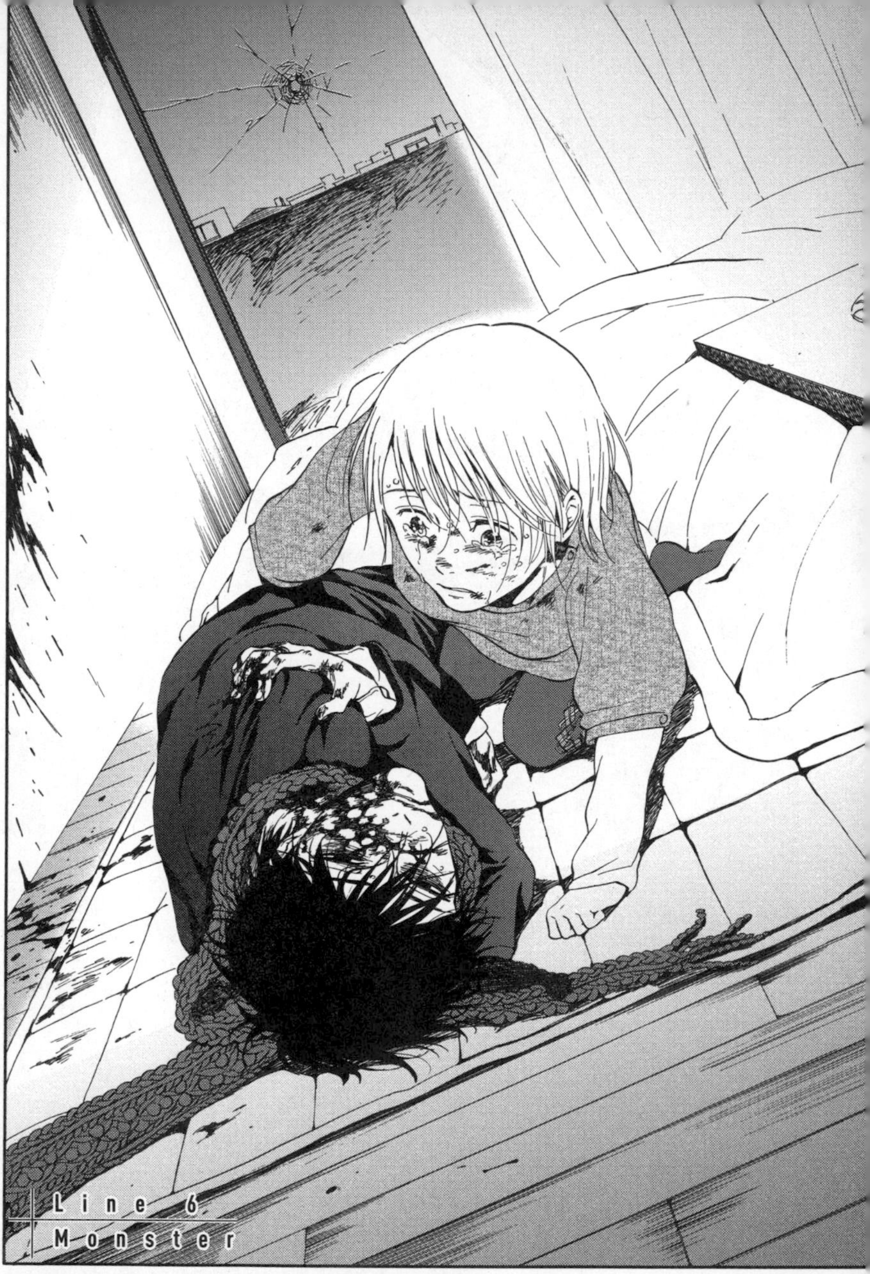
Line 6
Monster

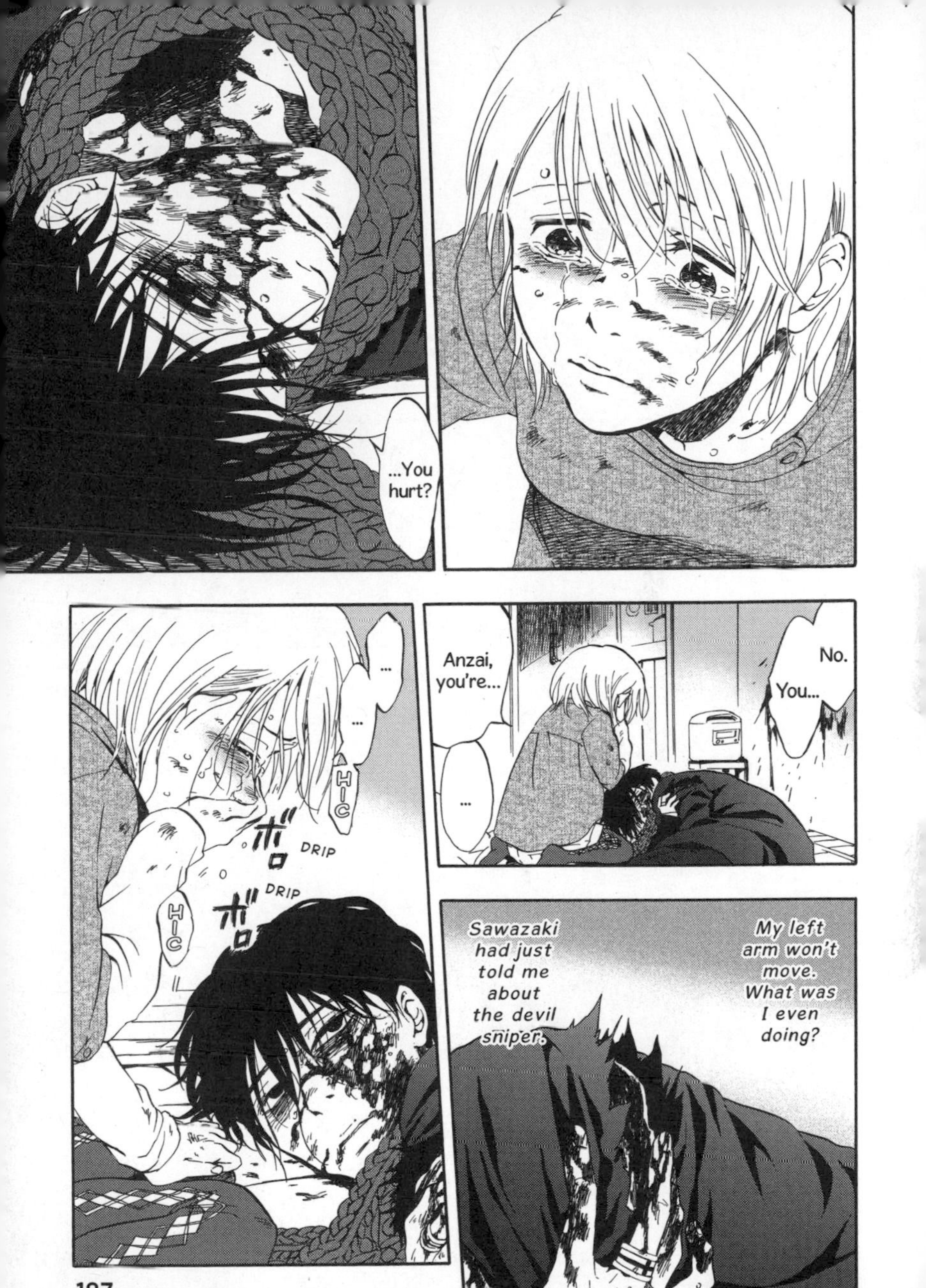
...You hurt?
No.
You...
Anzai, you're...
...
My left arm won't move. What was I even doing?
Sawazaki had just told me about the devil sniper.
...
...
HIC
ボロ DRIP
ボロ DRIP
HIC

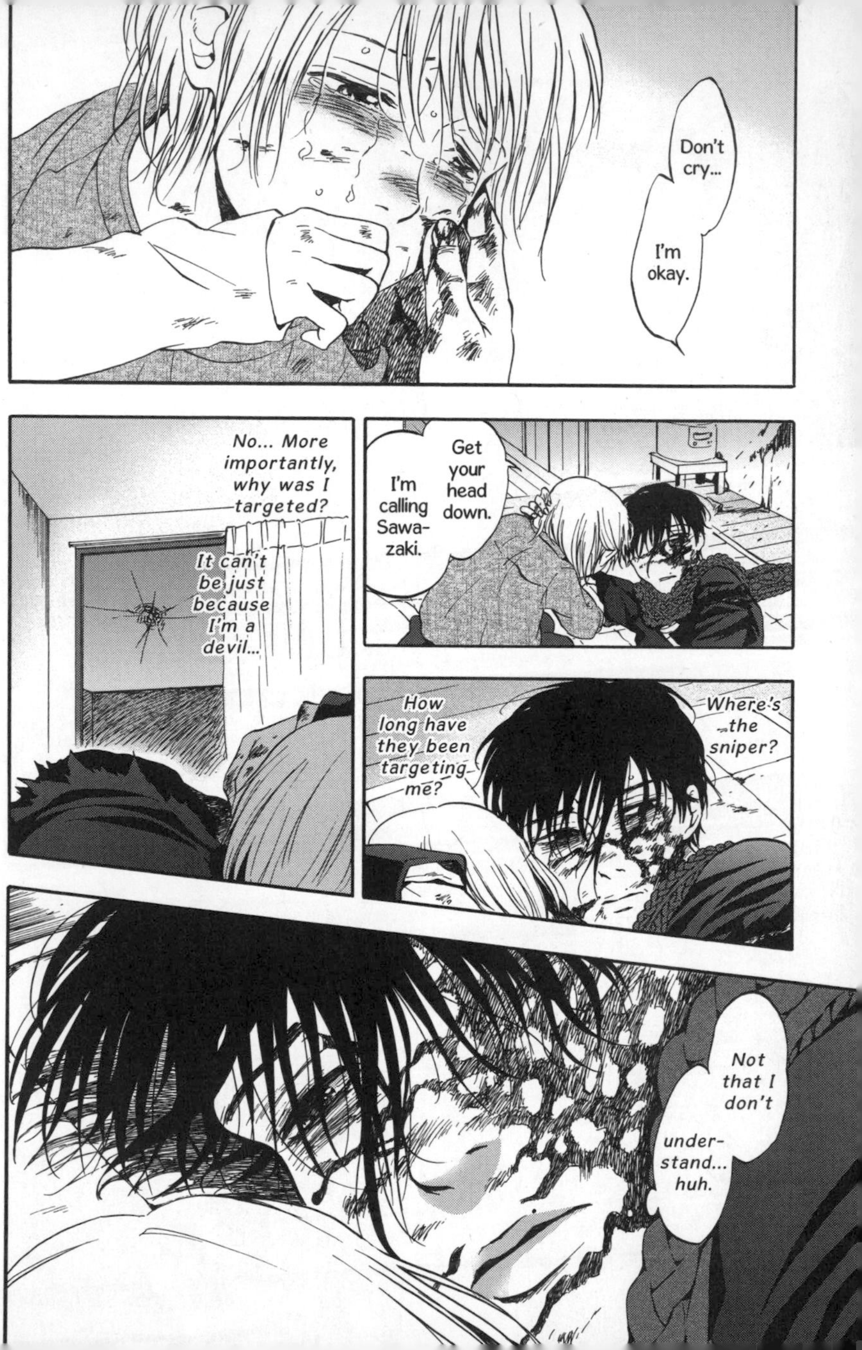
Don't cry...
I'm okay.
Get your head down.
I'm calling Sawa-zaki.
Where's the sniper?
How long have they been targeting me?
No... More importantly, why was I targeted?
It can't be just because I'm a devil...
Not that I don't
under-stand... huh.

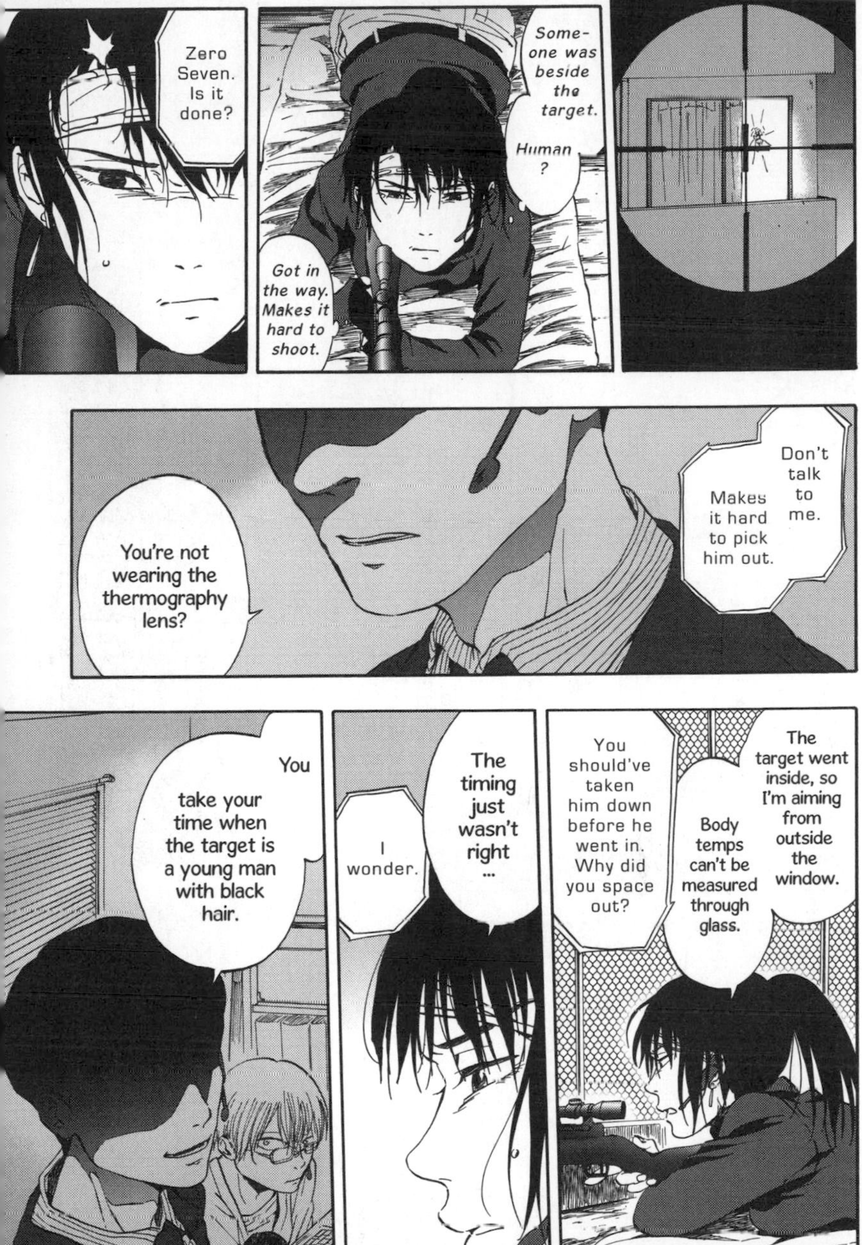
Some-one was beside the target.
Human ?
Got in the way. Makes it hard to shoot.
Zero Seven. Is it done?
Don't talk to me.
Makes it hard to pick him out.
You're not wearing the thermography lens?
The target went inside, so I'm aiming from outside the window.
Body temps can't be measured through glass.
You should've taken him down before he went in. Why did you space out?
The timing just wasn't right ...
I wonder.
You take your time when the target is a young man with black hair.

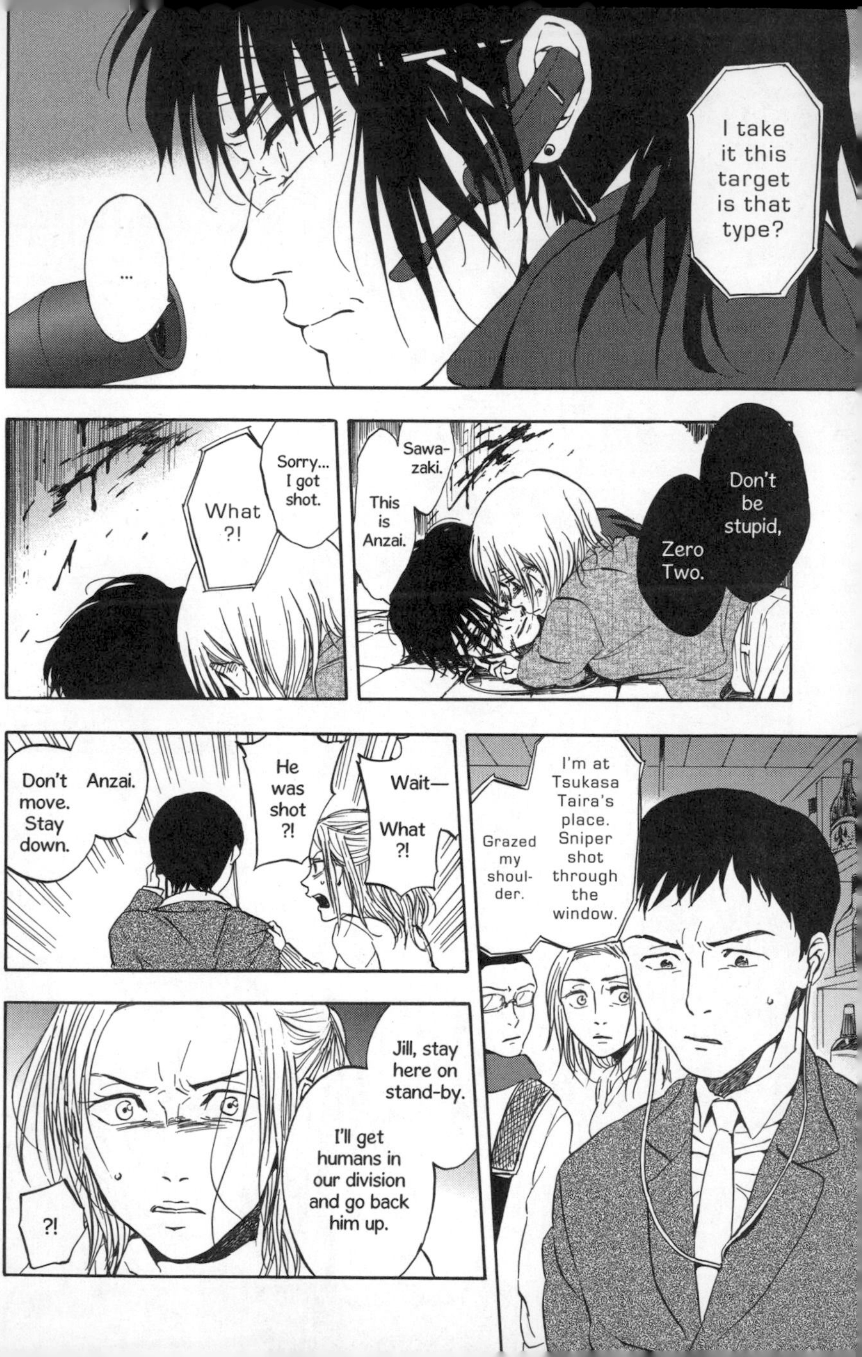
I take it this target is that type?
...
Don't be stupid, Zero Two.
Sawa-zaki.
This is Anzai.
Sorry... I got shot.
What ?!
I'm at Tsukasa Taira's place. Sniper shot through the window.
Grazed my shoul-der.
Wait—
What ?!
He was shot ?!
Anzai.
Don't move. Stay down.
Jill, stay here on stand-by.
I'll get humans in our division and go back him up.
?!

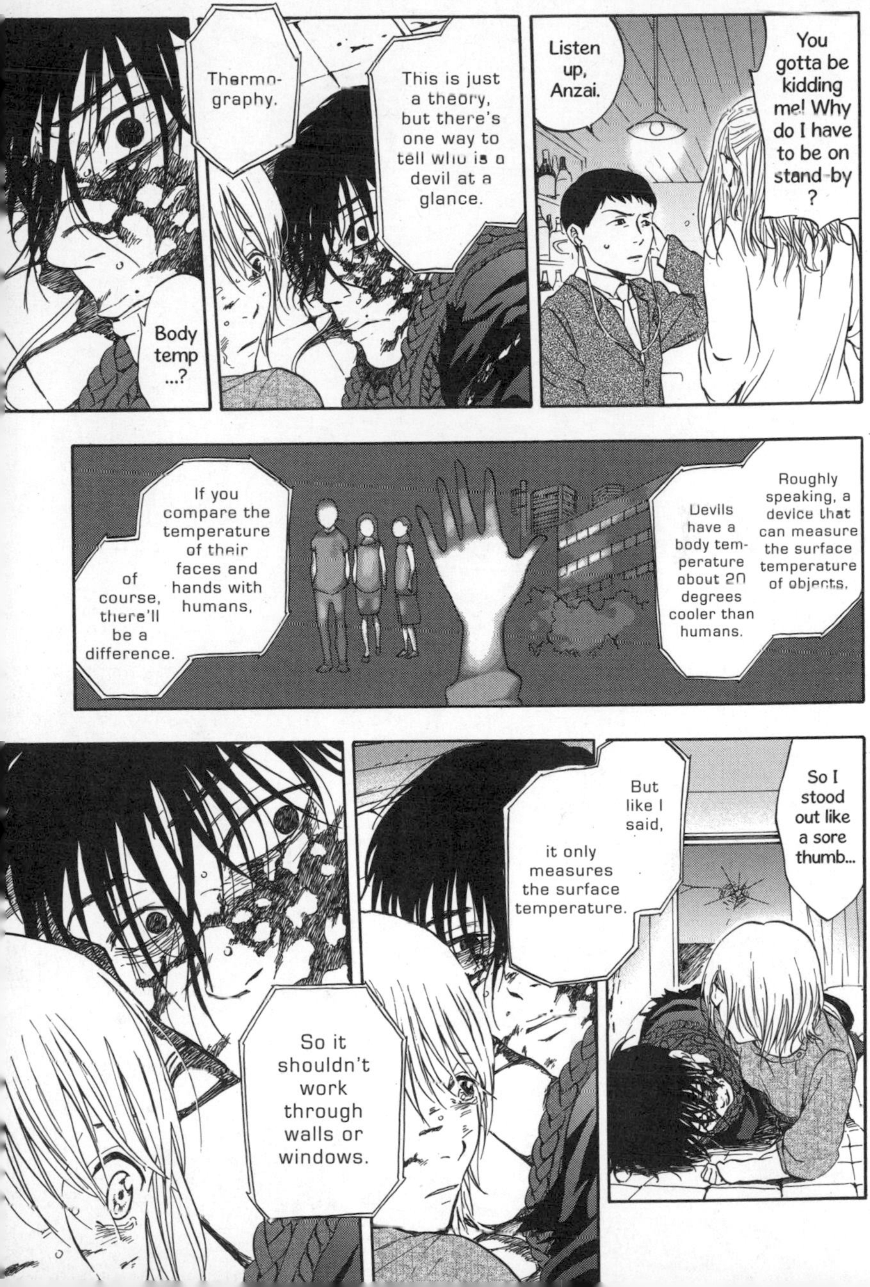
You gotta be kidding me! Why do I have to be on stand-by?
Listen up, Anzai.
This is just a theory, but there's one way to tell who is a devil at a glance.
Thermo-graphy.
Body temp...?
Roughly speaking, a device that can measure the surface temperature of objects.
Devils have a body temperature about 20 degrees cooler than humans.
If you compare the temperature of their faces and hands with humans,
of course, there'll be a difference.
So I stood out like a sore thumb...
But like I said,
it only measures the surface temperature.
So it shouldn't work through walls or windows.

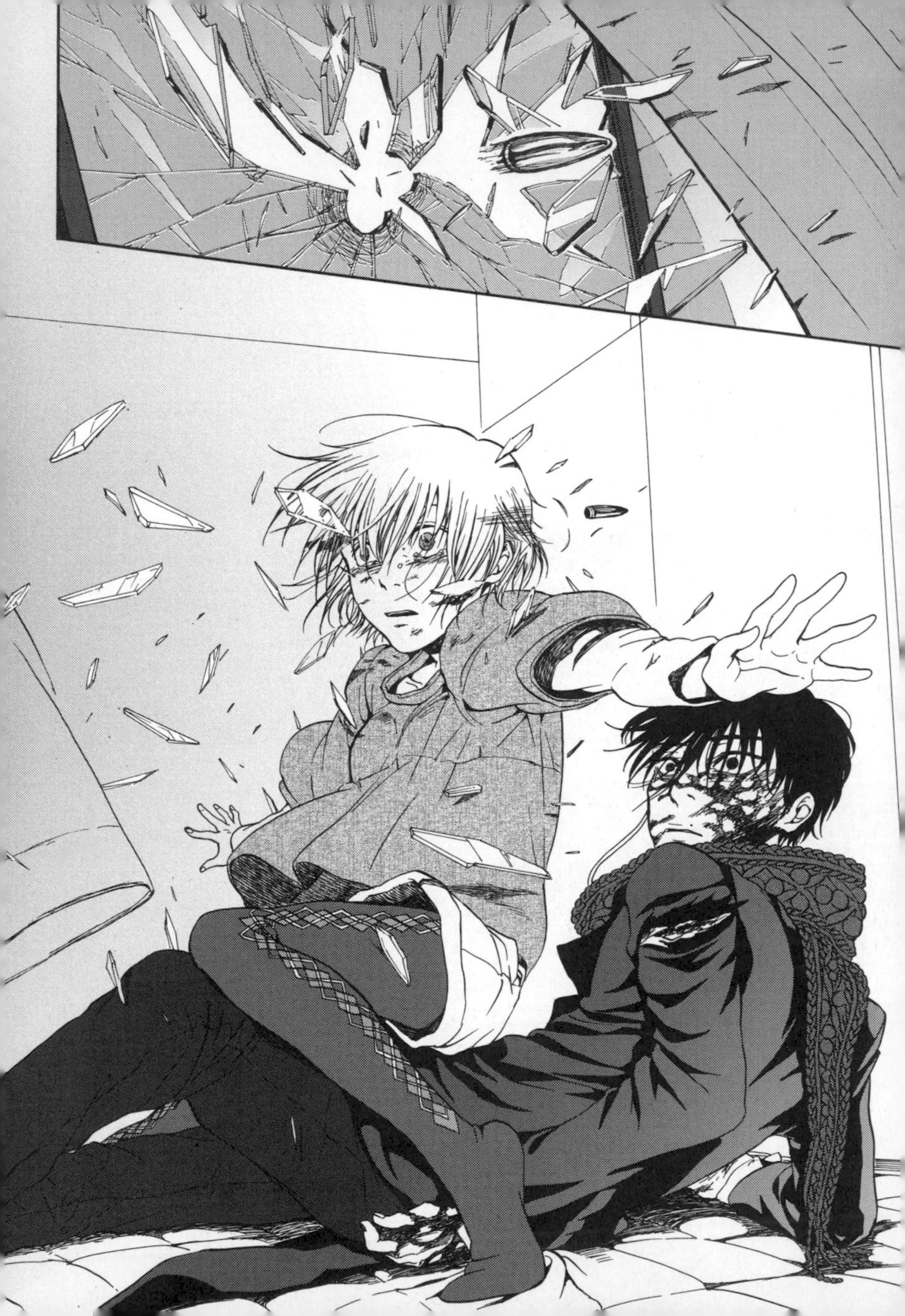

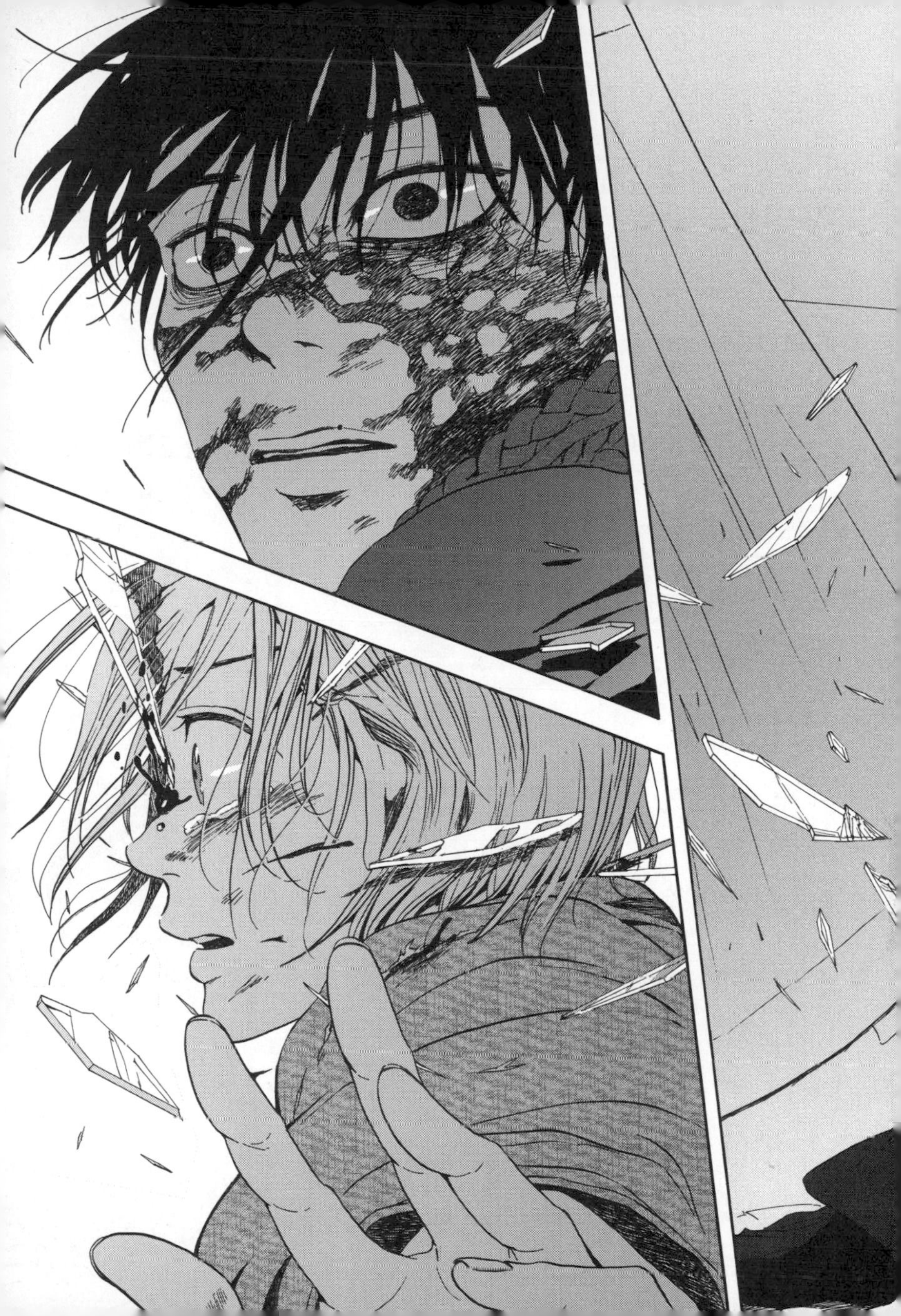

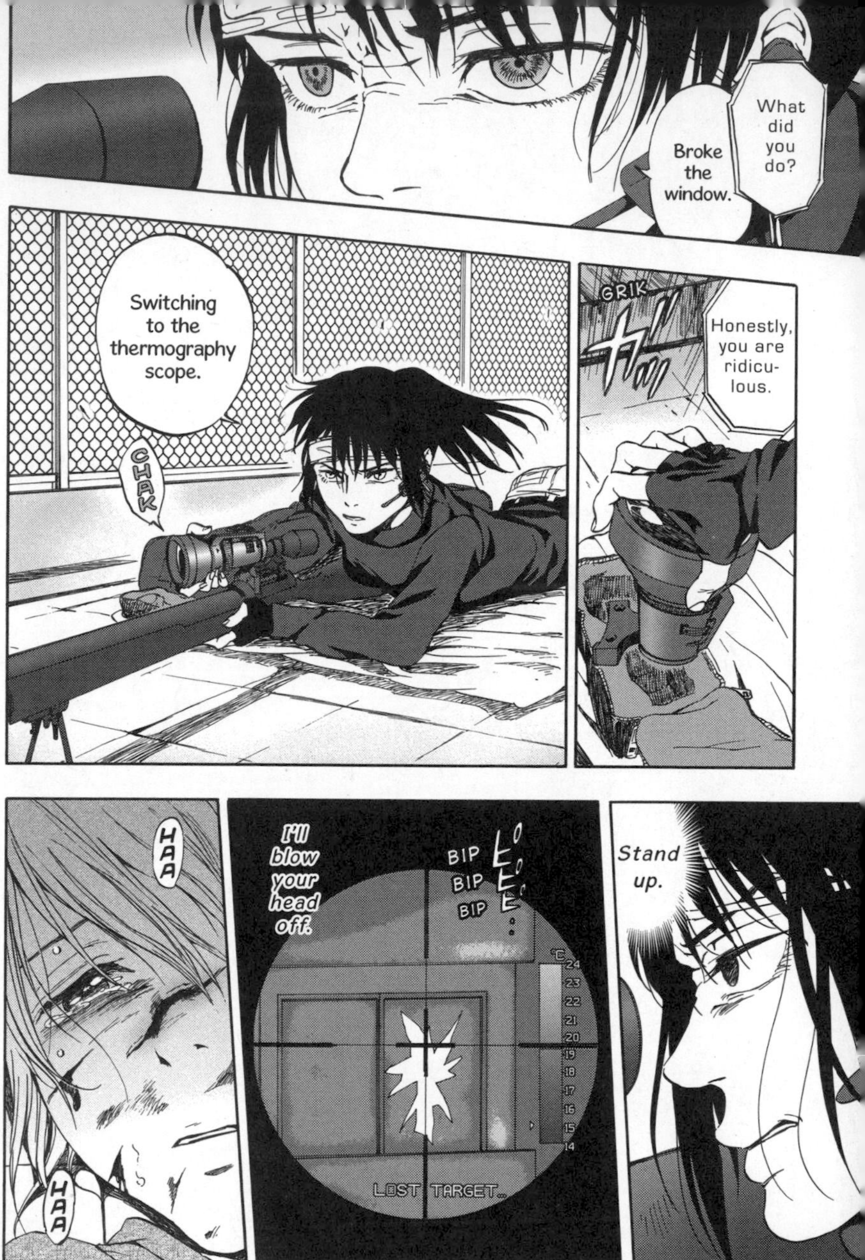
What did you do?
Broke the window.
GRIK
Honestly, you are ridicu-lous.
Switching to the thermography scope.
CHAK
Stand up.
I'll blow your head off.
BIP
BIP
BIP
°C
24
23
22
21
20
19
18
17
16
15
14
LOST TARGET...
HAA
HAA

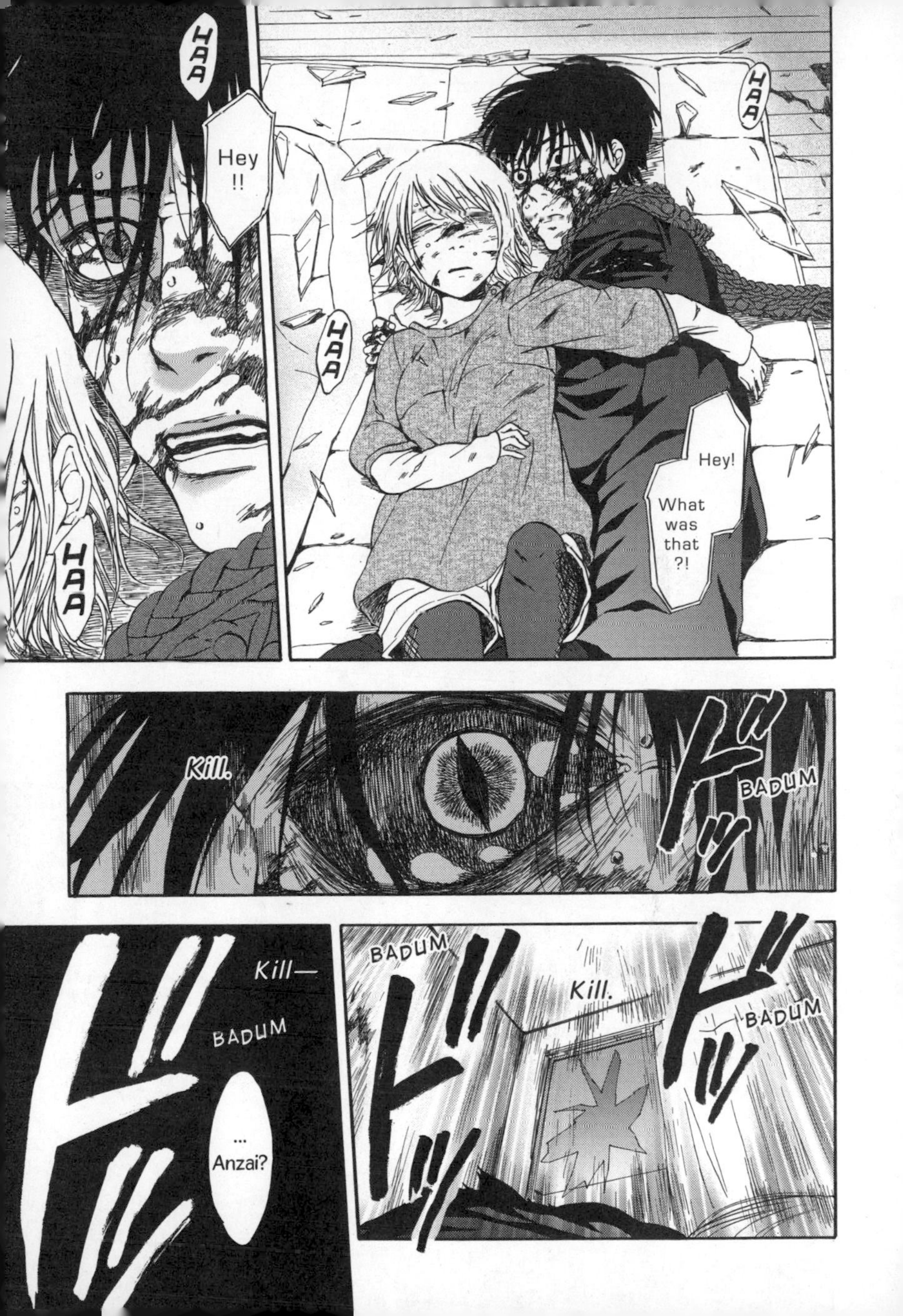
HAA
Hey!
What was that ?!
HAA
HAA
Hey !!
HAA
Kill.
BADUM
BADUM
Kill.
BADUM
Kill—
BADUM
... Anzai?

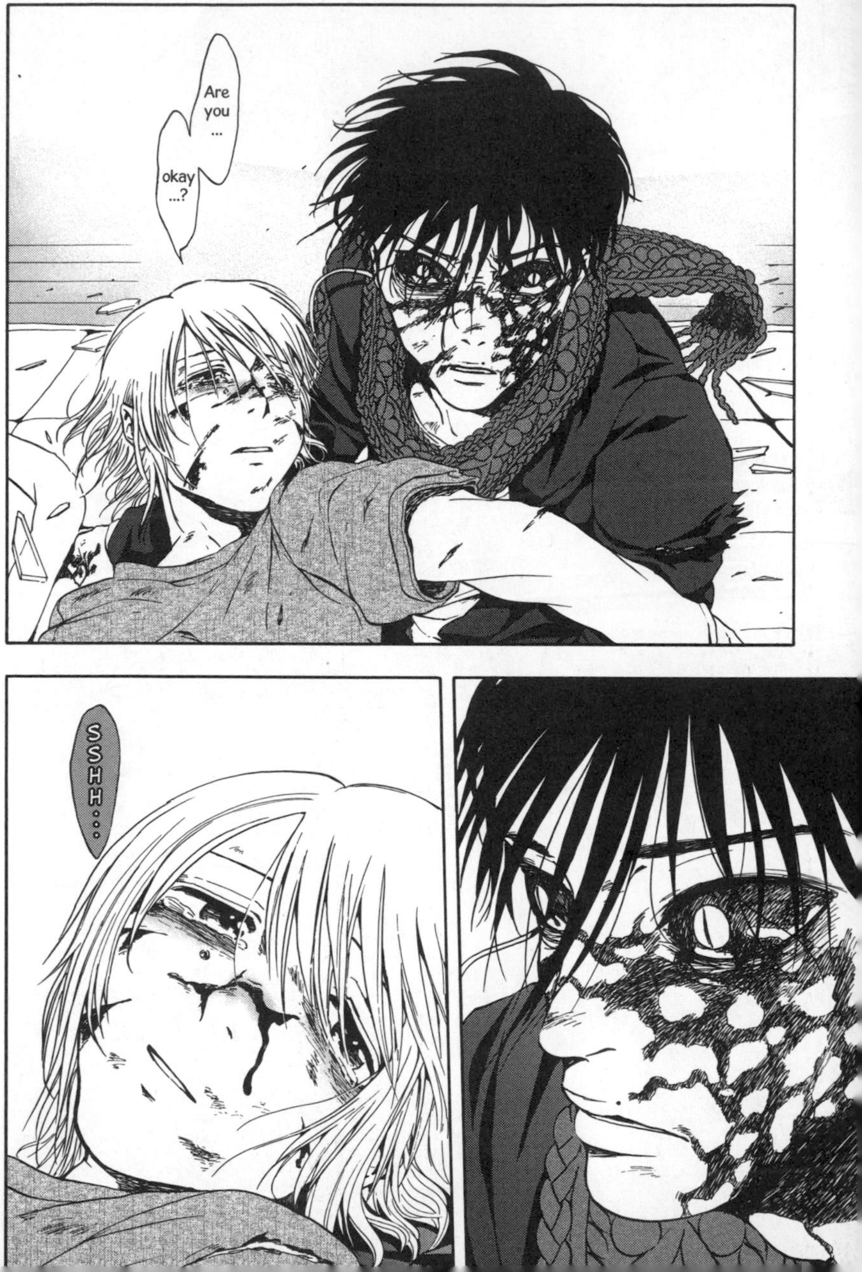
Are you ...
okay ...?
SSHH...

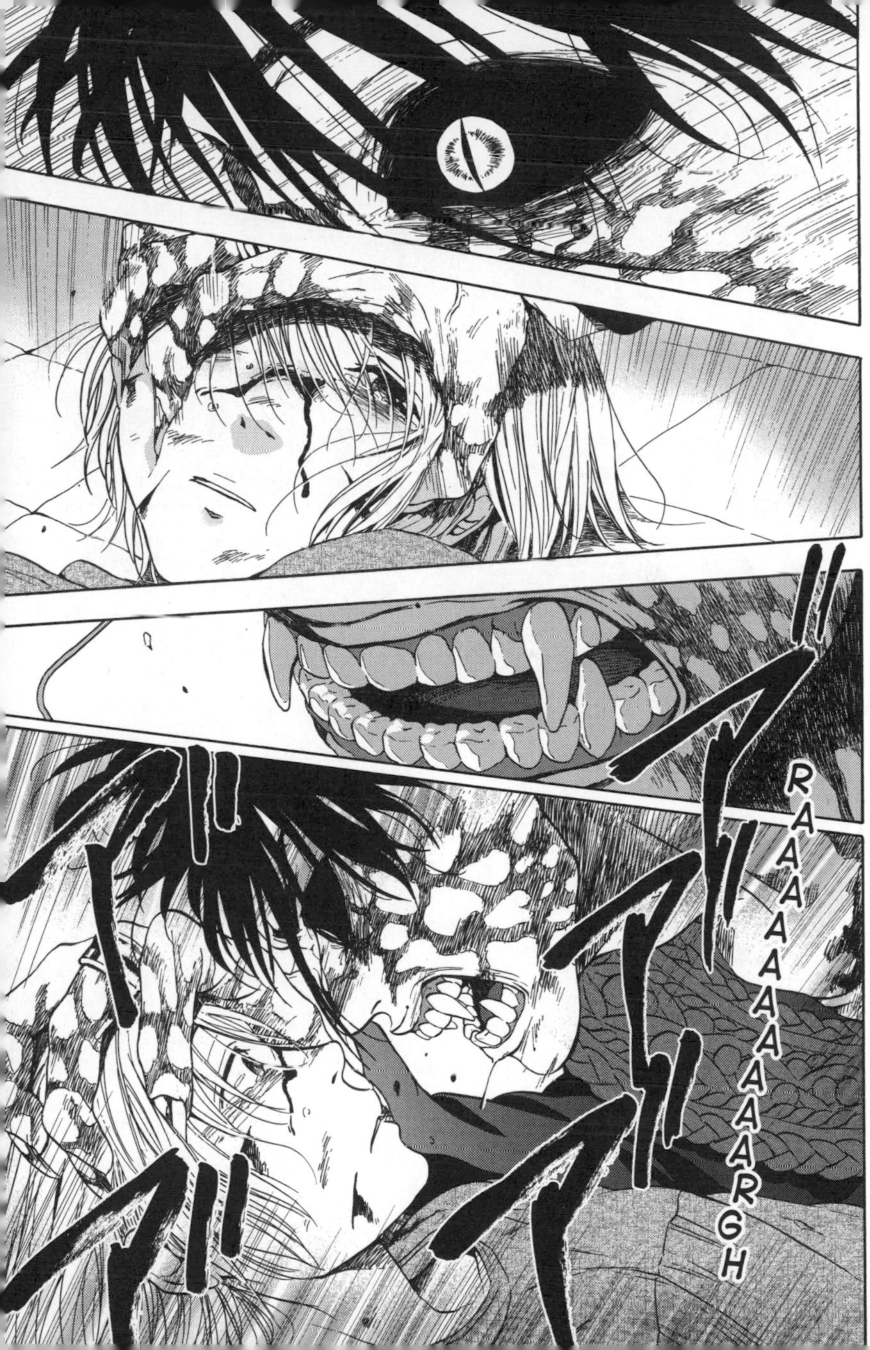
RAAAAAAAAAAAARGH

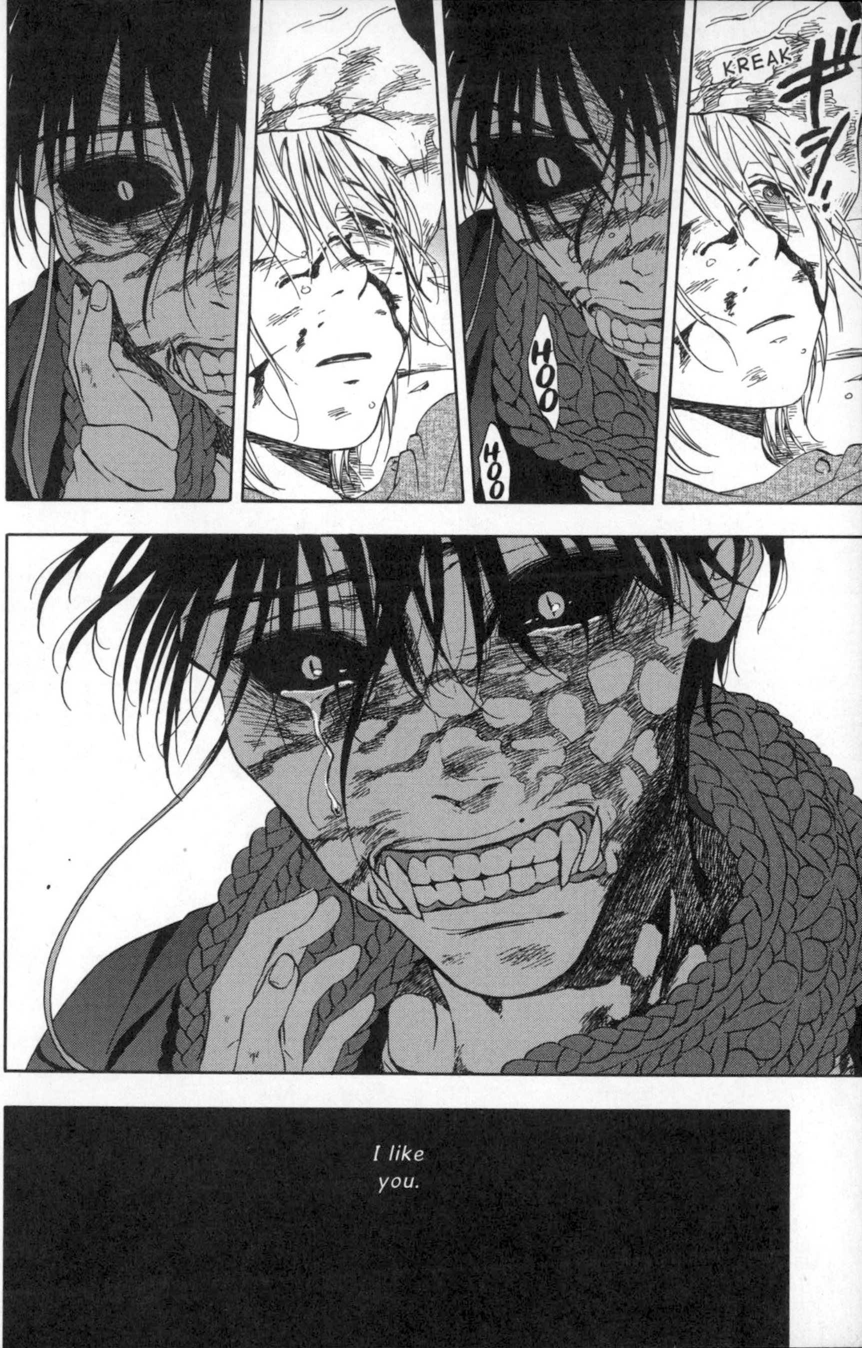
KREAK
ギシ!!
HOO
HOO
I like
you.

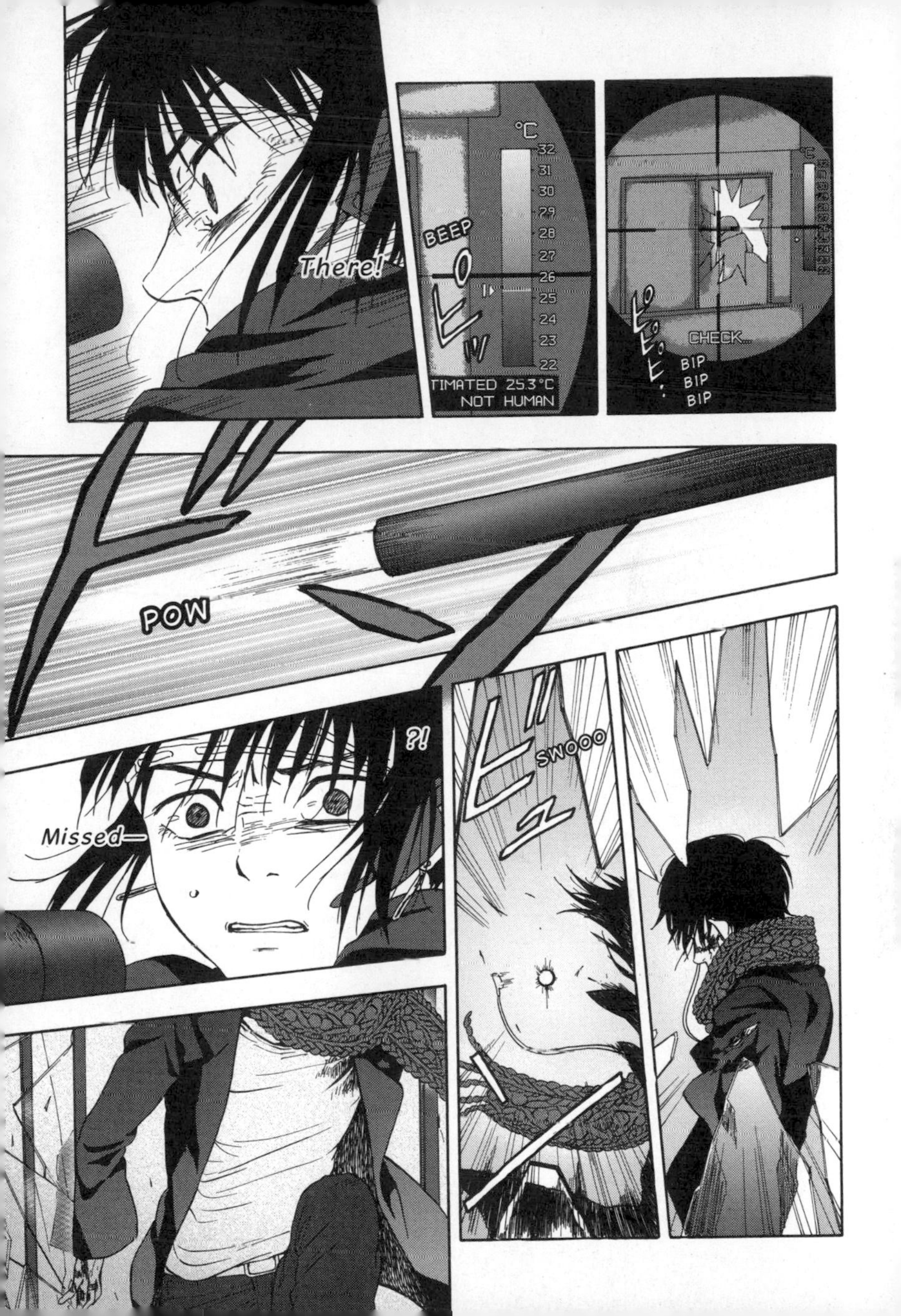

°C
CHECK...
BIP
BIP
BIP
°C
32
31
30
29
28
27
26
25
24
23
22
BEEP
TIMATED 25.3°C
NOT HUMAN
There!
POW
SWOOO
?!
Missed—

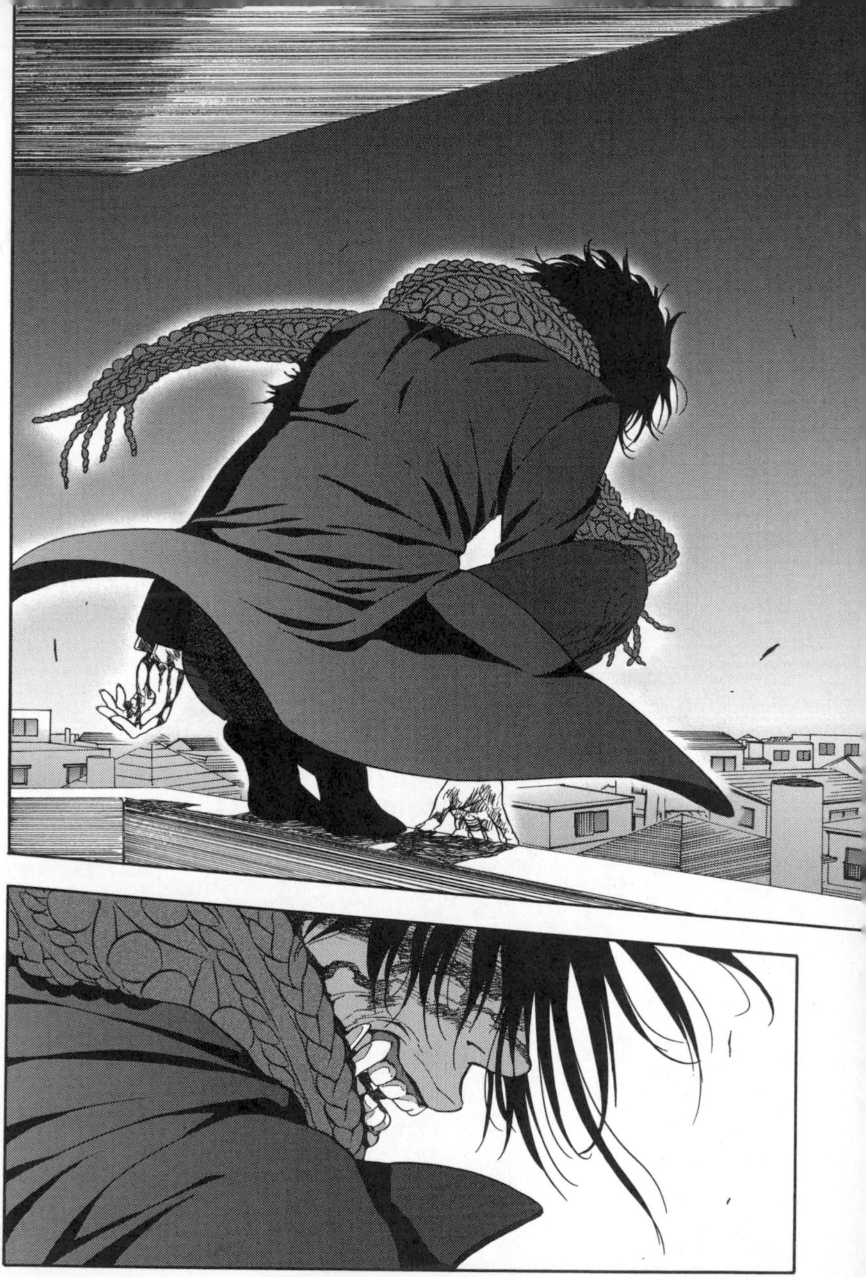

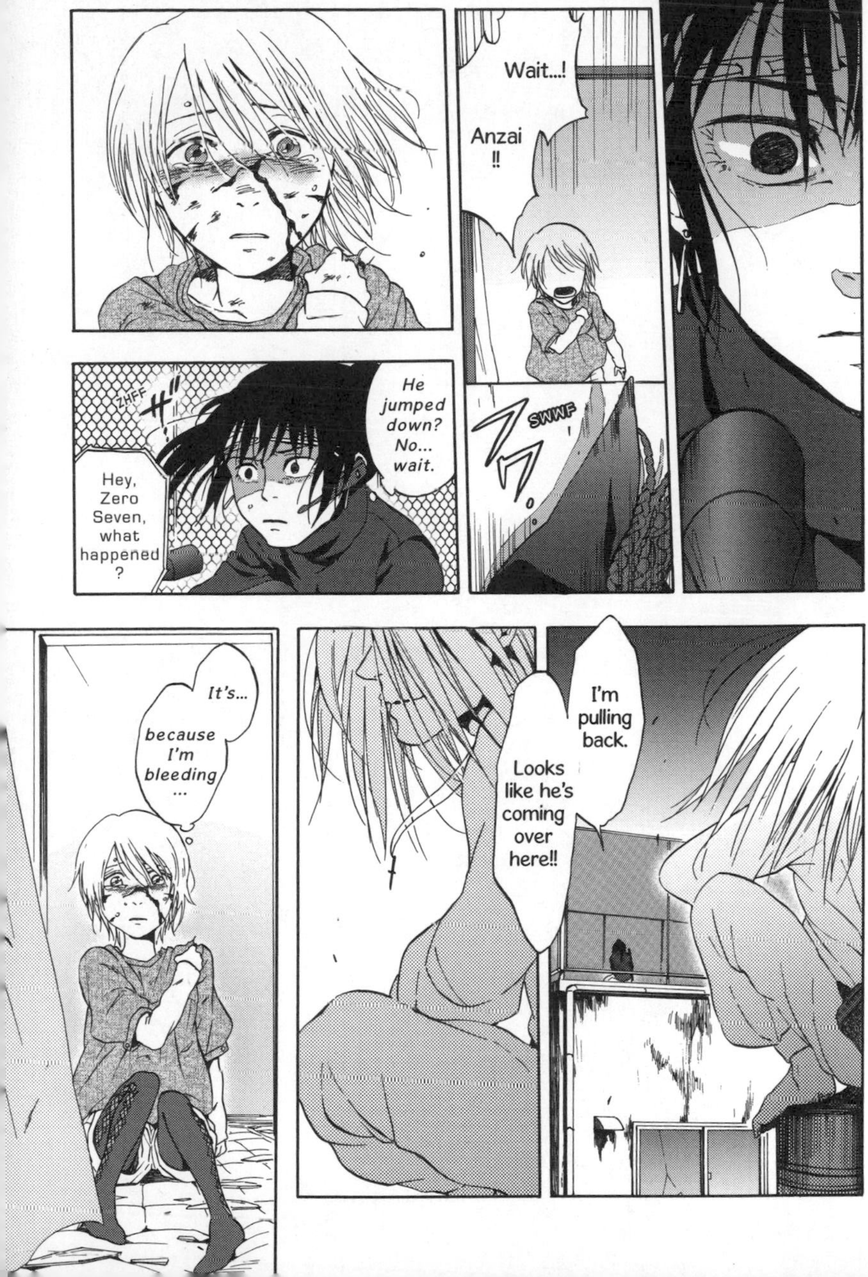
Wait...!
Anzai!!
SWWF
He jumped down? No... wait.
ZHFF
Hey, Zero Seven, what happened?
I'm pulling back.
Looks like he's coming over here!!
It's... because I'm bleeding...

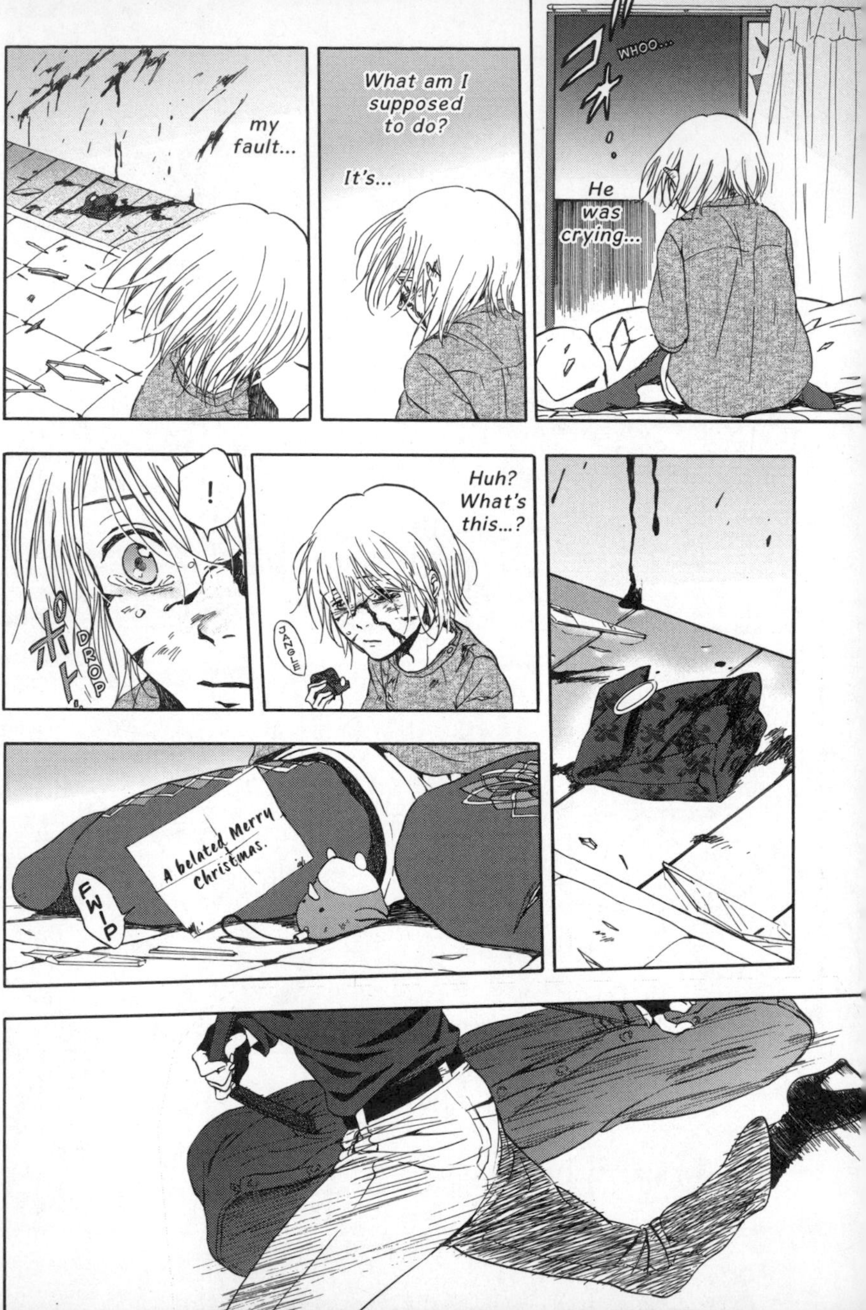
ゴォ
WHOO...
He was crying...
What am I supposed to do?
It's...
my fault...
Huh? What's this...?
JANGLE
!
ポト
DROP
A belated Merry Christmas.
FWIP

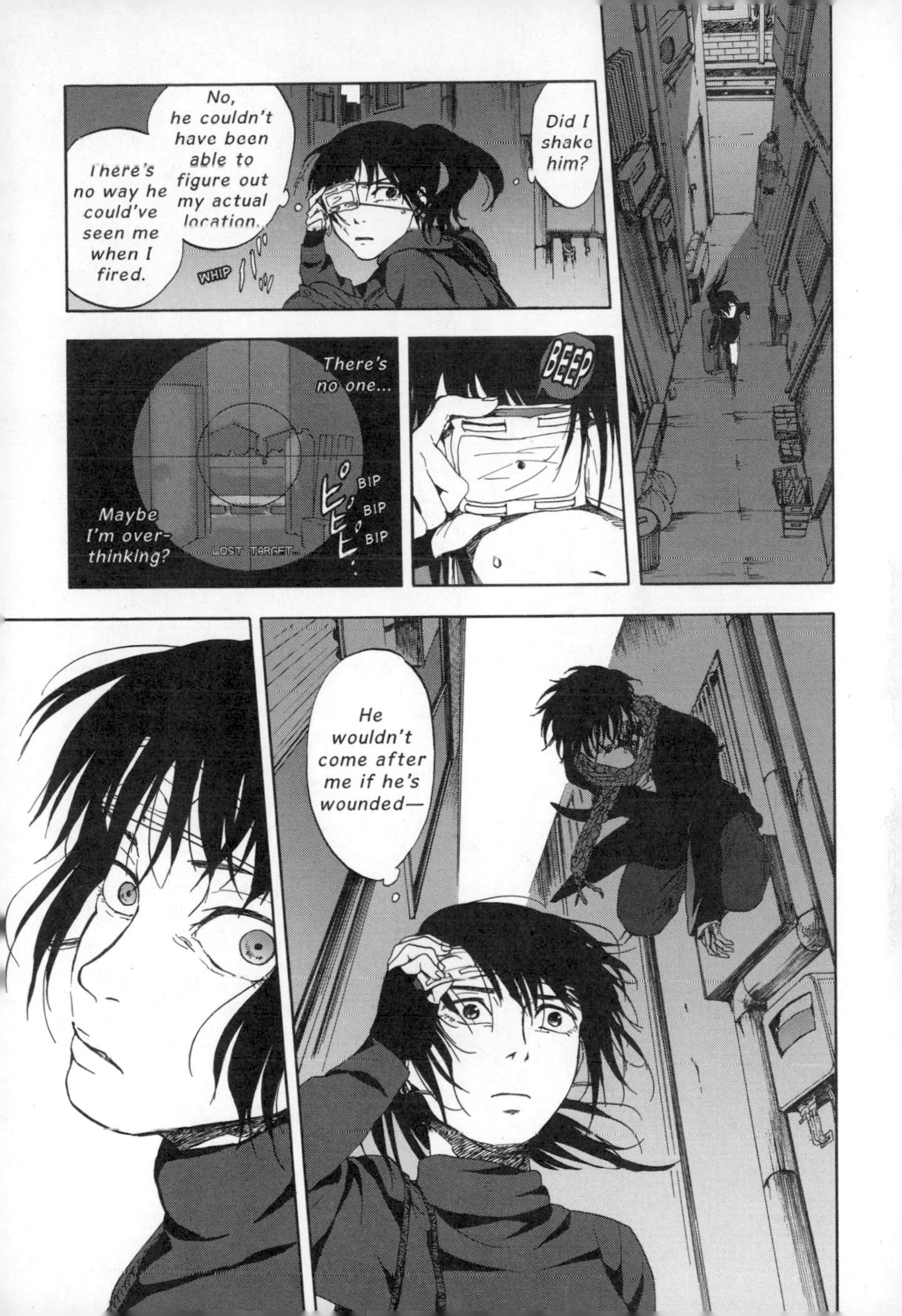
Did I shake him?
No, he couldn't have been able to figure out my actual location...
There's no way he could've seen me when I fired.
WHIP
BEEP
There's no one...
ピ、ピ、ピ
BIP BIP BIP
Maybe I'm over-thinking?
LOST TARGET
He wouldn't come after me if he's wounded—

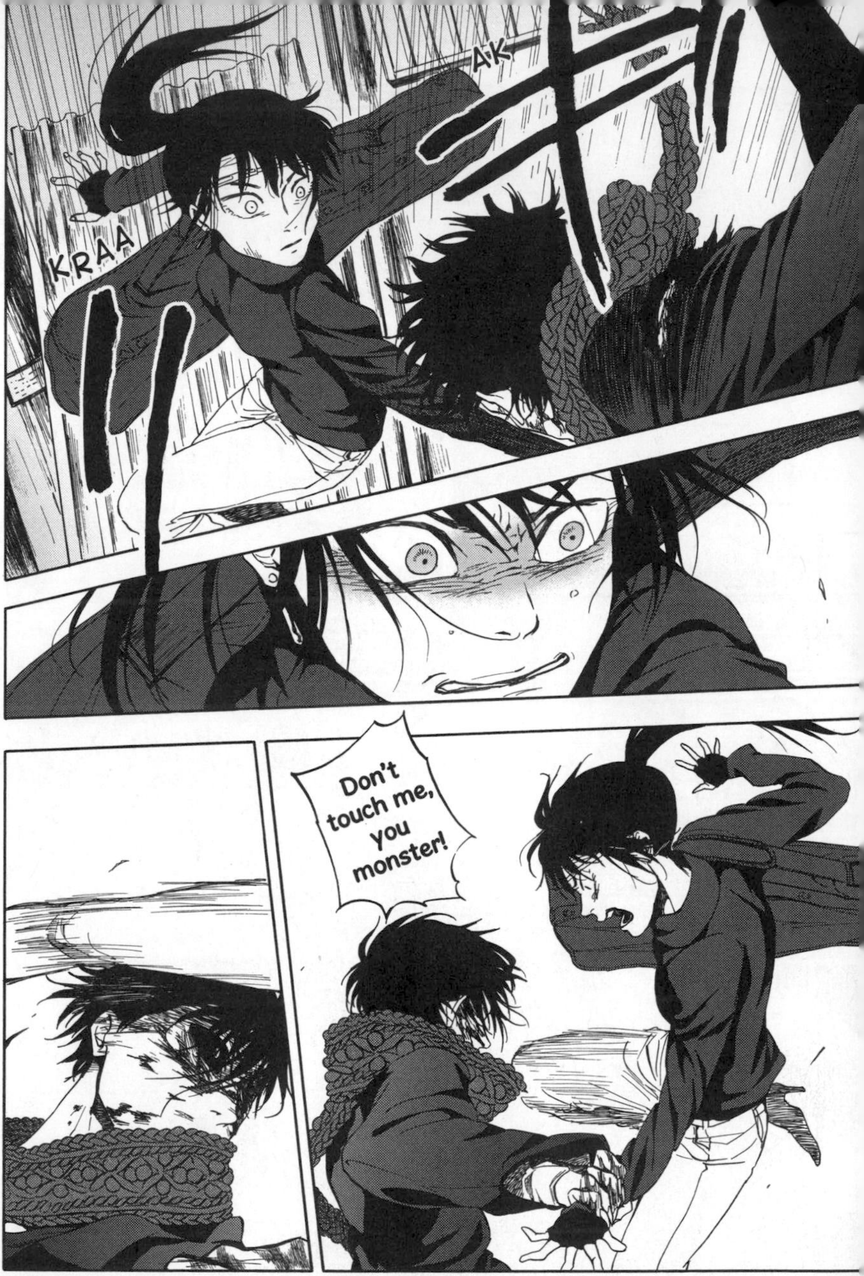
AK
KRAA
Don't touch me, you monster!

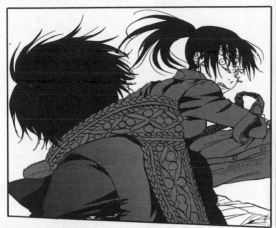
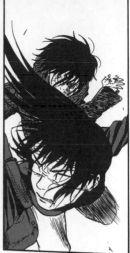
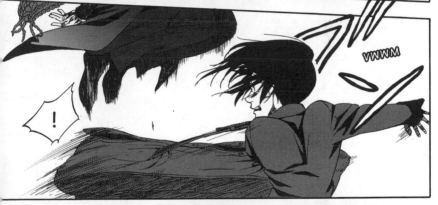

VWWM

!

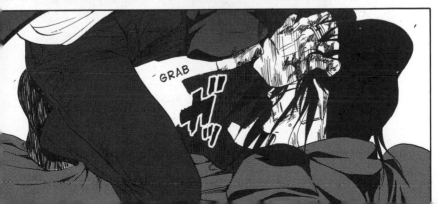

GRAB

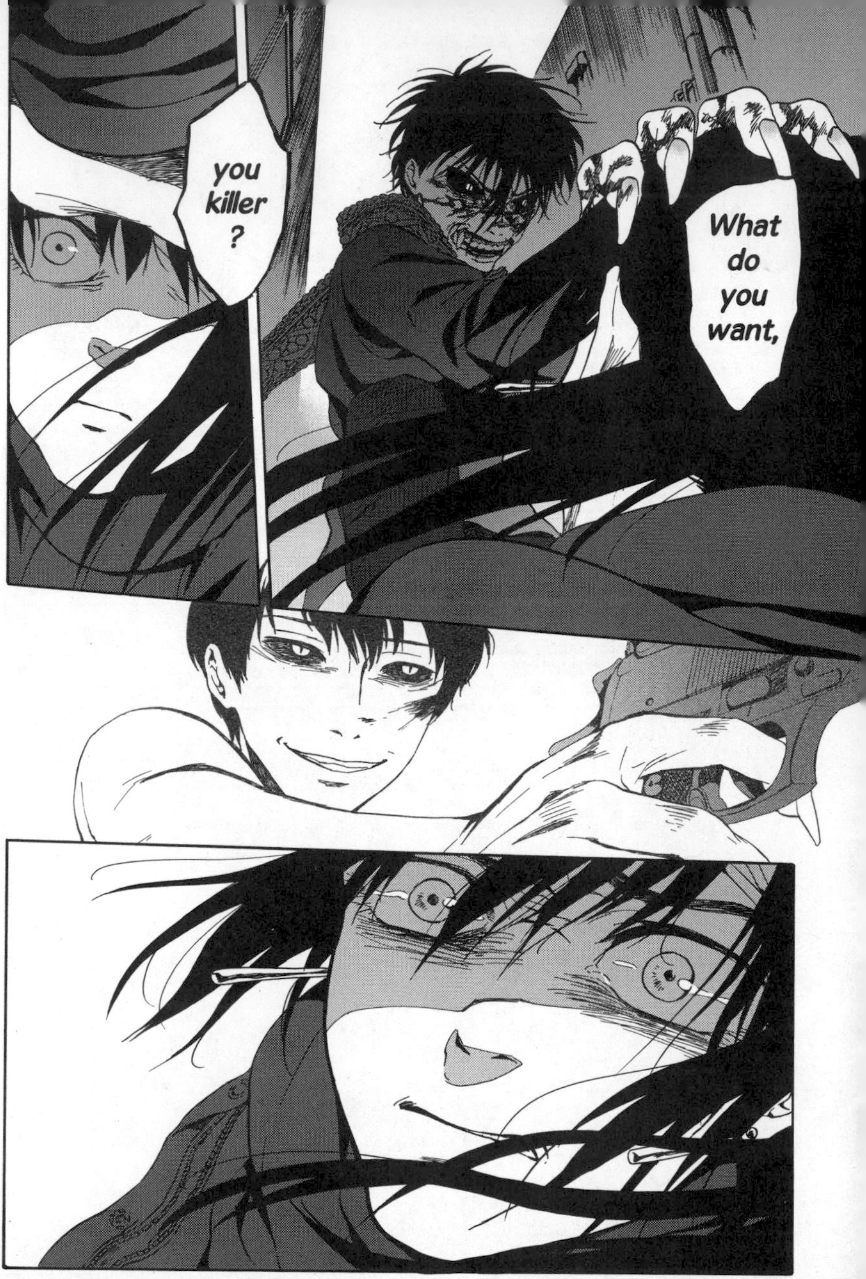
What do you want,
you killer?

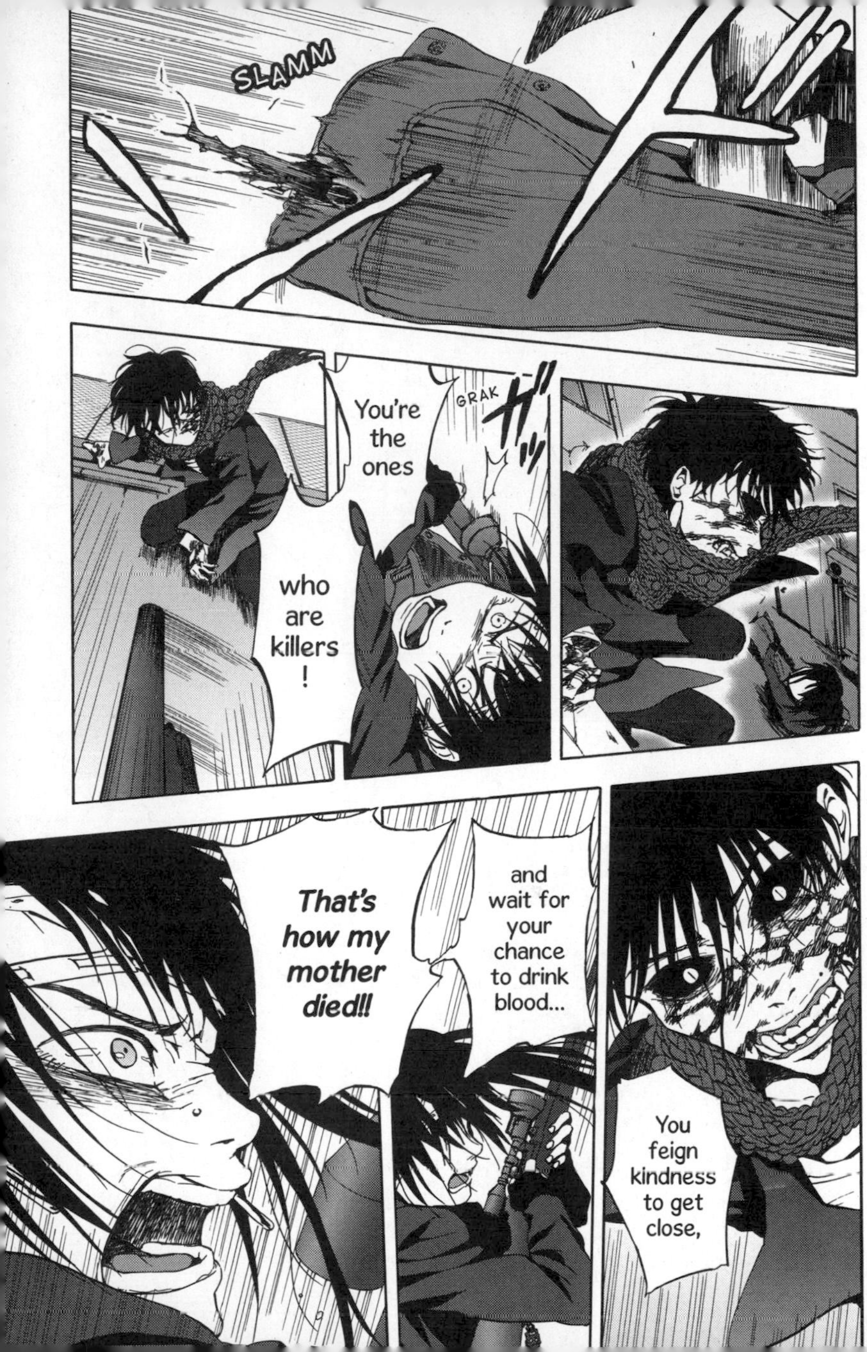
SLAMM
GRAK
You're the ones who are killers!
You feign kindness to get close,
and wait for your chance to drink blood...
That's how my mother died!!

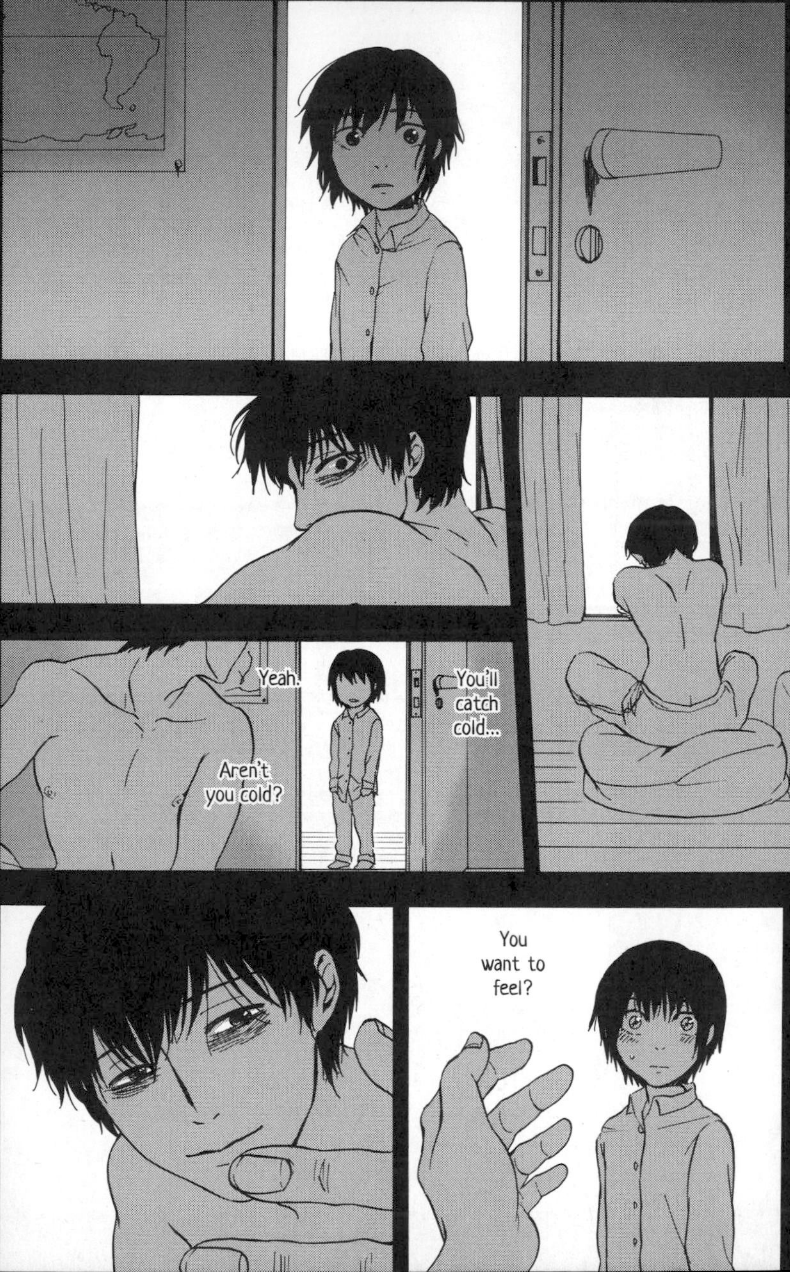
You'll catch cold...
Yeah.
Aren't you cold?
You want to feel?

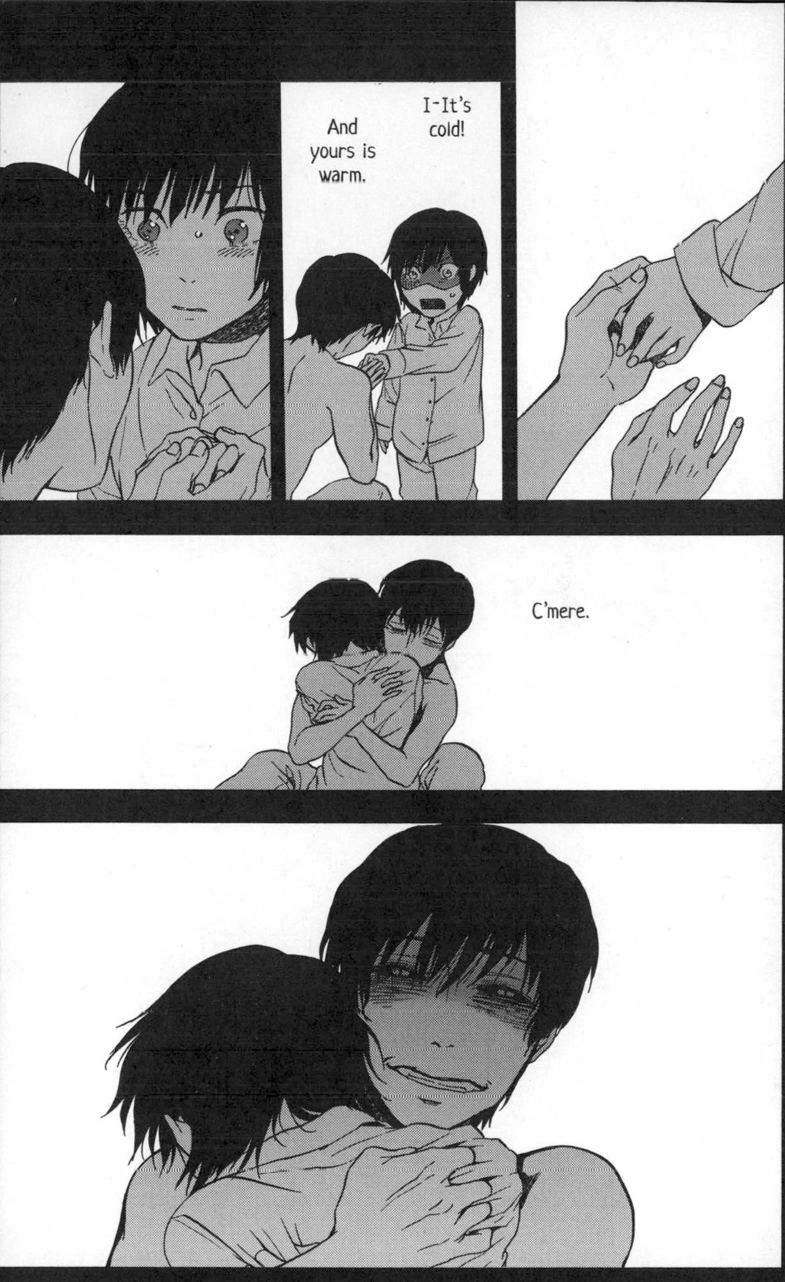
I-It's cold!
And yours is warm.
C'mere.

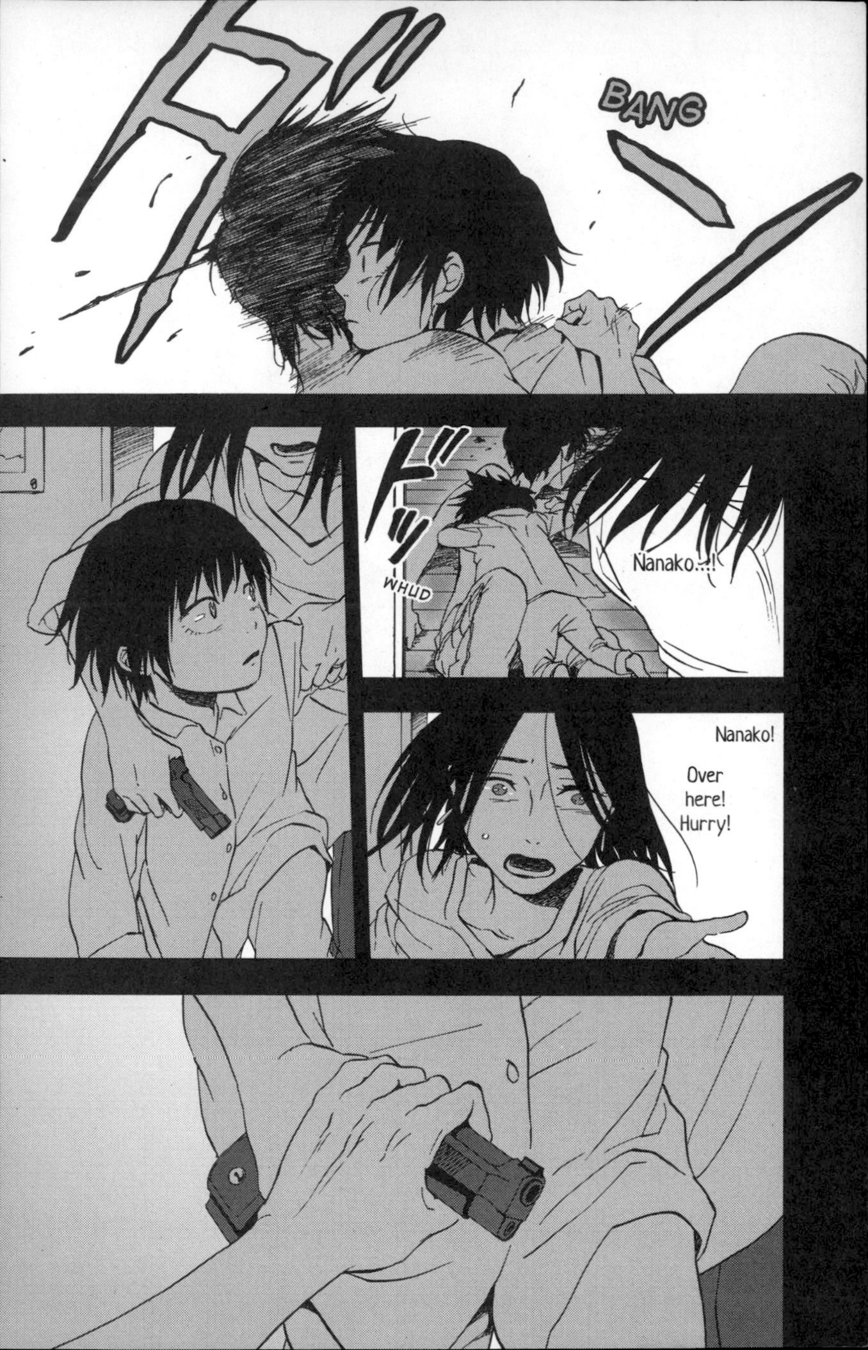
BANG
ドッ
WHUD
Nanako...!
Nanako!
Over here! Hurry!

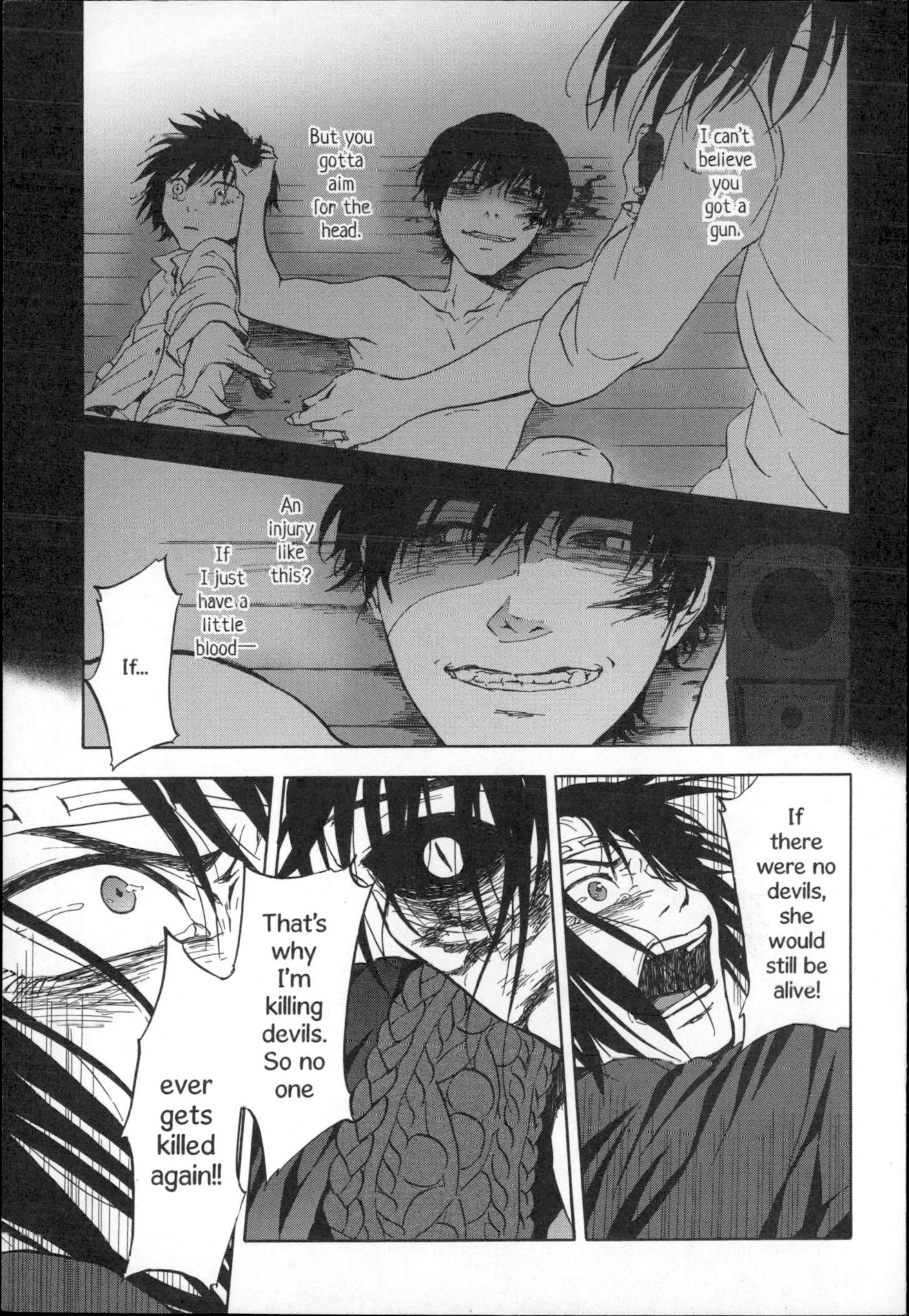
I can't believe you got a gun.
But you gotta aim for the head.
An injury like this?
If I just have a little blood—
If...
If there were no devils, she would still be alive!
That's why I'm killing devils. So no one
ever gets killed again!!

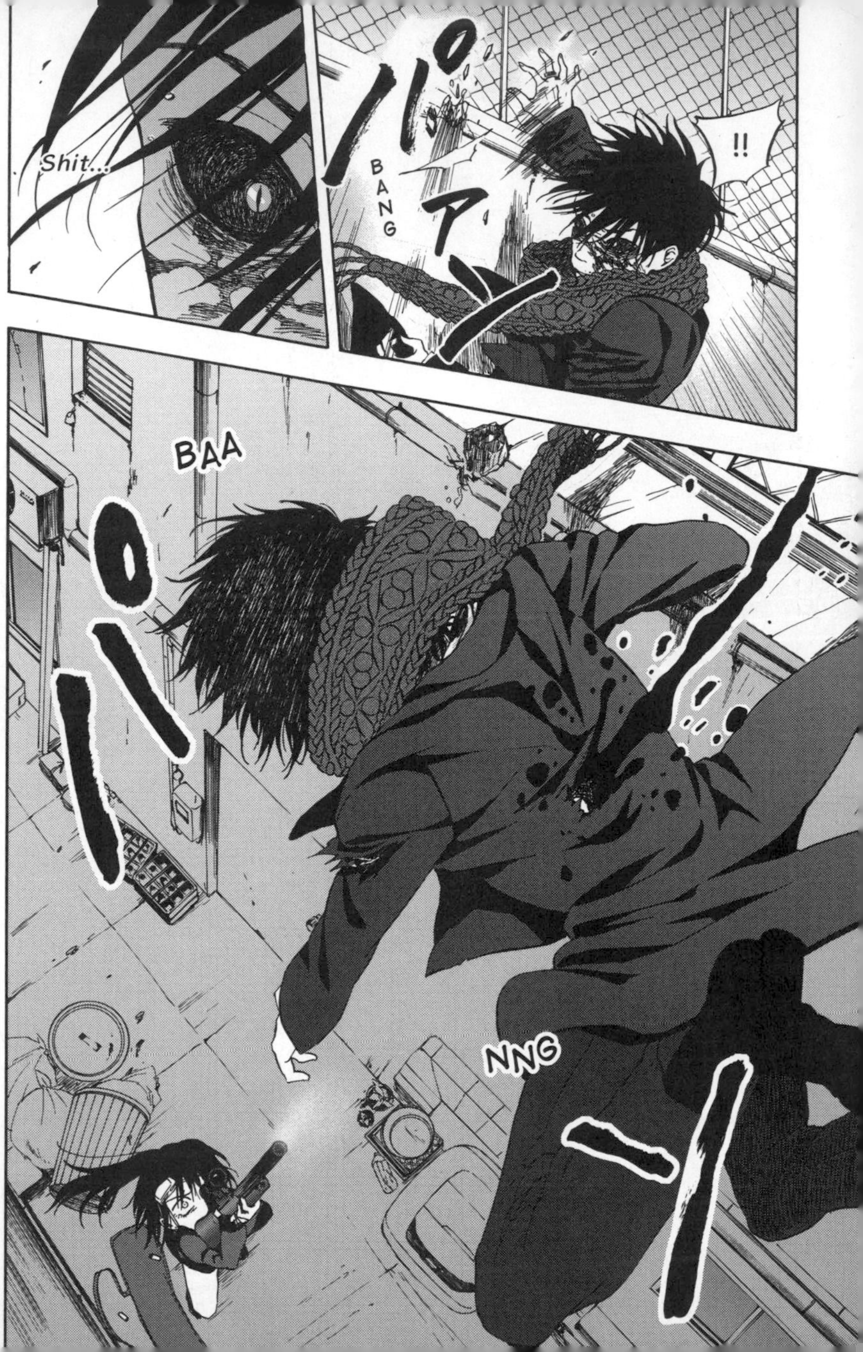
!!
パァン
BANG
Shit...
BAA
パー
NNG

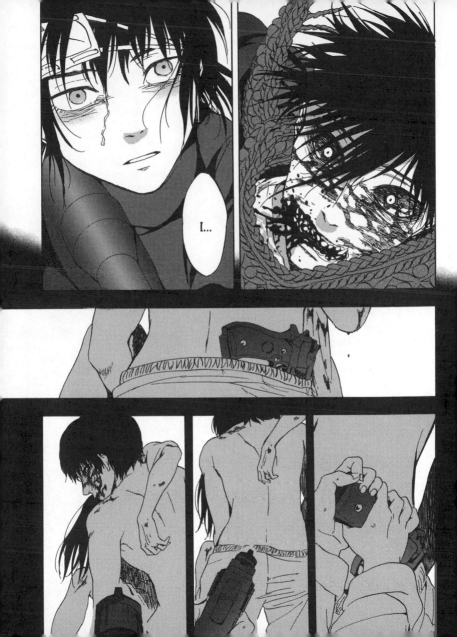

I...

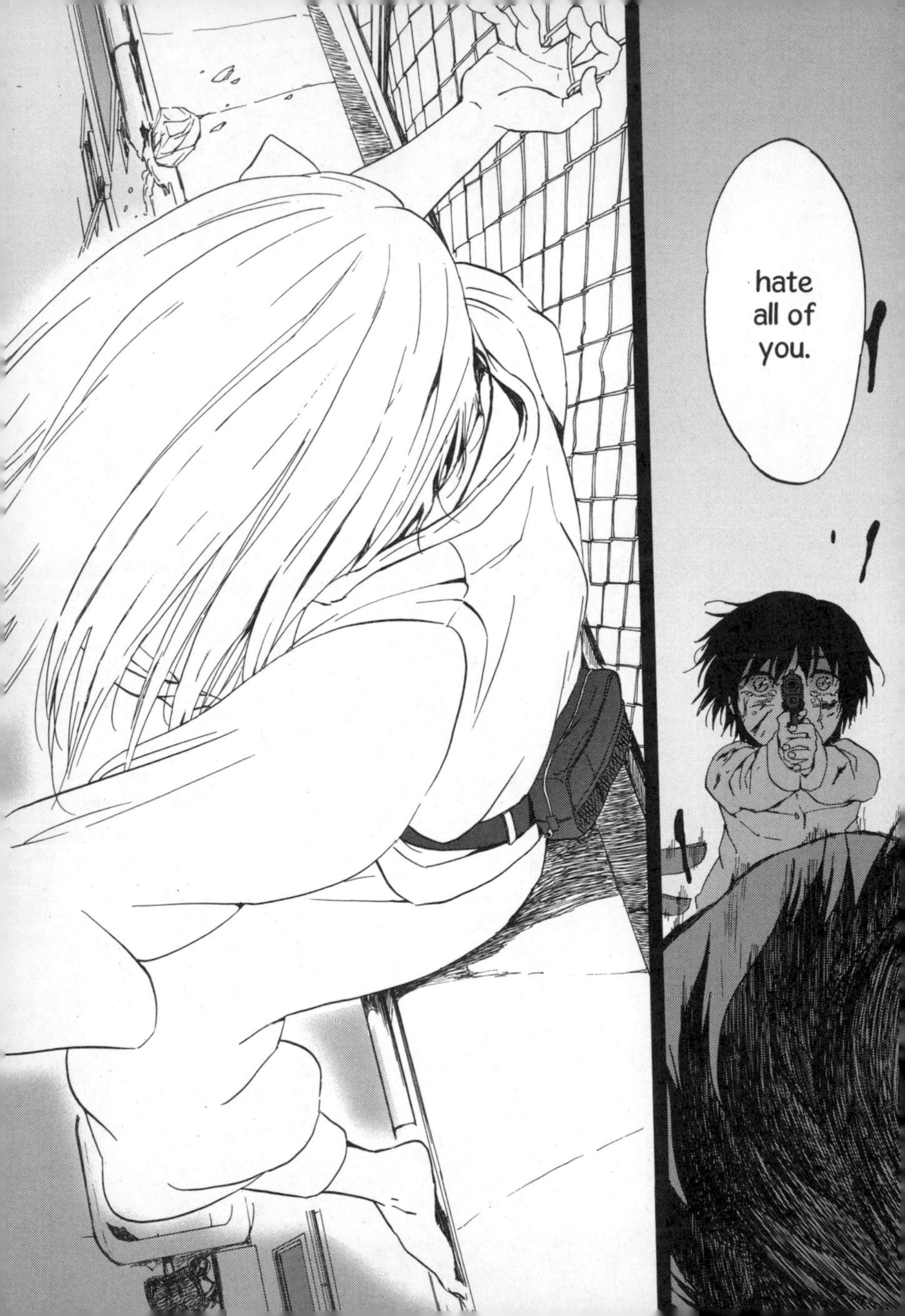
hate all of you.

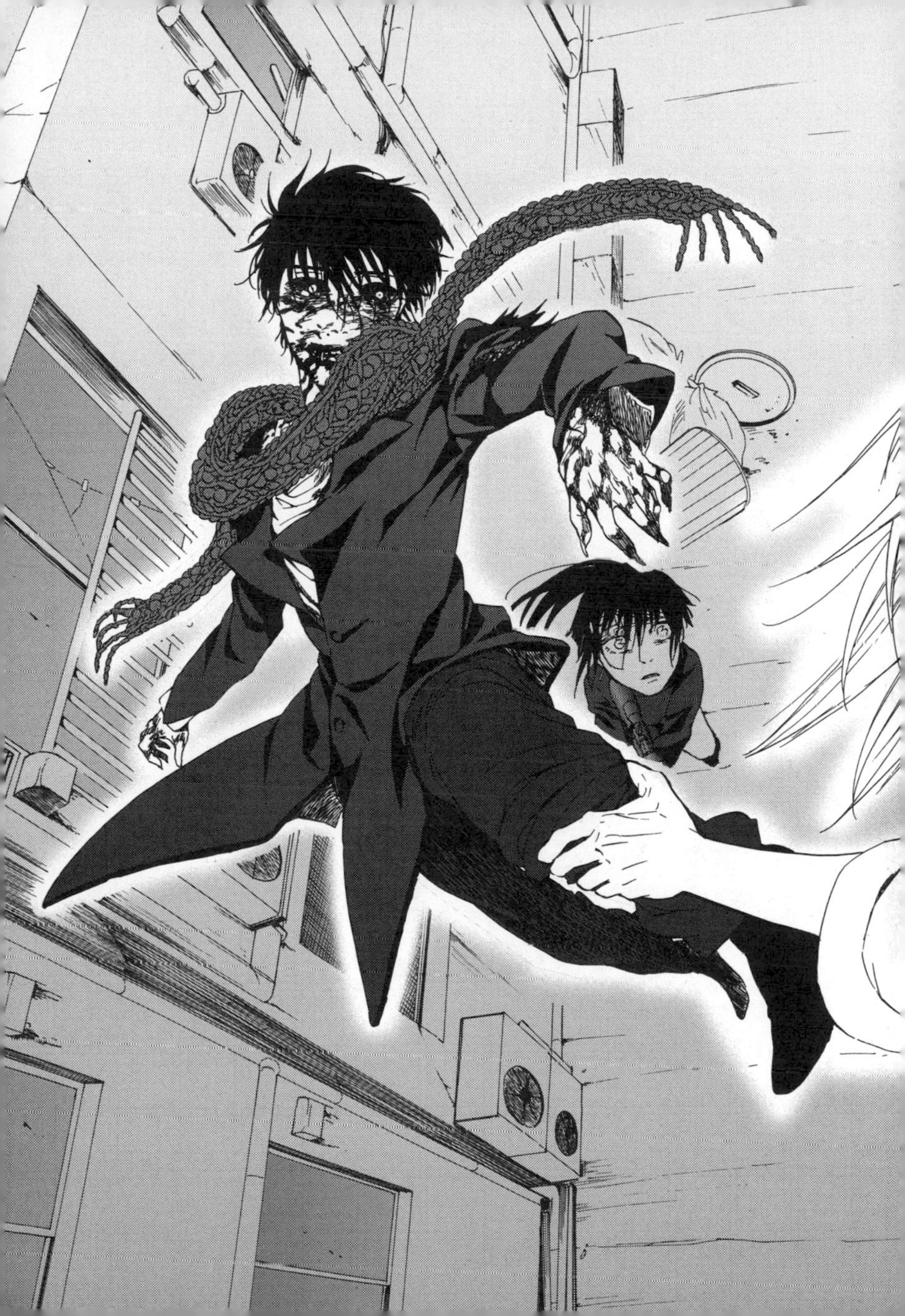

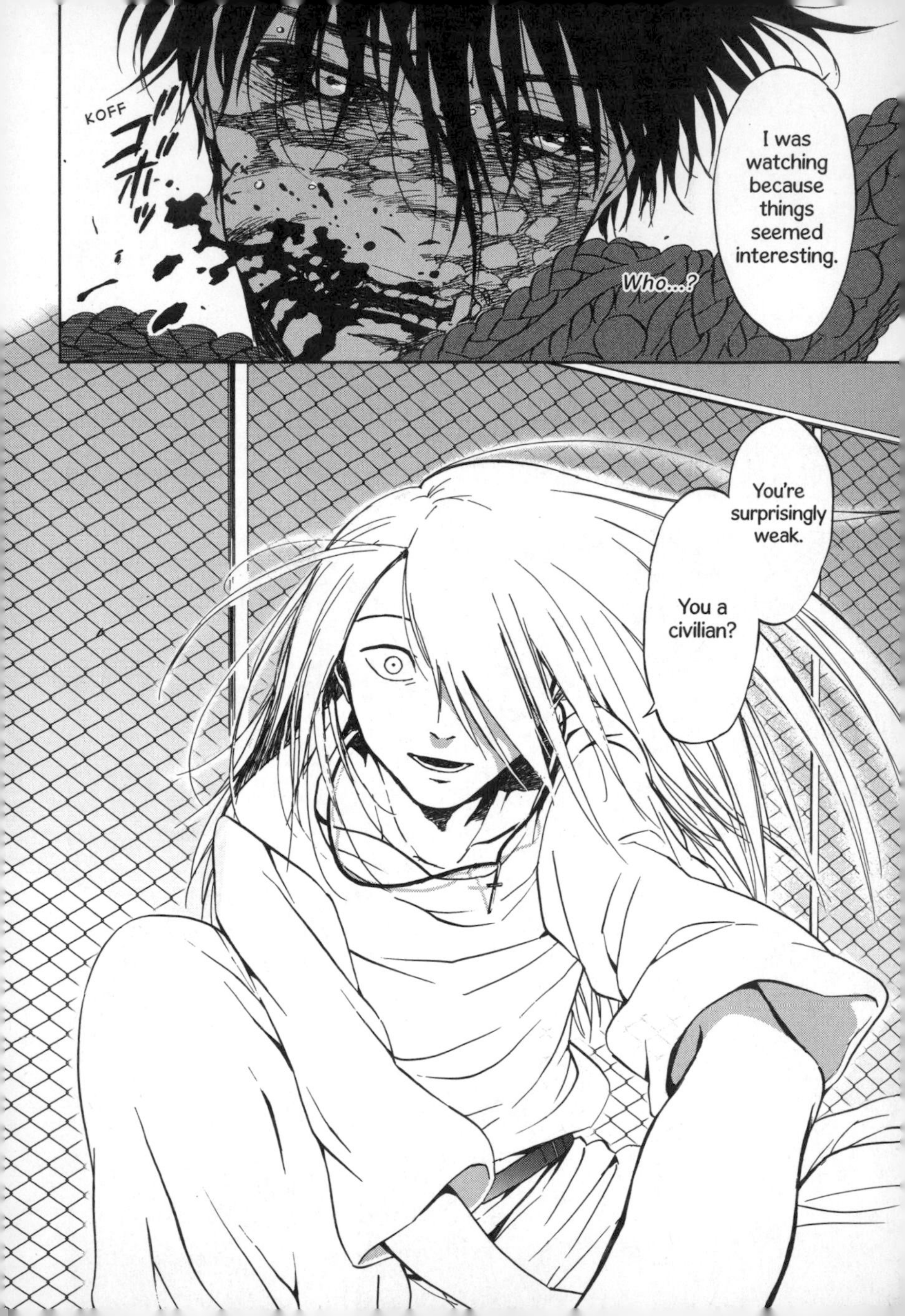
I was watching because things seemed interesting.
Who...?
KOFF
You're surprisingly weak.
You a civilian?

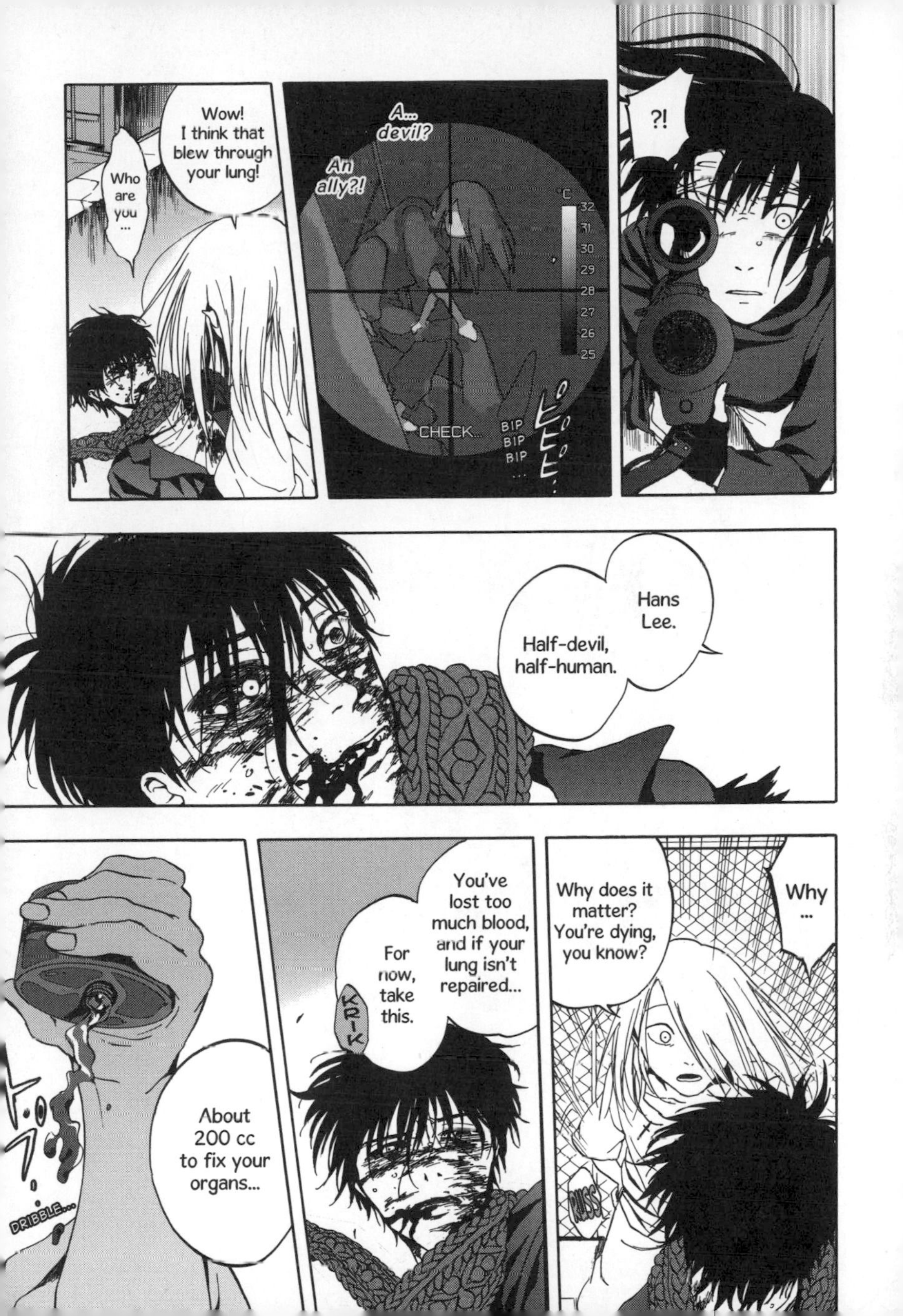
?!
A... devil?
An ally?!
°C 32 31 30 29 28 27 26 25
CHECK...
BIP BIP BIP ...
Wow! I think that blew through your lung!
Who are you ...
Hans Lee.
Half-devil, half-human.
Why ...
Why does it matter? You're dying, you know?
You've lost too much blood, and if your lung isn't repaired...
For now, take this.
KRIK
About 200 cc to fix your organs...
DRIBBLE...

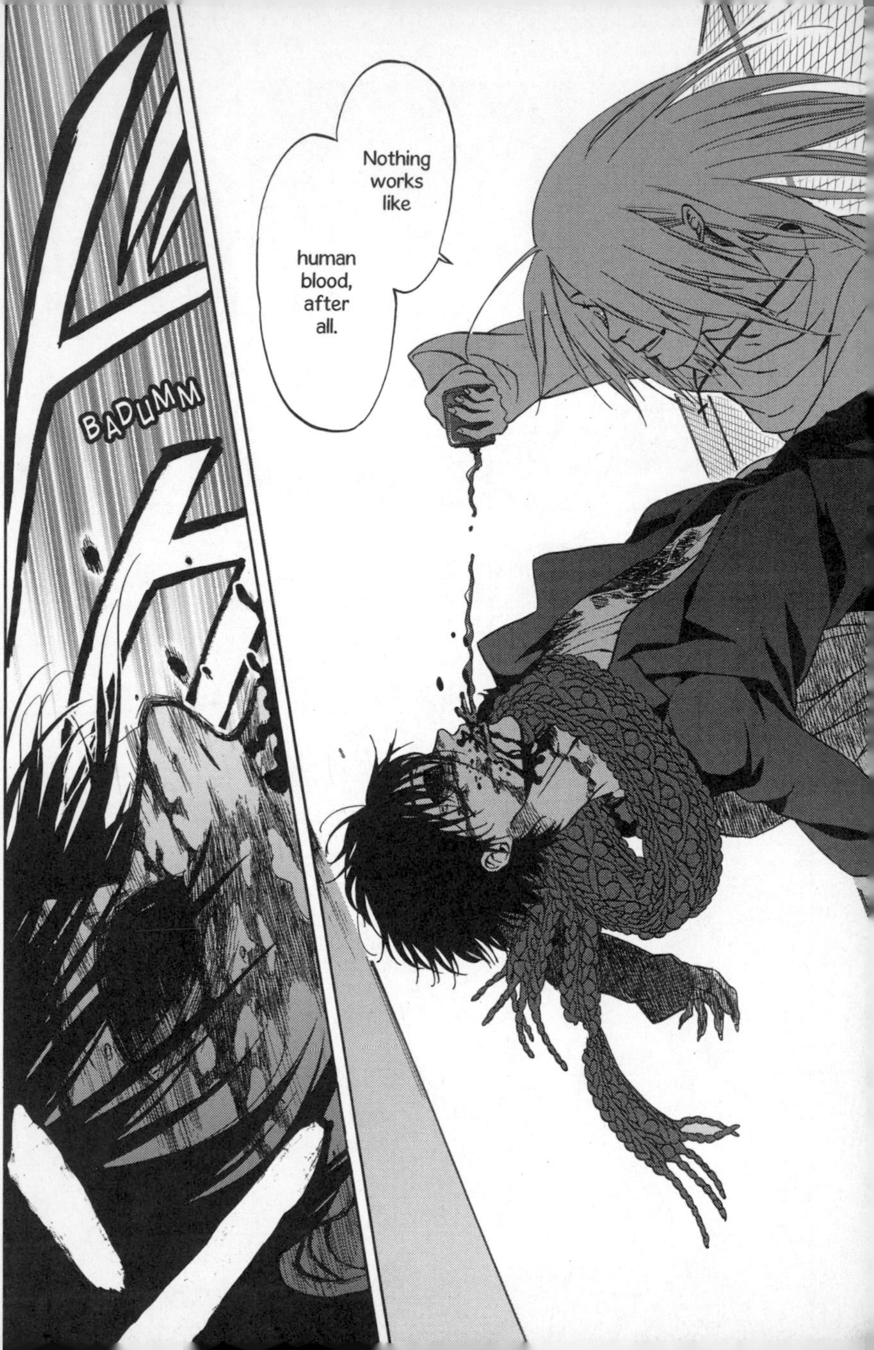
Nothing works like human blood, after all.
BADUMM

THE MYSTERY OF THE CHRISTMAS CARD

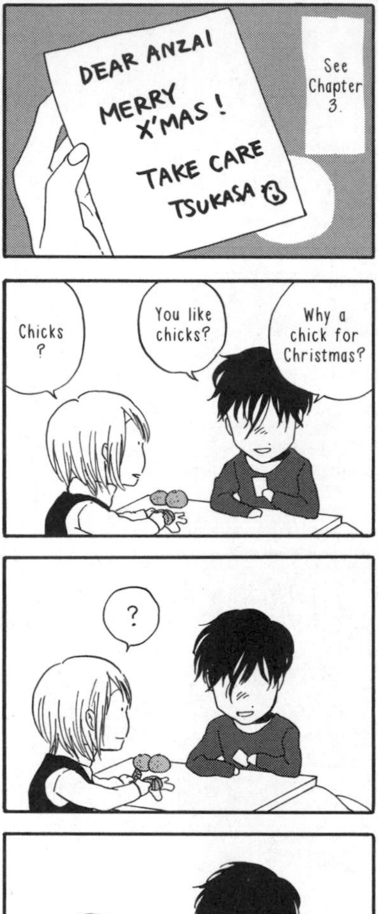
See Chapter 3.
DEAR ANZAI
MERRY X'MAS!
TAKE CARE
TSUKASA
Why a chick for Christmas?
You like chicks?
Chicks?
?
RUSTLE

MASTER ARTIST

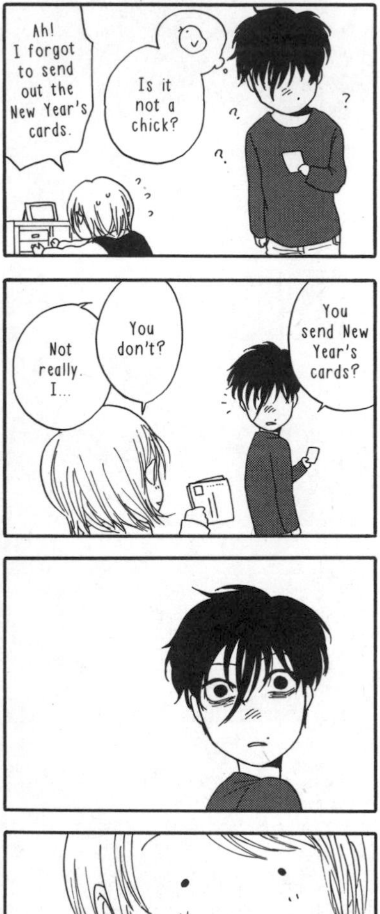
Is it not a chick?
Ah! I forgot to send out the New Year's cards.
You send New Year's cards?
You don't?
Not really. I...
2013
HAPPY NEW YEAR
SNAKE!!!
TSUKASA

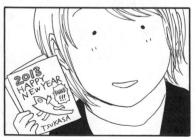

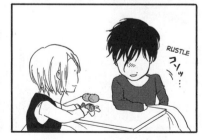

CLASSIC METHOD

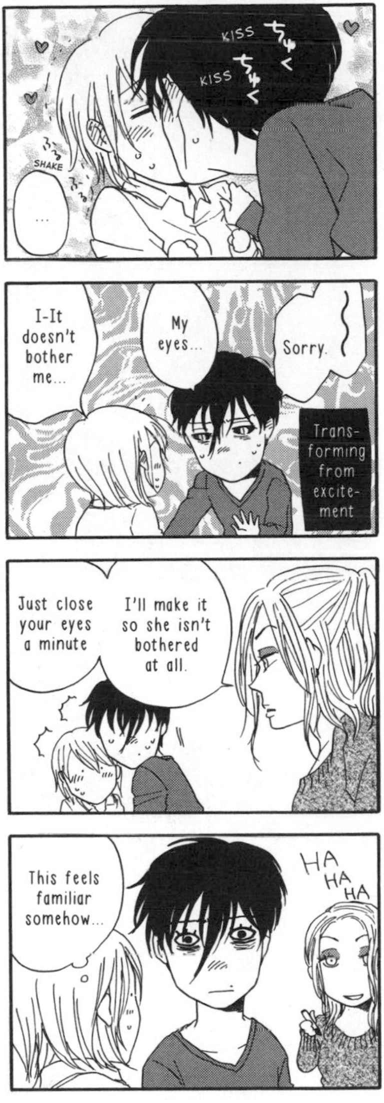
KISS ちゅく
ちゅく KISS
SHAKE ぷる ぷる
...
Sorry.
My eyes...
I-It doesn't bother me...
Transforming from excitement
I'll make it so she isn't bothered at all.
Just close your eyes a minute
HA HA HA
This feels familiar somehow...

FAIRLY DIFFICULT

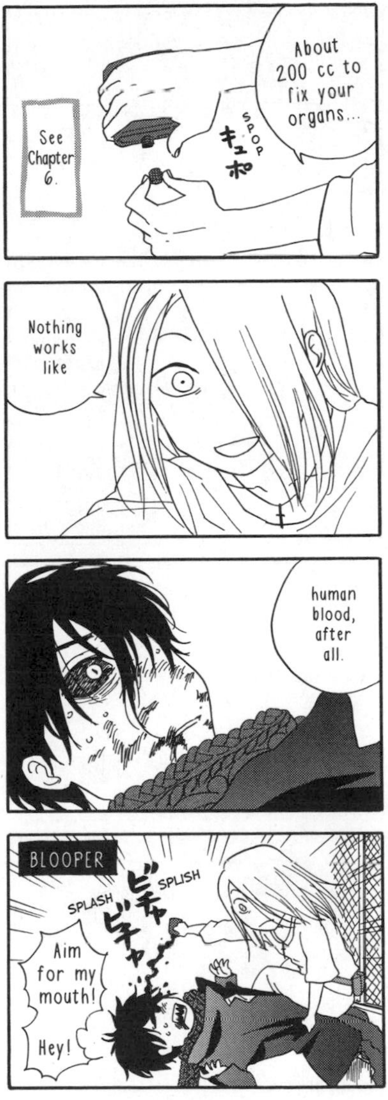
About 200 cc to fix your organs...
SPOP キュポ
See Chapter 6.
Nothing works like
human blood, after all.
BLOOPER
SPLISH ビチャ
SPLASH ビチャ
Aim for my mouth!
Hey!

CAN'T TAKE IT OFF

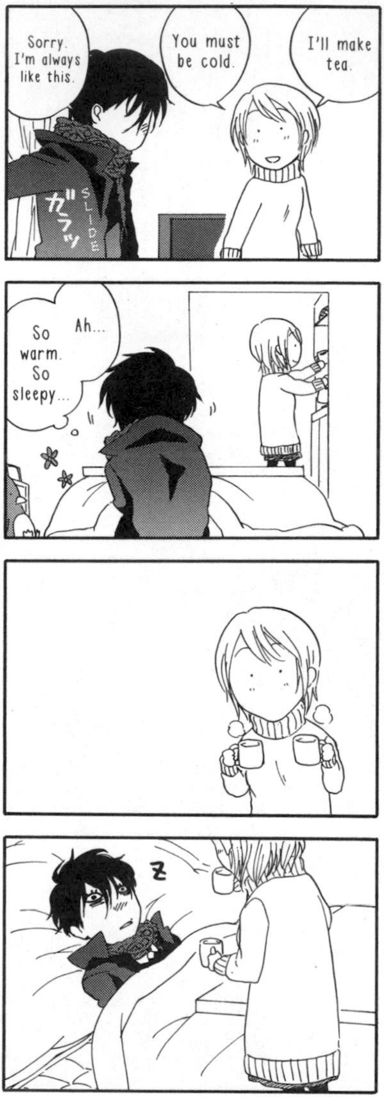
I'll make tea.
You must be cold.
Sorry. I'm always like this.
ガラッ
SLIDE
Ah...
So warm. So sleepy...
z

IT'S YOU, ISN'T IT?

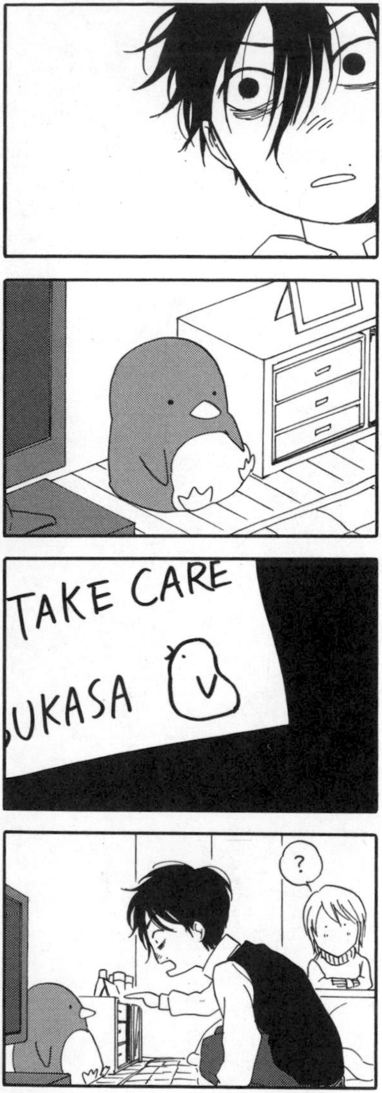
TAKE CARE
UKASA
?

DEVILS' LINE 1

A Vertical Comics Edition

Translation: Jocelyne Allen
Production: Risa Cho
Lorina Mapa

© 2016 Ryo Hanada. All rights reserved.
First published in Japan in 2013 by Kodansha, Ltd., Tokyo
Publication rights for this English edition arranged through Kodansha, Ltd., Tokyo
English language version produced by Vertical, Inc., New York

Translation provided by Vertical Comics, 2016
Published by Vertical, Inc., New York

Originally published in Japanese as *Debiruzurain 1* by Kodansha, Ltd., 2013
Debiruzurain first serialized in *Morning two*, Kodansha, Ltd., 2013-

This is a work of fiction.

ISBN: 978-1-942993-37-7

Manufactured in the United States of America

First Edition

Second Printing

Vertical, Inc.
451 Park Avenue South
7th Floor
New York, NY 10016
www.vertical-comics.com

Vertical books are distributed through Penguin-Random House Publisher Services.

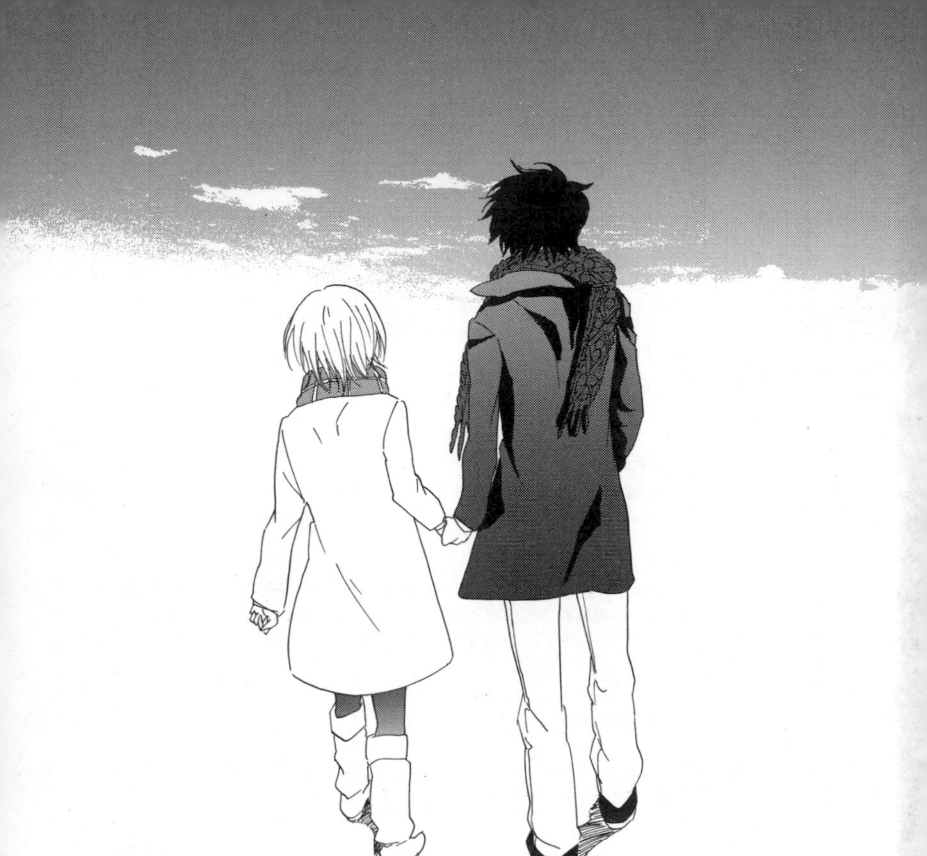

SPECIAL THANKS

MANAGING EDITOR——M-MURA
BOOK EDITOR——K-BAYASHI
DESIGN——HIVE HISAMOCHI

WEB COMIC POSTING AND BROWSING SERVICE——MANGA☆GET

AND ALL THE READERS!